NONCOOPERATION *in* INDIA

David Hardiman is Emeritus Professor of History at the University of Warwick and a founding member of the Subaltern Studies Group. He lived in India for many years. The author of *The Nonviolent Struggle for Indian Freedom, 1905–19*, he has also written extensively on Gandhi and Indian social history.

Praise for *Noncooperation in India*

'A vital, in-depth treatment of Noncooperation. Hardiman illuminates the politics of solidarity among Hindus, Muslims, and workers, the forging of unity and nonviolent discipline, and the tensions between ethical and strategic approaches to satyagraha. An important read for students of nonviolent resistance.'

— Erica Chenoweth, Berthold Beitz Professor in Human Rights and International Affairs, Harvard Kennedy School

'The most detailed and sophisticated study of Noncooperation yet. More than just an historical narrative timed for its centenary, Hardiman addresses the most important intellectual and political problems raised by the movement. Lucid, gripping, and wholly original.'

— Faisal Devji, Professor of Indian History and Director of the Asian Studies Centre, University of Oxford

'Examining the range of movements drawn into Noncooperation under Gandhi's leadership, Hardiman shows how tensions among elite leaders, and between them and popular movements, made it impossible to transform the upheaval into a coherent national movement. A welcome analysis illuminating "nonviolence" and the dynamics of Indian politics.'

— Judith M. Brown, Beit Professor Emeritus of Commonwealth History, University of Oxford

'Hardiman is among the foremost scholars of modern South Asian history. This work is highly original—a careful, and thoroughly fair, assessment of nonviolent politics. Much more than a new summation of existing research, it significantly expands the scope of what is usually understood as the Noncooperation Movement.'

— Partha Chatterjee, Senior Research Scholar in Anthropology and Middle Eastern, South Asian, and African Studies, University of Columbia, and author of *A Possible India: Essays in Political Criticism*

NONCOOPERATION *in* INDIA

NONVIOLENT STRATEGY *and* PROTEST, 1920–22

DAVID HARDIMAN

First published in the United Kingdom in 2021 by C. Hurst & Co. (Publishers) Ltd

First published in India by Context, an imprint of Westland Books, a division of Nasadiya Technologies Private Limited, in 2023

No. 269/2B, First Floor, 'Irai Arul', Vimalraj Street, Nethaji Nagar, Alapakkam Main Road, Maduravoyal, Chennai 600095

Westland, the Westland logo, Context and the Context logo are the trademarks of Nasadiya Technologies Private Limited, or its affiliates.

The translations from the Telugu of four nationalist songs are reproduced with the kind permission of Atlury Murali.

ISBN: 9789357765565

10 9 8 7 6 5 4 3 2 1

Printed at Nutech Print Services-India

CONTENTS

GLOSSARY

Acara	Transgression of an essential caste duty.
Adi-Dravida	Untouchable communities of Tamilnadu, particularly of the Paraiyar group.
Adivasi	Indigenous people considered to be 'tribal' by the British, being now classed as 'scheduled tribes' by the modern Indian state.
Ahimsa	Nonviolence.
Akhada	Gymnasium.
Amla	Rent collector.
Asahyog andolan	The Noncooperation Movement.
Avatar	A reincarnation of a deity in bodily form on earth.
Baba	Elder; learned or saintly person.
Babu	Originally a title of respect used in Bengal, but later applied pejoratively for an anglicised elite.
Baniya	Merchant caste.
Begar	Corvée labour.
Bhadralok	The 'respectable people' of Bengal, comprising the three upper Hindu castes of Brahman, Baidya and Kayastha.
Bhagat	Devotee.
Bhagchasi	Sharecropper, generally living in great poverty, in Bengal.

Bhajan	Devotional song, hymn.
Bhakti	Devotion to the divine.
Bharat	India.
Bharat Mata	Mother India.
Bhil	Adivasi community of western India.
Brahman	The highest, or priestly, caste among Hindus.
Burqa	Voluminous garment that envelops the body and the face, as worn by some Muslim women.
Chamar	Untouchable caste, chiefly of leather workers.
Charkha	Spinning wheel.
Chaukidar	Village watchman.
Dacoit	Bandit.
Dada	Respectful address to an older man, an elder brother, paternal grandfather, or pejoratively a bully, lout, neighbourhood boss, or gangster.
Dharma	Moral duty, law; more broadly, religion.
Dharmaraj	The rule of *dharma*.
Dharmic	Religious duty.
Darshan	Auspicious viewing that brings blessings on the observer.
Dhobi	Caste that specialises in washing clothes.
Draupadi	Wife of the five Pandava brothers in the Mahabharata.
Duryodhana	Major figure in the Mahabharata – the eldest of the Kauravas and the chief opponent to the heroes of the epic, the Pandavas.
Eka / Eki	Unity League.
Fakir	Religious ascetic who lives on alms, normally Muslim.
Fatwa	Opinion on a point of Islamic law given by a recognised expert.
Girasia	Poor cultivating community of southern Rajasthan.

Gurdwara	Sikh temple.
Haat	Weekly market.
Hartal	Form of protest involving a collective refusal to work or carry on trade for an agreed period.
Hijrat	Migration, including mass migration as an act of protest.
Ho	Adivasi community of eastern India.
Jagir	Landed estate.
Jagirdar	Holder of a *jagir* estate.
Jaikar	Exhortation of 'Long Live!'
Jat	Landholding caste of north-western India.
Jatha	Band of militant Sikhs.
Jihad	A struggle or striving for Islamic principles that may involve an outward fight against those seen as the enemies of Islam, or as an inward struggle for spiritual perfection.
Jotedar	Tenant with security of holding in Bengal.
Ka'aba	Holiest shrine of Islam in Mecca.
Kamma	Dominant peasant caste of Andhra.
karmi	Worker.
Khadi	Handspun and handwoven cloth.
Khatri	Middle-status caste of traders, mainly of Punjab.
Khilafat	Movement to save the Islamic Caliphate, a position that was held to be occupied by the Ottoman Sultan.
Ki jai!	Exhortation of 'Long Live!', preceded by an appropriate name.
Kirpan	Short sword or knife with a curved blade, worn as one of the five distinguishing signs of the Sikh Khalsa.
Kirtan	Devotional hymn.
Koeri	Cultivating caste of United Provinces.
Kshatriya	Caste of warriors and rulers.
Kurmi	Cultivating caste of northern India.

Lathi	Long stick with metal cap.
Lingayat	Dominant peasant caste of Karnataka.
Mahabharata	Great Hindu epic composed between 3rd C. BCE and 3rd C. CE. that narrates the struggle between the Kauravas and Paṇḍavas.
Mahant	Priest in charge at a temple or monastery.
Mahisya	Peasant caste of West Bengal.
Mantra	Word or sound repeated to aid concentration in meditation; statement or slogan repeated frequently.
Maratha-Kunbi	Dominant peasant caste of Maharashtra.
Maro!	Cry of 'beat!'.
Marwari	Hindu or Jain merchants of the Baniya caste originating in Marwar region of Rajasthan, but found all over India in modern times
Maulana	Revered Islamic scholar.
Maya	Illusion.
Merua	Derogatory Bengali term for a Hindi-speaker.
Muhajirin	Religious migrants (Islamic).
Mullah	Muslim scholar, teacher and leader of a mosque.
Murti	Image of a deity.
Mussalman	Term for Muslim often used in Central and South Asia.
Oraon	Adivasi community of eastern India.
Panchayat	Assembly of elders or representatives of village, town, caste or community, a popular council.
Pasi	Cultivating caste of the United Provinces, considered untouchable.
Patidar	Caste of respectable cultivators in Gujarat.
Pir	Islamic saint or holy person.
Prabhat pheri	Pre-dawn procession in which religious hymns were sung, and nationalist songs.
Praja	Subjects.

Qawwali	Form of Sufi Islamic devotional music – widely popular in South Asia.
Raja	King.
Rajput	Caste associated with rulers and warriors.
Rakshasa	Demon.
Rama	Legendary ruler of Ayodya, considered the seventh avatar of the deity Vishnu. His adventures are recounted in the Ramayana (5th C. BCE)
Ramcharitamanas	The story of Ram as recounted in the Awadhi dialect by Tulsidas in the sixteenth-century.
Ramraj	The rule of Rama; thus a righteous form of rule.
Ravan	The king of Lanka and the demon-figure of the *Ramayana*.
Ravanraj	The rule of Ravan; thus, a demonic form of rule.
Reddy	Dominant peasant caste of Andhra.
Sabha	An organised group such as an assembly, council, society, or association.
Sadhu	Holy man who has renounced worldly life. *Sadvi* is the female form.
Salaam	Gesture of greeting or respect typically consisting of a bow of the head and body with the hand or fingers touching the forehead.
Samiti	Association.
Sant	Saintly person.
Santal	Adivasi community of eastern India.
Sanyasi	Person who renounces material desire and prejudice, and who lives in a peaceful, love-inspired, simple, and spiritual way.
Sardar	Chief, headman, or leader; jobber in Bengal.
Satya	Truth.
Satyagraha	'Truth-force'; a method of conflict-resolution advocated by M.K. Gandhi – most typically involving nonviolent resistance.

Satyagrahi	Person who engages in *satyagraha*.
Seva	Service.
Sevak	Servant.
Shakti	Divine power.
Shanti	Peace.
Sharia	Islamic law.
Shuddha	Pure.
Sita	Wife of Rama.
Swadeshi	Self-help, self-production; a process of opting out of the imperial system and establishing parallel national economic and political structures.
Swami	Hindu ascetic, holyman.
Swaraj	Self-rule, freedom, liberation.
Taluqdar	Landlord.
Tapas/tapasya	Voluntary acceptance of bodily pain to achieve a higher end, primarily spiritual realisation; self-denial; penances.
Tehsil	Sub-district.
Thakur	Deity, lord, chief, landlord, person of rank or position. In Gujarati and Mewari – *thakor*.
Ulama	Islamic scholars.
Ustad	Honorific of a highly skilled person, often a teacher or guru-figure.
Wahhabi movement	Muslim reform movement that originated in the 18th century in Arabia under Muḥammad ibn ʿAbd al-Wahhāb that advocated a purification of Islamic practices, returning to the supposed fundamentals of the faith.
Zamindar	Landlord

INTRODUCTION

The Noncooperation Movement of 1920–22 that forms the subject of this book was directed against multiple aspects of British imperial rule in India. It was one of the major mass movements of modern times. Supported by people from every level of the social hierarchy, it united Hindus and Muslims in a way that was never again achieved during the Indian national struggle. It managed to hollow out British rule, shaking its authority to the core. In general, it was remarkably nonviolent.

In my previous volume,[1] I examined how nonviolent forms of resistance to imperialism were pursued under the rubric of 'passive resistance' during the first decade of the twentieth century. The technique was at the same time refined by M.K. Gandhi in South Africa in a campaign against the discriminatory treatment of Indians in that colony. Gandhi evolved a new practice that he called 'satyagraha', with a principled commitment to nonviolence at its heart. After his return to India in 1915, he campaigned to make such nonviolence a central commitment of the Indian National Congress, winning support for the idea through a small number of well-publicised local-level campaigns that he led successfully. Following from this, Gandhi launched his first all-India campaign in 1919 – the Rowlatt Satyagraha. The brutal repression of this protest in Punjab province created a 'backfire' against imperial rule, with mass alienation and a new vehemence injected into the nationalist movement. It paved the way for the campaign of 1920–22 that is the subject of this volume.

Hindu-Muslim unity was a crucial element in this movement, and we shall see how this came about in the first chapter. The second chapter examines how the campaign was conducted, with tensions always being there between the Gandhian ideal of ethical nonviolence and a more expedient or pragmatic approach, that tolerated a degree of violence and that anticipated an escalation towards violent resistance once the conditions were ripe (which was clearly not the case in the early 1920s). Whereas Gandhi conceived this as a movement to provide above all a moral regeneration of Indian society, the pragmatists saw their task as winning political independence by any means possible. Over the next three chapters we go on to describe and analyse the many local manifestations of the movement. These campaigns were against not only British imperial officials, but also British businessmen – such as industrial capitalists and factory managers, indigo planters and tea garden operators – and also against Indians who were closely allied to British rule, such as landlords and Sikh temple priests. These chapters will bring out how a range of different classes and communities from all walks of life participated in the movement. We shall try to judge how nonviolent these disparate groups were in practice. All recorded cases of violence will be noted scrupulously, and attempts made to put them in context. In this, it should be remembered that historians have relied on government reports and newspapers for much of their information. The authorities had a vested interest in emphasising a supposed 'violence of the masses' so that they could argue that the nationalist leaders were mobilising such groups in an irresponsible way. Newspapers, for their part, tended to amplify any stray acts of violence for sensationalist purposes. Many historians have gone along with these reports, holding that the masses had a tendency towards violence. I shall try to be more discriminating in my use of such source material.

Chapter 6 examines how these disparate protests gelled together under nationalist leadership. This is described as a process of 'braiding' and involved several elements. First, there was a shared challenge to the authority of the British, who had assumed a God-given right to rule that had hitherto been largely accepted. The first section will see how this encounter played out in practice. We shall then go on to see how the nationalist message was propagated, before looking at the leadership of the movement at three main levels – the national, the provincial, and the local. Chapter 7 examines the structures of popular nonviolence during what was known popularly as '*asahyog andolan*' (the Noncooperation Movement). We shall see how solidarities were forged, the main forms of protest that were deployed, the way that popular campaigns to reform and purify the lifestyles of the masses fed into the protest, and the importance of beliefs that supernatural forces had blessed Gandhi, and the Congress and Khilafat causes. There is a discussion of how historians should analyse the common assumption of that time that supernatural forces were playing an active role in the protest; in other words, had historical agency. The chapter concludes with some observations on the forms that popular nonviolence took at this time. Was such protest peculiar to India, or are there parallels with subsequent nonviolent campaigns in other parts of the world? Was this – perhaps – a force that emanated from deep within Indian society, or – rather – was this a political strategy that emerged from wider, more global processes of modernity? The conclusion starts by examining the reactions of different Congress and Khilafat leaders to Gandhi's decision to call off civil disobedience in February 1922 and goes on to evaluate the legacy of the Noncooperation Movement. Some observations are then made on the subsequent history of the Indian freedom struggle, and how independence was gained in 1947.

As in the previous volume, I shall be using the literature on nonviolent resistance to illuminate Indian history in a fresh way. Also, I shall seek to provide an intervention within it, raising questions about how the Noncooperation Movement fits its theoretical models. I shall also query the way that religious belief is handled within this field of study in the section in Chapter 7 on 'enchanted resistance'. The book ends by revaluating some of the findings of the *Subaltern Studies* project in the light of nonviolent theory.

1

KHILAFAT

In recent years, militant Islam has gained a reputation for great violence. It was not always like that, as the history of the Indian Khilafat Movement reveals. In this, a movement that asserted a pan-Islamic identity opted to use nonviolent strategies in pursuit of its agenda. In doing so, it was able to make common cause with the Indian nationalist movement that was led by Gandhi. In this chapter, we shall examine how this came about.

The Muslims who led the Khilafat Movement rejected the style of politics of the All-India Muslim League, founded in 1906. The initiative for the League had been taken by people associated with the Mahommedan Anglo-Oriental College started in Aligarh in 1875. This had sought to provide western-style education for a Muslim elite that might then serve in the bureaucracy or professions then dominated by Hindus. The League, which was based in Aligarh, petitioned for reserved seats and separate electorates for Muslims in the constitutional reforms of 1909. They also demanded a fixed proportion of Muslims for appointments in government service and local government bodies. The League was dominated by rich and respectable men who proclaimed their loyalty to the British. By 1910, however, a younger and more radical generation of Muslims were emerging from Aligarh who sought to challenge the old guard. They argued that although the 1909 Act had granted separate electorates, such lobbying had failed to prevent the reversal of the partition of Bengal in 1911 that went against the interest of Bengali Muslims. Also, in 1912, the British rejected the demand that Aligarh become a full university, which was taken as a snub to Muslim opinion. The young leaders saw that the Swadeshi agitation in Bengal had brought real gains – notably the reversal of the partition of Bengal – and felt that a more militant stance would benefit Muslims too.

Parallel with this, a new religious leadership was emerging that had been trained in reformed seminaries such as the one started in 1867 at Deoband in northern UP. Changes were made in these seminaries along the lines of English educational institutions, including a progression of classes, required attendance, examinations, and the granting of a degree at the end of a full course. They sought to build a cadre of *ulama* (Islamic scholars) who might spread traditional education, fostering Islamic principles and enforcing Islamic law – the *sharia*. In the early years of the twentieth century the predominant theology at Deoband became a more militant one, endorsing some fundamentalist Wahhabi doctrines. They did not however accept that the rule of the infidel should be opposed with violence, and there was openness to joining with Hindu nationalists to fight the British. Although the Muslim revivalist movement demanded Islamic purity, it was also a very modern movement, deploying the printing press for publication of journals and religious texts in Urdu, and establishing fund-raising networks and educational institutions. It also embraced a pan-Islamic consciousness that was largely new to India. Initially it claimed to be apolitical, but there was a clear political potential in the idea of a unity of Muslims throughout India and the Muslim world in general. By the time of the First World War they also were becoming dissatisfied with the politics of loyalism that many leading Muslims had pursued till then.[1]

The most prominent of the new leaders were two brothers, Shaukat Ali (b. 1873) and Muhammad Ali (b. 1878). Their forebears had served as elite administrators under the Muslim ruler of Rampur in western UP, and in this they had a similar background to Gandhi. Shaukat Ali earned his BA from Aligarh in 1894 and joined government service in UP as an opium agent. He financed the education of Muhammad in England after he graduated from Aligarh in 1896 with the aim of gaining entry to the Indian Civil Service. He was awarded a BA in History at

Oxford in 1902 but failed the ICS exam, and returned to India. Like Aurobindo Ghose, he took a post in Baroda State. From there, he kept in close touch with Aligarh and its affairs. He was an eloquent speaker and writer and popular among the Aligarh students and alumni. He believed that Muslims should campaign with Hindus in the national cause rather than allow themselves to be divided by the British. He left Baroda service in 1910, becoming a journalist and full-time politician. The brothers were involved in the campaign for Aligarh to be granted university status in 1910–11. Muhammad started an English weekly published in Calcutta called *Comrade* to campaign on this issue. The British rejected this demand in a ruling of 1912. The two brothers became active also in pan-Islamic affairs. They raised funds during the Tripolitan and Balkan Wars of 1911–12 for a Red Crescent Medical Mission to Turkey to help those wounded. Aligarh students helped in fundraising, and some students even went to Turkey in 1912 to help with medical relief. A photo of Muhammad Ali at this time shows him dressed in the military uniform of this mission, wearing a Turkish-style fez and with a pointed and waxed military-style moustache. Although the British were neutral during these wars, Indian Muslims wanted them to intervene in support of Turkey. Now, however, Britain and Russia were allies against the Ottomans. Muhammad Ali stated that as the British had previously been in the category of those who helped Islam, they could be loyal, but that this was no longer the case. In 1912, the year in which the government of India relocated from Calcutta to Delhi, the *Comrade* made the same move, and once in Delhi, Muhammad Ali started a new Urdu weekly called *Hamdard*. To increase circulation, he adopted a more strident tone in these weeklies. By 1913, they were attracting government attention and had to pay a stiff deposit as security. There was an emphasis on the world of Islam. With the declaration of war in August 1914 by Britain against the Ottoman Empire, many Indian Muslims came to believe that there was a plot by European Christian powers to dismember the Ottoman Empire – the last great Muslim power. They believed that Arabs were being stirred up for this end.[2]

The issue of the Islamic caliphate now came to the fore. The caliph was regarded as the spiritual and temporal leader of Sunni Muslims, responsible for the defence and expansion of divine justice on earth.

Exactly who the caliph was had been disputed over time. The Mughals had sought legitimacy in India by portraying themselves as caliphs, and rival Muslim rulers of the late Mughal period had asserted themselves by declaring their allegiance to a different caliph, the sultan of the Ottoman Empire. Tipu Sultan of Mysore sent an embassy to Turkey in 1785-90 in recognition of the sultan's position in this respect. After 1857, the British had demolished, in Minault's words, the 'whole symbolic system of authority' in India by ending the last remnants of Mughal rule. The Ottoman Sultan was left as the one remaining Sunni potentate who could be regarded as caliph. The Sultans themselves encouraged such pan-Islamic sentiment in India to bolster their position in European conflicts. They were under attack in the Balkans and feared the hostility of other European powers, claiming that this represented 'Islam in danger'. As Minault argues: 'The locus of the caliphate and the person of the caliph mattered little; it was the existence of the caliphate which was essential, as a symbol to which homage was rendered, as a banner for Muslim rulers to wave when threatened by conquest or internal dissention.' The acceptance of the Ottoman Sultan in this position at a wider pan-Islamic level was thus a late-nineteenth century phenomenon. Imams began to read his name on Fridays in mosques in India. Many Indian Muslims now supported the Ottomans in their wars.[3]

The Indian ulama became alarmed from 1911 onwards about the fate of the Ottoman caliph and a supposed threat to the Islamic holy places in Arabia, and increasing numbers became politically engaged. One such figure was Abdul Bari, a *maulana* (revered Islamic scholar) who was associated with another modernising seminary, the Firangi Mahal in Lucknow. He was an avid supporter of Turkey and had visited Constantinople in 1910–11. He and his students collected money for Turkish relief from 1911. He became associated with the Ali brothers in this work. The Ali brothers accepted him as their religious teacher, read the Quran in Urdu under his guidance and were deeply moved by it. Bari campaigned to unite Muslims around the demand to save the holy places of Islam. The three founded an organisation, the Anjuman-e-Khuddam-e-Ka'aba, in 1913 to campaign for the protection of the Ka'aba and other holy places of Islam. They claimed that this was a non-political organisation. They hoped to enrol as members 'every Muslim in India' who would take an oath on joining to give as much help as they were able in the service of Allah. Another activist who became involved in this work was Dr. Mukhtar Ahmad Ansari, who had trained as a doctor in Britain, and practised western medicine in Delhi. The Anjuman was based in Delhi with major branches in Lucknow, Bombay and Hyderabad (Deccan), and smaller branches in UP and Punjab. The leaders toured and held meetings, raising funds. The mother and wives of the Ali brothers and wife of Ansari held separate women's meetings. Members wore crescent badges, and the Ali brothers now dressed in flowing green robes that symbolised their Islamic identity. Many important ulama and Sufis became members and there was much enthusiasm. Plans were discussed to fund military equipment for Turkey – a clearly political objective. Poor Muslims were financed for the hajj. Bookkeeping was however poor, leading to accusations of improper use of the funds. This discredited the organisation. The body was suspended during the First World War, as the conflict with Turkey prevented the continuation of its work. The body had however provided a template for future cooperative work between the ulama and western-educated Muslims. It used religious symbols, such as the Ka'aba, the caliph, the green robes and banners. It reached out to Muslim women. It helped bring the ulama into politics and made many anti-British.[4]

Abul Kalam Azad of Calcutta was another significant leader. With a precocious intellect, he was a prolific writer, a talented Urdu stylist in both prose and poetry, and a persuasive orator. He was born in Mecca in 1888. His father was a respected Sufi of the Qadari and Naqshbandi orders who had migrated to Arabia, and his mother was an Arab. The family returned to India in the 1890s and settled in Calcutta. He was educated by his father, but after reading the writings of Syed Ahmad Khan saw that his traditional education was limited. He became highly critical of the existing ulama, who he saw as compromising religion for worldly gain. He became an erudite scholar who looked to the Quran to guide him in all aspects of life. He was impressed by the nationalist movement in Bengal in its Swadeshi phase and was enthused by the radicalism of groups such Jugantar and Anushilan. In 1908, he travelled through West Asia and met nationalists who were fighting Western imperialism in Iraq, Turkey and Egypt. He was inspired by their vision of a battle for the integrity of Islam waged out of necessity by different Muslim nationalities but united by a belief in Islamic universalism under an overall loyalty to the Ottoman caliph. He studied the Quranic concept of jihad closely and argued that each Muslim nation should wage its own jihad against western imperialism. In India, this meant uniting with Hindu nationalists. Muslims should not however follow Hindu nationalists blindly but be prepared to take the lead in the nationalist movement despite their comparative lack of strength in numbers. They could remedy their minority status through strong self-assertion and become equal partners in the nationalist project.

Azad made a living during this period as a journalist, initially with the influential Urdu paper *The Vakil* of Amritsar, and then as editor of *Al-Hilal* (The Crescent), which he started in Calcutta in 1912. He and other contributors deployed Urdu poetry to powerful emotional effect. He propounded his views on jihad as anti-imperial struggle, with extensive quotations from the Quran. He also wrote about history and events in Turkey and western Asia and extolled Muslims who were resisting European aggression in Tripoli and the Balkans. He began to feel that the Aligarh movement overemphasised rationality, when religion was above all a matter of the heart. In this, there was a strong element of Sufi mysticism in his thinking. While on the one hand he criticised the ulama for their narrow-mindedness, obscurantism and factionalism, on the other he chastised westernised Muslims for their imitation of all things European and the Muslim League for its loyalism. He saw however that a new leadership was emerging from Aligarh more in tune with his beliefs and reached out to men like the Ali brothers. The government forced *Al-Hilal* to close in November 1914 due to its strident pro-Ottoman sentiments. A year later, Azad started another paper *al-Balagh*, but this also had to shut down when in 1916 he was interned in Ranchi, where he remained until January 1920. While so confined, he worked on a translation of the Quran into Urdu.[5]

In 1913 there was an incident in Kanpur that was taken up by Muhammad Ali. The Kanpur Municipality had demolished the washing place of a mosque to make way for a new road in a congested part of the city and was accused of desecrating a holy place. The ulama of Kanpur issued a fatwa demanding its restoration. The lieutenant-governor of UP, Sir James Meston, dismissed the complaint, arguing that Muslims had entered the washing place with their shoes on so that it was hardly a sacred spot. Nonetheless, he agreed to go to Kanpur to hear the complaints. There was a mass demonstration of Muslims on 3 August attended by an estimated ten-to-fifteen thousand. They carried black banners as a sign of mourning. There was a passionate speech by a local maulana who depicted this as a threat to Islam and who exhorted them to be prepared to sacrifice their lives if necessary. The crowd then marched to the mosque and attacked the policemen on guard there, throwing bricks. The police fired, killing several demonstrators, while others were arrested. The dispute now became a national one for Muslims, with Muhammad Ali, A.K. Azad and Abdul Bari becoming involved. Appeals were made in their papers for funds for the bereaved families of Kanpur. Even otherwise loyalist Muslim Leaguers joined the protest. The Viceroy, Lord Hardinge, was asked to intervene. Muslim opinion was virtually unanimous on the issue. Hardinge, who felt that the UP authorities had blundered, went to Kanpur himself, and overrode Meston. Charges against the prisoners were dropped and the demolished area was restored. Shaukat Ali wrote to his brother on how Muslim unity had achieved remarkable results, revealing the potential for future Muslim political campaigns.[6]

At the start of the First World War, the British made a point of emphasising that they were not engaged in an attack on Islam, only on the Ottoman government. They promised that the Muslim holy places would be protected, and that there would be no interference with the hajj pilgrimage. Many Indian ulama gave their public support to Britain on this. The government believed that the Ali brothers were pro-Turkey at heart, and they forced their paper *Comrade* to close by forfeiting its security deposit. The brothers were then interned under the Defence of India Act in Chhindwara in a remote part of central India. As the war progressed, it became clear that the European powers were aiming to displace the Ottomans from west Asia and then dominate it themselves. Lloyd George declared the British entry into Jerusalem in December 1917 as 'the last and most triumphant of the crusades'. The Balfour Declaration of 1917, which promised a home for Jews in Palestine, revealed British support for the settlement of European Jews in a predominantly Muslim region. Radical Muslims in India began to feel that British promises of treating Islam fairly were a sham.[7]

Interned in Chhindwara, the Ali brothers studied the Quran and other religious texts in Urdu. Muhammad Ali was enthused by his reading. The brothers fully supported the Congress-League Pact, and although praising the moderate and secular Muslim leader Muhammad Ali Jinnah for achieving this, they pointed out that he was very aloof from the masses. They were also impressed by Gandhi, who had stated in a speech in Calcutta in 1915: 'Politics cannot be divorced from religion'. They saw him as a Hindu leader who might be sympathetic to Muslims and corresponded with him. They were shocked at the Arab revolt against the Ottomans, seeing it as an attack on the caliph that was encouraged by the British. They failed to appreciate that this might also be a form of nationalism against imperial oppression. They needed the figure of the caliph as a symbol that united the brotherhood of Indian Muslims. In 1917, Jinnah and the Muslim League supported Annie Besant's Home Rule League agitation. Besant demanded the release of Muslims interned during the war. Jinnah overcame his former distaste for mass politics and became president of the Bombay Home Rule League. The Muslim League elected Muhammad Ali as their president for the 1917 meeting when he was still interned, and at the session in Calcutta the president's chair was left empty except for his photo. His mother, Bi Amman, spoke in his place, giving an impassioned speech while wearing a *burqa*, which was perhaps the first time a Muslim woman had addressed such a large political gathering in India.[8]

The Muslim radicals now sought Gandhi's support for their cause and arranged a meeting between him, Abdul Bari and Ansari in March 1918. He was sympathetic to their argument that the Khilafat issue was a heartfelt grievance that united Indian Muslims. He agreed to campaign for the release of the Ali brothers and contacted the Viceroy to this effect. He was thus recognising the Ali brothers, Ansari and Abdul Bari as legitimate leaders of the Muslims of India.[9] Like many other non-Muslim nationalists at that time, Gandhi accepted the claims of the ulama with their scholarly quotations in Arabic, and was hardly aware that the notion that the Ottoman Sultans were caliphs only became widely accepted amongst Indian Muslims in the late nineteenth century.[10] He was not however concerned about the legitimacy of the claim, only that it was something that many Muslims felt strongly about and which he – as a champion of Hindu-Muslim unity – had a moral duty to support. Faisal Devji has written of how in taking up the issue, Gandhi was asserting what he understood as a defining principle of Indian civilisation namely the give-and-take between Hindus and Muslims in India that had underpinned their relations for centuries. Both saw it as a religious obligation (*dharma* or *farz*) to respect the beliefs and practices of those of the other faith. By upholding the demand of the Khilafatists, Gandhi hoped to restore what he saw as an earlier empathy between the two religious communities – one that had been put under strain in the preceding years by the emergence of communalist political divides.[11] In this, he sought to create a national polity that was bound together not by congruent 'interests', but by a sense of 'friendship', in which each group respected the beliefs, and even prejudices, of their fellow-citizens for the good of the wider whole.[12]

The annual session of the Muslim League was held in Delhi in December 1918, with Ansari as chair of the reception committee. He invited Abdul Bari and other ulama, who appeared for the first time at a League session. They demanded that the government represent the sanctity of the Muslim holy places and that all armed forces be withdrawn from Arabia, Syria, Mesopotamia, and other holy areas of western Asia. Ansari denounced British policy towards the Turkish ruler in strong terms, and the speech was subsequently proscribed by the government. They also demanded that the interned Muslim leaders be freed. Although the position of moderate Muslims in the League was weakened by all of this, the Muslim radicals did not regard the League as an appropriate vehicle for the Khilafat demand. It was an elitist organisation with only 777 members in 1919 and with little influence over the government. The Muslim radicals decided to start their own independent organisation and launched a Khilafat Committee at a meeting of 15,000 Muslims in Bombay on 20 March 1919. The president was a wealthy Bombay merchant, Seth Chotani. Sunnis and Shias of the city were both involved in this, even though Shias did not recognise the caliph, as all were concerned about the fate of the holy places under European domination over western Asia.[13] The Khilafat Committee then supported the protest against the Rowlatt Acts that followed immediately afterwards, which ensured a powerful inter-religious unity for the protest. However, while some Khilafat leaders such as Seth Chotani were adherents of Gandhian ethics, the radicals such as Abdul Bari and the Ali brothers viewed nonviolence as a matter of expediency in the circumstances of the day, rather than as a matter of principle. They used some bellicose and un-Gandhian language in their appeals, leading Gandhi to comment that such a tone was hardly designed to win over the hearts of their opponents, which he held to be essential to his method. There were thus from the start tensions between Gandhi and the Khilafat radicals. The Rowlatt Satyagraha did however demonstrate most strikingly the power of Hindu-Muslim unity, with the cry of 'Hindu-Musulman ki jai!' being a marked feature.[14]

By allying with the Muslim radicals, and particularly the ulama, Gandhi was endorsing a group that was often reactionary and divisive. Hamza Alavi has argued that this was a grave mistake on Gandhi's part, as it resulted in '...the legitimisation of the Muslim clergy at the centre of the modern political arena, ... Never before in Indian Muslim history was the clergy ever accorded such a place in political life.[15] In making this choice, Gandhi alienated some Muslim secularists who he also needed as allies in his fight for Hindu-Muslim unity, notably Jinnah, whose championship of a secularist and cosmopolitan politics for the Muslim League provided a counter to the claims of the Khilafatists to represent the Muslims of India. The Khilafat leaders were strongly hostile to Jinnah; at the Calcutta Congress of September 1920, Shaukat Ali even attempted to assault him physically, and he had to be wrenched away by the other delegates.[16] Gandhi was not in a position to bring the two sides together, as he also had alienated Jinnah profoundly when in October 1920 he demanded that the Home Rule League support the Noncooperation Movement. Jinnah, who was President of the Bombay branch of the League and a leading figure in the organisation since its establishment in 1915, argued that the body had been set up to fight for home rule for India by legal means, and that a two-thirds majority was required to change the League's constitution in this respect. Gandhi, who chaired this meeting, ignored him and pushed through a majority vote in his own favour. Jinnah was furious and resigned his membership.[17] Some of Gandhi's strongest Muslim supporters were greatly concerned by this turn of events. Abbas Tyabji, for example, warned Gandhi that the Ali brothers were effective as rabble-rousers, but that he would never want to have them in positions of responsibility or authority over him.[18] In this, he implied that people like Jinnah were more deserving of their trust.

Gandhi had, however, sided with the Khilafatists as they had mass support amongst Muslims, unlike Jinnah and the Muslim League. By doing so, he obtained the critical numbers needed to put intense pressure on the British. Erica Chenoweth and Maria J. Stephan have found in their analysis of civil resistance movements between 1900 and 2006 that when about one per cent of the population was mobilised about 25% of such movements succeeded. When the figure rose to one-and-a-half per cent or more of the population, the success-rate was 80% or over. A relatively small increase in percentage terms has thus greatly improved the odds of success.[19] With Muslims making up over one-fifth of the population of the sub-continent, mass involvement by them alone could have a huge impact.[20]

The real mistake was perhaps that the Muslim radicals adopted a cause that was doomed. They would have been better advised to have accepted that the Ottomans had had their day and that Arab (and Turkish) nationalism was the force to be supported against the British and French in their efforts to control western Asia through the mandate system. They might also have made an issue of the way that Jewish settlement was being encouraged in Palestine. These concerns had far greater long-term strength. The other mistake was that the radicals abandoned the Muslim League and diverted their energies into a separate organisation. They had a chance in 1919 to capture the Muslim League and use it as a vehicle to champion popular Islamic nationalism in alliance with the Congress. This might have provided a firmer base for long-term Hindu-Muslim unity in India.

A further meeting of the Khilafat Committee was held on 5 July 1919 at which it was resolved to start Khilafat branches all over India and exert stronger pressure on the government. An all-India Khilafat Day was held on 17 October 1919 that involved a hartal and mass meetings. It was a marked success, uniting Sunnis and Shias. Gandhi addressed a big meeting in Bombay, and 20,000 Muslims and Hindus met on the beach at Madras. Another large meeting was held in Calcutta addressed by Fazlul Haq, and there were meetings in most districts of Bengal. A monster meeting of some 50,000 in Delhi was addressed by Ansari and the Arya Samaj leader Swami Shraddanand. Urban Muslims were the main participants in all this, with some rural Muslims from Bengal and Sindh. Local Sufi leaders – the pirs – organised meetings in Sindh. An all-India Khilafat Conference was held in Delhi on 23-4 November 1919 to discuss a plan of action. About 300 attended, around half of whom were from UP. The ulama were heavily represented. Gandhi, Swami Shraddanand, Jawaharlal Nehru and M.M. Malaviya were there. It was resolved, first, to boycott the peace celebrations planned by the British for December, second for Muslims to withdraw cooperation from the government as a religious duty if the caliphate was jeopardised by the peace settlement, and third to boycott European goods. Gandhi and Chotani, and other moderate-minded merchants and moderate barristers, opposed this last resolution. The exact form that noncooperation would take was not spelt out at this stage, but a committee was established to discuss it. A delegation was appointed to go to England to plead the Khilafat cause. In his speech, Gandhi stated that Hindus supported Muslims over Khilafat as it was a just cause. He demanded national solidarity. This was all a victory for those who wanted mass agitation. The Ali brothers were released from internment at the end of 1919, in time to attend the Amritsar Congress in December. They had a triumphal procession from central India to Amritsar. It was clear that they were now the undisputed leaders of a popular Muslim movement.[21]

In early 1920, the Ali brothers threw themselves into a frenetic round of touring. They were received all over India as heroes, with slogans of 'Muhammad Ali-Shaukat Ali ki jai!' and 'Hindu-Musulman ki jai!' They were welcomed in Chandni Chowk in Delhi on 9 January by a crowd of 50,000. A.K. Azad was released from internment in January and he immediately joined up with the Khilafat, holding a big rally in Calcutta. His speeches were more cautious than those of the Ali brothers. He then went to Delhi, where he met Gandhi for the first time. An All-India Khilafat Conference was held in Bombay in mid-February 1920. The radicals tried to consolidate their hold against the Bombay merchants, headed by Chotani. Abdul Bari claimed that it was against their religion for Muslims to serve in the British armed forces as they could be deployed against Muslim rulers. He wanted a fatwa to this effect to be circulated among the troops. Chotani and the moderates were horrified by this suggestion, but it was hard for them to oppose an appeal to religion. However, the radicals needed the merchant's money, so a decision on the issue was postponed. The conference produced a Khilafat Manifesto and a new constitution for the body. The manifesto spelt out the Khilafat demands and hinted at dire consequences if the government failed to keep the Ottoman Empire and caliphate intact. The new constitution set out a framework of Khilafat Committee branches, the election of executives, raising funds, recruiting volunteers and electing delegates to the annual meetings. The aim was to make this into an all-India organisation.[22]

Muhammad Ali then led a Khilafat delegation to Britain that arrived in February. A photo of him taken in London shows him in a smart Western suit and tie, his Islamic identity being expressed through a fur karakul hat with a crescent and a smartly trimmed beard. The delegates met Lloyd George on 17 March and claimed to speak for the Muslims of the whole British Empire. Lloyd George asked them if they opposed Arab independence, and Muhammad Ali replied that they did and that the Arabs should accept ultimate Ottoman sovereignty. It was clear to Lloyd George that he had little appreciation of realities on the ground in western Asia. The terms of the treaty of Sèvres were published in May. This accepted the independence of the Arab countries from the Ottoman Empire. Syria, Palestine and Mesopotamia were made British and French mandates. Eastern Thrace and Smyrna were given to Greece, and the Dodecanese Islands to Italy. Constantinople was to remain Turkish, but the straits were internationalised. The Turks signed the treaty on 20 August 1920, and the Khilafat delegation returned to India having failed in their objective. Noncooperation was now the Khilafatists sole strategy.[23]

While the delegation was in London, a popular movement had emerged from Sindh and the northwest of India. This was led in Sindh by pirs who enjoyed a powerful position amongst the rural Muslims. They were the spiritual and often lineal descendants of the Sufi saints who had converted Sindhis to Islam. Their shrines owned large areas of land. They had acted as centres for protest from time to time. Many pirs now joined the Khilafat Committee and propagated the message in their localities. Even the smallest villages in Sindh were reached in this way. They preached that the infidel government had taken control of the holy cities of Islam and had defiled them by slaughtering pigs, drinking liquor, and walking with their boots in the sacred precincts. All Muslims had a duty of noncooperation with the government or be threatened with hellfire. Few rural Muslims knew about the Ottoman caliph, but they understood the idea that their religion was in danger and that the government was somehow responsible for this. Pirs who did not endorse this agenda found that they were losing influence and adapted accordingly. A Provincial Khilafat Conference was held in Sindh in February 1920 in which Shaukat Ali, Abdul Bari and other leaders shared the platform with pirs. Thousands of devotees attended and donated generously to Khilafat funds. During the summer of 1920 there was then a *hijrat*, or migration, movement, with Muslims of Sindh and the Northwest Frontier Province leaving for Afghanistan in protest at British policy towards the caliph. The hijratis believed that their religion was in danger in India, and that they should migrate to the land of a Muslim ruler. Abdul Bari and A.K. Azad issued a fatwa in favour of the migration, but not as a substitute for noncooperation. Thousands sold their property and migrated in July and August. The Khyber Pass was clogged with bullock carts, camels and people on foot carrying their possessions. Some were attacked and looted by tribesmen, others succumbed to hunger and thirst. With 30,000 on the move, the Amir of Afghanistan issued a proclamation urging it to stop. Eventually several thousand disillusioned *muhajirin* returned to India with nothing. Many had died on the migration. The Khilafat leaders had no control over this and stated that people should remain in India. The hijrat had however revealed the strength of religious feeling among rural Muslims as a force that could be tapped into. It also showed that the Khilafat leaders could easily lose control without better organisation and closer coordination with the ulama and Sufi pirs.[24]

Muhammad Ali arrived back in India on 4 October and immediately threw himself into the noncooperation campaign. He declared on his arrival in Bombay that Muslim interests could only be protected once India had self-rule. They would use noncooperation to secure that end.[25] The stage was now set for noncooperation to be embraced by the Congress also.

2

STRATEGIES OF RESISTANCE 1920–22

ETHICAL OR EXPEDIENT?

In the literature on nonviolent resistance, a distinction is frequently made between ethical and expedient approaches to nonviolence. Sometimes the distinction made is between the moral and the pragmatic. The ethical path is associated chiefly with Gandhi and his disciples. Nonviolence is said to work because of its moral superiority. Because this is so, it is imperative to maintain it even at the cost of short-term political failure. The expedient or pragmatic form adopts nonviolence as a means best suited to specific political situations – most commonly when the opponent has overwhelming control over the instruments of coercive force, so that violence is not a realistic option. Such pragmatists may tolerate a degree of violence in a movement for tactical purposes and will not rule out the use of violence when they consider it appropriate. We may say that pragmatists are hard-headed political realists, while ethicists maintain great faith in the psychological power of the purity of their approach. They also tend to have a longer-term vision of the sort of ethical society that they seek to build through such resistance. In practice, there tends to be a blurring of the lines between the two with protestors adopting an ethical approach at one juncture, expedient at another.[1] Nonetheless, this distinction was important during the campaign that was started in India by the Congress in 1920 – the Noncooperation Movement. While Gandhi sought above all to build an ethical alliance rooted in his principles, some other leading nationalists and their supporters embraced nonviolent methods at this juncture because it appeared to provide the best means to pressurise the British into devolving greater political power to Indians. The expectations of the two camps were generally reconciled during the first stages of this movement, but their different expectations led to conflict and disillusion at a later stage when Gandhi forced the Congress to accept his ethical approach at the cost of potential political advantage. In this chapter I shall focus on this tactical and strategic history and examine the British response.

There were two major grievances that were held to be behind the decision of the Indian National Congress to launch the Noncooperation Movement. The first concerned the way that so many British officers in India as well as significant groups in Britain had sought to justify the reign of terror in Punjab in 1919 as a necessary response to Indian nationalist protest. We have explored this in Chapter 5 of the previous volume. The second was the controversy over the caliph of Islam that underpinned the Khilafat Movement, which we examined in the previous chapter. This all gave rise to calls for a boycott of the first elections to be held under the Montagu-Chelmsford constitutional reforms of 1919. It was asserted that not only were the reforms inadequate, but that British officials would do their best to undermine them, given their hostility to Indian nationalists. Against this, many Congress leaders believed that a boycott would be a tactical mistake and it was preferable to fight their cause within the councils. Gandhi, however, could see that the political scene in India had shifted radically, with a new mass assertiveness making itself felt in the aftermath of the First World War. He knew that the Indian National Congress had to respond to this if it was to retain its credibility as a representative of the Indian nation, but – given the experience of April 1919 – he feared that it might lead to violence. He therefore sought to both mobilise and keep in check this popular explosion. In tapping this force in 1920, he managed to gain Congress support for the boycott of the elections to be held in November. Once the other leaders had agreed to this, they had little choice but to commit themselves to this new mass politics if they were to retain their political credibility. This history forms the subject of the chapter.

The Noncooperation Decision

Gandhi did not control the Indian National Congress in 1919; he had merely led one nationwide protest on an issue, the Rowlatt Acts, that had angered almost all nationalists, and which was not therefore controversial in Congress circles. Gaining control of the Congress for a campaign of noncooperation that would include the boycott of the new legislatures was another matter, as most of the leading nationalists of the day were, in 1919, firmly committed to fighting the elections due in November 1920 and taking their seats in the councils. How he managed to win a majority amongst them before the elections, and in doing so become the commanding leader of the Congress, forms the subject of this section.

Gandhi began by building up the support that he had enjoyed so far amongst many Muslim radicals – as seen in the Rowlatt Satyagraha. He went on to play a prominent role in the Khilafat Conference in Delhi in November 1919. Writing about this in his autobiography some years later, Gandhi described how he felt daunted about speaking before an audience who could express themselves in 'the faultless, polished Urdu of the Delhi Muslims'. Despite this, he went ahead in his 'broken Hindi', and made a powerful impression. He opposed the idea of a boycott of British goods along the lines of the Swadeshi Movement in Bengal as it was a punitive measure, and this went against his principles. It would be better, rather, to launch a campaign of noncooperation (*asahyog*). Gandhi said that he had come up with this term on the spur of the moment and had not thought through what it might exactly imply. His passionate delivery enthused Khilafat leaders and audience alike, and was followed by long and continuous applause, and a firm endorsement of his proposal.[2] Minault, by contrast, states that the idea of noncooperation was proposed at the conference by the Khilafat leader Sayyid Husain.[3]

A committee was set up to determine the form that noncooperation would take. Gandhi took the leading role on this. He managed to temper the demands of some of the more extreme Muslims, who were demanding hijrat – or migration to a Muslim country – and jihad – which in this instance meant a holy war. He argued in the committee sessions that, following the experience of 1919, the Indian people were not yet seasoned sufficiently in nonviolence for a campaign of mass civil disobedience. He believed that there had to be a gradual escalation of the protest in stages, with civil disobedience as the last one. He did not plan a boycott of British goods or the legislative assemblies initially, though some of the Khilafat leaders wanted this. He felt that though Indians should hand back their titles and resign from civil posts, it was premature to ask the military and police to quit their service. This would take place only at a later stage. Tax refusal would be the final stage. In May, Gandhi was still advising the readers of his weekly *Navajivan* on whom to vote for in the November elections. Early in June, however, Lala Lajpat Rai, who had also forged a good working relationship with the Muslim radicals, announced that he would not stand for election as he felt that the seat allocations announced by the British for Punjab were unfair to the urban interests that he represented. Gandhi decided to accept the election boycott as a part of the programme. This was a significant escalation, as it meant that career politicians of all religions throughout India who were intending to fight in the elections would have to decide whether to support Gandhi, Rai and the Khilafatists. Many mainstream Congress leaders were opposed to the idea but agreed as a compromise to call a special session of the Congress in Calcutta in September to debate the issue.[4]

On 4 July 1920, Gandhi announced that the Khilafatists would start noncooperation on 1 August. He first called on Indian soldiers to refuse to serve in Mesopotamia, as they were part of an occupying army that was resented by the Arabs of the region. He demanded that those who had intended to join the military should abandon their plans. He then set out a five-point programme:

1. Titles and honorary positions will be renounced.
2. Legislatures will be boycotted.
3. Parents will withdraw their children from government schools.
4. Lawyers will give up practice and help people to settle their civil disputes among themselves.

5. Invitations to government functions, parties, etc., will be politely refused, non-cooperation being given as the sole reason for doing so.

Gandhi noted that as Lala Lajpat Rai was boycotting the elections, it could be taken that the Punjab nationalists supported the programme, so that it now went beyond the Khilafatists alone. He went on to address some of the more contentious elements of this programme. On the issue of the legislatures, some – he said – had suggested that they fight the elections and then obstruct the government from within. He argued that as rulers could not govern without the support of their subjects, the most effective form of protest was complete withdrawal:

> So long as there is lack of understanding between the king and the subject, to attend the king's council is to strengthen his hands. A king cannot govern at all if he is not able to carry any section of his subjects with him. It follows from this that the fewer the subjects who co-operate with him, the less will be his authority. Hence, for those who accept non-co-operation, the total boycott of legislatures is the only right course.[5]

Here, he advanced what was to become a classic position of theorists of nonviolent resistance; namely that power rests in the people, and a ruler who has no support will inevitably fall.

The other highly contentious point for many nationalist leaders was the boycott of the civil courts, as a significant number were lawyers who depended on legal work for their incomes. Gandhi argued:

> It is my confirmed belief that every government masks its brute force and maintains its control over the people through civil and criminal courts, for it is cheaper, simpler and more honourable, for a ruler that instead of his controlling the people through naked force, they themselves, lured into slavery through courts, etc., submit to him of their own accord. If people settle their civil disputes among themselves and the lawyers, unmindful of self-interest, boycott the courts in the interest of the people, the latter can advance in no time. I have believed for many years that every State tries to perpetuate its power through lawyers.

In this, Gandhi referred to the position that he had adopted in *Hind Swaraj* (Chapter 11), namely that the British legal system encouraged lawyers to foment disputes as it enhanced their earnings, all of which undermined social cohesion.

He also addressed the issue of boycotting government schools. This was another self-denial that would hit elite nationalists particularly hard. He started by saying that the sort of education provided by such schools was harmful, and that Indians needed the 'right kind of education'. Here he was harping back to another of his arguments of *Hind Swaraj* (Chapter 18) on how the people were being enslaved by English education. He had argued that education in India should be entirely in the vernacular languages, with English studied merely as a foreign language. This would encourage critical thought in the languages of the people. Although he did not state it in his manifesto of 1920, he must also have had in his mind here the sort of nationalist education that Rabindranath Tagore had pioneered in Bengal during the Swadeshi Movement. Gandhi continued:

> But my purpose at present in calling for a boycott of the schools is different; I want to show the government by rendering the schools idle that, so long as justice is not done in regard to the Punjab and the khilafat, co-operation with it is distasteful. I know that this suggestion will be visited with a good deal of ridicule. But, with the passing of time, people will realise that if they refused to crowd the government schools, it would be impossible to run the administration.

Although he was justifying this aspect of the programme primarily in terms of paralysing the government, the symbolism of the elites giving up on another major privilege would have been apparent to all.

This programme clearly demanded a high degree of self-sacrifice from the English-educated higher-class nationalists. In this, they were to provide an example for the mass of the people. As it meant considerable hardship for them – with a loss of income and career-enhancing education for their children – many were at first disturbed by Gandhi's demands. Quite quickly, however, most came to see that such actions were necessary to build the parallel system of authority that could provide the necessary threat to British power. In place of the imperial institutions, they would now build up their own systems of civil arbitration and education.[6]

Gandhi and the Khilafat leaders launched the Noncooperation Movement on 1 August, with a day of hartal with prayers, fasting and meetings. There was to be no breaking of the law. They advised holders of imperial honours and titles to renounce them; and Gandhi took the lead by returning the medals that he had been awarded in South Africa and India.[7] In doing so, he made a formal announcement of his estrangement from the British Raj, and his belief that the time for compromise had passed. He was now a self-styled out-and-out opponent of British imperialism – something he had never stated unambiguously before. By taking this pre-emptive action, Gandhi and his Khilafat allies forced other nationalist leaders to adopt a position on the matter. Clearly, this was a gamble, as they would be side-lined and isolated if they then failed to carry the special Congress session due in September. Gandhi realised however that if what would be styled as collaboration with the British prevailed, those who had voted against his programme would appear as being weak, self-interested and vacillating – hardly qualities to further their future political careers.

Local Congress groups were now debating the issue. Motilal Nehru, the most prominent nationalist leader in UP, did not initially support the boycott of the legislatures, and was already planning his own election campaign. He nonetheless appreciated the emotional power of Gandhi's challenge, and sympathised with the idea of noncooperation. He came around to Gandhi's position after the matter was debated by the UP Congress Committee on 22 August. The UP nationalists decided to support the noncooperation programme in its entirety, including the election boycott. Nehru went along with this. In Bombay City, nationalists met on 15 August and voted for noncooperation – with the erstwhile Home Rule Leaguers who were closely aligned with Gandhi taking the lead in this. In Maharashtra, Tilak appears to have given some support for noncooperation, but kept his distance from the Khilafat leaders. He died on 1 August in Bombay City, before having to decide on the issue clearly. Several of his followers in Maharashtra opposed the boycott of elections, arguing that it was better to work within the councils. In Gujarat, on the other hand, a meeting of local nationalists held on 11 July voted in favour of Gandhi's full programme, as did the nationalists of Sindh. The Bengal Congress Committee met on 15 August and though supporting other aspects of noncooperation, came out against the election boycott. The Madras Congress Committee adopted a similar stance in three meetings in August, despite Gandhi and Shaukat Ali touring the Presidency in that month to win support for their programme. In Bihar, by contrast, where the Congress Committee was dominated by the strong Gandhian, Rajendra Prasad, Gandhi was promised full backing in a meeting at the end of August.[8]

This all meant that when the special session of the Congress met in Calcutta in September, support for noncooperation was by no means assured. Special trains were laid on to bring Khilafat supporters to the city from all over India, and as at that time there was no limit on delegates, they managed to gain control over the Subjects Committee – which was crucial in deciding the agenda that would be debated in the formal sessions. Muslim strength in Bengal itself was particularly critical in this respect. This was the first time that large numbers of Muslims had come to a Congress session. Also important was the support for council boycott given by Motilal Nehru, and the leaders of the Karnataka Congress, Gangadhar Rao Deshpande – formerly a leading supporter of Tilak. Even then, Gandhi won by only a narrow margin of 148 to 133 in the vote in the Subjects Committee. Without Khilafat support he would have had no chance of prevailing. This was crucial, as the vote in the open session could then be assured. The old Presidency leaders who supported the policy of obstructing the council from within had hoped to dominate the session and were both disconcerted and angry to see that they had been outflanked by Gandhi – something that they had not anticipated. The Bengal leader Chittaranjan Das was particularly upset. If Tilak – the most revered and influential of the old leaders – had been there and had opposed the boycott, the vote may possibly have gone the other way – but he was now dead. More important probably, as pointed out by Judith Brown, Gandhi managed to win support from what she calls the 'latent sources of political power' in India beyond that of the old nationalist elite, as seen in the way he had in the preceding years mobilised the urban middle classes in places such as Punjab and Bombay City, and the peasants in localities such as Champaran and Kheda. She writes: '...for the first time a leader tapped some of these latent sources to gain power at the apex of institutional politics'. Even then, Gandhi had to make some compromises. He agreed to include foreign goods in the boycott – something that he had opposed earlier – largely under pressure from Chittaranjan Das, who refused to abandon this iconic element of the earlier Swadeshi Movement in Bengal. Gandhi also agreed to a gradual withdrawal of pupils from schools and lawyers from courts, rather than the immediate complete boycotts that he had initially demanded. He also agreed that their stated goal should be that of 'Swaraj' – which could be translated into English to mean different entities – ranging from Dominion Status within the British empire, to complete independence, or – as Gandhi saw it – a freeing of the mental and institutional hold of British imperialism regardless of constitutional status. Once this was all agreed, the vote in the open conference was more overwhelming – 1,855 for the boycott and only 873 against.[9]

The details of noncooperation had to be worked out, and a sub-committee of the All India Congress Committee consisting of Gandhi, Motilal Nehru and Vithalbhai Patel was asked to do this. Patel, the older brother of Vallabhbhai Patel, was – in marked contrast to his sibling – opposed to the council boycott, having already built a distinguished career fighting the British from within the legislative councils established under the Morley-Minto reforms. He believed that they should act as Sinn Féin had done in Britain – by contesting seats and then refusing to take them up at the central level while implementing their programme as much as possible on local councils. When this sub-committee met later in September, Gandhi argued that the Congress had voted in Calcutta for all four stages of his noncooperation programme, up to and including tax refusal. This was rejected by the other two – it was to escalate only gradually. Vithalbhai Patel was worried that tax refusal would quickly lead to 'violence and riot', arguing that people were likely to react so when forced to pay up. Initially, there was to be a boycott of elections only to the imperial and provincial (but not local) councils and of foreign goods.[10] The All India Congress Committee then met in October to rule on this. What became clear here was that the old guard saw the council boycott as a one-off protest measure; they still expected to be fighting the next elections that would come in 1923. They were not in the meantime prepared to give up their legal practices or take their children out of government schools. After much debate, it was agreed that there would be a gradual and progressive boycott of courts and schools. The subsequent press statement nonetheless gave the appearance that the four-fold boycott – councils, foreign goods, courts and schools – was fully on course with Gandhi at the helm. Some pro-council Congress leaders resigned in protest. One of them, Jamnadas Dwarkadas predicted that the campaign would 'either fizzle out and make the Congress ridiculous or … if it is prolonged for some time … will inevitably bring disaster to the country'. Annie Besant fulminated against noncooperation, arguing that it was a 'channel of hatred' that threatened 'the very existence of India'. Gandhi was accused by others of being – variously – an impractical idealist, politically naïve, a conceited and ambitious upstart, a madman, and a rabble-rouser who would (in the words of G.A. Natesan) usher in a reign of 'chaos and anarchy'. People such as these had every intention of going ahead and fighting the elections and sitting in the councils. A group of them formed the National Liberal Federation that was dedicated to carrying on in the old way. In this, they broke decisively with the Congress. They were now known as the 'Indian Liberals', a group that was regarded with contempt by many nationalists as self-interested collaborators.[11]

The Reassertion of Bengal

The Bengali bhadralok elites had become accustomed to seeing themselves in the vanguard of the Indian nationalist movement, but they were now being outflanked by a charismatic Gujarati and a group of Muslim radicals. This irked them, and in late 1920, under the inspired leadership of Chittaranjan Das, they sought once more to gain the initiative.

Many in Bengal besides the Muslims were at that time spoiling for a fight with the British. During the First World War, some Indian businessmen in Bengal had made huge profits. To the fore in this respect were the Oswal, Agarwal and Maheshwari Baniya traders from the Marwar region of Rajasthan who had migrated to Calcutta from the mid-nineteenth century onwards, settling mainly in Barabazar. Known collectively as 'Marwaris', they had gradually replaced Bengalis as the chief collaborators with the British banking houses. They became the principle distributers of Manchester piece-goods in eastern India, and were prominent in the grain, oil-seed and jute trades – which were controlled ultimately by the big European managing agencies. They had not been involved in the Swadeshi Movement. The war had however given them greater financial power, and the grip of the European managing agencies had been loosened. According to Rajat Ray: 'From collaborators they turned almost overnight into competitors'. They gained control over the share market, and their speculative activities affected all areas of economic life in Bengal. Europeans accused them of gambling on the prices of essentials in an irresponsible manner and they began to compete openly with the European managing agencies, using their financial power to gain a dominant position in various manufacturing sectors. In 1919, they started building their own jute mills in 1919 and they now suffered from blatant racial discrimination by European businessmen. Their response was to support the nationalists, providing large sums for Congress funds. They were far more sympathetic towards Gandhi – a fellow Baniya from western India – than the Bengali bhadralok politicians. G.D. Birla, a leading Calcutta Marwari, became a particularly staunch Gandhian. The Marwari Chamber of Commerce supported the Noncooperation Movement and helped enforce the boycott of British goods.[12]

The European businessmen of Calcutta strongly resented the Montagu-Chelmsford reforms, taking them as a sign that they were losing their hold over British officialdom in India. Before then, they had always felt that their interests would be safeguarded by those who ran the Raj. Once the reforms were a *fait accompli*, they saw that they would now need to engage in politics themselves and try to keep in favour with Indian politicians if they were to protect their large financial assets. In fact, many British civil servants in Bengal continued to believe that European businessmen needed protection under the new order. The officials also argued that the Congress stood for the interests of the high castes alone and that the low castes of Bengal would be exploited unless they continued to protect them. The battle was now for the hearts and minds of the mass of the Bengali people. It was not a contest that the British were likely to win.[13]

During the Rowlatt Satyagraha, the Congress leaders in Bengal had been half-hearted in their support of the agitation. As yet, they had no proper organisation in the countryside. Only in Calcutta was there any real response. When news came of Gandhi's arrest on 10 April, the Marwaris and north Indians closed their shops, and trams were stopped by crowds in which Marwari youth took the leading role. Bengali Hindus took almost no part in the protest at Gandhi's arrest. Marwaris, Bhatias and Muslims were involved in rioting on 12-13 April. There was no disruption in the interior of Bengal. When information came through about the atrocities in Punjab – particularly about the massacre in Amritsar – there was an outburst of anger and revulsion, and Rabindranath Tagore took the lead in resigning his knighthood. Tagore stated in a letter to C.F. Andrews that the British had lost all moral prestige, and no longer could the people of India have any faith in British justice. Throughout July and August, there was steadily rising moral indignation over what had happened in Amritsar. The promised constitutional reforms were badly tainted by this. At the Amritsar Congress in December 1919, Chittaranjan Das moved a resolution that declared the reforms 'inadequate, unsatisfactory and disappointing'. Das was now being acknowledged as the foremost nationalist leader in Bengal.[14]

Chittaranjan Das was born in Calcutta in 1870 and was thus a year younger than Gandhi. He was from a wealthy family with a progressive reputation that came originally from Bikrampur in East Bengal. He was sent to Britain for education, where he failed the Indian Civil Service exam, but qualified as a barrister. He returned in 1892 to set up practice in Calcutta, soon becoming an extremely successful lawyer. He was involved in nationalist activity from his student days onwards and was part of the Swadeshi Movement, being close to Bipin Chandra Pal and Aurobindo Ghose and worked on the production of the weekly *Bande Mataram*. In 1910 he became a hero in the city through his painstaking defence of Aurobindo Ghose and his fellow-accused on terrorist charges. Das was a politician of great skill and was widely admired by his fellow bhadralok.

Das and other bhadralok leaders were not – in marked contrast to the Marwaris of Calcutta – much impressed with Gandhi as a person. C.F. Andrews noted in a letter to Tagore of 5 October 1920 how Bengal was the one province not captivated by Gandhi. He also noted how no Bengali leaders were regarded at that time with reverence by the masses. They were accustomed to living in a luxurious westernised manner and were not willing to give up this lifestyle. He had seen an article in the Calcutta-magazine, the *Modern Review*, that asserted Gandhi was the enemy 'of all civilisation and all the comforts which it brings' and that a life under Gandhi's Swaraj would be 'a veritable dog's life'. Andrews concluded: 'Mahatma Gandhi is, out and out, on the side of the poor. That is why the poor people have recognised him instinctively as their friend and champion.'[15]

Das and the Bengal Congress leaders were outflanked at the Calcutta Congress of September 1920 by Gandhi and the Khilafatists but managed to retain their integrity by putting their own stamp on the form that noncooperation would take. During the debates, Das asserted that he did not oppose noncooperation in principle but felt that each province should determine the form that noncooperation would take. He did not see it as a campaign for moral and material reconstruction, as Gandhi did, but as one primarily for Swaraj. Motilal Nehru agreed with this, and after discussions, Gandhi agreed to include the demand for Swaraj. Gandhi argued that the initial focus should be on getting the elites to renounce their privileges by resigning from government service and boycotting schools, colleges and law courts. The Bengali nationalists were not willing to do this. Gandhi agreed to substitute the word 'gradual' for 'immediate' boycott of schools, colleges and courts. The Bengalis wanted, by contrast, to prioritise an economic boycott of British goods, which they believed would hit British monopoly capital hard where it hurt most. Even before the Calcutta Congress, Bipin Chandra Pal had proposed that in Bengal there be an economic boycott, rather than boycott of government jobs and so on. Gandhi was reluctant to include strikes, *hartals* (mass protests) and boycotts as a core feature of the campaign at its start, as he was concerned about the potential for violence, as in 1919. He insisted that there had to be training in the methods of satyagraha before there were such confrontations. This training would be provided through constructive work.[16]

Once the council boycott had become a *fait accompli*, Das decided to put his own strong stamp on the movement. He sought to eliminate Gandhi's moral language and project it as a radical all-out attack on the British that would force them into granting further constitutional concessions. Having no ethical commitment to nonviolence, Das was prepared to accept that a predominantly nonviolent movement might be accompanied by a degree of violence. He had always had ties with the revolutionary nationalists of Bengal and was prepared to recruit them for the noncooperation campaign, hoping that they would instigate mass protest that would paralyse the whole machinery of government and bring it to its knees as quickly as possible. He felt that Gandhi was being far too cautious in projecting civil disobedience as a last resort, to be launched only after the recruitment of a large volunteer force that could maintain nonviolent discipline along with the careful preparation of the people chosen to break the law. Das was not concerned with such safeguards and wanted widespread civil disobedience to be inaugurated quickly. He and his fellow leaders wanted workers to strike in support of the movement – something that Gandhi was not prepared to countenance, as in western India that meant hitting mainly fellow-Indian capitalists. In Bengal, the target of such strikes would be European managers and plantation-owners. From his Bengali perspective, Das saw the domination of the British as racial as much as economic. As he wrote on 5 December 1920:

> Exploitation and administration being part of the same duty in the British government of India, any programme of non-cooperation to be effective must be both political and economic. On the political side it includes a boycott of the machinery of the present government, both legislative and executive, whether the services called for be honorary or stipendiary; on the economic side it means boycott of British goods and of British agencies in the import and export trade of the country, withdrawal of financial support from British enterprises and of Indian labour from its factories and, in the last resort, refusal to pay taxes.

He suggested that committees of traders and consumers be set up to consider the best ways of doing this. In this, Das was now instigating an upheaval considerably more radical than anything that Gandhi had been prepared to countenance.[17]

The Nagpur Congress of December 1920

The strategy to be adopted for the forthcoming struggle was debated and decided on at the Congress session held at the end of 1920 at Nagpur in the Central Provinces and Berar (CP & B); 14,582 delegates travelled there, the largest number ever to attend a session. Of these, 79% were from CP & B and Bombay Presidency – most of whom favoured noncooperation. Chittaranjan Das was supported by over 300 delegates who represented Bengal Districts. This included members of the Dacca Anushilan Samiti, whose fares Das paid himself. Many of these extremists had previously been in jail. Supporters of Gandhi were in a minority in this group. Of the 900 delegates from Bengal, only 100 were Muslim. Das's supporters were well-disciplined and willing to use violence to get their way. Before the Congress even started, the revolutionary Pulin Das led the pro-Das group in a physical altercation in the Bengal camp with the anti-Das group led by Jitendralal Bannerjea, who was supported by Marwari and Bhatia delegates from Bengal. The latter were beaten severely. Shaukat Ali sent a group of Punjabi and Gujarati volunteers to break up the fight. Gandhi then came and pacified the conflicting groups by telling them that a compromise had been reached between him and Das.[18] All of this revealed that Gandhi's leadership of the campaign was at times going to be challenged.

There were important initial debates in the Subjects Committee. The first major one was on whether they should now demand Dominion Status within the British Empire, or complete independence. Das and Lala Lajpat Rai headed a group wanting the former, while the Ali brothers insisted on the latter. Gandhi negotiated a compromise – they would demand 'swaraj' and leave the definition of the term unstated. Next day, Gandhi made it clear that he did not want to sever all ties with Britain unless forced to do so, to preserve their self-respect. The next topic to come before the Subjects Committee was that of the exact programme for noncooperation. Gandhi wanted a full boycott of schools and courts to be launched there and then, while Das demanded that it be implemented gradually. The resulting wording of the Congress resolution was something of a fudge, expressing merely a wish that parents make 'greater efforts' to withdraw their children from government schools, and for students at government colleges who believed it was against their conscience to stay in them to devote themselves either to the service of the campaign or study in national colleges. Lawyers were only asked to 'make greater efforts to suspend their practice and devote their attention to national service'. It was also agreed that there would be an economic boycott of foreign goods, but that it would be 'gradual'. A 'National Indian Service' was set up to implement this programme. It would all be funded by a collection that would be called the 'Tilak Memorial Swaraj Fund'. Congress Committees were to be established in each village or group of villages with a provincial central organisation co-ordinating them all. Rather than call directly for government officials, soldiers and policemen to resign their service, a vague statement was made about how they should consider where their loyalties lay and treat Congress protestors with respect and courtesy. The need for strict nonviolence was emphasised strongly, and it was stated specifically that violence was contrary to the growth of a spirit of democracy and would, if committed, be a grave setback to the movement. There was a call for strong Hindu-Muslim unity, and an end to the practice of untouchability. Finally, it was agreed that the stated aim of the movement was 'Swaraj in a Year'.[19]

Gandhi had first proposed the slogan of 'Swaraj in a Year' at the Calcutta Congress in September. He had stated then that it entailed 'such a state that we can maintain our separate existence without the presence of the English.' They might continue in a 'partnership' with the British, but it would have to be 'a partnership of equals'. 'To get swaraj is to get rid of our helplessness.' He stated that this involved freeing themselves from 'the threefold *maya* [illusion] of government-controlled schools, government law-courts and legislative councils, and truly control our own education, and regulate our disputes... (and) manufacture our own cloth...only by hand-spinning and hand-weaving'. If they could do all this in one year, they would have achieved what was in effect swaraj in that time.[20] For Gandhi, 'swaraj' was not defined in constitutional terms, but rather seen as entailing a broad cultural change in which the Indian people would shed their fear of the British and subservience to their values and institutions. The slogan suggested that if the Indian people embraced Gandhi's methods they could, through a sheer act of will, prevail against the Raj. Gandhi talked in terms of a spiritual miracle. There was a mystical element in this that provided a hostage to fortune.[21] Despite this, the slogan was ambiguous, as for many nationalists 'swaraj' still meant self-government through a popularly elected legislature that was free from any control by the British, rather than a more amorphous spiritual and mental liberation. The slogan provided, nonetheless, an inspired rallying cry. Compared to his early protests in India, Gandhi was adopting a far more confrontational stance. The downside to this from the perspective of the satyagrahi was that it allowed for less chance of a constructive dialogue with his opponents that might lead to a compromise satisfactory to both parties. Here, one key element of his technique was being side-lined, for the time being at least.

Some historians, such as Judith Brown and Gopal Krishna, have seen this all as a triumph for Gandhi; others, such as Rajat Ray, have argued that Das's approach had in fact won the day.[22] The evidence here is mixed. Das was certainly far less cautious than Gandhi on the matter of confrontational mass civil disobedience, and his demand for an economic boycott carried the day, as did his programme for only a gradual disengagement from British institutions. Nonetheless, the informing demand of the campaign – that of 'Swaraj in One Year' – had come from Gandhi. Ray – in contrast to Gopal Krishna – attributes the restructuring of the Congress organisation, the creation of the special fund, and a membership drive to Das.[23] Ray's argument here is not borne out by the evidence. The idea of a 'Swaraj Fund' had been set out by Motilal Nehru, Gandhi and Vithalbhai Patel in their report of 22 September 1920.[24] Three days later, on 25 September 1920, Gandhi had written to the Chairman of the All India Congress Committee arguing the case for changes to the Congress constitution. This was in response to the resolution passed at the Amritsar Congress at the end of 1919 that a committee be appointed to review this matter. The three-person committee failed to meet face-to-face, and issues were discussed through correspondence, and the letter of 25 September explicitly expressed Gandhi's opinion, which appears to have been all that counted. While the other two committee members favoured keeping existing arrangements about delegates to the Congress, Gandhi argued that it should act more as a 'representative body' by selecting delegates 'scientifically'. While the existing Congress constitution stated that they should campaign only in 'constitutional' ways, Gandhi suggested that this be replaced with 'legitimate and honourable' methods – which allowed for its support of civil disobedience.

Gandhi also proposed that the provincial Congress committees be reformed to reflect linguistic boundaries, rather than the boundaries of the existing British provinces, many of which incorporated multiple language areas. This would allow their work to be carried on at the provincial level in a more democratic way, using local vernaculars.[25]

Gandhi had first announced that he wanted to do this on 28 April 1920. In this, he had sought to strengthen the areas which had responded particularly well to his political programme, and thus limit the power within the movement that the old Presidency politicians had formerly enjoyed. In Bombay Presidency, for example, the Congress had been dominated by Maharashtrians led by Tilak. By carving five separate Congress areas out of this British province – namely Gujarat, Bombay City, Sindh, Maharashtra and Karnataka – Maharashtra was marginalised. Similarly, in Madras Presidency, the new Congress regions of Andhra and Kerala could challenge the domination of the Tamil politicians of Madras City. Only in Bengal Presidency was this not possible, as this was one linguistic region; but Gandhi nonetheless managed to win backing in 1920–22 from the Muslims of East Bengal who sympathised with his support for the Khilafat cause, providing a counter to the bhadralok politicians of Calcutta City led by Chittaranjan Das. In all of this, Gandhi proved that he had a greater all-India visions than the erstwhile Congress leaders of the three Presidencies – who were predominantly Hindu bhadralok in Bengal, Maharashtrian Brahmans in Bombay, and Tamil Brahmans in Madras. Until then, they had managed largely to limit the power and influence of politicians from outside their own elite circles and language areas.[26]

All of this and more was implemented at the Nagpur Congress, making it a much more effective fighting organisation. There were to be 21 provincial Congress Committees, each of which could send one delegate to the annual Congress session for each 50,000 of the inhabitants of the province. This would prevent Congress sessions being swamped by the delegates of certain provinces, as had been the case on some critical occasions in the past. For example, 14,582 delegates attended the session before the new constitution came into effect, only 4,728 in the one after. The membership of the All-India Congress Committee (AICC) – an already-existing body – was raised to 350 members selected by the provincial committees, with numbers in proportion to their population sizes. In addition, there was to be a Working Committee (WC) – an entirely new body of fifteen members – that would act as an executive responsible for the day-to-day running of the Congress. It was to meet roughly once a month. Gandhi understood the AICC to be like a parliament, and the WC its cabinet. He clearly understood this to be a parallel government with an authority that rivalled that of the British. Once the WC met, it formulated further rules, such as establishing tiers of committees, stretching from individual villages and towns upwards. Any person who was 21 years or more of age could become a member on payment of a very low fee of four annas (a quarter of a rupee). This allowed it to become a genuinely mass organisation.[27]

Although Gandhi was clearly in the driving seat in 1920, the overall strategy bore many of the marks of Aurobindo Ghose's manifesto of 1908, 'The Doctrine of Passive Resistance', which was published in his weekly *Bande Mataram*. At that time – during the Swadeshi Movement in Bengal – it had not been implemented in a systematic or all-India manner. We have already examined this manifesto in the previous volume.[28] Gandhi was aware of Aurobindo's writings in *Bande Mataram* when he was in South Africa. It is significant also that Gandhi sent his son Devdas to meet Ghose in Pondicherry at the end of 1919 to request his help in the coming campaign. Aurobindo turned the request down.[29] Clearly, Gandhi had Aurobindo's programme as a guide as he formulated his strategy in the following months. Aurobindo had called for a parallel government that would exist alongside the imperial structure of power, with political bodies at village, town, district and provincial levels. He had demanded a new constitution for the Congress to this effect, something that the Moderates refused to countenance at that time. The 'passive resistance' that Ghose advocated involved the boycott of foreign goods and British-controlled institutions such as schools, colleges and law courts. They should refuse to serve in the bureaucracy or police. They should aim to be self-sufficient as much as possible. Aurobindo had emphasised the importance of a campaign of tax-refusal. As this posed a great threat to the whole system, the authorities would either quickly come to an agreement, or try to repress the movement in ways that would merely 'give greater vitality and intensity to the opposition'. This agenda was embraced by Gandhi in 1920, providing the blueprint for the forthcoming movement.

There were however significant differences between Aurobindo and Gandhi. The first involved what Aurobindo described as the nationalist strategy of 'self-development and self-help'. Gandhi used a different term – that of 'constructive' work – but they were dealing largely with the same issue. Aurobindo argued that such work was unlikely to succeed while the British held power, as they would always sabotage attempts to build alternative institutions and economic structures. While boycott – that is refusal to participate in British institutions and forms of economic life and to provide nationalist alternatives – was an important element to the passive resistance that he advocated, such initiatives would only come to fruition once they had gained political independence. Therefore, the fight for freedom had to take precedence over any such nation-building activity. Gandhi, by contrast, regarded such work as having to be carried out before there could be any meaningful independence. He sought to do this through a range of programmes, such the self-production of indigenous items of daily use (notably khadi cloth), the encouragement of small-scale and appropriate industries, establishing a system of nationalist education, improving sanitation, campaigning against the consumption of alcoholic drinks and encouragement of a simple diet and lifestyle, the abolition of untouchability, and active work to create harmony between religious groups. The village provided an exemplary site for such activity. While many nationalists saw such work as either a distraction from the more important task of winning freedom or denigrated it as a celebration of 'backward' forms of socio-economic organisation, Gandhi believed that his programme provided the necessary condition for genuine swaraj. He also believed that it provided a means to build a new nonviolent polity. Rather than gain power and force socio-economic reforms on the people through statist means – e.g. through legislation and coercion – he wanted to create a climate in which it would be accepted willingly, nonviolently, and in a creative way even before political freedom was won. India was riven by inequalities and injustices, but these took many local forms, and sweeping measures imposed from above once power was gained would lead merely to resentment, reaction and polarisation, thus stoking civil conflict and violence. Sensitive issues such as disparities in landholding and caste inequalities required careful local handling if they were to be resolved in ways that had lasting value. Action, for Gandhi, began at the local level in an intimate world. The constructive programme was for Gandhi the most important part of noncooperation.[30]

Another issue was that of Aurobindo's advocacy of social boycott of those who failed to support nationalist agitations. As he had stated: 'It is therefore necessary to mete out the heaviest penalty open to us in such cases—the penalty of social excommunication. We are not in favour of this weapon being lightly used; but its employment, where the national will in a vital matter is deliberately disregarded, becomes essential.' During the Swadeshi Movement, there was widespread social boycott of this sort, usually involving caste sanctions. Adherence to the nationalist agenda was claimed as a matter of *dharma* – religious duty – and any violation of it as *acara* – or transgression of an essential caste duty. Consuming foreign goods was treated as ritual pollution, and offenders were in some cases made to shave their heads as an expiation for their 'sin'. Others were denied the use of everyday services by people such as priests, barbers, washermen and so on. Both Aurobindo and Surendranath Banerjee advocated this form of social coercion. Rabindranath Tagore had criticised this as both obnoxious and violent; he believed that people should participate in the struggle of their own free will. In pointing this out, Ranajit Guha has noted that genuine popular consent was limited – the masses had to be compelled to support a protest that was largely in the interests of the bhadralok elite. This all revealed, in his opinion, the shallow base there was to Indian liberalism.[31]

Gandhi, like Tagore, condemned the use of such social pressure. During the Kheda Satyagraha of 1918 he had emphasised: 'We are not to boycott or treat with scorn those who hold different views from ours. It must be our resolve to win them over by courteous behaviour.'[32] During the Rowlatt Satyagraha, he had stated that 'boycott was totally inconsistent with satyagraha'.[33] Writing in March 1920, he asserted: 'Boycott, in my opinion, is a form of violence.'[34] Writing a month later, he adopted a more realistic tone:

> …ostracism to a certain extent is impossible to avoid. I remember in South Africa in the initial stages of the passive resistance campaign those who had fallen away were ostracised. Ostracism is violent or peaceful according to the manner in which it is practised. A congregation may well refuse to recite prayers after a priest who prizes his title above his honour. But the ostracism will become violent if the individual life of a person is made unbearable by insults, innuendoes or abuse.[35]

Later that year he assented with some reluctance to the demand from Chittaranjan Das for a boycott of foreign goods. He now made a distinction between 'political' and 'social' forms of boycott. Writing in December 1920, he said that it was wrong to try to enforce solidarity through social boycott: 'Ostracism of a violent character, such as the denial of the use of public wells is a species of barbarism, which I hope will never be practised by any body of men having any desire for national self-respect and freedom.' They had to persuade people through argument only. It was however acceptable to boycott members of the new Legislative Councils – this was a 'political boycott'.[36] In an article in *Young India* in February 1921, Gandhi voiced his severe reservations about the use of what he called an 'age-old institution' that could be deployed to 'terrible' effect. In effect, he said, it meant excommunication from the community. If it meant merely refusing to interact socially with those with whom one disagreed, it was unobjectionable. If it involved refusing people services that were essential for life, it was not acceptable. He mentioned a case from Jhansi, in which an ostracised person was refused the service of a doctor when very ill. This was, he said, uncivilised and inhuman, being comparable to an act of murder. It should never be deployed in such a way when opinion was divided – as it was over the merits or demerits of noncooperation. When so used it became 'a species of unpardonable violence'. It was of course acceptable to boycott the government and its institutions, as this involved self-denial.[37]

In May 1921, Gandhi made a distinction between 'civil' and 'uncivil' boycott. 'Civil' boycott entailed a refusal to avail of the services of people who did something that was contrary to one's truth – e.g. selling liquor. Such a boycott was conceived out of love. 'Uncivil' boycott was designed to punish another, and it was rooted in hatred.[38] This advice was however widely ignored during the Noncooperation Movement. In this, many nationalists implicitly followed Aurobindo rather than Gandhi.[39]

The issue of ostracism led into another major difference between Aurobindo's and Gandhi's agenda – that over nonviolence. In August 1920, Gandhi had published an article titled 'The Doctrine of the Sword'. In this, he set out the reasons why he considered that 'nonviolence is infinitely superior to violence'. He argued that he was not deploying nonviolence while secretly planning to use violence when the time was ripe – as some alleged – but because he believed in its moral and practical superiority. He did not – as had also been stated – adopt this approach out of cowardice, but because he saw it as being if anything more courageous. Given a choice between cowardice and violence, he would advise violence; but it was far better to be courageous and nonviolent. He exhorted the people: '...give nonviolent noncooperation a trial'.[40] Aurobindo, by contrast, had envisaged an armed wing of the movement existing side-by-side with the campaign of passive resistance, ready to step in to provide any necessary force when the time was ripe. Chittaranjan Das, a staunch follower of Aurobindo during the Swadeshi period, continued to think in this way and cultivated his links with the revolutionaries of Bengali groups such as Anushilan Samiti. They were to participate actively in noncooperation in an ostensibly nonviolent way, but still be ready for armed action when this was required. For Gandhi, of course, this was anathema – nonviolence was to be the guiding ideology of the whole movement, and any serious lapse in this respect would mean his withdrawal from the campaign. When Gandhi sent his son Devdas to meet Aurobindo in late 1919, he had explained the principles of Gandhian nonviolence. Aurobindo was not impressed and asked him rather flippantly what he would do if the Afghans attacked India through the Khyber Pass. The followers of Aurobindo who reported this encounter claimed that Devdas had no reply. In common with many of his fellow Bengali bhadralok, Aurobindo was sceptical about many of Gandhi's dearly held principles. For example, when Devdas chided him for his addiction to tobacco, Aurobindo merely retorted: 'Why are you addicted to non-smoking?'[41] In all this, there was a clear emotional gap between the two men; which – most importantly – was of a similar quality to the emotional distance that prevailed throughout the Noncooperation Movement between two of its most charismatic leaders – Gandhi and Chittaranjan Das.

Because of his experience in 1919, Gandhi did not trust the masses to be nonviolent when mobilised in support of a nationalist demand. This was a not something had concerned Aurobindo at all, so this represented another major difference in the agendas of these two nationalists. Gandhi, unlike Aurobindo, insisted that if there was widespread violence he would advise that the campaign be stopped. Initially, he was particularly concerned about the Muslims of north-western India, whom he believed – stereotypically – to have a strongly martial and thus violent culture. He toured Sindh and Punjab in July 1920, preaching his creed. Speaking in Rawalpindi, he praised the courage of Muslims, but said that they tended to be headstrong. They knew how to wield 'the sword', but as mercenaries. In this, he was referring to the fact that many Muslims of these regions served the British as soldiers in the Indian Army. Instead, he told them: 'I have found a way by which you can fight while keeping your swords sheathed'. Nonviolent noncooperation was 'a strong form of jehad [sic]'. In this, they needed to learn to 'fight with discipline, with intelligence and courage'. They should obey the orders of their leaders.[42] Going on to Sindh, he called for 'soldiers with spiritual power; soldiers who stand their ground and do not run away'. They could not oppose the British with force of arms but would certainly be defeated, as 'they have arms, aeroplanes and machine-guns'. He closed by emphasising that: 'No force should be used'.[43]

Gandhi was very concerned about the question of what he called 'the mob'. In an article of 8 September 1920 titled 'Democracy "versus" Mobocracy', he argued that India was still at a 'mob-law stage'. This, he said, had been all too apparent in the Rowlatt Satyagraha. 'It represented undisciplined destruction and therefore it was thoughtless, profitless, wicked and harmful'. He had continued to witness such 'mobocracy' as he toured India during 1920.[44] He reported how in place after place he was being met by unruly crowds who caused much injury to people and property when they pushed and jostled to see their 'heroes'. The noise had been 'unmusical and harsh'. Jostling crowds had wilfully ignored the commands of volunteers in charge of crowd-control and even treated them as their enemy. In Madras, for example:

> ...the crowd was large, the noises they made were so terrific that the directions given by the volunteers could not be heard at all. All was chaos. My poor toes were every moment in danger of being crushed to a pulp. I often very nearly lost my balance through the jostling of the very volunteers who were trying to protect me. And but for the very great care with which they guarded me and the assistance rendered to them by the stalwart Maulana Shaukat Ali, I would have fared much worse than

> I did. The atmosphere was suffocating. Thus struggling it took us nearly three quarters of an hour to reach the motor car, whereas ordinarily it need not have taken three minutes to walk out of the station to the porch. Having reached the car it was no easy job to get into it. I had to be shoved into it in the best manner possible. I certainly heaved a sigh of relief when I found myself in the car, and I thought that both the Maulana and I deserved the ovation we received from the crowd after the dangerous exercise we had gone through. With a little forethought this mobocracy, for such it was, could have been changed into a splendidly organised and educative demonstration.[45]

Gandhi observed that so long as what he called the 'mob' was with you everything went well, but 'immediately that cord is broken, there is horror'. He emphasised that his faith in the people was 'boundless', and that given proper leadership and guidance they could achieve wonders. He asserted: 'We must then evolve order out of chaos.' Rather than 'mob-law' they required 'the people's law' – in other words a movement that served the interests of the masses in a controlled and ordered manner. This was to be achieved by training volunteers in crowd-control methods.[46]

Ranajit Guha has argued that 'mobocracy' was 'an ugly word greased with loathing, a sign of craving for control and its frustration'.[47] If we go to the Oxford English Dictionary we find that 'mobocracy' was a word that dated back to the mid-eighteenth century, meaning (1) 'Mob rule, government by a mob; an instance of this', and (2) 'The mob as a ruling body or political force; a ruling or politically powerful mob'. During the French Revolution, some English commentators had contrasted 'mobocracy' with 'democracy'. 'Mob' was an older English word that denoted a disorderly and riotous assembly of the common people. Guha argued that in using such a term Gandhi – for all his assertions to the contrary – revealed his profound distrust of the masses. Although he wanted to deploy their energy, he had learnt to be wary of them. He thus sought to mobilise them in a controlled and limited manner. Guha acknowledges that Gandhi was not seeking to order the 'mob' through armed force, as the British did. His method differed in very important respects, for he wanted to inculcate a spirit of self-regulation. Guha goes on to argue that the crowd had its own discipline: one that emerged from the subaltern and not elite domain of politics. They followed 'rules of association' that were seen in the ways they conducted their work and spiritual life.[48] This latter point is hardly convincing. There was a world of difference between the order seen in peasant production and worship with that of the surging crowd of the modern metropolis with its sudden and unpredictable swings in mood. Crowds can become murderous in seconds, venting their anger on unfortunate people and groups who are suddenly labelled – often by provocateurs – as their 'enemies'. We need to recognise this as a force that is as liable to be unjust as just and acknowledge that Gandhi had good reason to demand order and discipline. It is in general a sound principle that resistance is more effective and fruitful if controlled, coordinated and guided than if not. Nonetheless, there was the troublesome issue of Gandhi's implicit support for elite interests during this period – something that will be addressed in later chapters.

The Campaign 1921–22

The strategy that had been thrashed out by December 1920 was put into effect over the course of the next fourteen months. This process did not always run smoothly or to plan. The various boycotts of British institutions and products enjoyed mixed success. Very few government officials resigned their posts and hardly any titleholders relinquished their honours. While almost no soldiers resigned, some policemen did – though the numbers were hardly substantial. A moderate number of lawyers stopped practising in the British courts – it was estimated that 180 did so throughout India during the first two months of the campaign. This figure included Chittaranjan Das and Motilal Nehru – both of whom had extremely lucrative legal practices – and their renunciation consolidated their reputations as elite nationalists who were prepared to sacrifice their careers for the good of the nation. Some other prominent nationalist leaders, however, continued to practice in the courts. Parallel nationalist arbitration courts had some success, particularly in Bihar, where large numbers of cases were withdrawn from the official courts and heard in front of the new popular assemblies. The boycott of secondary schools and colleges was far more successful. During this period in British India as a whole, arts colleges lost 12.4% of their students and secondary schools 3.3% of their pupils. The number of children in government primary schools, by contrast, rose by 2.9%. Nationalist institutions were opened as a substitute. There were two nationalist universities and an estimated 1,255 such schools – though most proved short-lived. In general, the advantages of government education proved too strong to resist for more than a few months. Nonetheless, a significant number of the students who quit their studies went on to become nationalist leaders in the following years.[49]

The boycott of foreign cloth was particularly successful, with the value of imports declining from Rs 10,200,000 to Rs 5,700,000 during this time. There were bonfires of foreign cloth, and shops dealing in such cloth were picketed by nationalist volunteers, with many merchants agreeing under pressure to stock only Indian-made cloth. In most cases they did this unwillingly and returned to selling foreign cloth as soon as the movement subsided in 1922. From April 1921 onwards, Gandhi put much of his energy into encouraging Indians to take up spinning cotton-thread on *charkhas* (spinning wheels) and giving the thread to weavers to be turned into khadi cloth on their handlooms. He exhorted people to wear only such cloth. Spinning and khadi-wearing became a way of demonstrating commitment to the nationalist movement and the Gandhian way of life, and the white *khadi* cap that was devised by Gandhi at this time became the uniform of Indian nationalism. The other main product that was boycotted was liquor, with shops being picketed by volunteers. Considerable social pressure was placed on people to give up alcoholic drinks. Gandhi encouraged women, in particular, to carry out the picketing as he believed that they were less likely to respond violently to provocation by outraged drinkers. The excise from liquor – all of which had by law to be sold in licensed liquor shops – was by this time the single most important tax-earner for the British, and the boycott hit the rulers hard. By February 1922, for example, the loss of such revenue in Madras Presidency had led to a deficit of Rs 650,000 in state funds; in Punjab, the deficit was Rs 330,000, in Bihar and Orissa Rs 100,000, and Bombay Rs 60,000.[50]

The All India Congress Committee met on 31 March 1921 in Bezwada to consider the next step. It was decided to focus on enrolling ten million members for the Congress, on fundraising, and on propagating spinning wheels. When civil disobedience was suggested Gandhi countered that it was premature to escalate the movement in that way at that juncture – they should consolidate it in the other spheres first. They had, he insisted, to be certain that there would be no violence when civil disobedience began. Not all agreed, but he had his way. Over the course of the next few months, the nationalist leaders toured India putting pressure on their supporters to donate as generously as they could to the Tilak Swaraj Fund. The merchants of Bombay gave particularly generously, donating about Rs 3,750,000. The people of Gujarat donated about half a million rupees. Most of this money came from urban rather than rural areas. By 1 July, ten million rupees had been received, which met the target set at Bezwada. The spinning-wheel campaign also met its target of two million new wheels. They did not reach the membership target, however. Many rural areas remained beyond the reach of the nationalist organisation.[51]

In early April, the Ali brothers made speeches that appeared to advocate violence.[52] The government discussed prosecuting them, but decided against it at that juncture, lest Gandhi then escalate the movement in protest. The new Viceroy Lord Reading – who had replaced Chelmsford in April – agreed to a series of meetings with Gandhi in Simla in mid-May 1921. A leading British Liberal and a consummate political operator, his appointment was popular with Indian moderates, who felt Reading might soon be open to further constitutional reform. Reading had experience of dealing with nationalists in Ireland and the Middle East and understood the power of their appeal. He saw that the Noncooperation Movement was building a strong momentum and was wary of making the mistake of crushing the protestors as British hard-liners were demanding, rather than negotiate with them first. He believed that it was possible to lower the political temperature through frank face-to-face meetings. He also believed that it might be possible to divide the Khilafatists from the Congress. When he met Gandhi, he appreciated his clarity of expression and his command of English and was impressed by his admirable moral views and sincerity, though felt that his desire to reform all his followers to embrace 'non-violence and love' was quixotic. Gandhi had – Reading remarked in a letter to Montagu – accepted into his fold many who did not believe in such principles, and had a hard task in keeping them all together. Reading's judgement was shrewd; he had identified a fault in the movement that might lead to its eventual fracture. During the meetings he managed to persuade Gandhi that there was a contradiction in his support for the Ali brothers when they used violent rhetoric. Gandhi said that he would ask the Ali brothers to apologise for their speeches and promise not to advocate violence in future. Gandhi then persuaded the brothers to issue a public apology, which appeared on 30 May. This, as Woods states, 'was a triumph for Reading and a political embarrassment for Gandhi and the Ali brothers'.[53]

At the same time as he was identifying with the Khilafatists, Gandhi was projecting himself as a highly orthodox Hindu of the Sanatanist persuasion and depicting the movement as a Hindu crusade. He took up the issue of cow protection, calling it the central fact of Hinduism that symbolised the Hindu's reverence for all of God's creation.[54] When he was criticised by Goswami Shri Gokalnathji Maharaj, a leader of the Vallabhacharya Vaishnavites, for his opposition to untouchability, Gandhi argued that he was as orthodox as any. 'Do not conclude that I am a polluted person, a reformer. A rigidly orthodox Hindu, I believe that the Hindu Shastras have no place for untouchability of the type practised now.'[55] On a visit to a Swaminarayan temple in 1921, he exclaimed: 'At this holy place, I declare, if you want to protect your "*Hindu dharma*", non-cooperation is [the] first as well as the last lesson you must learn up.'[56] He used Hindu imagery for swaraj, such as '*dharmaraj*' (the rule of Hindu religion), and often referred to Ram and Sita, declaring that their goal was '*Ramraj*' (the rule of Rama) and the defeat of '*Ravanraj*' (the rule of the demon-king Ravan). With appeals such as these, Gandhi managed to rally a significant number of Hindu nationalists behind him during this phase of the movement. The Arya Samaj leader Swami Shraddananda had thrown in his support behind Gandhi in 1919. Previously he had distrusted the motives of politicians, but he felt that Gandhi's politics were different, being enthused with the spirit of religion. For a time, the Swami became a leading proponent of Hindu-Muslim unity, and was even invited to preach at the Jama Masjid in Delhi.[57] Gandhi sought to win such people to a more tolerant and inclusive nationalism, insisting, for example, that cow protection should not be made a pretext for any antagonism against Muslims – their support for this cause should be won through love.[58] Nonetheless, despite all Gandhi's skills in holding together the coalition of Hindu and Muslim nationalists, there were ongoing tensions that pushed and pulled the movement in different directions as it progressed. Many Hindu nationalists were suspicious of the Ali brothers, who appeared to valorise a pan-Islamic over a national identity, as well as the ulama who provided key support to Khilafat in their commitment to sharia law over and above any national law. For their part, many Muslims resented having to campaign alongside Hindus using Hindu religious imagery. They in turn were mobilising Muslims using religious imagery, but the message of nonviolence was often lost in the process.

To try to reconcile the tensions within its own ranks, the Khilafat Committee held several meetings in mid-1921 that sought to emphasise a firm gap between them and the Congress. At the Gujarat Provincial Khilafat Conference held in Bharuch, Gujarat, on 2 June 1921, Muhammad Ali restated his commitment to Gandhian nonviolence, but added that they were of different religions and that Islam permitted the use of force. Indeed, it was obligatory in cases of self-defence. They thus reserved the right to take up arms against the enemies of Islam if noncooperation failed. The All-India Khilafat Conference was held in Bombay on 15 June, where it was declared that it was the duty of Muslim soldiers to refuse to serve the British government in any war with Turkey. A group of ulama that included A.K. Azad and Abdul Bari issued a fatwa that stated it was unlawful to serve in the military or police as it involved fighting one's Muslim brethren. The Quran was cited: 'One who kills a Muslim deliberately will be subjected to eternal hellfire.' The Prophet had said: 'Whoever takes up arms against Muslims, he ceases to be a Muslim.' This fatwa was published and widely distributed by Khilafat volunteers on trains and to police barracks and army camps.[59]

By mid-1921, the campaign was taking on its own dynamic. We shall examine these multi-faceted developments in detail in later chapters. Gandhi feared that some of the protests – for example the refusal to pay rent to landlord in UP and Bihar – had the potential to escalate in violent ways, and he was unwilling to give his support to them. He stressed that all should focus on opposing the British rather than their fellow Indians, however exploitative they may have been, to obey the law, and follow instructions from the police until civil disobedience was announced.[60]

The AICC met in Bombay in July 1921. The decision on civil disobedience was once again deferred and it was decided to focus on the boycott of foreign cloth. The Ali brothers then raised the temperature at the All-India Khilafat Committee in Karachi in July when they publicly supported a *fatwa* that called on Muslims to stop serving in the army. Muhammad Ali gave a strong speech that called for the British to be driven out of India. A resolution was passed that Indian Muslims would shirk 'no sacrifice' to uphold the Khilafat. One resolution stated that 'the Holy Shariat forbids every Muslim to serve or enlist himself in the British army or to raise recruits for it.' Muslims were duty-bound to carry this message to every Muslim in the British Indian army. There was talk of striking out independently of the Congress and adopting widespread civil disobedience. The government decided to take out a conspiracy case against the leading Khilafatists at Karachi – seven in all, including the Ali brothers and Dr. Kitchlew. They did not arrest them immediately but waited on events.[61]

It was announced at the AICC meeting held in Bombay on 28–30 July 1921 that the Prince of Wales would be boycotted on his visit to India at the end of the year. In the meantime, they were to focus on the campaign against foreign cloth. Gandhi proposed a target of 30 September for a complete boycott in this respect – which was later extended to 31 October. He inaugurated this phase by personally setting alight a massive bonfire of foreign cloth, including many luxury items. This action was imitated in hundreds of other places. It provided a dramatic form of protest that provided a substitute for civil disobedience for the time being. The bonfires symbolised the wealthy making sacrifices for the cause – as the Tilak Swaraj fund had done also. They also helped to channel urges towards violence. Gandhi said of this that 'It is with the utmost effort, that I find it possible to keep under check the evil passions of the people. The general body of the people are filled with ill will because they are weak and hopelessly ignorant of the way to shed their weakness. I am transferring the ill will from men to things'.[62] He himself began wearing only a loincloth made of khadi at this time.

In August 1921 there was a massive outbreak of communal violence in Malabar District, a British-ruled area in northern Kerala, when Muslim tenants rose against Hindu landlords. There was a long history of revolt by this group, who were known as the Mappilas. In 1918 there had been a local rising by some tenants against arbitrary eviction by Hindu landlords, but there had been no reform in the law. Congress leaders in Calicut had organised a Tenants' League with branches all over Malabar District. The situation continued oppressive for the tenants. The monsoon failed in 1921 and the crops were poor. Many Muslim soldiers had been demobilised and had returned to their villages. They were trained in acting together and in using weapons and provide the nucleus for groups of Khilafat volunteers. They dressed in khaki and carried knives and spears. Meetings were held supporting Khilafat demands and calls were made for strong, even violent, action against the landlords. Congress leaders saw what was going on and organised a meeting to encourage nonviolent noncooperation. The local authorities banned the meeting, but when it went ahead arrested four noncooperators and sentenced them to six month's imprisonment. All political meetings were banned in Malabar District. In this way, the government silenced the moderating voices.[63]

In late July, a police party tried to arrest some people suspected of burgling a landlord's house. An armed group prevented them from doing this. The police believed that the local Khilafat leaders were behind this, and on 20 August searched a mosque where it was believed they were hiding. A rumour was spread that the mosque had been desecrated or even destroyed, and the police were then surrounded by 3,000 angry people and had to fight their way out. The whole district then erupted. Railway lines were torn up, telegraph wires cut, post offices and police stations burnt, and money and arms captured and carried into the hills. The rebels adopted guerrilla tactics, and civil authority collapsed. Martial law was imposed, but the Mappilas now had the area under their control. Khilafat flags were in evidence, and in a couple of villages 'Khilafat republics' were proclaimed. The rebels killed landlords with a bad reputation, pillaging and burning their houses, while sparing landlords who were known for their relative benevolence. Poor Hindus were generally left alone. Some Hindu temples were burnt down and there were some forcible conversions to Islam. Martial law was in force for six months, and many starved as the movement of food was badly hampered. The authorities gradually regained control. When at this stage some Hindus helped the British forces, the rebels turned on them as a community, converting a predominantly anti-landlord revolt into a communal battle. The government responded viciously. Official figures stated that during the repression of the revolt 2,339 Mappilas were killed, 1,652 wounded, 5,655 captured, and 39,348 gave themselves in. One particularly notorious atrocity occurred on 21 November 1921, when one hundred captured Mappilas were crammed into an airless railway carriage to be taken to jail and 64 died of asphyxiation.[64]

The government claimed that Mappila leaders had heard a speech by Muhammad Ali that led them to believe that the Amir of Afghanistan would come to help them in their revolt. Both the Congress and Khilafat leaders disowned the rebels. They said that the issue was primarily an economic one, rather than a result of nationalist propaganda and Khilafat activity. The Mappilas had, they said, gravely misunderstood the movement. If the noncooperators had been allowed to work in the area freely, they could have propagated nonviolence. A.K. Azad and Abdul Bari expressed horror at the forcible conversions, pointing out that proselytising with the sword was against Islamic law. The insurgents, for their part, denounced Gandhi and the Ali brothers as infidels when they appealed for them to renounce violence. Many Hindus were alarmed by the revolt, seeing in it a pattern of supposed Muslim fanaticism and lack of commitment to the nationalist cause, and went on to argue that Muslims could not be trusted. Bari retorted that the government wanted to promote the Hindu-Muslim divide, and that they must resist it. He felt that the government may well have provoked it all for this end. Many of the ulama claimed that the accounts of forcible conversion were false and designed to cast a slur on Muslims.[65]

Soon after this, in September, the Khilafat leaders were arrested and after a theatrical and well-publicised trial were sentenced in October to two years' imprisonment. Gandhi and other Congress leaders promptly courted arrest by issuing a statement that it was against national dignity for Indians to serve the government, whether as civilians, police or soldiers. The Congress Working Committee endorsed this next day.

T.B. Sapru, an Indian moderate who was a member of the Viceroy's Council, argued that it would be a grave mistake to overreact to this provocation. He noted that Gandhi had won over nearly all classes in India except the landowners, and even the moderates who disagreed with noncooperation still admired Gandhi as a person. If Gandhi was jailed, many others would repeat his statement and court arrest, thus filling the prisons. Unless they had public opinion behind them, the arrest of Gandhi would backfire. He also doubted whether the Indian Legislative Assembly would support such a move. They should therefore wait until Gandhi put himself further in the wrong before arresting him. Reading and his Council accepted this argument and agreed to leave Gandhi free at that juncture.[66]

There was now the matter of the forthcoming visit of the Prince of Wales, which Congress intended to oppose in a vociferous manner. The visit had already been postponed once before, and it had become a matter of prestige for the government. The decision to now allow the visit to go ahead gave the Congress a strong bargaining chip. M.M. Malaviya played this hand in a meeting with Reading on 9 October, when he suggested that the Viceroy could defuse the situation by offering to hold a round table conference to discuss further constitutional reforms. Reading was receptive to this suggestion and raised the matter with Montagu. Montagu, however, felt that Reading was allowing Gandhi dangerous leeway, and after putting the matter to the British Cabinet, advised Reading to arrest him forthwith. He also said that it was premature to be thinking of any round table conferences at that juncture – the reforms had to be given a chance to bed in. He communicated this all to Reading on 13 October, but Reading ignored him.[67]

In an article in *Young India* of 3 November 1921, Gandhi said that he was prepared to support a campaign of civil disobedience in any district in which ninety per cent of the population had boycotted all foreign cloth and were manufacturing all the cloth they required through handspinning and hand-weaving. In addition, all religious groups should be living in perfect harmony and there should be no practice of untouchability. He hoped that there might be several such districts. He cautioned that if there was the slightest outbreak of violence anywhere, then he would deem that it was not be safe to continue the campaign. This was to be a symbolic action – one that Gandhi could control.[68]

In the meantime, he had identified a sub-district in his own Gujarat – Bardoli Taluka in Surat District – which he was confident would meet such conditions. Initially, he had considered selecting a sub-district of Kheda, as he had previous experience of leading a protest there. Kheda had responded strongly to noncooperation, with many national schools and generous donations to the Tilak Swaraj Fund. Gandhi however resolved on Bardoli after being advised by Vithalbhai Patel that it would be a better choice. Bardoli, like Kheda, was an area dominated by Patidars, and the caste had a strong association, the Patidar Yuvak Mandal, that had already given firm support to the nationalist cause and noncooperation. There was no turbulent underclass in Bardoli, unlike Kheda, where the poor and landless peasants had a history of sometimes violent disputes with the dominant landholders. In Bardoli, the Patidars largely cultivated their land with bonded labourers who had no history of conflict with those who controlled and exploited them with an iron hand. There was almost no recorded crime in the area. Vithalbhai Patel felt that the likelihood of achieving complete nonviolence was better than in Kheda. Gandhi went there to see for himself, and accepted Patel's suggestion.[69]

The AICC met on 4–5 November in Delhi. P.C. Bamford, the Deputy Director of the Intelligence Bureau of the Government of India, reported that most of those who attended were restless, wanting a dramatic escalation of the protest. They reluctantly accepted Gandhi's dictates for the moment out of personal regard for him – at least till the end of the year in which he had promised 'swaraj'. After that, Bamford believed, more radical leadership would probably assert itself.[70] At the meeting, Gandhi said that he was pleased that that there had been no violence over the arrest of the Ali brothers, and he agreed that the AICC could authorise provincial Congress committees to launch both individual and mass civil disobedience. As few Congress leaders had experience of leading such a campaign, they were prepared to accept Gandhi's guidance in this matter. He announced that he would start the first such campaign in Bardoli on 23 November. An all-India hartal was also announced for 17 November, the day that the Prince of Wales was to arrive in India at Bombay.[71]

Gandhi was in Bombay on the day of this hartal. Nationalists who had come out to protest clashed with loyalists who were welcoming the prince, leading to three days of street rioting that will be examined in Chapter 4. Gandhi, who had gone into the thick of the crowd to try to restore order, was left distraught. He fasted for five days in penance and announced that the launch of civil disobedience in Bardoli was to be delayed.[72] Elsewhere, the hartals passed off peacefully. The protest in Calcutta was particularly successful with the city being closed for 24 hours. Congress and Khilafat volunteers patrolled the streets, effectively controlling the city. The shops and markets were all closed, and no trams or other transport ran. There was hardly any violence, and the armoured cars that patrolled the streets were not attacked. It was the most successful hartal ever held there, and it revealed the organisational skill of Chittaranjan Das and his lieutenants. There were similar hartals in towns throughout Bengal on 17 November. This all caused serious alarm amongst the European businessmen of Calcutta – the state had lost control for 24 hours. There was talk in such circles of a 'revolution', and the Bengal government was told it should take strong action to prevent any recurrence. The Bengal government passed on its concerns to Delhi.[73]

Responding to this pressure, Reading told the provincial governments that they could declare volunteer organisations illegal and prosecute anyone they wished. This was just what these authorities had been pushing for so long, and they reacted with alacrity. Political meetings and volunteer organisations were banned, and numerous arrests were made. In UP, the Congress organisation responded by publishing in the newspapers lists of volunteers who were prepared to go to jail. Motilal Nehru headed the first such list. Some 75,000 volunteers stepped forward in this province alone. They paraded openly, picketed shops, and organised demonstrations creating a feeling of euphoria. The aim was to fill the jails, jamming them up in a way that the government found hard to handle. The arrests began in early December. Both Motilal and Jawaharlal Nehru were arrested in Allahabad, along with all 55 members of the UP Provincial Congress Committee. Others who had played no role in the movement before that moment courted arrest – even government officials – showing that the repression might be counter-productive for the authorities. Youths often insisted in getting into the police vans along with arrested Congress activists, refusing to move when ordered to and demanding that they also be imprisoned. When the Prince of Wales visited Allahabad city a few days later, there were deserted streets and a solid hartal.[74]

During December and January about 30,000 nationalists were imprisoned throughout India. This included most of the top leaders, with the notable exception of Gandhi. Local officials arrested nationalists freely, e.g. merely for wearing a Gandhi cap, or selling khadi, or shouting '*Mahatma Gandhi ki jai*!' Previously there was a stigma attached to going to prison, but now it became a matter of pride. The crackdown of November 1921 created a 'backfire',[75] as it alienated many moderates. According to Woods: 'The result was probably more drastic than the government intended.' The Indian Association in Calcutta 'complained of indiscriminate arrests, including the arrests of ladies, the maltreatment of arrested prisoners and assaults and rude behaviour of officers against innocent persons.' The Association objected to the use of Part Two of the Criminal Law Amendment Act of the Seditious Meetings Act and complained of a 'state of terrorism'. It concluded by asking whether Bengal ministers had been consulted before the action was taken, and did they agree to it? The Lucknow Liberal League in UP protested, as did the moderates and in Allahabad. There was a sense of outrage across India that respected leaders could be arrested and imprisoned. Reading admitted on 18 December that there were probably cases of over-reaction by officers who might have acted too punitively. Noncooperators were deliberately courting arrest, and the number in jail was becoming an embarrassment to the government. Reading told Montagu on 17 December that there was a general feeling that the government was being 'purely repressive' and moderates were becoming critical of the government as a result. He felt that the pendulum had swung too far 'in the direction of enforcing law', but that he also did not want to demoralise the police and local authorities.[76]

Sapru, the Law member, suggested to Reading in early November the idea of a round-table conference of Indian leaders followed by a meeting with government. Malaviya and Jinnah supported this idea, and on 14 November, Malaviya met Reading, who told him he was prepared to consider the proposal. Malaviya felt that Gandhi would respond positively. Sapru sent two liberals, Jamnadas Dwakadas and

H.N. Kunzru, to Ahmedabad to sound Gandhi out. They reported – perhaps over-optimistically – that Gandhi seemed to be open to the idea. Feelers were also put out to Chittaranjan Das and A.K. Azad, who were both keen to have a conference. Reading sent a telegram to Montagu hoping for Cabinet approval, and to provincial governors informing them of what was going on. The Cabinet in London however repudiated the proposal, at least in the immediate future. The experience of Ireland was fresh in their mind – once talks had been started there with the nationalists a momentum had built up and the government had granted concessions that they had not originally intended. Indeed, some Indian nationalists took the Irish case as a sign that the British government might be similarly generous with them. The British Cabinet felt that Reading was acting over-hastily so as to defuse the situation before the Prince of Wales reached Calcutta on 24 December. Also, Reading was vague on the terms of the conference – was it merely to set out respective positions, or to negotiate a substantial amendment of the 1919 Act on a path towards Dominion Status? The Cabinet ruled that there was to be no revision of the 1919 Act in the near future. In India, while the Governors of Bengal, Bihar and Orissa, and the Central Provinces and Berar were in favour, all other governors were opposed. Willingdon in Madras and Lloyd in Bombay were particularly vociferous in their disapproval. Gandhi then informed Reading by telegram that he would only attend a round-table conference if the Khilafat leaders were released from jail first. He feared that if he did not make this a condition, he would alienate Khilafatists everywhere. Reading took this as meaning that the proposal was now a dead letter. He also turned down a suggestion by Das that if all political prisoners were released, he would call off the planned protests against the Prince of Wales on his arrival in Calcutta. Reading stated, nonetheless, that he detested 'repression' and was still prepared to hold some sort of negotiations if necessary.[77]

Reading was worried that if the visit of the Prince of Wales to Calcutta went badly for the British it would sour relations at all levels and make an eventual compromise harder to achieve. The Bengal authorities were meanwhile doing all they could to prevent a recurrence of the successful hartal of 17 November. Four armed cruisers were anchored outside the harbour and special battalions of troops posted in every part of the city. Europeans, Eurasians and Indian loyalists organised civil guards. Congress volunteers and similar bodies were declared unlawful associations, prosecutions were instigated against leading politicians and newspapers, and public meetings were prohibited for three months. Das ordered that Congress activists choke the jails by courting arrest. Many did so from 5 December onwards, both in Calcutta and the Bengal interior. Bengalis, north Indians, Muslims and Sikhs all participated. Bengali women took part openly in the protest for the first time, when a small group led by Basanti Devi Das, Das's wife, courted arrest. On 8 December, Harrison Road was blocked by demonstrators in a way that alarmed and demoralised the Bengali police. Arrests had to be made by European police officers. The military was posted there on the 9 December. Large crowds gathered at Barabazar, leading to 190 people being arrested by the infantry. On 10 December, Das, A.K. Azad, S.C. Bose, and other top leaders were arrested. In all, 753 had been apprehended up to that time, mainly students. After 10 December, students were replaced increasingly in the jail-courting movement by mill-hands and lower-class Muslims. On the afternoon of 23 December, the day before the prince arrived, 650 arrests were made in Bowbazar and Barabazar, which filled the jails to capacity. On the night of 23/24 December, the civil guard took over the whole of south Calcutta, allowing the police and army to concentrate on the north of the city. There was a hartal and shops and markets were closed, and there were no disturbances, as there had been in Bombay. Trams were able to run, due to the police and army presence. Many people, including Indians, came out on the streets to greet the prince. The welcoming crowd of 27 December was particularly impressive. In this way, the government regained the initiative. Das's tactic of courting arrest from early December had proved inspirational, but its downside was that there were few experienced Congress workers available to organise the protest at the prince.[78]

The Congress session of December 1921 was held in Ahmedabad in conjunction with sessions of the Muslim League and Khilafat. Many of the top leaders could not attend as they were in jail. Gandhi announced that he would launch civil disobedience in Bardoli Taluka early in 1922. Tensions between Khilafatists and the Gandhian Congress were revealed when Hasrat Mohani stated that 'Swaraj in a Year' had proved a mirage and that they should scrap the insistence on nonviolence in favour of an immediate declaration of 'complete freedom' from Britain and the use of violence if necessary. He and other ulama criticised the oath to observe nonviolence that all volunteers were required to take, maintaining that their religion permitted violence under certain conditions. Gandhi took a strong stand against this, arguing that they had failed to fulfil the conditions he had laid down for Swaraj, and the resolution was voted down by a large majority. Gandhi also met a group of ulama privately to try to persuade them of the need for complete nonviolence. Mohani then tried to get the Muslim League Council to declare for complete independence but was voted down in that forum by 36 to 23. In the Khilafat Conference, Mohani's motion was ruled out of order by Hakim Ajmal Khan, who had to adjoin the meeting to avoid a fistfight between the noncooperators and Mohani's supporters. This revealed the severe tensions that were building up both within the Khilafat movement, and between Muslim hardliners and the Congress.[79]

With civil disobedience looming, the Governor of Bombay Presidency, George Lloyd, asked Reading for permission to arrest Gandhi immediately. Reading refused to allow this, stating that it was better to arrest him once he broke the law actively through civil disobedience – when the government would be able to argue a better case for it. Some of the moderates were still hoping to be able to organise a conference and discussed this at a meeting in Bombay on 14–15 January. Gandhi came and announced that as far as he was concerned the Khilafat leaders had to be released before there could be any negotiations. As a result, the initiative came to nothing. After observing this, Reading told Montagu that: 'the tactical advantage Gandhi gained in December . . .had been lost by his latest action', and that the government was in a much stronger position. He still resisted pressures from the British government and provincial governors to arrest Gandhi. On 1 February 1922, Gandhi sent an ultimatum to Reading: if he failed to reverse the policy of repression he would launch a campaign of civil disobedience in Bardoli in seven days' time. Reading felt now that Gandhi should be arrested once the Prince of Wales had visited Delhi on 14 February.[80]

It was at this juncture that there was an act of violence that for Gandhi represented the last straw. Local volunteers in the area around Mundera in eastern UP had been picketing shops selling meat, fish and liquor. There was a strong belief there that Gandhi had forbidden all consumption of meat and fish, as well as liquor. The police came and broke up the demonstrations, in the process beating up one of the activists. Outraged volunteers flocked in from the surrounding areas, and on 4 February marched to the police station at nearby Chauri Chaura and demanded an explanation from the police for their oppressive action. Outnumbered, the police tried to intimidate the crowd by firing in the air. This had the opposite effect to that one intended – the crowd believed that: 'Bullets have turned to water by the grace of Gandhiji'. They rushed at the police and started beating them. The police fired, killing three protestors, but had to retreat into their station. The building was splashed with kerosene and set alight. Twenty-three policemen either died in the blaze or were battered to death when they tried to flee.[81]

News of this reached Gandhi on 9 February, and the following day he decided to halt the plan to launch civil disobedience in Bardoli. He stated that as the 'message of non-violence' was being ignored, the time was not yet ripe for such a protest.[82] On 11 February the Congress Working Committee met at Bardoli and endorsed this decision. The 'conduct of the mob at Chauri Chaura' was deplored and condolences were extended to the families of the policemen who had died. Every time they had been moving towards mass civil disobedience, it had had to be postponed because 'some popular violent outburst has taken place'. People should stop courting arrest, taking out processions, and carrying on picketing (except of liquor shops), though there could be hartals wherever they could be sure that there would be no violence. Peasants were told to pay all their taxes to the state, and rents to landlords. The 'laxity' that prevailed in the selection of nationalist volunteers and their lack of commitment to the principles of the cause – in particular, nonviolence – was deplored. Congress organisations should now focus on enlisting Congress members, though nobody should be recruited who was not fully committed to the belief 'in non-violence and truth as indispensable for the attainment of swaraj'. They should also popularise the spinning and weaving of khadi, organise national schools, collect funds, carry out social work to improve the conditions of the 'depressed classes' (e.g. untouchables), and conduct local arbitration courts.[83] In other words, nationalist activists were to focus on constructive work – which was in Gandhi's opinion the most important element of the whole campaign.

After hearing the news of the massacre at Chauri Chaura, but before the news of the climbdown, Reading had decided, as we have seen, to order Gandhi's arrest. In the light of the Bardoli decision, and heeding Sapru's advice, Reading agreed to postpone the arrest. D.A. Low has argued that Reading acted astutely in this respect as it provided time for the movement to collapse before Gandhi was arrested eventually in March.[84] Woods, by contrast, says that although this was true in one respect, it was a costly decision as it enraged the British hardliners who then moved into a concerted attack on the British Liberal position on India. Important provincial governors were furious with what they saw as Reading's vacillations and resented what they perceived to be Sapru's hold over the Viceroy. Their sentiments in the latter respect were represented by the UP Governor, Butler, who wrote to the ex-Viceroy Lord Hardinge on 22 December 1921 that: 'The Viceroys' evil geniuses are Sapru, the Law Member, who hates the British more than anyone in India, and Madan Mohan Malaviya who is the most double dealing man in India.' Lloyd, the Bombay Governor, felt badly let down in February 1922, as he had been on the brink of carrying out Gandhi's arrest in his own province. He and the Madras Governor, Willingdon, both considered resigning their posts. Reading met the Bengal Governor Ronaldshay and Lloyd in Delhi at the end of February. Lloyd brought up the vacillation over Gandhi's arrest, and complained that he had not had a chance to put his views before a decision was reached. Lloyd complained in a letter to Montagu of 3 March that Reading had negotiated in secret with Gandhi through Malaviya 'under my very nose in my own Presidency'. Lloyd said that he left Delhi 'sick at heart and with my confidence in Reading much impaired'. Under this sort of pressure, Reading agreed that Gandhi's arrest should proceed.[85]

The Liberal position in India was undermined even more gravely by the resignation of Edwin Montagu as Secretary of State for India on 9 March. For some time, Montagu had been in constant conflict in the coalition cabinet with Conservatives who advocated a hardline policy for India. They had never liked Montagu or forgiven him for his strong condemnation of those responsible for the atrocities in Punjab in 1919. The Foreign Secretary, Lord Curzon opposed the Indianisation of the civil service and army and was highly critical of the way that Reading had handled noncooperation. The Secretary of State for the Colonies, Winston Churchill, felt it was wrong to grant democratic institutions, to – as he stated on 9 February 1922 – 'backward races which had no capacity for self-government'. Churchill argued that the forms of autocracy found in the native states were more appropriate for India as they were 'in harmony with the ideas of Indians to whom European democratic institutions were generally repugnant'. Prime Minister Lloyd George's hold on power was at the same time slipping, with the Conservatives in his coalition government increasingly flexing their power. They despised the concessions granted to nationalists in Ireland, India, Egypt, the Middle East, and Turkey. They accused Montagu of flinching from firm action – unfairly as he had for some time been urging Reading to arrest Gandhi. In early March, they blew up a minor issue of Cabinet confidentiality and demanded his resignation. He complied on 9 March, the day before Gandhi was arrested. Ironically, he had been forced out of office just after Reading's administration had prevailed against Gandhi and the noncooperators. The Conservative Lord Peel was appointed to replace Montagu, bringing a much more reactionary flavour to British policy on India. Peel had no background in Indian affairs. The Indian Liberals were horrified by Montagu's ousting, as they had placed all their trust in him. They now felt very isolated. Sapru said that they had lost the only statesman in England who believed firmly in reform in India.[86]

Gandhi was arrested on 10 March. On 18 March he and a fellow nationalist, Shankarlal Banker, were brought before the Sessions Court of Judge Robert Broomfield in Ahmedabad, where they were treated with great respect. They were charged with exciting disaffection against the government, with certain articles that Gandhi had published in *Young India* being cited in evidence. Both men pleaded guilty to the charges and Gandhi asked that he be awarded the highest sentence under the law. He was allowed to read out a long statement that set out his position and reasons for his disaffection. British rule had rendered the Indian people helpless and poverty-stricken. This was, he said, 'a crime against humanity'. Their exploitation was underpinned by a legal system that served imperial interests.

> In ninety-nine cases out of hundred, justice has been denied to Indians as against Europeans in the Courts of India. This is not an exaggerated picture. It is the experience of almost every Indian who has had anything to do with such cases. In my opinion, the administration of the law is thus prostituted consciously or unconsciously for the benefit of the exploiter.

The tragedy was that Englishmen and their Indian collaborators were unaware of the crime that they were committing.

> I am satisfied that many English and Indian officials honestly believe that they are administering one of the best systems devised in the world and that India is making steady though slow progress. They do not know that a subtle but effective system of terrorism and an organised display of force on the one hand, and the deprivation of all powers of retaliation or self-defence on the other, have emasculated the people and induced in them the habit of simulation. This awful habit has added to the ignorance and the self-deception of the administrators. Section 124 A under which I am happily charged is perhaps the prince among the political sections of the Indian Penal Code designed to suppress the liberty of the citizen. Affection cannot be manufactured or regulated by law. If one has no affection for a person or system, one should be free to give the fullest expression to his disaffection, so long as he does not contemplate, promote or incite to violence.

Gandhi emphasised that he held no ill will against any individual administrator, or indeed the King, but he was 'disaffected towards a government which in its totality has done more harm to India than any previous system'. He asserted that he was in fact doing a service to the British people by showing them how they could escape from an 'unnatural state' that was causing great harm to them also. He called on Broomfield to either inflict on him the highest penalty under the law or refuse to be complicit with 'evil' and resign his position.[87]

In his judgement, Broomfield thanked Gandhi for pleading guilty. He accepted that Gandhi was a person of exceptional quality who was regarded by millions of his fellows as a great patriot. 'Even those who differ from you in politics look upon you as a man of high ideals and of noble and of even saintly life.' He was in any case not passing judgement on his exemplary character, but only the fact that he had broken the law and had pleaded guilty to it. He then made an extraordinary comparison that appeared to make him complicit in the whole drama:

> I propose, in passing sentence, to follow the precedent of a case, in many respects similar to this case, that was decided some 12 years ago, I mean the case against Mr. Bal Gangadhar Tilak under this same section. The sentence that was passed upon him as it finally stood was a sentence of simple imprisonment for six years. You will not consider it unreasonable, I think, that you should be classed with Mr. Tilak, and that is the sentence, two years' simple imprisonment on each count of the charge, i.e., six years in all, which I feel it my duty to pass upon you and I should like to say in doing so that, if the course of events in India should make it possible for the government to reduce the period and release you, no one will be better pleased than I.

Shankarlal Banker was given only six months, as he had acted out of loyalty to his 'chief'. Gandhi replied in the same spirit, thanking Broomfield for doing the honour of putting him in the same category as Tilak, and for his great courtesy. The report of the trial published five days later in *Young India* concluded: 'Then the friends of Mr. Gandhi crowded round him as the Judge left the court, and fell at his feet. There was much sobbing on the part of both men and women. But all the while Mr. Gandhi was smiling and cool and giving encouragement to everybody who came to him. Mr. Banker also was smiling and taking this in a light-hearted way. After all his friends had taken leave of him, Mr. Gandhi was taken out of the Court to the Sabarmati jail. And thus the great trial finished.'

The court case provided an extraordinary drama, and the poet and Indian nationalist Sarojini Naidu, who was present, sought to inflate its importance by comparing it to a trial that had been conducted two thousand years before in Jerusalem. 'I realised now that the lowly Jesus of Nazareth, cradled in a manger, furnished the only parallel in history to this invincible apostle of Indian liberty who loved humanity with surpassing compassion…' She concluded: 'In the midst of this poignant scene of many-voiced and myriad-hearted grief he stood, un-troubled, in all his transcendent simplicity, the embodied symbol of the Indian nation – its living sacrifice and sacrament in one.'[88] This was a blatant exaggeration, for while the first trial had ended in brutal tragedy, that of 1922 provided a demonstration of British legality and gentlemanly liberalism. Gandhi was to serve only a relatively cosseted two years in prison before being released on compassionate grounds after falling ill. The British hardly came out of this looking bad, but they did not repeat the mistake of providing Gandhi with such a platform: in future they would simply arrest and jail him without trial.

In the next three chapters, we shall examine the various local level campaigns that braided with the wider movement during 1920–22. We shall start with the no-rent campaigns waged by agrarian tenants against landlords who were, as a rule, allied closely with British rule.

3

STRUGGLES AGAINST LANDLORDISM

The Kisan Sabha Movement in Awadh

Awadh was a region of northern India that was annexed by the British in 1856, leading to the deposition of its ruler, the Nawab. It was integrated into the British-ruled United Provinces (UP). The imperial state established a firm hold over the area by granting extensive rights to the local aristocracy, known as the taluqdars, or sometimes zamindars. In the time of the nawabs, these people had been responsible for tax collection and maintaining law and order in a locality. The British turned them into landlords with full ownership rights in their areas of influence. This meant that most peasants who had previously held their land on a customary basis that gave them generally accepted rights of occupancy now became tenants-at-will in the eyes of the law and were thus subject to arbitrary eviction by the landlords. Such displacements, usually enforced by the hired strongmen of the landlords, became a means through which the taluqdars routinely hiked the rents that they took from the peasants. On top of this, the taluqdars demanded a wide range of extra cesses on one pretext or another, as well as making the people work for no pay on their own personal lands – a practice known as *begar*. This was all resented strongly by the cultivators. The British regarded the taluqdars as a pillar of their rule, and to keep them on their side refused to provide any meaningful rights of occupancy for the peasants. As the Governor of UP, Sir Spencer Harcourt Butler, commented to the new Viceroy, Lord Reading, in June 1921: the taluqdars were 'the most loyal body in India and a break water between trouble in the Punjab and trouble in Bengal'.[1] They were, in other words, seen as the chief bulwark against nationalist agitation in the eastern part of UP. The peasant movements of this time were driven by the demand for occupancy rights – and thus freedom from eviction – and an end to extra cesses and demands for free labour.[2]

In 1917, two peasant farmers of Rur village in Pratapgarh District of Awadh called Jhinguri Singh and Sahdev Singh formed a *kisan sabha*, or peasants' association. Jhinguri Singh's forebears had been prosperous cultivators, but the family had fallen on hard times, and he was raised as a common peasant. He and Sahdev Singh were of the Kurmi caste, considered of middling-to-low status in the hierarchy. The Kurmis were in a majority in several villages of this area, and they had a reputation for strong community solidarity. They were known as excellent cultivators and market gardeners who maintained the fertility of their soil through careful husbandry and irrigation from the wells that they often owned. Pratapgarh District had 52 taluqdars, most of whom were heavily indebted due to their extravagant lifestyles and mismanagement of their estates. They were constantly increasing rents and cesses to pay their debts. Eighty per cent of the population of the district was engaged in agriculture, and although the large majority were highly efficient in their work, they struggled to meet the ever-increasing demands of the landlords. Indeed, many tenants could only pay up with the help of remittances sent by family members who had taken jobs elsewhere in India. There were 114,061 tenants in 1918, 91.34% of whom had no secure right of tenure. Most were either of middling-to-low status castes, such as the Kurmis and Ahirs, or of untouchables castes, such as the Pasis and Chamars (the latter alone made up 42.82% of the population in 1921). The landlords regularly ejected a few tenants each year so as to keep them subservient as a class, and this was a major grievance.[3]

The Rur Kisan Sabha soon attracted the attention of a remarkable activist called Baba Ram Chandra. He was born in 1864 into a family of Maharashtrian Brahmans who lived near Gwalior, his original name being Shridhar Balwant Jodhpurkar. Leaving home at an early age due to abuse by family members, he lived initially as a labourer and petty vendor. In 1905, he went to Fiji as a contract labourer. When doing this, he changed his name to Ram Chandra Rao to conceal his Brahman identity as the British were suspicious of members of this supposedly 'seditious' caste. He became active in fighting for the rights of his fellow-workers in Fiji and had to flee in 1916 to avoid arrest. He settled in eastern UP – a region from which many of the contract labourers were recruited – and agitated there about the conditions of such work. While doing this, he became aware of the way in which the taluqdars oppressed the cultivators of this area. He tried initially to persuade the landlords to tone down their demands, but found his efforts spurned. He then decided to organise the people in a more active resistance.[4]

As a Brahman, he was steeped in religious literature, and he applied this to the cause he had now adopted. In Awadh there was a deep reverence for the mythical Lord Ram who, according to legend, had been unjustly expelled from the city of Ajodhya in Awadh that he should have ruled, and forced to wander with his wife Sita for fourteen years in exile. After various adventures, which included the rescuing of Sita after her abduction by the demon king Ravana, he eventually returned to his rightful kingdom, which he governed with fabled justice. A version of the legend written in the Awadhi dialect by the sixteenth-century sage Tulsidas – the *Ramcharitamanas* – was particularly revered by the people of this region. The peasants who began to organise themselves from 1917 onwards used to convoke meetings with a cry of 'Sita Ram'. Baba Ram Chandra quickly grasped the power of such an appeal when mobilising the peasantry. He learnt the local dialect so that he could converse easily with the people. As soon as he entered a village, he would 'blow the whistle of Lord Ram' to collect an audience and then recite appropriate verses from the *Ramcharitamanas* in a way that encouraged the peasants to organise themselves to resist the landlords. He likened the British to Indra, the king of the gods, who continued to wage war oblivious to the suffering of the common people. In the words of Tulsidas about Indra: '...there is no limit to his guile and rascality; he loves another's loss and his own gain'. Also: '...you make good evil and evil good, with a heart that feels neither grief nor joy... But now you shall receive a due return for your act'. The landlords were associated by Ram Chandra with the subsidiary gods whose devious manoeuvres led to Ram being banished from his rightful kingdom. He quoted another verse that spoke of the futility of petitioning an evil ruler – it would bring no redress. Such a ruler had to be stood up to, for 'only by threats will he learn humility'. He cited verses that condemned Ram's great enemy, Ravana, and said that the peasants should regard themselves as being like the monkey army that fought alongside Ram against Ravana. Although the battle that the monkey army fought was extremely violent, Ram Chandra himself did not advocate that method – he asked of the peasants only that they should display a similar courage in their struggle against the taluqdars. He travelled the region speaking to the peasants in this vein. His normal practice on arrival in a village was to string up a hammock between the branches of trees as a platform and speak to the crowd without any loudspeakers. Ram Chandra told them that if anyone was in distress and needed help, they could shout *Sita Ram*. The cry would be relayed from village to village, with people coming to help from over a large area. This he believed would discourage the talukdars from acting oppressively.[5]

When Jhinguri Singh and Sahdev Singh saw how effective and popular Ram Chandra was in the area, they invited him to take over the leadership of their Kisan Sabha at Rur. They were not confident that they had his ability to lead a major campaign against the landlords. Together, they organised a march to the office of the Deputy Commissioner (DC) of Pratapgarh (in parts of northern India such as UP, officers in charge of districts took this title; one that was equivalent to the 'District Collector' of other regions). About a thousand men and women were on the march. The DC ordered Ram Chandra to stop encouraging such protests – he refused to do so. Ram Chandra contacted the leaders of different castes who were already organising local campaigns, such as boycotts of the landlords, and with their help began opening branches of the Kisan Sabha. By mid-1920 there were about fifty in the district, with support from a wide range of peasant castes. As entreating the authorities had gained nothing, Ram Chandra decided to escalate the movement by advising the tenants to pay only what they considered a fair rent, to refuse to pay all extra cesses, and to stop providing any free labour for the taluqdars. He also encouraged them to raise their productivity by digging more wells, enlarging village reservoirs, planting orchards, and developing a cotton industry by sowing half their land with cotton and opening a cotton mill in each *tehsil* (sub-district) to employ those thrown out of work. He encouraged the education of women by itinerant women teachers. He told the people of Gandhi's campaign in Champaran, where the peasants had fought the planters with Gandhi's help, and he requested Gandhi and other like-minded nationalists to come to provide advice and leadership. He even organised a march of about five hundred peasants – both Hindu and Muslims – to the provincial capital of Allahabad, which lay on the southern border of the Awadh region, to request such help. Ram Chandra had heard that Gandhi himself would be in that city in early June – as he indeed was – but he had left before they reached there. Instead, they met with nationalist leaders, such as M.M. Malaviya. Malaviya had been instrumental in setting up an organisation at the time of the Home Rule League agitation in 1917 that styled itself the UP Kisan Sabha. In this, he and some other nationalistic lawyers of the city were advancing a claim to represent the peasants, even though they had no active organisation in rural areas. Ram Chandra and his peasant colleagues only came to know of this body in 1920. It arranged to accommodate the marchers in the city. Ram Chandra requested the nationalist leaders to examine the condition of the peasants and to campaign for them. He pestered them to do so, refusing to leave without a promise of help, just as Raj Kumar Shukla had done to persuade Gandhi to intervene in Champaran in 1917. The urban leaders were reluctant to give such support. In the end, Jawaharlal Nehru agreed to go and see for himself.[6] In all this, it was clear that Ram Chandra wanted his movement to be a part of the mainstream nationalist campaign led by Gandhi, fully in conformity with its nonviolent agenda.

Jawaharlal Nehru was joined by Malaviya's nephew, Krishna Kant Malaviya, and two leading Congressmen of Allahabad, Gauri Shankar Misra and Purshottamdas Tandon. Nehru wrote later in his autobiography of how this tour of the remote villagers of Pratapgarh was a 'revelation to me'. He was astounded how the cry of '*Sita Ram*' filled the air, bringing ever-swelling crowds to meet him and his colleagues. 'We found the whole countryside afire with enthusiasm and full of a strange excitement.... [The peasants] were in miserable rags, men and women, but their ... eyes glistened and seemed to expect strange happenings which would, as if by a miracle, put an end to their long misery'. They appeared to regard the four nationalists as 'the guides who would lead them to the promised land'. Nehru felt ashamed at the easy life he enjoyed in the big city and inadequate – even 'frightened' – in the face of such high expectations.

> I listened to their innumerable tales of sorrow, their crushing and ever-growing burden of rent, illegal exactions, ejectments from land and mud hut, beatings; surrounded on all sides by vultures who preyed on them – zamindar's agents, moneylenders, police; toiling all day to find what they produced was not theirs and their reward was kicks and curses and a hungry stomach. Many of those who were present were landless people who had been ejected by the landlords and had no land or hut to fall back upon. The land was rich, but the burden on it was very heavy, the holdings were small, and there were too many people after them. Taking advantage of this land hunger, the landlords, unable under the law to enhance their rents beyond a certain percentage, charged huge illegal premiums. The tenant, knowing of no other alternative, borrowed money from the moneylender and paid the premium, and then, unable to pay his debt or even the rent, was ejected and lost all he had.[7]

Baba Ram Chandra and Jhinguri Singh then wrote a pamphlet in the Avadhi dialect that was published under the name of Gauri Shankar Misra, in his capacity as vice-president of the UP Kisan Sabha. It was titled *Kisan Pratigya* (the peasants' solemn affirmation). It urged the peasants to follow certain principles in their struggle. They were to tell only the truth about their conditions and to stand up to any abuse by the landlords or their hired men. If so abused, they were to reason with the abuser, and if necessary take him to their *Thakur* (this word was ambiguous, as landlords were often known as *Thakurs*, though it could mean their own leader, e.g. Baba Ram Chandra). They agreed to pay their rent at the proper time, going in a bloc to the landlord's house and demanding a formal receipt, but to pay no cesses and provide no free labour. They would refuse to eat if anyone was compelled by the taluqdars' strongmen to labour, abstaining so long as the enforced work continued. They agreed not to quarrel, but if there was a dispute would settle it with a village panchayat. They stated that they would not fear government policemen and would refuse to submit to any tyranny. The last principle stated: 'We shall trust God and with patience and zeal we shall try to end our woes'.[8] These principles were ones that Gandhi should not have had any difficulty accepting, though, as we shall see, he soon came to distrust these peasants.

Urban leaders such as Motilal Nehru and M.M. Malaviya wanted to take advantage of this rural upsurge to gain votes for themselves in the forthcoming elections for the UP legislative council, which in June 1920 they were still anticipating fighting. They did not want to alienate the taluqdars unduly, as the lawyers amongst the urban leaders often represented them in legal cases and their relationship was generally comfortable. Their main plan was first to obtain peasant votes, and then to try and negotiate some sort of settlement with the taluqdars that would grant the tenants a few concessions. Jawaharlal Nehru, who had been genuinely moved by what he had seen on his tour of Pratapgarh, was too junior a political figure at that time to have much sway over the top leaders, including his own father, Motilal. Meanwhile, Ram Chandra and Jhinguri Singh were organising mass meetings at which increasingly radical demands were voiced. They threatened anyone who refused to join the movement with social boycott. As a result, many of the wavering joined them, even if under duress.[9] We have already in the previous chapter discussed how Gandhi did not regard such forms of social coercion as being in accord with his understanding of 'truth'. This did not however necessarily mean that it was an invalid method to use in nonviolent movements – many activists regarded it as vital for solidarity. As it was, the use of the method in Awadh in 1920 was in line with most previous mass movements in India.

The landlords were by now becoming seriously alarmed. They saw this as a matter of prestige, believing that if they yielded in any way the floodgates would be opened. They accused the peasants of behaving like the Irish or Russian peasants and spoke of a possible 'mutiny' far worse than 1857. Following this mindset, the leading pro-British newspaper of the region, the Allahabad *Pioneer*, translated 'Kisan Sabha' into English as 'Soviet' and claimed that 'Soviets' had been set up by villagers. The movement was thus depicted as a form of Bolshevism. This all stoked an alarmist atmosphere. The taluqdars held meetings at which they denounced the activists as 'irresponsible agitators' who were inflaming the people, and they demanded that the British authorities take strong action to crush the protest. On 28 August 1920, the DC responded to their pleas by arresting Ram Chandra and 32 other tenant leaders. When the authorities attempted to bring them to trial in Pratapgarh, there were such strong protests in the town by people of the surrounding area that Ram Chandra had to be released to defuse the tension, followed later by the 32 others.[10]

Harcourt Butler then attempted to calm the atmosphere by appointing the DC of Pratapgarh, V.N. Mehta, to enquire into the grievances of the peasants. Mehta was known to be relatively sympathetic to the tenants, and it had only been while he was on leave in August that his temporary replacement made the botched effort to have Baba Ram Chandra and the other peasant leaders locked up on a dubious charge. Mehta now consulted Baba Ram Chandra, regarding him as the mouthpiece of the peasants. An uneasy peace prevailed for nearly three months while the enquiry went on. During this time, the Congress leaders toured the rural areas urging the peasants to boycott the elections in November and preaching patience. Motilal Nehru held a meeting at Pratapgarh on 17 October at which he announced that a new Awadh Kisan Sabha was to be formed that would lead a campaign to refuse demands by landlords for cesses on top of the legitimate rent, to refuse to cultivate any land from which a tenant had been evicted, to socially boycott anyone who failed to adhere to these two points, and to decide disputes through popular councils (*panchayats*). In this, it is apparent that the top Congress leader of UP had no problem with social boycott. With the help of the Congress organisation, the Awadh Kisan Sabha managed to get 330 local kisan sabhas affiliated to it by the end of October. Motilal Nehru had taken this initiative to sidestep his leading rival in the UP Provincial Congress Committee, M.M. Malaviya. The result was two separate organisations that were in competition with each other. In his eventual report, V.N. Mehta documented many cases of abuse by the taluqdars. Butler was unhappy with this as he was sympathetic towards the landlords and had hoped for a whitewash. Accusing Mehta of ignoring many complexities of the case, he refused to print the report in its entirety. He also ordered that Mehta be transferred away from Pratapgarh and replaced by a European DC, believing that he would be more malleable.[11]

Meanwhile, Baba Ram Chandra had been invited to start work in the neighbouring district of Rae Bareli, where only 3.63% of tenants had secure tenure. The invitation came from Matabadal Koeri, a tenant famer of Rasulpur village who was in dispute with his landlord over rent payments. He was a Koeri, a caste similar to the Kurmis with a reputation for being excellent market gardeners. The rent collector was a corrupt man who was in the habit of taking the rent in full, recording a much lower sum in the rent book, and appropriating the rest for himself. Koeri had managed to expose this abuse, but in the following season was evicted as a punishment. He then went to Baba Ram Chandra for help, who then came and founded a Rae Bareli Kisan Sabha on 28 October 1920. Ram Chandra toured the district preaching the Congress creed of Hindu-Muslim unity, the use of swadeshi products, education of children, and boycott of the council elections. He went on from there to other districts of Awadh, travelling on foot and opening new branches of the Kisan Sabha; he worked with Kedar Nath and Deo Narain Pande in Faizabad District, and with Pandit Ramlal Sharma in Sultanpur District. Kedar Nath had already formed a local Kisan Sabha in September 1920, and he proved to be a talented organiser. Deo Narain Pande had previous links with Malaviya's Kisan Sabha, but now shifted his loyalty to Baba Ram Chandra.[12]

While Baba Ram Chandra was away from Pratapgarh, a new and more aggressive leader, Thakur Din Singh, emerged in that district. He was a Rajput by caste – traditionally the ruling group – and had been employed by the Raja of Parhat, a taluqdar of the district. In 1920, he resigned his post and established himself as a champion of the tenants. The police tried to arrest him when holding a meeting at which he was advising the peasants to seize the granary of the landlord. The people turned on the police and prevented him from being captured. Thakur Din then announced that the British Raj was at an end in the area, and that tenants had no need to pay their rent. Peasants began to harvest the crops from the personal holdings of the landlords that were traditionally cultivated with their free labour. They also appropriated grain from the stores of the Baniya merchants and usurers, which was then distributed among the people. The landlords retaliated by launching a reign of terror, with their strongmen going into the villages and beating up peasants, molesting women, and looting the houses. The police either watched this without intervening or they participated themselves. Thakur Din was soon captured, and he and some of his main supporters were sentenced to four years in jail. Baba Ram Chandra felt that Thakur Din's militancy had been counter-productive, isolating him and his followers, so that they could be crushed relatively easily. He believed that if Thakur Din had joined the Kisan Sabha and worked under his supervision much more could have been achieved.[13]

Gandhi was in Allahabad from 28 November to 1 December 1920. In his speeches in the city, he emphasised 'the great necessity for unity' – but stated this mainly in terms of Hindu-Muslim relationships. Like Baba Ram Chandra, he appealed to the story of Ram – comparing the British government to that of the demon-king Ravana. He reminded an audience of women that Sita had worn rough garments of tree-bark in her fourteen-year exile with her husband Ram and asked them to practise a similar self-denial by wearing coarse khadi cloth. He stressed the need to fight the violence of this state with 'soul-force', by which he meant 'non-violent non-co-operation'. On 29 November he carried out a fleeting visit to Pratapgarh accompanied by Motilal Nehru, Shaukat Ali and A.K. Azad. They gave speeches advocating noncooperation and swadeshi. Nothing was said about peasant grievances, and Gandhi did not meet any Kisan Sabha leaders. Instead, he met some taluqdars.[14]

The Awadh Kisan Sabha organised a meeting at Ajodhya, which was in Faizabad District, on 20 December. The landlords warned the peasants to keep away, but their threats were largely ignored. An estimated 50–100,000 people poured into the city carrying banners demanding an end to taluqdari oppression and shouting 'Baba Ram Chandra Ki Jai' and 'Sita Ram Ki Jai'. The priests allowed them to stay in the temples, with Hindus and Muslims sleeping alongside each other in harmony. Baba Ram Chandra made a passionate speech, appearing theatrically tied in ropes and comparing the condition of the peasants to that of prisoners bound by 'government, taluqdars and capitalists'. He said he was prepared to go to the gallows or *kalipani* (e.g. to be transported to the Andamans) for their cause, and that he would only untie the ropes when the peasants assured them of their unity in the struggle against these triple evils, which they did. Gauri Shankar Misra presided, emphasising the need for swadeshi and noncooperation in his speech. The people were well-ordered throughout and returned to their villages filled with enthusiasm, conscious of the strength they had in numbers. The districts of Pratapgarh, Faizabad, Sultanpur and Rae Bareli were to the fore in all this. Some people of Barabanki District had attended the Ajodhya meeting, and one of them, Kashi Prasad, invited Ram Chandra to go there. He toured the district for two weeks giving speeches, receiving a hero's welcome from Hindus and Muslims alike. He told the people to stand up to the oppression of the landlords, to use swadeshi goods, wear khadi cloth, and donate money to found national schools. A branch of the Kisan Sabha was inaugurated there. In all this, Ram Chandra intertwined his anti-taluqdar agenda with the programme of the mainstream Congress – although officially the Congress had kept silent on the issue of landlord oppression.[15]

In early January 1921, some peasants of Pratapgarh and Rae Bareli Districts started going from one estate to another, surrounding the landlords in their mansions and in some cases destroying their crops. The shops of Baniya merchants and usurers were also raided. This gave a licence for some known criminals to join in under the guise of being members of the Kisan Sabha. In Rae Bareli District, for example, a well-known *dacoit* (bandit) of Nasirabad village called Mahabir Gadaria headed a band that claimed to be acting in support of the peasant movement. In one week of January 1921, thirty-seven cases of banditry were recorded in Rae Bareli District alone. In this way, criminals sought legitimacy as Robin Hood-style local heroes. This was not how the mainstream Kisan Sabha activists regarded them, as was revealed when Shah Naim Ata – a leader in the area in which Mahibir Gadaria was active – went to the DC to apologise for what was going on and promised to work with the government against such miscreants.[16]

On 5 January, Baba Janki Das led a group of peasants to the mansion of a notoriously oppressive taluqdar of Rae Bareli District, Tribhuwan Bahadur Singh of Chandania, demanding an end to enforced 'gifts' and evictions. After the taluqdar rejected their demand, the peasants surrounded the mansion. The DC had been forewarned and he arrived on the scene with a party of police. They attempted to arrest Janki Das and two other leaders, but the peasants lay down in front of the police to prevent them. Janki Das told them to allow their arrest, stating that they would get justice in the court in Rae Bareli. The peasants then allowed the three to be taken away. Janki Das had thus managed to ensure that the peace was kept. He was charged with extorting gold ornaments from the taluqdar and sent to Lucknow jail to await trial.[17]

On 6 January, a crowd of between 300 and 400 people gathered at the market at Fursatganj in Rae Bareli District to protest about the high price of grain and cloth, and the tyranny of the taluqdars. They shouted 'Ram Chandra Maharaj Ki Jai', 'Mahatma Gandhi Ki Jai', and 'Shaukat Ali Muhammad Ali Ki Jai'. The Baniyas were accused of profiteering and they were told to sell at a fair price. The numbers rapidly swelled to perhaps 10,000. The police fired in the air to try and disperse the crowd, but to no avail. They then fired on the crowd, killing six and injuring many more. They claimed that they had opened fire as the peasants had started looting the shops, but the only supposed 'loot' subsequently recovered was a little tobacco. Twenty-six of those with injuries were arrested – they were of many castes, including one Brahman. On the same day, the property of taluqdars was allegedly looted at four other places in Rae Bareli District.[18]

Meanwhile, the message had gone around the village that 'Babaji' had been arrested at Chandni on 5 January. Many believed that this meant Baba Ram Chandra himself rather than the local leader Baba Janki Das. Some even said that Mahatma Gandhi had been arrested, and that all of them were lodged in the prison at Rae Bareli town. In fact, Baba Janki Das and his two colleagues had been taken to Lucknow jail. Large numbers marched to Rae Bareli, gathering just outside at Munshiganj Bridge, to show solidarity with their leaders and put pressure on the authorities to release them, as they had managed to do on previous occasions. The DC of Rae Bareli District, Sherreff, was determined to face them down, and gathering police and military reinforcement, blocked the way into the town, and started making arrests. No attempt was made by the people to resist. Meanwhile a group of largely poor Pasi peasants led by a *fakir* called Rahmat Ali Shah who was of the same caste entered the town from a different direction and approached the jail demanding the *darshan* of Babaji and an end to taluqdari oppression. Sherreff drove up in his car accompanied by Sardar Birpal Singh, who was a member of the UP Provincial Council and a prominent local taluqdar. Singh was a Sikh whose ancestor had been given land confiscated after the revolt of 1857 as a reward for their loyalty to the British at that time. Sherreff told them that the 'Baba' was an absconding offender, that he was not in Rae Bareli jail and would not be released. He rebuked the peasants for coming as a 'mob' and making impossible demands. The protestors were being pressed by the police to their front and an ever-swelling crowd from behind. When the Municipal Commissioner, Bhagwati Prasad, tried to reason with the crowd to disperse, he was arrested on the grounds that he had been inciting the people. Mounted police were then sent in to disperse the crowd, driving them back a short distance despite some resistance. Jawaharlal Nehru, who had received news that a serious situation had developed at Rae Bareli and that leadership was required, had rushed there, arriving at this juncture. Sherreff was advised to take Nehru's help in quietening the crowd, but he said that he was not prepared to give any such role to a 'firebrand' and sent a note ordering him to leave by the next train. Nehru replied that unless the legal status of this order was stated he would not obey it, and he then tried to walk to Munshiganj Bridge but found his path blocked by the military. By now, the police had started firing on the crowd. Nehru was surrounded by frightened peasants who had been separated from the main crowd and managed to reassure them. He found out later that the main body of peasants at Munshiganj Bridge had refused to disperse without any directive from a leader whom they trusted and had remained there peacefully in the face of the police guns. Many were shot by the police. Nehru was convinced that if he had been allowed by Sherreff to address them, they would have dispersed. He later stated: 'He could not permit an agitator to succeed where he had failed. That is not the way of foreign governments depending on prestige.'[19]

The British claimed that they had only started firing at Munshiganj Bridge after stones were thrown at them by the crowd. Sherreff and the District Superintendent of Police (DSP) claimed that a soldier had fired initially in self-defence, though the soldier himself said that his gun had gone off accidently. Sherreff and the DSP also said that they would have been overwhelmed by the crowd had they not fired. In fact, not a single policeman or soldier was injured that day. The crowd had, by most accounts, behaved in a firmly nonviolent manner. Several witnesses later testified that the local taluqdar, Sardar Birpal Singh, had fired first. One of them, a Chamar called Basanta, stated that a white car had driven up and Sardar Birpal Singh had got out and told them that he would 'scorch' them if they did not retreat. He then took out a gun and shot Pancham Pasi. Basanta began to flee but was hit and had to limp away. He heard frequent firing behind him after that. He insisted that Birpal Singh had been the first to fire. This account was denied by the government, claiming that it was fabricated to malign the taluqdar. Sherreff later described Birpal Singh as his 'friend, philosopher and guide' and said he had been with him all day, and that he had fired only one shot from his pistol. Others claimed that the taluqdar had not fired a single shot. Birpal Singh was praised for his composure in restoring order and a courage worthy of his Sikh heritage. Officially, four died and fourteen were wounded in the firing at Munshiganj Bridge. The urban politicians said that they had seen six dead bodies heaped on a horse-drawn carriage near the bridge. Locally, it was believed that about a hundred had been killed and that their bodies were taken at night by lorry and thrown into the Ganges River. There was much anger at this 'miniature Jallianwala', meetings were held in protest and the nationalist press condemned it as an atrocity. Harcourt Butler, for his part, praised the authorities for restoring order, and singled out Birpal Singh for special praise. Butler later remarked in an unpublished autobiography that he believed that in India trouble had to be squashed through 'overwhelming force', which meant a willingness to take quick action by firing low and lethally into crowds.[20]

Baba Ram Chandra learnt about the events at Munshiganj Bridge in Lucknow, where he had gone to talk to the Khilafat leader, Abdul Bari. Bari regarded Ram Chandra as a troublemaker, and telegrammed the Ali brothers in Bombay asking for advice – should he remain aloof from the Kisan Sabha movement or take measures to stop Ram Chandra? Shaukat Ali cabled in reply that Ram Chandra should pacify the peasants 'according to our non-violent creed', and that coolness was required. Bari then ordered his servants to prevent the peasant leader from leaving his residence. He cabled Gandhi informing him of this and asked for his advice. Gandhi sent a cryptic telegram that stated: 'You should certainly intervene for securing peace.' Abdul Bari took this to mean that he should continue to detain Ram Chandra, and he told him that he would not be allowed to go anywhere for the time being.[21]

As it was, the peasants continued to fight for their rights under local leadership. In Fyzabad District, Deo Narain Pande took the initiative in this respect, encouraging the landless labourers to strike for higher wages. He was a local Brahman who was a staunch follower of Gandhi, and was accordingly known by some in the area as 'Mahatma'. This district had the highest number of agricultural wage workers of all districts of Awadh. Many of them were Chamars, an untouchable caste. There was also little security for tenants – only 1.88% of the tenancies being secure in the district. From 12 January onwards, poor and largely landless peasants of mainly Ahir and Bhar castes carried out raids on the taluqdars, rich peasants, Baniyas and goldsmiths in villages of Tanda sub-division. A message had gone around that Gandhi himself had ordered such raids, and they accordingly shouted 'Mahatma Gandhi Ki Jai' as they helped themselves to the property of the exploiters. According to Jawaharlal Nehru, the servants of a taluqdar who had a feud with another taluqdar had spread this message maliciously to cause trouble for their rival. Crowds of a thousand or more were involved in this, with women following the men and carrying off the goods. Some upper caste women were subject to humiliation, maltreatment and abuse by groups of lower caste women. Armed police arrived on 15 January, and along with the hired men of the landlords tried to recover the goods and punish those who had taken them. Three hundred and forty six were arrested and much of the property recovered. It was officially estimated that 114 houses were raided in thirty-one villages. Deo Narain Pande was assaulted by a Brahman landlord at Baskuri on 19 January as he was seen to be responsible for the raids – which as a firm Gandhian he was not. Next day, he sat outside the police station demanding an apology, as he believed that the police had instigated the attack on him. As the news spread, 7,000 to 10,000 people flocked to the place in his support. Pande spoke to the crowd and told them to be patient. When the authorities complained that the people were armed, Pande collected 300 *lathis* (long heavy wooden stick) and deposited them at the police station. They refused, however, to disperse. As more were thought to be coming, the Deputy Commissioner made a compromise with Pande – there would be an enquiry into the affair if he told the crowd to go. The findings would be announced on 27 January, when the crowd could reassemble. The people then left on the command of their leader.[22]

Jawaharlal Nehru was outraged when he heard that the peasants in Faizabad had been raiding exploiters in the name of Gandhi and went there immediately. He held a meeting attended by five or six thousand people. He condemned them for 'the shame they had brought on themselves and our cause' and he demanded that all those involved in looting should confess in public. He later remarked that he had in those days been full of the spirit of Gandhian satyagraha, and that he had acted unwisely in this respect, as those who confessed were then arrested by the police. In his words: 'I began to regret having exposed these foolish and simple folk to long terms of imprisonment.'[23]

The only recorded killing of a policeman by a crowd at that time in Awadh occurred at Sehagaon Panchimgao village in Rae Bareli District on 23 January. The local taluqdar, Gauri Shamkar, a Kurmi by caste, was very oppressive and unpopular among the peasants, many of whom were also Kurmis. According to the peasantry, the taluqdar had, some years previously, relocated the local market onto his own land, which allowed him to levy heavy taxes on it. The peasants took advantage of the situation in 1921 to announce that they were moving the market back to its original place in defiance of the landlord. The taluqdar had requested that the police come to stop this happening. When the peasants assembled at the place that they considered the rightful one for their market, they were fired on by the police, injuring twelve. They had retaliated, attacking the police with their lathis, and in the fracas a policeman was killed by a blow. According to the police version, two peasants who had a grudge against the taluqdar had instigated a mass attack on the police on that day, with peasants rushing at them with their lathis while women threw brickbats from the surrounding roofs. The police then fired in self-defence. The two alleged ringleaders were arrested and later sentenced to death.[24]

On 27 January Jawaharlal Nehru presided over a meeting in Fyzabad attended by some 30,000 to 40,000 peasants. Speeches were directed at the government, with landlords being spared. Gandhi was praised in the speeches for his struggle for *Bharatmata* (Mother India), and for his attempts to cure the many ills of Indian society. The peasants were told to consider Gandhi as their raja. They refused however to consent to a resolution that condemned the raiding of the previous weeks, and they left in a deflated mood. The Congress leaders were trying hard to restrain the more radical local leaders such as Deo Narain Pande and Kedar Nath who wanted to establish a parallel administration with their own unauthorised DC and other officials, and people's police. The Commissioner for Fyzabad Division reported that these leaders were able to summon a large crowd at short notice, and that the people would carry out their orders, even if it involved violent attacks on the police. As it was, there is no evidence that the two leaders ever encouraged such attacks.[25]

There was a yet more radical leader in that area who had been active since 1918 called Suraj Prasad, who was a Pasi by caste. He was known as *Chotta* (little) Ram Chandra. In 1921, he established a Kisan Sabha and declared himself ruler of a tract that was demarcated with flags. He dressed in a saffron robe and claimed to be a follower of Gandhi. He ordered that no police should be allowed to enter the area, and one policeman on patrol was accordingly detained. He said that no rent should be paid to the landlords and he announced that all landlords' rights were abolished and tenants who had been ejected were to be reinstated. He fined government servants and pensioners. Several thousand peasants, predominantly of low caste, regularly attended his meetings. These were held mainly in villages under the Khapradih estate of Kesari Prasad Singh in Fyzabad District. The taluqdar sent hysterical telegrams to the authorities demanding that Prasad be arrested. Other local leaders found Prasad to be too militant, and Deo Narain even declared him an imposter. Prasad was arrested by a party of 70 armed mounted policemen on 29 January and taken to Fyzabad jail. The news of the arrest spread rapidly and several thousand went to Gosaiganj railway station as they assumed he would be taken there. They squatted on the track to prevent any trains leaving but fled when the police opened fire.[26]

In early February, Motilal Nehru ordered Abdul Bari to have Baba Ram Chandra escorted in secret to his residence in Allahabad. Two of Bari's armed servants took him disguised in a *burqa* and he was then detained. On 7 February, Malaviya's UP Kisan Sabha announced a meeting to be held in Allahabad that same day. Nehru and the other Congress leaders knew that Malaviya wanted the Rent Act to be amended in favour of the tenants, which went against the Congress policy of ignoring the legislative councils and seeking to negotiate a solution through mutual agreement between landlord and tenant. Nehru and his colleagues planned to disrupt Malaviya's meeting, and – getting wind of this – the secretary of the UP Kisan Sabha – Indra Narain Dwivedi, a known opponent of Gandhi – hastily changed the venue. The Congress noncooperators then held their own meeting on 7 February at which Baba Ram Chandra was produced to give a veneer of legitimacy. He was not given a chance to speak, and though distressed by this turn of events felt it best to remain silent. A new Kisan Sabha was announced that was to be led by Motilal Nehru. In this way, the elite politicians of Allahabad split the Kisan Sabha movement at the provincial level. Ram Chandra later described Motilal Nehru as 'an advocate of taluqdars', and he believed that it was in the interest of the Gandhian Congress for the kisan movement to be disrupted and the discontent diverted into Congress channels.[27]

With Baba Ram Chandra's whereabouts now being known, Jhinguri Singh, Matabadal Koeri and other local leaders managed to secure his release from Nehru's clutches. Governor Butler had however already given the order for Ram Chandra's detention. This was effected on 10 February in front of 80,000 people at the opening ceremony of the Kashi Vidyapith at Banaras, which he was attending at the invitation of Gauri Shankar Misra. He was charged with sedition and promoting enmity between classes. Gandhi was also at this ceremony, and the British had calculated that his presence coupled with the fact that Banaras was well away from the Awadh region would make any disturbance unlikely. The day before, Gandhi had asserted in a speech at the town hall in Banaras: 'Do not be frightened of jail. People who seek release of those who have gone to jail show cowardice and their fear of jail. We should go to jail cheerfully'. Next day, he described the arrest of Ram Chandra as a 'sacred event' and advised the peasants not to protest as Ram Chandra would not want to be released. On the same day, Gandhi went on to Faizabad, and in a speech expressed appreciation for Kedar Nath, the local kisan leader who had been arrested a few days before. He went on to criticise the kisans who had said he had acted violently, saying that violence was a 'sin against God and man'. He condemned 'all attempts to create discord between landlords and tenants and advised the tenants to suffer rather than fight, for they had to join all forces for fighting against the most powerful zemidar [sic.], namely the government.' Their priority should be, rather, to win swaraj through *shanti* (peace), the spinning wheel, non-cooperation and money. He also issued a list of nineteen rules for the peasants of the region which revealed that he had no time for some core elements of their struggle, such as refusing to pay their rents, stopping railways trains and travelling without tickets, trying to prevent the arrest of their leaders, and applying social boycotts to maintain solidarity. He condemned the use of 'undue pressure' being applied to opponents and told them that they had to win them over through 'kindness'. Their aim should be to turn the landlords into their friends. Motilal and Jawaharlal Nehru and Gauri Shankar Misra reinforced Gandhi's message by circulating a leaflet signed by them titled: *Peace, Patience, Non-Cooperation*. They asserted that nobody should be unhappy at Ram Chandra's arrest and they should not try to get him released. The best way to ensure the results they wanted was through peaceful noncooperation. Although the Congress leaders had not engineered Ram Chandra's arrest, it served their purpose well. It allowed them to strengthen their hold over the peasant movement and preach accommodation with the taluqdars rather than confrontation. The British transferred Ram Chandra to Lucknow secretly and tried him there. He was sentenced to two year's rigorous imprisonment and a fine of Rs 200, or an extra six months in default.[28]

The Governor, Harcourt Butler, was determined to show who was in charge in Awadh and ordered a squadron of Indian cavalry and two companies of British infantry to march through Fyzabad and Sultanpur District led by the DC of Fyzabad District. Those who refused to provide free provisions to the troops were punished with fines. Villagers, including children, were made to line up by the road and *salaam* the troops as they passed. Village leaders were arrested systematically and Kisan Sabha meetings were banned. Butler reported in March 'we are prohibiting meetings and serving notices all over the province', and that the situation was now under control.

This boosted the morale of the landlords throughout the region, and they unleashed their strongmen on their tenants. Peasants were beaten up, peasant women were molested and abused, houses were looted and burnt. Many tenants were evicted as a punishment. Those who refused to perform free labour were beaten. The landlord's men were often assisted in this by the police. Large numbers of cooked-up cases were also lodged against peasants, who were arrested and taken to jail to await trial. This reign of terror effectively crushed the movement in Awadh by the end of March 1921.[29]

Historians who have examined the Kisan Sabha movement in Awadh have tended to characterise this as a violent outbreak. W.F. Crawley talks of 'the outbreak of rioting' that was associated with Gandhi's name, but which Gandhi subsequently repudiated for its violence.[30] Majid Siddiqi describes it as a series of riots, clashes and looting initiated by the peasants to which the police merely responded.[31] Gyan Pandey, in a generally excellent study of this movement, begins by stating that 'peasant violence – the looting of bazars (as at Fursatganj), attacks on landlords, and battles with the police – broke out around this time'. Later, he talks of 'the violence of their actions' and the 'widespread rioting' of January 1921. He starts his conclusion by stating: 'When peasant violence erupted in January 1921...' His general argument is that the violence of the peasantry increased as they gradually developed a better understanding of their needs as a class, so that by the later stages of the movement they were attacking the landlords and police with growing impunity. It appears in this account that peasant violence was a central, ever-escalating feature of the whole affair.[32] In arguing this, Pandey tends to accept British official accounts of the violence of the people at face value, adopting their use of terms that suggest crowd aggression, such as 'riot', 'clashes', 'looting', 'attacking', 'erupted', and so on.[33] To take an example, he describes a confrontation between the police and the people at Karhaiya Bazaar in Rae Bareli District on 20 March 1921, in which some of the protestors were shot, claiming that 'the peasants battled with the police, trading brickbat for buckshot'. He holds that this violence on the part of the peasantry came as a consequence of the new political awareness that they had acquired over the previous months.[34] Kapil Kumar's more detailed account of this incident reveals that the violence began when the police arrested two prominent peasant leaders of the district, Brijpal Singh and Jhunku Singh. Their followers managed to secure their release by throwing brickbats and using lathis. The police then escalated the violence by opening fire on the crowd of some seven hundred people, killing one person and injuring others. Outnumbered, the police fled into the mansion of the local landlord, which was surrounded by the crowd. Although the peasants shouted threats, such as *maro!* (beat them), they did not attempt to storm the building. The terrified police then began firing from the rooftop on the unarmed people below. Police reinforcement led by the DC Sherreff arrived late that evening and the crowd was told to disperse. Brijpal Singh complained to Sherreff of the earlier firings by the police, and he appealed to his sense of fairness. He told the crowd to stage a sit-down protest to reinforce their demand for justice. When the DC ignored this appeal, Singh loudly entreated the Indian policemen to side with the people as they were their 'brothers'. The stand-off continued through the night, and early next morning the peasants brought two of their dead and some wounded people to demonstrate the brutality of the police. Brijpal Singh demanded a doctor to treat the wounded, and when one was found went with him to a nearby village to attend to them. There, he was seized by the British and taken immediately to the jail at Rae Bareli. Jhunku Singh was also arrested, and while this was being carried out, the police again fired on the crowd. In all, four peasants were killed and twenty wounded, while the police suffered no casualties at all.[35] The detailed account reveals that most of the violence came from the police, and that the people were remarkably restrained in their reaction.[36]

In contrast to Pandey, Kapil Kumar has argued in his full-length study of the movement that the peasants of Awadh did not employ lethal violence against the oppressors – e.g. take human life. No taluqdar was killed in crowd action. Those who carried out raids on the property of landlords and other oppressors did not generally see these as violent acts.[37] Kumar states: 'Thus, as far as the peasants [sic] interpretation of non-violence was concerned, they were perfectly non-violent.' Gandhi, he argues, used the notion of nonviolence instrumentally – he made it an issue when the class interests of the upper classes were challenged. Gandhi was also, Kumar holds, swayed by the letters he received from landlords that spoke of the violent temperament and lawlessness of the people of this region.[38] There is also evidence to suggest that some of the more violent acts perpetrated against landlords during the upsurge were committed by criminals who took advantage of the situation to loot and rob. As it was, almost all the violence at this time came not from the Kisan Sabha but from the police, army and taluqdars' strongmen. Only one case of lethal violence is recorded in Kumar's extensive account – the killing of a policeman by a *lathi* blow at Sehagaon Panchimgao village in Rae Bareli District on 23 January 1921. There appears to have been extreme aggravation by the police in this case, and the peasants were acting mainly in self-defence. For the most part, the peasants showed great restraint in the face of continuing provocation.

The issue therefore was not so much that the peasants were too violent, but that their movement did not conform to the Congress agenda at that juncture, which was to build a united front of all Indians, with the rich fighting alongside the poor for freedom from British rule. Taluqdars and peasants were meant to unite against the British. This agenda was woefully misguided when applied to areas such as Awadh – for the power of the taluqdars rested entirely on their close alliance with the British. The British regarded the taluqdars as vital allies, and did all they could to support them, even if this entailed the ruthless suppression of entirely just and legitimate demands by the people. There was no way that the landlords were going to be persuaded by force to abandon their greatest allies, the British, and develop a new and unprecedented sympathy for their tenants, as Gandhi argued would be the case if the peasants acted in the way that he demanded.[39] As the interests of the British and the taluqdars were one, they were a legitimate target for any movement that claimed to stand for the people-nation against imperial oppression. As Pandey points out: 'The days were gone when the Raj could pose as an impartial referee, standing on high and whistling "foul play". Local struggles tended more and more to get caught up in the general wave of anti-imperialism sweeping through India.'[40] In demanding that the peasants support nationalist protest while refraining from their struggle against landlord oppression, Gandhi, the Nehrus, and other top leaders were 'standing for the *status quo* … against any radical change in the social set-up'.[41]

In so acting, the leaders of the Noncooperation Movement were betraying the movement that they were supposed to be championing.

The Congress leaders of UP were particularly reprehensible in all of this. Initially, people such as M.M. Malaviya and Motilal Nehru had adopted a populist agenda in fishing for rural votes. Once the elections had been abandoned, they reverted to their old ways, acting as the spokesmen of the landlord classes.[42] This led to some shameful behaviour, such as the detention of Baba Ram Chandra in January 1921 by Abdul Bari and then Motilal Nehru. While Nehru and Malaviya then squabbled as to who represented the real Kisan Sabha in the province, the actual peasant movement was crushed brutally. Neither had anything of substance to say on this. Motilal's son, the young Jawaharlal Nehru, had been moved by what he witnessed in Awadh in the first weeks of 1921, but when he later wrote about the decline of the movement in the following two months he merely commented: 'The Indian *kisans* have little staying power, little energy to resist for long…they began to weary a little and the determined attack of the government on their movement ultimately broke its spirit for the time being.'[43] Nehru was here implying that the peasants were unable to sustain their protest as they above all lacked the moral fibre of their betters. On the previous page he had called them 'foolish and simple folk'. Ultimately, his attitude towards them was both patronising and dismissive.

This account of the movement in Awadh brings out, first, that there were layers of leadership, ranging from the all-India/Khilafat figures (such as Gandhi and the Ali brothers), to the regional (e.g. the Nehrus and Baba Ram Chandra in the United Provinces), to local (e.g. *Chhota* Baba Ram Chandra in the Khapradih estate in Fyzabad District). While some of these leaders had a reputation that could assume mythical and even fantastic proportions, others relied for their popularity on their claim to be acting as allies of the people in their many life struggles. Second, it shows that the strategies of these leaders were generally determined by considerations of caste, class and religion, and that there were many tensions between leaders at different levels, and sometimes conflict. Thirdly, it reveals that the ideology of nonviolent resistance was still in a state of development, being contested and defined though the process of struggle.

The Eka Movement in Awadh

The decline of the Kisan Sabha movement did not bring an end to anti-landlord protests in Awadh. Another such campaign – the Eka, or unity, movement – began towards the end of 1921 in the north of the region. Eka stood above all for the unity between Hindus and Muslims, and there was a strong Muslim component in the movement. The Khilafat leaders of Malihabad town of Lucknow District, and particularly Kwaja Ahmad, had encouraged the tenants of the area, including in neighbouring Hardoi District, to resist the illegitimate demands of their taluqdars. The local Congress had supported this. An Eka Association was formed, and those who joined took a thirteen-point oath. These points included an insistence on receiving receipts when paying rents, to pay only the recorded rent, to refuse various cesses, to resist illegal ejections from holdings, to provide no unpaid labour, to refuse to tolerate insults by the taluqdars and their hired men, to resist oppression by them, and to form panchayats and abide by their decisions. Peasants who refused to join were ostracised. In some cases, it was resolved to harvest the crops from the land of the landlords. The taluqdars were boycotted socially by washermen, barbers and sweepers. The oath was taken over Muslim holy scriptures or holy Ganges water. They were told to conform to Gandhi's programme of demanding swaraj, use of swadeshi goods, to spin on the charkha, and to boycott government courts, all of which was to lead to Gandhi raj. It was commonly believed that under such a rule, Gandhi would ensure lower rents. The peasants of the area understood swaraj as liberation from the taluqdars and other oppressors.[44]

Madari Pasi soon emerged as the most influential and talented of the leaders. He was a Pasi, a caste considered untouchable. He claimed to be a reincarnation of the fifteenth-century Sufi saint Madar Shah, a holyman who preached syncretism and who was revered in this region by Hindus and Muslims alike, and whose shrine, or *darga*, was at Makanpur in neighbouring Kanpur District. Madari Pasi recited a mix of Hindu and Muslim holy scriptures at meetings such as the *Bagavad Gita*, *Quran*, *Katha Sat Narain* and *Milad Sharif*, and he was treated with reverence, even by local Brahmans. He held many meetings to promote the Eka agenda. He established his base at Sandila in Hardoi

District, as he wanted to be able to act independently from the Khilafat and Congress leaders of Malihabad. The movement spread rapidly in Hardoi in early 1922, and then to the districts of Bahraich, Sitapur, Kheri, and Bara Banki. The leaders were touring the region as self-styled rajas, protected by archers and spearmen. Large groups of tenants moved about the area demanding an abolition of rent in grain. They sometimes surrounded oppressive taluqdars and forced them to apologise for their misdeeds. Grain was also removed rather than left on the threshing-floor for division by the landlord's hired men (a process in which the peasants were invariably cheated), and there was a case of two taluqdars' agents who tried to resist such removals being beaten up in Bahraich District. A leading landlord of Sitapur District, the Raja of Mehmudabad, employed nearly 100 Gurkhas armed with rifles to guard his properties. Private militias such as these worked with the British police when the situation arose. On 1 April 1922, a Brahman agent of this landlord was killed with a sickle by a Kurmi tenant who was unable to pay his rent and had been branded as a 'bad tenant'. The Kurmi was arrested and sentenced to death – later reduced to six years on appeal. In one group of villages of Sitapur centred on Laharpur, the people established their own government with a 'Deputy Commissioner', judge and other officials. When a Congress worker in Kheri District was arrested, a large crowd besieged the police station and secured his release. In March 1922, about a hundred Pasis armed with lathis were reported in *The Leader* newspaper to have attacked a police party that had come to their village shouting 'kill, kill' – the police opened fire and killed two of the attackers. A landlord's rent collector who was particularly hated by the local tenants was murdered in Bara Banki District in early February 1922. Officials were boycotted as well as landlords – for example no barber would shave the Sub-Divisional magistrate.[45]

The Congress leaders of UP came to the area in response and tried to persuade the tenants to include taluqdars in the Eka. Madari Pasi was in accord with this, allowing many petty landlords to join. Motilal Nehru visited Hardoi on 13 March and told them to stop fighting the landlords. Swaraj, he claimed, would be obtained only through the unity of peasants and landlords. The Eka leaders ignored him, as well as the Bardoli Resolution that called off civil disobedience, and continued their struggle. The UP Congress then disowned the movement. Already, orders had been given by the government for Madari's arrest, but this proved impossible to effect as he went everywhere surrounded by several thousand supporters. A force of two thousand men was deployed to catch him, with fifty motor vehicles at their disposal. Madari then went into hiding, only being caught some months later. A reign of terror was unleashed by the British in northern Awadh, with columns of Sikh soldiers being marched around the villages to overawe the peasants. Villages were plundered by policemen and those who protested were beaten up or punished, e.g. by being ducked repeatedly in village ponds. Money was extorted as a supposed fine. Women were molested. The landlords encouraged men described in a Congress report as 'hooligans', 'bad characters' and 'dacoits' (bandits) to raid and loot villages, with the peasants having to flee to avoid being hurt. These 'bad characters' were in some cases assisted by the police. Under such an onslaught, the Eka movement dissolved from April 1922 onwards.[46]

This movement was predominantly nonviolent, with demonstrations, social boycotts, and refusals to tolerate the unjust exactions of the landlords. Five acts of violence were recorded, namely the beating up of a couple of landlord's agents who tried to stop tenants removing harvested grain, the murder of two rent-collecting employees of the landlords, and an allegedly murderous attack on a police party in which two peasants were killed but no policemen. These acts were isolated and untypical of the movement in general. Madari Pasi moved around protected by armed men, but they are not recorded as having ever used force. In general, the violence was almost entirely from the side of the landlords, their men, and the British police. As in the case of the Kisan Sabha Movement, the top Congress leaders of UP refused to back the protest, leaving it isolated when suppressed.

Movements in Eastern India

In the Darbhanga region of Bihar, eastern India, there was, in 1919–20, a strong movement against a prominent landlord, the Raja of Darbhanga. This was led by an educated man from a family of relatively prosperous tenants called Bishnu Bharan Prasad. He had become a religious mendicant, assuming the name Swami Vidyanand, and had started championing the right of tenants. There were meetings attended by large numbers of peasants – some attracted between ten-to-twenty thousand people. Vidyanand encouraged the tenants to pay their rent in cash rather than as crops in kind, which gave less scope for swindles by the landlords. Besides doing this, they also began to demand rent receipts, as this provided proof of occupancy and thus a basis for claims for security of tenure. They also refused to supply free goods to the landlords. Vidyanand admired Gandhi and looked to him and the Congress for support. However, as in Awadh, the local Congress leaders refused to provide this. Rajendra Prasad, the leading Congressman in Bihar, asserted that Vidyanand could not be trusted, that he was falsely projecting himself as a follower of Gandhi, and was a charlatan who was whipping up the tenants merely to further his own career. This left the movement isolated, and the Darbhanga administration managed to defuse it, in part through repression, which was assisted by the British, and in part by dividing the protestors through granting concessions to some of the more prosperous peasants. The lack of rich peasant support and leadership was often critical in breaking the opposition. The movement had largely ended before noncooperation got fully under way in 1921. In his account of this protest, Henningham states in passing that there were 'some violent incidents' but does not describe them. As it is, the details provided in the text suggest that it was largely nonviolent.[47]

The predominantly Muslim tenantry of northern and south-eastern Bengal protested against their landlords, inspired and instigated initially by Khilafatists and local Wahabi sect leaders. The movement was strongest in districts at the periphery of the province, such as Jalpaiguri, Rangpur, Mymensingh, Tippera, and Chittagong, where there were few large, powerful Hindu zamindars. In Mymensingh, the Muslim peasants declared 'that they live in the land of God and are His creation and are not to pay anything to anybody in the world'. In Tippera, the authorities had lost control over the villages by late 1921. No rents or taxes were being paid. Although the peasants concerned were all Muslim, they were not driven primarily by religious sentiment, their main aim being to assert themselves against local landlords and the state. In February and March 1922, the authorities tried to reassert their power using the armed police, with the brutal crackdown culminating with three peasants being killed in a firing of 9 March. Officials reported that nationalist activists had tried to restrain the people in this incident to no avail. The bhadralok leaders of the Congress were relatively relaxed about opposition to landlords in such areas, for as a class they had few vested interests there.[48]

In the districts of the East Bengal heartlands such as Dacca, Faridpur and Bakarganj – which had contributed strongly to the earlier Swadeshi Movement – the large bhadralok landlords, in alliance with the bhadralok politicians who controlled the Bengal Congress, managed to discourage and stifle popular dissent that was liable to turn against them. In Medinipur District, western Bengal, there were no movements to refuse rent to zamindars unless the landlord was either the government, as was the case with some estates in the Kanthi area, or the Medinipur Zamindari Company, which was controlled by British capitalists. In areas with strong movements, the more prosperous peasants were to the fore in the campaign and they linked up with the Khilafat and Congress workers. Generally those with secure tenancies – the *jotedars* – they organised and led the poorer tenants – usually those who had no security of tenure. They later turned against the movement when it began to slip out of their control.[49]

Although the anti-landlord protest in Bengal was generally nonviolent, there was a higher level of violence there than in the anti-landlord movements of Awadh and Bihar. In Rangpur District, for example, a Wahabi leader called Abdullahal Baqi had begun by organising the drilling of Wahabi volunteers, which was a new, militaristic feature of the movement. There was a systematic boycott of government servants, police and *chaukidars*, and this soon developed into a movement to refuse to pay rent to the landlords. Nilpahari was the worst-affected subdivision, and a 'Swaraj Thana' (police station) was opened there by Gayesuddin Ahmed, who was known there as the 'Gandhi *daroga*' (police chief). He used a bugle to call volunteers together. On 21 December 1921, armed police were attacked in Nilpahari market, and they fired back, inflicting some casualties. The District Collector then patrolled the area with an armed force. On 20 February 1922, an official who tried to clear away a prohibited market at Ulipur was attacked by a crowd armed with bamboo sticks and clods – three were wounded in police firing. The Congress volunteers tried to help the police and persuade the crowd to disperse, but they were ignored.[50]

Abdullahal Baqi was also popular in the neighbouring districts of Rajshahi and Dinajpur, and he led similar opposition to the landlords there. Another area of strong opposition to landlordism was in the eastern-border district of Tippera. There, local landlords and moneylenders came under attack from the Muslim peasantry, with fierce class conflict. The landlords and moneylenders had to take police protection in some areas. The police were in turn attacked on five occasions between 13 February and 9 March 1922. For example, after a riot on 2 March, the District Magistrate and District Superintendent of Police carried out a house search on 9 March with 48 constables. They were attacked by a crowd of four hundred armed with lathis and *daos* (axes). Nationalist volunteers tried to restrain the crowd, to no avail. The police opened fire three died and five were wounded. As Ray states: 'Neither the Congress nor the government had any control over the area.'[51]

In Chittagong District, the Congress leader J.M. Sengupta was alarmed by the way that the Muslim masses of the district had taken the movement into their own hands. He told the Bengal Provincial Conference that met in Chittagong in April 1922 that he had moved among the Muslims of the district during the past months and had found a strong hatred amongst them for the British. He was worried that they might turn on the higher classes in general, with Indian landlords, merchants, traders and the middle classes being attacked. Although Gandhi had by then called off civil disobedience, protest continued until July in the remote tracts of Tippera and Chittagong. There was class conflict in July and August 1922 between landlords and tenants in north Bengal (Pabna, Rajshahi, Dinajpur, Rangpur), with tenants refusing to pay illegal cesses to landlords, and with meetings to organise opposition. In August there was a determined attack by 800 tenants on a special police force sent to Char Khalitpur in Pabna, with six tenants being injured in firing. As the upper classes had now withdrawn from the movement, there was no longer any central coordination or Congress backing for such protest.[52]

There was a strong no-rent campaign in Kanika, a large zamindari estate of coastal Orissa. This area had a longstanding tradition of peasant dissent led by village leaders, known as *mustagirs*. From August 1921, a protest was organised against the Raja of Kanika by a young nationalist called Rama Das Babaji. He dressed in saffron in the garb of a sadhu and was an inspiring orator who gained a lot of influence among the masses. He was arrested in September 1921. Leadership was taken up by Congress activists of the Orissa Provincial Congress Committee, who established a Swaraj Ashram at Kanika as a base for the struggle. Many peasants were enrolled as four-anna members of the Congress, and branches were established in several villages. A no-rent campaign was launched in January 1922. The zamindar had increased rent-rates in 1914, which had been a continuing grievance for the peasants. About four thousand peasants from over a hundred villages took part, with the organisation and mobilisation being largely by peasant leaders. People who paid rent were boycotted and intimidated. They believed that once swaraj was gained, nobody would have to pay rents. It was rumoured that Gandhi was marching from Ranchi in Bihar at the head of an army to liberate them. Although the Congress leaders tried to halt the protest in February in response to Chauri Chaura, the peasants ignored them and carried on their movement. The raja waited until April before unleashing his men against the dissidents, backed fully by local British administrators. On 18 April about four-hundred protestors mobbed the police and freed some of their colleagues who had been arrested. The police then gathered their forces. They surprised a demonstration of about a thousand protestors on 23 April, and opened fire, killing three and injuring about a hundred and forty-four. Two of those who died were local leaders; one was a small cultivator and another a washerman. The police then toured the area looting houses and beating up peasants. Many women were assaulted, and several of those who were pregnant at the time gave birth prematurely as a result. Large numbers were arrested and tried at the mansion of the raja, where they were forced to admit their guilt. They were punished by being made to walk a long distance tied with ropes. A collective fine of ten thousand rupees was imposed on the villages, and those who refused to pay their rent or the fine were thrown off their land and expelled from the state. This broke the movement. There were no-rent movements in some other parts of Orissa at this time, though they were nowhere as strong as that in Kanika.[53]

Rajasthan–Gujarat Border Region

In the previous volume, we saw how the peasant movement against the jagir of Bijoliya that began in 1917 carried on until 1922.[54] In the latter stage it was clearly associated with the Noncooperation Movement. Pathik and his colleagues in Ajmer had firm links with the Congress, and they actively guided the movement in Bijoliya and other estates of Mewar. One nationalist who toured Bijoliya at this time described how he was met by the nationalist cry of 'Bande Mataram' wherever he went. The British Agent in Rajasthan reported at the end of 1921 that Pathik and other nationalists were leading no-rent campaigns in the Mewar State jagirs of Bijoliya, Parsoli, Begun and Basi. Popular panchayats had been formed in each village and over them was a general committee that took decisions on civil, criminal and revenue cases. They met on fixed days and refused to admit the authority of the jagirdars. They enforced their will through boycott, excommunication, and fines. Large weekly meetings of cultivators armed with lathis were being held in each jagir. Volunteers with belts and badges had been posted in villages, and they were refusing to allow officials to enter the villages. The movement was spreading. At the end of December 1921, Pathik led a delegation of 250 people from these estates to Ahmedabad to attend the annual Congress session there. Thus, although Gandhi refused to associate actively with the movement in princely states at this time, on the grounds that they were fighting the British and not the princes, peasants in Rajasthan were rebelling against their overlords in the name of the Indian nationalist movement.[55]

The movement that we will focus on in this section straddled the border region between Rajasthan and Gujarat – that is southern Mewar and Sirohi States in Rajasthan, and Idar, Pol and Danta States in Gujarat. It affected mainly Bhil cultivators who were ruled by feudatories of the Rajput princes, known there as thakors. The movement was led by a Baniya of Mewar called Motilal Tejawat. Born in 1885, he was educated to fifth standard, and then from 1912 worked as a storekeeper at

Jharol, for a Rajput thakor who was a feudatory of Mewar. Motilal was witness to the way in which the thakor and his henchmen maltreated the people. They were forced to carry out free labour, and beaten, even tortured if they failed to satisfy the demands of their overlord. Women were often abducted and raped. Disgusted by what he saw, Motilal quit service in 1920 and went to work for a Baniya shopkeeper in the city of Udaipur. Soon afterwards, however, the shopkeeper sent Motilal to Jharol on business. While there, the thakor tried to confiscate some the shopkeeper's property, and when Motilal protested he was arrested, imprisoned, beaten up and made to eat dirt. His employer, an influential man in Udaipur, managed to have him released soon after. The experience proved a formative one, for Motilal then gave up his job in Udaipur and devoted himself to full-time political activity, his mission being to carry out social reform amongst the Bhils and to champion their demands against the oppressive landlords.[56]

Motilal was inspired by the peasant movement in Bijoliya. He copied an anti-landlord pamphlet from this movement and circulated it in the Jharol area. This met with a good response from the people, who respected him for the stand he had taken against the thakor, and they agreed to form an *eki*, or unity, league. He and some leading villagers of the estate put together a list of demands against the thakor, and in June 1921 he led a march of around ten thousand cultivators to Udaipur, where they camped before the palace of the ruler, Maharana Fateh Singh, demanding an audience. They threatened to stop all produce from being brought into the city if their grievances were not investigated. They had to wait several days before Fateh Singh agreed to receive a delegation. The peasants complained of various oppressions carried out by local Rajput chiefs and state officials, being careful not to condemn the ruler himself. In this, they followed the old convention of refraining from directly criticising their ruler, merely pointing out the abuses that were being carried out by his feudatories. The Maharana discussed the grievances and agreed to remedy some of them. These were, however, too minor to satisfy the peasants. Motilal told them to boycott the thakors and their officials, to refuse rents, and to establish their own councils to settle disputes. They were told to join the *eki* (union), swearing an oath of loyalty on the blade of a sword.[57]

Motilal was a religious man who believed that his actions enjoyed divine support. Besides championing the grievances of the predominantly Bhil peasantry against the landlords, he also felt he had a religious duty to persuade them to give up drinking liquor, to stop killing animals, and to refrain from stealing. Some other Baniyas of the region joined him, and in doing so they were linking up with a longstanding religious reform movement of the region, known as the Bhagat Movement. This involved Bhils taking an oath to abstain from all crimes and acts of violence against other humans as well as animals, and to abjure liquor and take a daily bath. They were to maintain their livelihood through agriculture.[58]

Motilal saw his protest as being a part of the wider movement for independence, then at its height during the Noncooperation Movement. In speeches he stated that once 'Gandhi raj' was established they would only have to pay one anna in the rupee to the state. Some of his followers took to wearing white caps. He clearly believed that in trying to wean the Bhils away from violence he was following the programme of the Gandhian movement closely. As yet, however, Gandhi knew nothing of him or his movement.

In August 1921, Motilal was arrested by the thakor of Jharol. Six to seven thousand Bhils from sixty-two villages gathered together, marched into Jharol and forced his release. Thousands more Bhils then came forward to take the oath of *eki*. Bhils who refused to do so found themselves subjected to social boycott. They came not only from Mewar, but also from the adjoining states of Sirohi, Idar, Danta and Pol. Besides Bhils, there were many of a similarly depressed community – found mainly in Sirohi – called the Girasias. In early 1922, Motilal began touring this entire area, accompanied always by several thousand Bhils and Girasias armed with bows and arrows, issuing demands for reform to the local thakors and ruling princes. There were some minor clashes, with aggressive state policemen and officials being beaten. There is no record of anyone being killed by the Bhils – by their standards they were protesting in a remarkably nonviolent manner.

This was not however how Gandhi saw it when his attention was drawn to the matter in early 1922. His information came from the chief minister of Sirohi State, Ramakant Malaviya, who was a son of the leading UP nationalist, M.M. Malaviya. The Maharao of Sirohi had appointed Ramakant as chief minister in October 1921 in the hope that he would deflect possible nationalist protest against the state.[59] In late 1921 he had joined with the British Agent in Rajasthan, Robert Holland, in negotiating with Vijay Singh Pathik terms for the suspension of the Bijoliya movement that was advantageous to the Mewar peasantry. He was thus seen in a positive light in nationalist circles at that juncture. As is clear from an article in *Young India* of 12 January 1922, Gandhi had great affection for the Malaviya family; in this article he lauded both Malaviya and another of his sons, Govind, who had been imprisoned for his nationalist activities.[60] When Ramakant wrote to Gandhi, pointing out to him that Bhils and Girasias wielding bows and arrows and spears were refusing to pay their taxes to an Indian prince in his name, his immediate reaction was to condemn the protest. Writing in the 2 February issue of *Young India* under the heading 'Danger of Mass Movement', he stated that Malaviya had 'kindly' told him about the protest and that 'he tells me that great mischief is being done in my name'. Gandhi denied that Motilal was any sort of disciple and condemned him for his allegedly 'destructive work'. The movement was violating his code of nonviolence, as Motilal's followers were carrying arms. They should state their grievances to the Sirohi authorities in an orderly way. They had a right to refuse to pay their dues if they believed them to be excessive, but such an act was to not to be undertaken lightly, and they needed to get public opinion behind them. 'If they do not take these precautions they will find everything and everybody arrayed against them and they will find themselves heavy losers in the end.'[61]

As Denis Vidal has pointed out, Gandhi's reaction and subsequent position taken by the nationalist leadership in relation to the *Eki* movement has to be seen in the context of the internal politics of the Indian National Congress at the time.[62] M.M. Malaviya, who was on the conservative wing of the Congress, was on good terms with Rajput rulers in Rajasthan, notably the Maharana of Mewar, and believed in the intrinsic benevolence of – as he saw it – these Hindu rulers. These considerations were important in the choice of his son as chief minister of Sirohi. Gandhi himself had much sympathy at that time for Malaviya's position on the Indian princes, believing that they could be persuaded to reform their societies in more benevolent directions, and that they did not provide a legitimate target for nationalist attack.

Gandhi sent one of his leading followers in Gujarat, Manilal Kothari, to Sirohi to carry out further enquiries. Kothari met Motilal and advised him to keep the movement strictly nonviolent, for any violence on their part – he warned – would invite severe reprisal from the British: they would 'all be slaughtered like dogs.'[63] At this juncture, the Bijoliya leader Vijay Singh Pathik became involved. He also travelled to Motilal's camp and gave him advice similar to that of Manilal Kothari. Motilal replied that he would not act in a way that would cause any trouble. Next day they all proceeded together to Abu Road, a town on the railway line between Ahmedabad and Delhi. There they came face to face with Sirohi State troops with Ramakant Malaviya at their head. Kothari and Pathik met Malaviya and promised that Motilal and his Bhils would leave the state. This they did on 7 February, returning to Gujarat, to the princely states of Palanpur and Danta.

There, Bhils and Girasias continued to flock to Motilal's camp, offering their unwavering support. On 10 February, the British political agent in charge of this area reported that the roads were being blockaded and the people were refusing to pay their taxes, but so far there had been no acts of violence. Pathik was still with Motilal urging him to maintain strict nonviolence. By now, he had become doubtful about Motilal's ability to control the movement. He saw that his followers were a law unto themselves, not following Motilal's advice when it conflicted with their agenda. For example, it was beyond Motilal's power to persuade them to stop carrying a weapon that marked their very identity – a Bhil or Girasia male would have felt naked without his bow and arrow.[64] In Bijoliya, Pathik had maintained a tight control over the movement; it had been relatively free of violence, particularly in the later stages, and the moral pressure thus maintained had – he believed – brought highly positive results. Seeing the Bhils and Girasias *en masse* – armed with their traditional weapons – Pathik believed that violence could easily be triggered, providing an excuse for the British to crush the movement ruthlessly. As Motilal was linked in the popular mind with Gandhi, such violence could discredit the nationalist movement, as had been the case with the Chauri-Chaura debacle a short time before.[65]

Manilal Kothari was however more sympathetic towards Motilal and the Bhils. He sent a telegram to Gandhi: 'Five days in hills, met Moti Lal hundreds of Bhils in Danta Forest; your message duly communicated, much appreciated.'[66] On 11 February, Motilal forwarded a letter to Gandhi through Kothari:

> In whichever place I work, I work for *satyagraha*. I do not work for any other thing. The fact is that the Bhils and Girasias follow me in the same way as the whole of India is following you. They have bows and arrows and swords. These are their traditional weapons. They are farmers in the hilly tracts and are peaceful. They are truthful and righteous people. They are perfectly innocent and are lovers of religion (*dharma*). When I started *satyagraha*, these people gave me full cooperation with good faith. The same thing has displeased the officials. They want to suppress the Bhils by beating them and making them give bribes. But the Bhils are steadfast and intelligent. They know their self-interest. Now, neither the states nor the English are listening to my petitions. You are my only helper. Help me. I am ready to die for these poor people. Send somebody who can provide publicity for our cause. These people are ignorant and very simple. Manilal Kothari knows this fact very well. Do pay attention to my request.[67]

Motilal had been both upset and disheartened when he had learnt of Gandhi's disavowal of his activities in the *Young India* article of 2 February, for – as is apparent from this letter – he saw himself as a faithful follower of Gandhi. It is however clear from this letter that he knew he could not prevent his own followers from carrying arms – with all the possible dangers which that entailed. He argued that despite this, Gandhi should view them favourably as an intrinsically peaceful and religious-minded people who were suffering from the oppression of autocratic and corrupt state officials.

Gandhi gave his response in *Navajivan*, published in Gujarati on 26 February. He accepted that Motilal had been trying to reform the Bhils morally, and that through his work there had been an 'awakening' within the community. He argued, nonetheless, that Motilal was wrong to expect the British to intervene in his favour. 'The British have nothing to do with the issue and the matter ought to have been brought to the notice of the States concerned in a proper manner. Shri Manilal says that in Palanpur, Danta and Shirohi States, he, Manilal, had received full co-operation from the authorities... I hope that the *Bhils* will be satisfied if the States listen to their complaints and redress their grievances.'[68]

Though more sympathetic in tone than in his earlier article in *Young India*, Gandhi's tone was still frosty towards his self-avowed disciple, Motilal Tejawat. His argument that the princes and their officials would respond positively if the grievances of their subjects were stated in a clear and non-threatening manner was highly questionable. There was no evidence that the Sirohi officials were prepared to tackle the complaints of the Bhils and Girasias in a serious manner; Gandhi was placing great faith in the goodwill of Ramakant Malaviya – a faith which was to prove misplaced in the light of the subsequent brutal repression of Motilal's movement by the government headed by this man. The Mewar state had, it was true, sought to remedy the grievances of the peasants of Bijoliya, but only after the British had intervened by forcing the abdication of the Maharana in mid-1921 and having his more amenable son put on the throne. Also, the political agent in Rajputana, Holland, had personally negotiated this settlement. All of this brings out a serious flaw in Gandhi's argument that the British had 'nothing to do with the issue.' As the Bhils well knew, the British pulled the shots in Rajasthan.[69] It was quite clear that nothing of any consequence could happen in the princely states without the direct involvement of the British political agents, who were in direct touch with and controlled by the government of India in Delhi.

The crucial figure in all this was in fact the Agent in Rajasthan, Robert Holland. He was strongly committed to reforming the feudal polities of the princely states, realising that the peasants had valid grievances against the princes, their jagirdars and their thakors. It was for this reason that he had, in the previous two years, engineered the abdication of not only the Maharana of Mewar, but also the Maharao of Sirohi State, who he had forced to step down in 1920 because of his failure to deal with a widespread rural protest directed mainly against the Baniya usurers of the state.[70] When faced with the movement led by Motilal Tejawat, Holland realised that he had a difficult situation on his hands. He knew that the grievances of the agitators were warranted, and he knew also that the local rulers and thakors would repress their protest savagely if they had the power to do so, and that they could only have such a power if they were backed by British troops. The fate of the movement thus rested in British hands. In the initial stages, neither Holland nor his superiors in Delhi wanted a violent confrontation with the Bhils, for this was a time when the government of India was still hoping to be able to defuse the Noncooperation Movement through negotiation. Holland decided to bide his time, hoping that the movement would remain relatively nonviolent, while working behind the scenes, trying to persuade the local rulers and thakors to agree to some concessions that might defuse the movement. He gave orders to his subordinates 'to avoid a conflict if possible.'[71]

Because of this, the movement was able to gather steam over the winter of 1921–22 without any significant confrontation. Then, on 16 February 1922, Motilal wrote to the British – his first direct communication with them – stating that he had done no more than what was the policy of the Congress. On 21 February, Holland wrote to his superiors in Delhi:

> Moti Lal has been disowned by Gandhi. I hear that he is nervous about his own safety, and now wishes to be allowed to quit Bhil country and settle near Ahmedabad. He undertakes not to interfere any further with Bhil affairs. Since Moti Lal has not committed any very serious offence in their territories Sirohi and Mewar Darbars would have no objection to this course...[72]

By this, Holland meant that he supported such a course of action, and that the states concerned would follow his advice. His strategy – to offer a safe pass to Motilal should he choose to leave the Bhils and go into exile in British Gujarat – was an astute one. Motilal was in fact under pressure from his Gandhian contacts to do this so that he could receive instruction in the techniques of satyagraha direct from the hands of Gandhi at his ashram in Ahmedabad. Motilal, seeing himself as a disciple of Gandhi, was strongly tempted in this respect.

This strategy was not however acceptable to the government of Bombay Presidency. The governor, Sir George Lloyd, informed the government of India in Delhi that he did not want the agitator in his territory, and that he deserved to be punished harshly. He urged 'that in the interest of the Bhils this course will be the best.'[73] This argument was based on Lloyd's belief that subaltern action of the sort seen amongst the Bhils was engineered by extremist agitators who were manipulating poor and ignorant rustics to further their own nefarious designs. Holland knew that the truth was more complex, but it was the

Governor of Bombay who was to prove to have the ear of the Viceroy, Lord Reading, in this matter.

On 2 March, Lloyd wrote to Reading that he had proof that Gandhi was in direct contact with Motilal through 'an extremist' (namely Manilal Kothari). Barely a month before, Kothari had led a protest against Lloyd when he was on an official visit to Rajkot State, so that there was much personal pique in his comment. The governor concluded:

> From this it is apparent that Gandhi is not entirely unconnected with the Bhil affair and confirms me in my view that no compromises should be made with Moti Lal who should be severely punished even if he surrenders.[74]

Reading replied to Lloyd that he agreed entirely with him, and that:

> We have instructed Holland to demand unconditional surrender of Moti Lal and troops are in readiness to act in support of the demand when called on by local authorities.[75]

This hardening in the position of the government of India came at a time when it was realised that the nationalist agitation was flagging following Gandhi's withdrawal of civil disobedience after Chauri-Chaura. Lord Reading now believed he could move in on the nationalists, arrest their leaders and crush their resistance without suffering any very grave political consequences.

It was at this fateful juncture that news came that Motilal and his followers had decided to return to Mewar to once more put their grievances to the Rana. The British-run militia that was stationed close to the border between Gujarat and Rajasthan, the Mewar Bhil Corps, was ordered to proceed immediately to intercept Motilal. They did this on 7 March, arriving on a hill overlooking the camping-place of Motilal and his followers. According to the official version, the force was attacked by the Bhils and had to fire in self-defence, killing 22 and wounding 29. One British official claimed that the Bhils had to be quelled in this way as they were a '...people little removed from savagery...childishly ignorant and inflammable...' The Bhils themselves claimed that they had only shouted slogans at the troops, who then opened fire. Those who survived, including Motilal, fled the scene. The Bhils claimed that 1,200 to 1,500 had fallen in the barrage of rifle-fire, of whom about a third were women. Vijay Singh Pathik made his own enquiries in the following days, concluding that 'scarcely a Bhil used his weapon'. Why, he asked, had no soldier suffered any injury if the Bhils had attacked first? He claimed that the Bhil casualties were over one thousand. He accused the British of spilling much innocent blood in a thoroughly 'blood-thirsty' manner, after which they had covered up the carnage.[76]

Despite claims by the authorities that the firing had had a salutary effect on the Bhils of the region, the situation remained tense. In late March, the Bhils of three estates besieged their thakors in their mansions, the sieges being lifted only after the appearance of Mewar State soldiers under the command of a British officer. The troops then marched through the region to impress on the Bhils the power of the state.[77] Motilal himself had fled back towards the Sirohi side, where he remained in hiding.[78] In Sirohi State, the movement escalated, with widespread refusal by Bhils and Girasias to pay their rents and dues. Troops were mobilised under the command of a British officer and punitive raids were carried out on several rebellious villages, with houses being burnt and stocks of grain destroyed. Villages were shelled with artillery and machine-gunned, with many of the inhabitants killed. The headmen were caught and forced to renege on their unity oath in public.[79]

In early 1922 the British had a choice, to either force the local princes and thakors to change their ways profoundly and remedy the grievances of the people, or to suppress a largely peaceful and morally justified protest through force. The chose the latter course, and the violence – when it came – was vengefully one-sided. Although the massacre of 7 March was by all accounts an atrocity on a par with that at Amritsar three years before, it never gained the notoriety of the earlier outrage and was soon largely forgotten by the outside world (though not by the local Bhils). This was above all because the nationalists – with the exception of Pathik and his colleagues in Rajasthan – made no attempt to make an issue of the matter. One reason for this was that they were in disarray after Gandhi's arrest on 10 March – only three days after the shooting – and subsequent sentence to six years in jail on 18 March. But more important still was the fact that they had no great interest in taking it up. Motilal's movement was peripheral to their concerns, which were centred on the British-ruled areas. The grievances of subjects of princely states against their rulers were not at that time on their agenda. Gandhi had taken some interest in the movement during February and early March as it had, as he saw it, a violent potential that could reflect badly on the Congress. He had therefore sent Manilal Kothari to wean Motilal away from a looming disaster. This strategy nearly succeeded with Holland's attempt to gain permission for Motilal to leave his followers and join Gandhi in his ashram in Ahmedabad. The failure of this initiative led to the massacre. Little could be done, so far as the Congress was concerned. Even if they could have sent a team to carry out an investigation on the spot – something which was not easy, seeing as they would have been hindered at every turn by the local rulers and thakors – there seemed to be little point in the exercise.

Conclusion

Throughout India at this time, powerful peasant movements against landlords were supressed, often brutally, by the British and their Indian collaborators. In general, Gandhi and many of his fellow leaders in the Congress preferred to condemn the tenants rather than champion a plight that should have been as much a cause for nationalist solidarity as any of the other issues that were made targets for protest during 1920–22. In November 1920, for example, on a visit to Awadh, Gandhi, Motilal Nehru, Shaukat Ali and A.K. Azad preferred to meet up with the taluqdars rather than any Kisan Sabha leaders, and although they gave speeches advocating noncooperation and swadeshi, they said nothing about the grievances of the tenants. Despite tenants throughout India adopting the rallying cry of 'Mahatma Gandhi Ki Jai', the Mahatma regarded them with suspicion, seeing them as stoking social disharmony and lacking in commitment to nonviolence. When he visited Awadh in February 1921 he condemned those who created discord between landlords and tenants, stating that they should regard the taluqdars as potential friends. The best way to achieve their ends was through peaceful noncooperation against the British. Provincial leaders such as Motilal Nehru and M.M. Malaviya in UP and Rajendra Prasad in Bihar acted in ways that tended to undermine rather than strengthen the tenant movement in their regions. In Bengal, the Congress leaders discouraged protest against bhadralok landlords while encouraging resistance to British-controlled managing agencies that rented land to tenant farmers. The agencies represented only a small proportion of the body of landlords as a whole. In East Bengal, the Khilafat Movement inspired many Muslim tenants to campaign against their largely Hindu landlords, but in this they received no active support from the top Khilafat leaders, and the campaigns remained isolated. They succumbed eventually after the wider movement collapsed in 1922. In Rajasthan, the Gandhian Congress had been sympathetic to the longstanding movement in Bijoliya, but in 1921–22 insisted that it should not be regarded as a part of the Noncooperation Movement. The Congress had, it was asserted, no quarrel with Indian princes and their feudatories. Subsequently, there was far less sympathy towards the movement led by Motilal Tejawat.

In January 1922, Gandhi issued a directive to tenants throughout India:

> I hear the talk even of refusing payment of rent to zemindars. It must not be forgotten that we are not non-co-operating with zemindars, whether Indian or foreign. We are engaged in a fight with one big zemindar – the bureaucracy – which has made of us and the zemindars themselves serfs. We must try to bring round the zemindars to our side, and isolate the big zemindar. But if they will not come to us, we must be patient with them. We may not even proclaim a social boycott against them. That is to say, we may not refuse social service such as dhobi, barber, etc., to them. In areas under permanent settlement, therefore, there can be no non-payment campaign except in respect of cesses that might be payable directly to the government.[80]

This message was reinforced in the following month in a couple of resolutions by the Congress Working Committee. 6 and 7 concerned landlords:

> 6. Complaints having been brought to the notice of the Working Committee that ryots are not paying rents to the zemindars, the Working Committee advises Congress workers and organisations to inform the ryots that such withholding of rents is contrary to the resolutions of the Congress and that it is injurious to the best interests of the country.

> 7. The Working Committee assures the zemindars that the Congress movement is in no way intended to attack their legal rights, and that even where the ryots have grievances, the Committee's desire is that redress should be sought by mutual consultations and by the usual recourse to arbitrations.[81]

All of this sent a clear message to the tenants of India that their cause would not be one adopted by the Indian National Congress, at least at that time. A potentially powerful element within the nationalist movement was thus being disavowed. It was a policy that weakened the entire movement profoundly.

4

POLITICAL ACTION BY INDUSTRIAL WORKERS 1920–22

In *The Politics of Nonviolent Action*, Gene Sharp lists two major forms of what he calls 'economic noncooperation' – economic boycotts and strikes. Chapter 6 focuses on the strike. He defines this as: '…a refusal to continue economic cooperation through work'. Though mainly associated with industrial labour, strikes can be staged by anyone who works for wages for any type of employer. In nonviolent movements, strikes often take a symbolic form, with stoppages for limited periods, such as a day. This is designed to send a message to those in power, and it acts as a warning that there may be more serious disruption if there is no adequate response. Such temporary shutdowns also serve to educate workers, who generally attend protest rallies while out of the workplace. In this context, Sharp specifically mentions the hartal in India, in which the economic life of a place is brought to a halt for a limited period. There is an emphasis on the voluntary nature of the protest, and support may be obtained from employers. Shopkeepers and businessmen may support the hartal. Sharp notes now Gandhi deployed the hartal for gaining support for a struggle, to test feeling on an issue, and as a form of purification for participants. He mentions protests of this sort from elsewhere in the world that preceded the Noncooperation Movement in India. They include the wave of temporary strikes during the Russian Revolution of 1905, when different trades stopped work on certain days, and a 24-hour general strike in Ireland on 23 April 1918 in support of the demand for Home Rule, when factories, shops and bars were all closed. It brought almost the entire country to a halt, with the notable exception of Belfast. Such strikes may have provided a model for Indian nationalists.[1]

Another form of industrial action examined by Sharp is the slowdown, which may take the form of a work-to-rule. It lowers output and hits the profits of employers, who may then put pressure on the government to deal with the issue. There might be a refusal to carry out certain types of work that is considered objectionable for one reason or another. Glasgow dockers used this method with success in 1889. It was an important element in syndicalism, with its first recorded use in this respect being by Italian railway workers in 1895. Austrian railways workers applied a work-to-rule with good effect in 1905–07. Workers in St Petersburg refused, in 1905, to work more than eight hours each day. Such methods may be used when dissidents are being crushed by a ruthless state, as it can be done in a clandestine manner. Sick-leave or absenteeism can be deployed in this way.[2]

More serious for any government is a third form of political action that can be taken by workers – the general strike. This spans several major industries and aims to bring economic life to a halt until the demands are conceded. It can be confined to one city or be nation-wide. It may be called to obtain a stated economic or political demand from a government. The Chartists dreamed of staging one in the 1830s and 1840s, though they never came close to pulling it off. The American anarchist Benjamin R. Tucker (1854–1938) was an influential theorist of the general strike. He supported violence in self-defence but saw passive resistance as being the more potent force, and argued that it was the most effective weapon for the working classes. Georges Sorel (1847–1922) – the major theorist of the syndicalist movement – embraced this principle. Although he believed in revolutionary violence, he saw the general strike as a crucial weapon in the struggle. Syndicalism became a major force in Italy from 1900 onwards. In 1904, Italian workers staged a general strike in protest at the killing of workers and peasants in the south and in Sardinia. There were similar strikes in Belgium in 1893, 1902 and 1913 to demand universal male suffrage. There were general strikes with a revolutionary intent in

Russia from 1902 onwards – initially confined to certain cities but becoming nationwide in 1905. The Great October Strike of 1905 was the most powerful of these. Railway transport was halted, the telegraph fell silent and most public activity stopped. In the same year in Finland there was a general strike over the demand for Finnish autonomy from Russia – a liberal-nationalist rather than revolutionary demand that was supported by Finnish employers, who continued to pay the wages of the workers. Trains and other forms of communication were stopped, shops, offices, restaurants and schools were closed, and factories empty. There was no bloodshed at all. It united the people of Finland as a nation and was a major element in their obtaining most of their demands in that year. In Germany, the influential theorist Rosa Luxemburg (1871–1919) advocated the general strike in her pamphlet of 1906 *The Mass Strike: The Political Party and the Trade Unions*. There was a successful use of such a method in Weimer Germany in March 1920, when some right-wingers supported by the military tried to stage a coup d'état against the government. Known as the Kapp Putsch, it failed after four days due to widespread strikes by civilians from all walks of life that effectively paralysed Germany.[3]

What this brings out is that in the climate of 1920–22, industrial action was widely perceived as providing a powerful way of bringing strong pressure to bear on a government in support of political demands. The modern industrial sector had become pivotal in the economic life of many countries, giving its workers a political weight that was out of proportion to their numbers alone. Their concentration also in the major centres of government enhanced this effect. There had already been stirrings in this respect in India. In 1905–06, industrial and transport workers in Calcutta had brought Calcutta almost to a standstill during the early phase of the Swadeshi Movement.[4] In 1908, the workers of Bombay's textile mills downed tools for six days when they heard the news that Tilak had been sentenced to six years' imprisonment as a punishment for his nationalist activities. Lenin is said to have taken it as evidence of a new political awareness among Indian workers.[5] As it was, there were no more such political strikes in India until the period of the Noncooperation Movement. In this chapter, we shall examine the dynamics of such action during 1920–22. To what extent did Indian nationalists understand its potential, and to what extent was the modern industrial working class able to be deployed in support of the nationalist struggle, and – if so – with what success?

We shall confine our inquiry here to workers in the major large-scale capitalist industries, namely in textile mills, steel mills, coal mines, and on the railways – both in rail workshops and on the rail network itself. As Dilip Simeon has pointed out, capitalists have, since the time of the industrial revolution in Europe, sought to build 'a world created in the image of capital'. In this milieu, the new working class develops 'spheres of perception and action which are its own'. In this, workers retain a degree of recalcitrance that may occasionally lead to confrontation.[6] The British and their Indian allies understood that the smooth operation of this sector was of particular – indeed vital – importance to the country as a whole, and they were extremely sensitive to any disruption in it.

It should be noted that we are not dealing, in this chapter, with the politics of the urban poor in general, for there were far larger numbers employed in a great variety of other jobs. Many worked in small units that processed foodstuffs, pottery, glass, metal, jewellery, paper, tobacco, or which specialised in printing, dyeing, tailoring, laundering, and so on. Labourers worked on construction sites, in the ports, local transport, and as market-carriers, many being employed casually. Others worked for municipal councils, for example as street-sweepers and cleaners. Many lived from selling food and other products on the streets as hawkers and peddlers. There were large numbers of domestic workers. Much of this work was very insecure and most such workers lived in great poverty. We should also note that it is not always easy to differentiate the urban poor, as there was considerable fluidity of occupation. In general, we may say, the politics of this wider urban poor was rooted in the neighbourhood and market, while in the modern industrial sector the concentration of labour and a clearly defined system of management provided a focus for dissent and action. Despite this, as we shall see, the neighbourhood also provided a crucial theatre for working-class politics and conflict, so that there were always crossovers between these two political domains.[7]

The Indian Working Class

Although large-scale capitalist industry in India was located mainly in large cities, this was not always the case –the Tata Steel works were in a remote region of southern Bihar that was not hitherto urbanised, and railways by their nature encompassed town and country. This was a rapidly growing area of economic life. Between 1892 and 1923, the number of factories in India increased from 956 employing 316,816 workers to 5,985 with 1,409,173 workers – an increase of 626 per cent of factories and 445 per cent of workers. The largest single industry involved spinning and weaving of cotton textiles. The sector consumed large amounts of coal, and the railways were crucial for carrying the coal and its raw materials and then distributing its manufactured products.[8] Bombay City was the foremost centre for the cotton industry, followed by Ahmedabad (where the sector grew particularly rapidly between 1900 and 1914) and Madras, and then to a lesser degree by smaller cities such as Sholapur and Kanpur. In 1921, Bombay – a city with a total population then of 1,244,934 – had 606 cotton mills that directly employed 16.2 per cent of the male and 9.2 per cent of the female population, with a yet larger number depending on this industry in indirect ways. Engineering workshops serviced these mills, leather workers provided belts for machines, sawmills and wood-workshops provided spindles and bobbins, and electricians and blacksmiths carried out repairs. Tailors stitched the textiles unto clothing. In times of high demand, mill-manufactured yarn was supplied to city-dwelling hand-weavers to process on temporary contracts. In this way, the cotton industry had by 1921 come to dominate the economic life of certain cities more than any other single sector.[9] As with cotton in Bombay, Calcutta City became renowned at this time for jute production. The boom years for this industry were from 1890 to the 1920s, with huge profits being earned during the First World War One. By the 1920s, there were about 300,000 workers employed in the jute mills of the city and adjoining areas.[10]

The railways employed large numbers, both in workshops and in operating trains. For example, in Bombay City, the railway workshops were among the largest industrial employers – the Great Indian Peninsula Railway employed 5,000 in the locomotive works and 6,000 in their carriage and wagon departments, and the Bombay, Baroda and Central India Railway employed about 5,000 in their locomotive and carriage shops. These assembled imported steam engines, and manufactured carriages and various parts. As demand fluctuated, a lot of this labour was employed casually. The more skilled workers had the most secure employment, as there were fears that they might be recruited by rival concerns if made jobless.[11]

Coal was vital to power the steam engines that were being used increasingly in India during the nineteenth century for transport and industrial production, and for military purposes, which included steam-powered ships. Coal extraction started in Raniganj in the Burdwan District of Bengal in 1814. The Jharia coalfield of southern Bihar was surveyed in the years after 1860, and mines were opened there in the 1890s. It soon became the most productive coalfield in India. Between the late 1890s and the 1916–20 period, coal production in India increased from 4.7 to 19.3 million tons.[12] Steel was also a vital requirement for modern industry, with most of it being imported until the early twentieth century. The Bombay-based firm Tata began to manufacture steel at a factory that it constructed at Jamshedpur in southern Bihar in 1907 – an area with plentiful supplies of cheap iron ore – and production took off in a major way as demand increased during the First World War.

These industries were owned by both European and Indian capitalists, and generally run by managing agencies that operated across several sectors. This system allowed for the capital to be raised from diverse sources, and then placed in the hands of professionals to carry on the day-to-day running of complex factories. Thus, the capital could be Indian, while the factories themselves were managed by Europeans. In Bombay Presidency, the capital underpinning the cotton mills was largely Indian, and although many top managers were also Indian, Europeans were also hired in this role. In Bombay City, most of the mills were owned and run by Parsis, Bohras and Bhatias, all Gujarati-speaking groups. The Parsis were the first major group to open mills, and among them the Petits and the Wadias were the greatest of such magnates. The Currimbhoys were the most important of the Bohra mill-owning families with a chain of factories. The firms of Mulji Jetha, the Tairsees, the Khataus, and Goculdas were owned by Bhatias. The Bombay Mill Owners' Association acted as a lobby group for their dealings with the state, and to press for their interests against those of Lancashire. However, according to Kumar, the mill owners 'were a disorganised and opportunistic group', working in their own interest first and foremost and often refusing to cooperate with other mill owners. They were incapable of responding strongly as a group. At best, those of a common caste or community might try to work together. In the Bombay mills themselves, the lower managerial grades and higher supervisory posts were dominated by Europeans, largely from Lancashire, and Parsis – who were regarded as being close allies of the British. The relationship between the workers and these superiors was, according to Chandavarkar, riven with 'suspicion, jealousy and antagonism'. In this, the workers could understand the way that they were oppressed within an imperial system. In Calcutta, the jute industry was dominated by both British capital and a dozen or so British managing agencies, who were able to defend their interests with much greater solidarity. The cotton industry was dominated in Madras by two mills that were established with British capital and run by the British-controlled Binny managing agency. About half of the coal industry of eastern India was controlled by seven British managing agencies that were also involved in jute production in Calcutta and tea plantations. Indians generally owned and ran the smaller and less important mines. The railways, on the other hand, were largely British-financed and run, with Europeans in the top managerial roles, and Anglo-Indians as lower-level managers and train operatives. What this meant was that Europeans played a leading role as either capitalists or managers across modern industry. Indian industry and British capital were thus tightly entangled, though more so in the east and south of India than in the west.[13]

The central role of Europeans in management and supervision created a situation in which the Indian workers were often treated in a racist manner. Physical punishment was frequently meted out to workers who were seen as slow in their work or insubordinate. The Europeans felt empowered as they were considered members of the ruling race, were paid so much more than the Indian workers, and lived in far superior conditions. This was the case in the two Binny mills in Madras, where the European supervisors were renowned for their arrogance and brutality toward workers. Over the years, there were occasional fracas when Indians who could bear no more retaliated with violence. One such case in 1918, saw the weavers in one of these factories, the Carnatic Mill, demanding that they be both paid more and treated with greater respect. When their demands were ignored, they attacked an unpopular European spinning master, and then a few days later stoned the European mill manager. Binnys closed the mill until the anger had dissipated.[14] Similarly in the railway workshops, the managers and supervisory subordinates were recruited mainly from Britain, while the lower-paid workers were Indians. The foremen were usually British, and the chargemen Anglo-Indians, Parsis and Goanese. There was considerable racial discrimination on the railways in relation to appointments, pay, promotion and the allocation of housing, all of which created continuing animosity.[15] Even in the Indian-owned Tata steel works, there were, in 1920, five hundred European staff who were paid far more than Indians in similar positions. The European supervisors often beat the Indian workers to force them to work longer hours in this often-dangerous work. In September 1920, the European staff on higher salaries were granted a twenty per cent increase. This infuriated the workers, as they had been told that the company could not afford to pay them more. During the rest of 1920 and 1921, there were several walkouts and even physical confrontations with the European supervisors.[16]

The workers were in most cases migrants from rural areas who retained firm links to their villages of origin. In Bombay City in 1921, for example, 84 per cent of the population had been born outside the city. It was, in other words, a city of migrants – and this phenomenon went well beyond the working class itself. Many returned to their villages for the harvest or when field-labour was required. The insecure nature of employment in the city encouraged workers to maintain strong connections with their villages as a fall-back. Most in any case withdrew from the workforce after ten to fifteen years, as the work was physically gruelling, and would then return to their villages if possible. In general, the workers were recruited from the villages by intermediaries who acted as jobbers. Once in the city, the jobbers determined when and where they would be employed, and the workers paid a commission for this service. Workers often took money-advances from the jobbers and obtained accommodation through their help. The jobbers employed their own strongmen who might use violence to force workers to repay their debts and rents. The jobbers tried to maintain good relations with the management of the factories and negotiated pay-rates for the workers with them. All of this made the workers highly dependent on the goodwill of their jobbers.[17]

From the start, there was a history of strikes by workers – particularly in the cotton textile mills of Bombay and Madras. Most lasted only a day or two, with just a fraction of the workers being involved. A common grievance was the reprimand or dismissal of a jobber by the mill management. As the workers were under the sway of the jobbers, they would protest for them if told to do so. Such strikes were at short notice, with demands that were not thought through, and confined often to one department of a factory. The first labour union in India was the Bombay Mill-Hands Association, founded in 1890. This was a loose body with no clear aim or constitution. It mainly acted as a pressure group on government. Before 1918, workers in general lacked any strongly established unions that could coordinate strikes across entire industries. Unions tended to come and go, lasting for the duration of a strike only.[18]

Congress and the Workers

Members of the elite with nationalist leanings took an interest in the industrial working classes from the late-nineteenth century onwards. In Bengal, socially conscious members of the bhadralok publicised the poor conditions for workers in the jute-mills. Bankim Chandra Chattopadhyay was a pioneer in this respect. During the Swadeshi Movement, some nationalist leaders took up the cause of the workers and supported strikes in Bengal printing presses, on the railways and in railway workshops. Nonetheless, although the government was collecting evidence on the conditions of industrial workers in India in 1907–08, and the Indian Factory Bill was being discussed in the Imperial Council, there was not a single resolution on any labour issue in the Congress sessions of 1908, 1909 or 1910. In Bombay City, the Kamgar Hitvardhak Society (Society for the Amelioration of Workers) was founded in 1910 to carry out welfare work for mill workers and sometimes its members acted as arbitrators in disputes, but it did not initiate or lead any industrial action by workers. A leading figure in such activity was a member of Gokhale's Servants of India Society, N.M. Joshi. He had founded the Social Service League in Bombay in 1911 – an organisation that sought to provide welfare and education for the industrial and other workers.[19]

Nationalists became involved in more active union work towards the end of the First World War, a period of rapid inflation, massive profits for mills, and a reluctance by industrialists to allow their returns to be eaten into by adequate wage increases. There was continuing resentment among workers of their discriminatory treatment by European managers and supervisors, and this fed into the burgeoning nationalist fervour of that time. It was the experience of racism that united many Indian workers with nationalists of a very different class at that time. A Parsi lawyer and ardent Home Ruler called B.P. Wadia formed the Madras Labour Union in April 1918 due to his anger at the racism of the white staff towards Indian employees in the two Binny mills. He accused them of treating the workers in 'the ways of Germans, who are haughty, arrogant and careless of Freedom and Justice'. He was threatened by Binnys with legal action for defamation. Wadia was a close ally of Annie Besant, who had been a union leader in Britain before she came to India, and she advised him on establishing the union. Wadia did not at that time call for a strike, arguing that it would hamper the war effort. The Madras Labour Union was primarily for textile workers, but it later became a general union for all workers. It was the first union in India to have a regular membership paying a subscription, and with a relief fund, and workers played an active role in its running.[20]

In the same year, Gandhi led a strike by the Ahmedabad mill workers. He established certain principles, namely that demands should be voiced with care only after the situation had been thoroughly examined and the workers were sure that that they had a good case. Strikes should be the last resort, with arbitration being always preferable. There should be peaceful and nonviolent behaviour on the part of the workers and no ill-will should be shown towards employers. As the mill owners in Ahmedabad were all Indian, there was there none of the racial antagonism felt in Madras. Projected by Gandhi as a variety of satyagraha, strikers were expected to stick to their resolution despite hardships and act truthfully and with courage. Workers should be aware of the responsibility they had for the industry in general. A formal union, the Textile Labourers Association (TLA) was established in the city in 1920, and by the end of that year it had 16,450 members and a fund of Rs 54,797. By the end of 1921, over half the factory workers of the city were organised. Only Madras and Ahmedabad had stable unions in 1920–22.[21]

With the passing of the Montagu-Chelmsford reforms in 1919, the government in India was for the first time prepared to accept the legitimacy of moderate trade union organisation. It was willing to initiate legislation that would legalise such activity and provide protection for workers. The British wanted to ensure that the unions were controlled by moderates rather than those whom they considered 'rabble-rousers' or communists and were prepared to grant limited concessions that strengthened the hold of such leaders. Gandhi was viewed as a moderate in this respect for his work in Ahmedabad, also N.M. Joshi in Bombay and B.P. Wadia in Madras.[22]

It was in this climate that the All India Trade Union Congress (AITUC) was founded in 1920 by nationalists who sought to coordinate union work throughout India. This quickly went beyond the moderate limits that the British considered acceptable in such matters. Lala Lajpat Rai was the first president of this body, and its first session in October 1920 was attended by Annie Besant, Motilal Nehru, C.F. Andrews, and Vithalbhai Patel. In his address, Rai asserted that India had been bled white by capitalists, and they were connected closely with imperialism. Indian labour had to organise itself, agitate and educate. 'We must organise our workers, make them class conscious.' For a time, members of the intelligentsia would have to provide leadership, but eventually the workers would produce their own leaders. The AITUC manifesto urged workers to support the nationalist movement. Rai was concerned that the rivalries of local union leaders would undermine the strength of these organisations and wanted to provide a way of going beyond this. He also understood that while the government and capitalists had all-India resources at their disposal, the trade unions did not. He acknowledged however that it would be many years before the AITUC was likely to become a genuinely all-India organisation that could claim to speak on behalf of the mass of Indian workers. B.P. Wadia supported the initiative, believing it would strengthen the growth of democracy at the national level if workers learnt to organise and operate in democratic ways through unions linked to the nationalist movement. He envisaged peasants and plantation workers learning to work democratically in this way also. Otherwise, Wadia argued, democracy in India would mean merely the transfer of power from the British to Indian elites. Joseph Baptista, a Fabian socialist at Cambridge and then a prominent Bombay-based lawyer and follower of Tilak, became chairman of the AITUC in 1921, and was its president in 1922. He was an active leader of several Bombay unions at that time. His vision was for a Congress labour section in which cooperatives, trade unions and socialists would be represented. This, he argued, would help the workers to assert themselves through unions, strikes and boycotts. Congress leaders such as Chittaranjan Das, Subhas Chandra Bose, Motilal and Jawaharlal Nehru all presided over the AITUC at one time or another. Gandhi, however, focused his union activity on Ahmedabad, arguing that it was premature for the Textile Labourers Association to join the all-India union. In general, the nationalists sought to provide a climate in which trade union work could thrive. This connection was, however, resented by many employers, and it allowed them to claim that strikes were now politically driven rather than being rooted in workplace grievances. Initially, the AITUC was merely a body that met annually in December to discuss issues and pass resolutions, and – in contrast to the local trade unions – it was not actively involved in organising workers. Four years had passed before it produced a constitution.[23]

Although the Congress was reaching out to industrial workers in these ways at the time of the Noncooperation Movement, it was also concerned not to alienate the Indian capitalist class. Since the time of the Swadeshi Movement, Congress leaders had valued the contribution that Indian capitalists could make in building an independent economy. They valued the funds that the capitalists provided for the Congress organisation, and admired their management and accounting skills, believing that these should be replicated within the wider society. As they wanted to build a popular front in which labour would also be a part, they emphasised the idea of a partnership of capital and labour against the British. Tilak had argued this in 1918 when confronted with a wave of strikes by the mill workers of Bombay – both should unite against the imperial state. Lala Lajpat Rai, in his presidential address to the first AITUC in 1920, had stated that labour and capital must work equally to develop Indian industry, though at present the capitalists were not treating their workers fairly. Joseph Baptista also talked of a 'partnership' in which the well-being of workers should be accorded full due. This would promote the general welfare of society. Gandhi spoke a similar language, demanding, in 1920, that that the Ahmedabad mill hands identify themselves with the interests of mill owners. He eschewed the idea that strikes should be used as a threat or to coerce. Where Gandhi went beyond these other nationalists was in his development of a coherent code of ethics and a philosophy of practice to govern industrial relations. This was rooted in the idea of the interdependence of labour and capital.[24]

Gandhi saw strikes as being like a dispute in the family. In Ahmedabad this was literally the case, as the mill owner Ambalal Sarabhai was the brother of the Gandhian activist and union leader Anasuyaben Sarabhai. This was however a unique case. Gandhi made one of the clearest statements of his approach at a talk in Jamshedpur in 1925, where European managers of the Tata steel works were among his listeners:

> It is my ambition to see one of the greatest – if not the greatest – Indian enterprises in India, and study the conditions of work there. But none of my activities is one-sided, and as my religion begins and ends with truth and non-violence, my identification with labour does not conflict with my friendship with capital. And believe me, throughout my public service of 35 years, though I have been obliged to range myself seemingly against capital, capitalists have in the end regarded me as their true friend. And in all humility I may say that I have come here also as a friend of the capitalists—a friend of the Tatas.... At Ahmedabad I have had much to do with the capitalists and workmen, and I have always said that my ideal is that capital and labour should supplement and help each other. They should be a great family living in unity and harmony, capital not only looking to the material welfare of the labourers but their moral welfare also, capitalists being trustees for the welfare of the labouring classes under them.

Gandhi held that the demands of workers should be based on an appeal to justice, and that they should not act in any way that would undermine the financial health of the industry. Disputes should always, if possible, be settled by advisors or arbitrators who would work to achieve an outcome that was both fair and respected by both sides. If a strike was resorted to, it should be in the interests of the whole industry, so that the employers would come to appreciate the justice of the demand. However, as Chandavarkar points out, the problem here was that the mill owners were not normally willing to be transparent about their financial situations – they tended to argue that the market could not bear a wage-rise, even when it could. Arbitration tended to favour the stronger side – namely the mill owners. Indeed, advice by an arbitrator that was disliked by the mill owners was liable to be ignored.[25]

Chandavarkar has also noted that many capitalists viewed Gandhi with suspicion. They feared that his campaigns would disrupt business and treat a climate of lawlessness in the cities. They resented the way that he encouraged workers to be develop self-respect and stand up for their rights. They were annoyed when he told them that the workers were as much the proprietors of the mills as the shareholders and that the owners had no right to 'lord it over the labourers'. They did not appreciate it when he told them that because the prosperity of the capitalist was based on the hard work of the labourers they should hold their factories as a trust to be used in the interest of the whole 'family' of workers and capitalists. Gandhi accepted that while the capitalists brought business skill and acumen to the running of the mills, something the workers then lacked, in time they might develop such abilities and be able to inherit the 'father's' wealth. To achieve this, they had to organise themselves and learn to be assertive as to their rights. Workers could take such ideas and extend them in radical directions. The bosses were right to be worried, for such talk had parallels with the syndicalist demand for workers' control. Gandhi's was not therefore a doctrine that demanded quiescence or worked in the narrow interests of the capitalists. In this respect, he hardly succeeded in acting as an ideologue for capital.[26]

Gandhi did not, however, believe that workers should stage political strikes, except for limited periods – as in hartals – and then only when the management of their factory had given permission for them to do so. He made this clear right at the start of the Noncooperation

Movement in 1920, when giving instructions for the inaugurating protest: 'The Committee advises *full* hartal on the first of August. Mill-hands, however, are requested not to abstain from work, unless they receive permission from their employers…'[27] Clearly, the hartal was not to be quite as 'full' as he made out. His advice in this respect remained consistent throughout the campaign. When planning a week of protest to commemorate the second anniversary of the Jallianwala Bagh massacre, he stated: 'We should observe hartals on the 6th and the 13th. No compulsion should be used on anyone. Mill-hands too should arrange in advance to take leave for these two days. Those who may not get leave should certainly not stop work.'[28]

Gandhi made his views on this matter very clear in an article in *Young India* of 16 February 1921. He noted that there was a wave of strikes at that time in India and accepted that the grievances of the workers were genuine. Yet, the people who came forward to act as 'advisers and guides' were 'not always scrupulous' or wise in their advice. Many sought to engineer strikes for political purposes. Although he was aware that strikes could serve political ends, they had no place in the Noncooperation Movement. It was dangerous for workers to withhold their labour in this respect so long as they lacked an understanding of the political condition of their country or what was for 'the common good' of India. They would not be in such a position until they had first improved their conditions of life, become 'better informed', and had become 'part proprietors' in the industries in which they worked. In the present circumstances, political strike action would merely 'retard the fulfilment of the great national purpose'.[29] In a further directive written four months later, Gandhi stated: 'We want no political strikes. We are not yet instructed enough for them.' Political strikes unleashed 'unruly and disturbing elements' in society and created 'an atmosphere of unsettled unrest'. In this, they hampered rather than furthered the cause of freedom. While it was acceptable to support strikes that were purely about wages and working conditions, they should 'sedulously avoid all other strikes'. 'We seek not to destroy capital or capitalists, but to regulate the relations between capital and labour. We want to harness capital to our side. It would be folly to encourage sympathetic strikes.'[30]

The drawback to Gandhi's caution in this respect was that the atmosphere in many Indian industries had become explosive at this time, and many nationalists believed that they could turn the anger of the workers against the British in a way that would greatly strengthen the movement and in the long run benefit the workers. Food grain prices had almost doubled between 1914 and 1918, with most of this increase taking place in 1918. In Bombay City, for example, the wages of the mill workers had been increased by only 15 per cent. They now were spending about two-thirds of their wages on basic foodstuffs and were faced with starvation. This was at the same time as the textile magnates of that city were making huge profits. Dividends in the mills shot up from 6 per cent in 1914 to 30 per cent by 1917. The workers were aware of this and knew that the capitalists could afford to pay them much higher wages. The workers were also affected by the economic fluctuations of the post-war period, meaning that employment became increasingly insecure after 1918. About one-third of the workers in the cotton textile mills in Bombay were hired on a casual and daily basis. The system depended on the availability of a surplus labour force to ensure that when the demand for products was high, output could be increased relatively easily. The price of raw cotton formed a major proportion of the cost of production and much entrepreneurial skill was required in obtaining it at a good quality and reasonable price. If good cotton could not be obtained at an acceptable price, it made economic sense to cut back on production rather than keep workers employed. The workers were made to bear the brunt of these fluctuations.[31]

All of this provided an opening for working class organisation and – in 1920–21 – considerable militancy that in several cases linked up with the Noncooperation Movement in ways that often ran counter to Gandhi's advice. I shall now provide case studies of working-class involvement in the cities of Bombay and Madras, and in Bengal, before concluding the chapter by addressing some of the major issues involved.

Bombay City

The first strike to affect the entire cotton industry of Bombay City took place in early 1919, with 83 factories employing 140,000 workers being closed by the action. It was initiated and organised largely by the workers, without any significant leadership or guidance by nationalistic union leaders. It began over a wage-dispute at the Century Mills, which was owned by the Parsi capitalist C.N. Wadia and managed by a Britisher, J.G. Anderson. The workers demanded a 25 per cent wage increase because of rapid price inflation at a time when the mills were generating huge profits. They also demanded a month's salary as bonus. Wadia refused to accept the demand. The workers asked a sympathetic radical lawyer – H.B. Mandavale – to represent them, but Wadia refused to accept him as a spokesman. They struck work on 31 December. Wadia was chastened by this and he agreed to set up an arbitration committee of himself and L.R. Tairsee, a prominent Gujarati businessman. The workers agreed to return to work on 7 January while the committee appraised their demands. Once back in the mill, they were however treated with racist contempt by Anderson, which suggested to them that the committee was unlikely to concede their demands in any significant way. On 8 January, they gathered at the gates of a neighbouring factory, the Textile Mills, and as the workers left the factory, persuaded them to stage a sympathetic strike. They succeeded in this. Now twice the number were on strike. These mills were both in Parel, and the workers lived in *chawls* (tenement blocks) close by. The close proximity of residential and workplaces facilitated united action that spread rapidly across the industry. On 9 January, the workers from the two mills toured Parel and neighbouring mill districts persuading the workers of other mills to come out. They staged orderly demonstrations at the gates of factories in a way that was intended to enlist the support of their fellow workers rather than antagonise the managers. In most cases, the managers closed their factories as they saw that it was futile to resist. The few managers who refused to do so were subjected to volleys of stones and brickbats. This was however rare. By and large, the strikers achieved their objective with little injury to persons or property. By the end of the 9 January, the great majority of Bombay textile workers were on strike and out on the streets. They were, for the most part, orderly and well behaved. Kumar writes of this phase: 'The methods they adopted in bringing the textile industry of Bombay to a grinding halt were peaceful and effective in equal proportion.'[32]

As neither the workers nor mill owners were well-organised, there were problems in negotiating a resolution to the strike. The jobbers acted as the leaders, and on the first day of the strike they approached the Commissioner of Police for the city, C.A. Vincent, and asked him to arbitrate. He told them that if they formulated their demands, he would put them to the mill owners. Over 4,000 workers, led by their jobbers, met on the morning of 10 January to do this. Mandavale also attended and urged them to appoint their own delegates to put their case to the owners. He also advised them to form a trade union that could act in the name of the workers. The workers decided to demand a 25 per cent wage increase. On the same day, the Mill Owners' Association met and resolved to, take a hard line. They asserted that they would not negotiate unless all workers returned immediately to the factories. This caused a deterioration in the situation. On 11 January, 55,000 workers held a meeting in Parel. Some nationalists, such as the Dwarkadas brothers of the Home Rule League, and Umar Sobhani, a later Khilafat leader, spoke. They urged the workers to return to work and then negotiate. This advice was too timid for the workers, who insisted that their wage increase be granted before they went back. They decided to march in a group to Tardeo, where a couple of mills were still operating. Vincent sent a police party to stop them, but it was swept aside by the large crowd. Armed police were sent and the workers halted, with one being killed in the police action.[33]

The workers were made more determined by this killing. The dissatisfaction was now spreading to other employees in the businesses of the city, such as clerks, salesmen and accountants, who were also suffering from the price inflation. These were often Gujaratis who worked on very low wages for their caste-fellows. There were no fixed times for their work – they had to do whatever the big businessmen ordered them to do, at any time. They had supported the Home Rule Leagues, believing that the 'freedom' they promised meant better working and living conditions for them. On 12 January, 6,000 of these subordinate staff went on strike, demanding a 33 per cent increase in their wages. Then on 16 January, some 10,000 workers in the naval dockyards came out on strike demanding higher wages. The next day, they took out two processions through the streets of the city, shouting slogans and damaging property before being dispersed by the police. That same day, 7,000 employees in the workshops of the Great Indian Peninsula Railway at Parel came out for higher wages. The strike spread rapidly to the workshops of the Bombay, Baroda and Central Indian Railways, also located in Parel. The managers of these railway companies offered immediate wage increase of 10 per cent and more liberal vacation rules, after which they returned to work within a few days. Other workers in the city also went on strike at this time.[34]

On 17 January, a meeting of workers was held under the presidentship of N.S. Velkar, the head jobber of the Petit Mills. The workers made it clear that they did not trust the verbal assurances of the owners. There was thus a stalemate. Vincent then arranged to see a delegation of 300 jobbers and other strike-leaders in his office in Parel. They presented their grievances, and Vincent encouraged them to put their demands to the Governor of Bombay, Sir George Lloyd. Lloyd held liberal views on industrial relations. He had already launched a programme for housing workers and established a Bureau of Labour to collect statistics on the urban poor. He believed that the state should act as an impartial arbitrator between labour and capital when there were disputes that threatened public order; and that large profits should be reflected in higher wages. He favoured trade union organisation as providing a mechanism for this, so long as the unions did not become the tool of political agitators. Lloyd received the delegation of jobbers at the secretariat and heard their demands. He told them they had a good case and assured them that having met the Mill Owners' Association on the 17th, he believed that they were now prepared to award a pay-increase. If they went back to work peacefully, he would use his influence to ensure that this happened. The delegation reacted favourably, but its members lacked any institutional means to get the mass of workers to accept. As it was, most of the workers wanted to stay on strike until they had a written guarantee of wage rises. On 21 January, the Mill Owners' Association announced a wage increase of 20 per cent and a special bonus to offset the increased cost of food. When Vincent announced this to a large crowd, there was great joy. Vincent was hailed as a saviour, with cries of 'Vincent Maharaj ki jai!' Within a few days, the mills were working as normal.[35]

It was clear that in 1919 the nationalists of the city had very limited support amongst the workers. This was in marked contrast to Ahmedabad, where Gandhi had managed to intervene in March 1918 on behalf of the workers with great success in a similar dispute, and consequently enjoyed widespread support amongst this class in the following years. In Bombay City it was the British Commissioner of Police and Governor who carried out the crucial arbitrating role. The weakness of the nationalists in this respect was emphasised again three months later, during the Rowlatt Satyagraha. As we have seen in the previous volume,[36] Gandhi had encouraged the workers to stop work for one day, on 6 April 1919, so long as their employers supported their action. With only eleven bosses agreeing to do this, hardly 15 per cent of the workers came out on that day. The riots that then occurred in the city on 10 and 11 April were largely by Gujarati and Muslim traders, with workers playing almost no part. In all this, there was a clear ethnic divide between Gujaratis and Muslims of the city, who were strongly nationalistic, and the mill workers, who were almost all Maharashtrians in an industry controlled by Gujarati-speaking capitalists.

The inauguration of noncooperation on 1 August 1920 coincided with the death of Tilak. Although the mill workers had remained in the factories during the initial hartal in support of noncooperation, once news came of Tilak's death, they came out in a block as a mark of respect to this Maharashtrian hero. They attended the cremation of Tilak's body on the sands at Chowpatty Beach and remained out on 2 August. Thereafter, for the next year, they failed to come out on strike in support of the movement, even on days when city-wide hartals were declared by the Congress. For example, when such a hartal was held on 6 April 1921 to mark the start of 'Satyagraha Week' in memory of Jallianwala Bagh, the protest was only partially observed, with just a few shops being closed, while the mills worked as usual. Peace prevailed on the day. On 7 April, a public meeting was held for the mill hands at Chinchpokli and neighbouring areas. Lala Lajpat Rai and others spoke, encouraging workers to join the Congress. About 3,500 workers attended. On 10 April, Gandhi addressed a meeting for mill workers at Elphinstone Road, at which he exhorted them to contribute to the Tilak Swaraj Fund and join the Congress as paid-up members. Many donated to the fund as it was named in memory of their dead hero. Gandhi also told them to boycott foreign cloth and use the spinning-wheel. Despite this, the hartal declared for the last day of that week – 13 April – was similarly patchy with no significant response from the workers.[37]

On 31 July 1921, Gandhi attended a rally in the compound of the Elphinstone Mill, which was owned by the Khilafat leader Umar Sobhani. Sobhani gave his full support to this meeting at which foreign cloth was burnt. About ten to twelve thousand were present, and the affair was entirely peaceful and orderly.[38] The mood began to shift from September 1921 onwards. When Shaukat Ali was arrested that month there were spontaneous strikes in certain mills, starting on 17 September, with 19,000 workers out by 19 September. They returned to work after seven ringleaders were arrested. There was a further bonfire of foreign cloth at Elphinstone Mill, on 9 October 1921, that Gandhi attended. The same venue saw another such ceremony staged by Gandhi on 17 November 1921, the day on which the Prince of Wales landed in Bombay to start his tour of India. Now, there was a much larger turn-out than on the previous two occasions, with an estimated 25,000 workers being there as a pile of foreign cloth was lit. Gandhi addressed the meeting, stressing the need for nonviolence even in the face of great provocation. At the same time, the Prince of Wales was proceeding through streets lined with crowds of cheering loyalists – many of whom were Europeans, Anglo-Indians, Parsis and Jews – on the way to Chowpatty Beach. When the meeting at Elphinstone Mill ended, the workers made their way to Charni Road and Marine Lines stations where they met crowds of loyalists returning from welcoming the Prince, many of whom were in trams. The workers rushed the trams, beating up their occupants. Many trams were set on fire. Anyone wearing hats that were seen to be 'loyalist' – whether solar topees, felt hats, or the Parsi *phenta* – was singled out for attack. Their headgear was snatched, piled up in the street and burnt. Europeans and Anglo-Indians were singled out because they were associated with the mill supervisors who often treated the workers in a racist and violent manner. They were now on the receiving end of the kicks and blows. The Parsis were attacked because they were known for their loyalism to the British,[39] as they owned and operated several mills, and as many of the liquor shops in the city were run by members of this community and they had refused to close them despite nationalist picketing. The relatively small Jewish community of the city was associated with the capitalist elite. When news of what was going on spread, workers came out from other mills and joined the fray. Some were heard to cry 'Mahatma Gandhi ki jai' as they assaulted the loyalists. Even Parsi women were not spared – several were assaulted and had their saris torn from them. Two Anglo-Indians, two Parsis, and one American were killed in the turmoil. During the disturbance, four liquor shops were burnt down and a further 135 looted or damaged by the crowds. Intense fighting continued into the early hours of 18 November, with six policemen being killed. Congress volunteers who tried to stop the violence were themselves beaten; some so badly that they died. Although martial law was declared, workers continued in the next few days to roam the streets attacking those whose headwear and clothing marked them as loyalists. Some Parsis and Anglo-Indians retaliated by forming their own bands, which toured the streets snatching Gandhi caps and attacking people considered to be pro-Congress, while the police looked on and even helped them. At the same time, nationalist leaders and volunteers joined with groups of public figures who went around the city exhorting people to stop the violence, and by this means order was eventually restored.[40]

Gandhi was left distraught by all this, especially as he had put so much stress on the need for complete nonviolence in his speech that day to the workers. He had rushed immediately to the scene on hearing of the rioting, where he was told 'the most painful and humiliating story of molestation of Parsi sisters'. One elderly Parsi pleaded with him to save them. He was surrounded by crowds chanting 'Mahatma Gandhi ki jai!', a sound that – he said – merely grated on his ears. He appealed for them to go home. When a report came to him of violence in another part of the city, he went there and called for calm, persuading the crowd to disperse. He estimated that about 20,000 people were involved, and not all were mill hands. He felt that they knew what they were doing, being 'bent upon mischief and destruction'. He wrote late that night: 'We have a foretaste of swaraj. I have been put to shame.' Next day, 18 November, he reported that Hindu and Muslim volunteers who had tried to intervene with workers in Parel had been turned on. He had personally seen them on their return with their heads broken and bleeding. Some had 'lacerating wounds'. He accused the mill workers of leaving their factories in 'criminal disobedience of the wishes of their masters'. 'We claim to have established a peaceful atmosphere, i.e., to have attained by our non-violence sufficient control over the people to keep their violence under check. We have failed when we ought to have succeeded.' He felt personally culpable, as he had encouraged a spirit of defiance that he had been unable to control.[41]

Early next morning, Gandhi announced that he was to go on a fast until peace had been restored between the different communities. He stated: 'The swaraj that I have witnessed during the last two days has stunk in my nostrils'. The fast continued during the 20th and 21st as he issued appeals for peace. The riots had subsided by 22 November, and he broke his fast that morning. A meeting of the Congress Working Committee was held in the city on 22 and 23 November at which the violence was deplored. The committee felt, nonetheless, that it had exposed a 'weak spot' that revealed a need for efforts to obtain better control over 'all turbulent elements in society'. Congress outposts were to be established 'in every street, in every lane' in which volunteers would be based who would maintain peace. Only those who had taken a pledge of nonviolence were to serve in such a capacity. Gandhi left Bombay on 26 November.[42]

During these years, the Bombay workers proved well able to mobilise themselves in a nonviolent action, as was seen during the strike of January 1919. Here, the jobbers were in control, and they managed to maintain a discipline that worked to their advantage in obtaining their demands. This was not the case in November 1921, when more violent forces were in the ascendant. I have not myself seen any evidence that reveals clearly what those forces were. We do not, in other words, have any detailed analysis by any commentator or subsequent historian on how the Bombay crowd was directed and controlled in November 1921. It is not enough to merely assert that the workers 'lost their heads', for the violence was directed and with meaning, and there must have been some people at the helm at critical junctures. We may note in this respect that the everyday world of the workers was often a violent one, and that people whom they looked up to who had a reputation for getting their way through violence could well have provided leadership in this case. There was huge competition in the city between workers for good jobs and housing, and this created rivalries and divides. Groups vied to control neighbourhoods. In the previous section, we have already referred to the strongmen whom the jobbers worked with to maintain their power in these respects. In Bombay, these neighbourhood bosses were known as *dadas*. Chandavarkar states that they enjoyed 'a reputation for physical prowess or for getting things done.' They established a reputation through street violence, and were often associated with gymnasiums (*akhada*), where they exhibited their fighting prowess. The *dadas* cultivated a virile and aggressive persona that was designed to overawe and command obedience; they worked for a variety of patrons, helped jobbers to control their clients and might help them in organising strikes and enforce strike-discipline. They collected house or room rents for landlords and debt repayments for moneylenders and grain-dealers, or whipped up support for politicians. In some cases, they were even hired by mill owners to break strikes. They cultivated a reputation for generosity towards those who were under their control, protecting them when in need and helping them find work. Relationships with the lower ranks of the police were fostered, and they intervened when their clients were arrested, sometimes by providing surety. On occasion they were called in to arbitrate in neighbourhood disputes. And they often patronised local shrines, temples, and mosques and organised religious festivals, so as to try to gain legitimacy and respectability.[43] It is quite likely that people of this sort were in control of the Bombay crowd in November 1921, using the opportunity created by the anger against loyalists to settle a range of scores.

Their perceived antagonists in the events of November 1921 were Europeans, Anglo-Indians (who were frequently described at this time as 'Christians'),[44] Parsis, and Jews. Significantly, there was no antagonism between Hindus and Muslims. It is significant in this respect that Hindus and Muslims often worked out at the same *akhadas* at that time. These gymnasiums provided an important arena for male working-class culture. Young men learnt wrestling and how to fight with lathis and they could then be called in to either protect their neighbourhood in times of trouble or fight those seen as their opponents. Gymnasiums were social centres that were used for meetings to discuss local problems and for political work attended by prominent public figures. In this way, local *dadas* could form relationships with elite politicians. The *dada* could mobilise the gym students in various causes, ranging from participating in and guarding religious processions, protecting neighbourhoods, attacking rivals in riots, mobilising votes and supporting political protests and nationalist campaigns. Up until the mid-1920s, Muslims and Hindus often attended the same gymnasiums, with *ustads* of both faiths in charge of the training. They invoked both Hanuman and Moula Ali – considered the strongest man in the world. It was only in the period after 1922, with the growth of religious nationalism in India, that *akhadas* began to be formed that were patronised by only Hindus or Muslims. This set the stage for the clashes between Hindus and Muslims that were to become a feature of urban politics from the mid-1920s onwards. This was not, however, the case in the working-class politics of the city in 1920–22.[45]

Chandavarkar has pointed out how even those designated as Congress 'volunteers' could be associated with gymnasiums or be *dada*-figures: '...individuals came to acquire a reputation for their excellence at wrestling, or their ferocity in street fighting, their shrewdness in dealing with the police or their range of connections within the neighbourhood...' They were driven by notions of honour and correct conduct. 'The mainstreams for political action were located within the daily patterns of social life.'[46] Though many Congress workers risked their safety, and even lives, in trying to stop the violence in 1921, not all may have so acted, and some may even have stoked it.

A working-class culture was being created at this time in Bombay City, with inputs from a range of sources. In part, it was forged from the rural experience of workers who maintained firm links with their villages in Maharashtra, and in part from the social and political realities of the large city. When engaged in industrial or political action, the workers might act in a way that was reminiscent of a peasant *jacquerie* – as Ravinder Kumar has pointed out was the case during the strike of January 1919.[47] In this case, as in much rural protest, there was little violence directed against opponents. The mass of the workers gained confidence from the fact that their jobbers were in the lead, as would have been the case if the dominant peasants had assumed such a role in the rural equivalent. Or, they might respond in the more violent way of the big city, with its *dadas*, macho culture and street-fighting. The latter culture appears to have been to the fore in November 1921.

The Bombay workers had an ambivalent attitude towards Gandhi. Many felt that – as a Gujarati – he was more likely to sympathise with the bosses of the city than its workers. Although the workers generally respected his nationalism, they found his nonviolence irrelevant to their social and political life. All of this provided an opening for Maharashtrian radicals who believed in strikes as political weapons and who were not committed to nonviolence. Prominent amongst these was S.A. Dange, a young Maharashtrian Marxist who in 1920–22 had thrown his support behind the movement led by Gandhi.[48] Even then, he was troubled by what he later described as Gandhi's 'obscurantist outlook on socio-economic matters'. He and his fellow-radicals wanted to push the movement forward with strong working-class action in Bombay. When the movement in Bombay faltered as a result of the violence of November 1921, they directed their attention to building a strong independent base amongst the working class. Over the following years they set up and ran the Girni Kamdar Union, which in 1928 and 1929 led a series of massive strikes by the textile workers that paralysed the city. In this way, they and the majority of workers of Bombay broke decisively with the Gandhian Congress.[49]

Madras

In a previous section of this chapter we have already seen how the moderate nationalist B.P. Wadia formed the Madras Labour Union in 1918. As this union adopted a restrained approach, the managers of the two Binny Mills were able to ignore it with impunity. In early 1920, faced by a rapid inflation in prices, the workers demanded higher pay. The new Governor of Madras Presidency, Lord Willingdon, persuaded the management to agree to a government-appointed enquiry into the situation, which, on 8 March, recommended wage increases of between 20 and 30 per cent Binnys agreed to this but refused to backdate the increase, after which the workers declared a strike and walked out. A compromise was reached, and they returned to work. The workers had taken this action themselves as they felt that the union had not been active enough in their interests. Wadia was at that time abroad and played no part in it.[50]

Once noncooperation began, Congress politicians tried to take over the Madras Labour Union and use it in support of their movement. This led to a split in the union. One group was headed by Wadia and was supported by most worker leaders. Though sympathetic to the nationalist cause, they did not want the union to become a mere tool of the Congress as they felt it would prevent any dialogue with Binnys and the Madras government. A smaller group was led by Singaravelu Chetti, a lawyer of the fisherman caste who later became a leading Communist organiser, and a Brahman lawyer, E.L. Iyer. This led to some small strikes, as the rival unions vied for support. The managers and other British businessmen of the city accused the nationalists – whether moderate or radical – of being Bolsheviks who favoured violent revolution, and even complained to the government of India about the inaction of the Madras government in all this. Although the local authorities held that the managers should increase wages in line with the cost of living, they also felt that the burgeoning industrial action posed a threat to law and order, and they began to intervene on the side of management.[51]

Matters came to a head in October 1920 when a jobber of the Buckingham Mill who was active in the union was refused promotion. Other jobbers were offered the post, and when they refused, were dismissed. In protest, some workers marched in a body to the office of the European mill manager, who produced a revolver. The workers confiscated this, whereupon a lockout was declared by Binnys. This led to a strike that that began on 20 October. Wadia supported the workers, congratulating them on their nonviolence. Over the next week, Binnys tried to break the strike using members of the Adi-Dravida community (Dalit groups) as blackleg labour. In this way, they exploited communal divides amongst the lower classes of the city. Forty-six per cent of the mill workers were caste Hindus who had been recruited from rural areas close to Madras, 39 per cent Adi-Dravidas, 8 per cent Christians, and 5 per cent Muslims. Each caste or community tended to live in its own cluster near the mills. There was much solidarity among the caste Hindus, while the Adi-Dravidas – who lived in segregated slums in very poor conditions – had little to do with the other workers. For example, they were made to eat apart from caste Hindus in the mill dining hall. They tended to be employed in the harder and more demanding jobs. The Christians were mostly converts from low castes or the untouchables, and they also lived in the slums in a way similar to the Adi-Dravidas. The Muslims were Urdu speakers who were economically depressed and lived in close proximity to the

Adi-Dravidas. They were sometimes in conflict with them. These three disadvantaged groups lacked the links to villages of the caste Hindus, and thus did not have this fall-back during strikes. The strike of October 1920 was supported by all workers, including the existing Adi-Dravida employees. Binnys set about recruiting labour from Adi-Dravidas who had not hitherto been employed by them, transporting them to the mills in lorries that had to make their way through picket lines. The initial nonviolence evaporated as furious workers hurled rocks and other missiles at the strike-breakers. Binnys then made a claim against the union through the courts for Rs 75,000 for malicious injury to the company. There was no trade union legislation in India at that time that prevented such a claim. On 2 December, the English judge found for the company and banned Wadia and other union leaders from having anything to do with the workers. This verdict led to riots in which a young worker was killed in police firing. Binnys offered to reopen the mill on 6 December, though would not promise to reinstate all those dismissed. The firm offered to pay the wages of the workers for the period 20 to 31 October, except those in the weaving department, where the strike had started. The offer was rejected at a meeting of the union attended by workers. They demanded that the court order be withdrawn by Binnys and that their union be recognised by the company. Binnys ignored this and continued to try to employ strike-breakers. There was more violence on 7 and 8 December when lorries carrying Adi-Dravidas came under heavy attack from large groups of strikers. On 9 December, one of the lorries broke down in the middle of such a crowd, and the policemen who were inside protecting the strike-breakers found themselves isolated. They opened fire, killing two young mill workers and wounding sixteen others, including ten mill workers.[52]

The nationalist press of Madras compared this event to the Jallianwala Bagh massacre, and the Governor, Lord Willingdon, to Michael O'Dwyer (Punjab Governor in 1919). The funeral of the two young men became a nationalist procession in which both Hindus and Muslims participated. The mill workers became more involved in nationalist protest as a result of this. They participated in the Congress-sponsored boycott of the Duke of Connaught when he visited Madras in January 1921. The dispute widened on 17 January

1921 when the workers of the Carnatic Mill joined those of the Buckingham Mill in a sympathy strike. Wadia was no longer taking any active part in all this, due to the court order. He felt demoralised by it all, and on 25 January resigned from the Madras Provincial Congress Committee. He believed that he was no longer able to act effectively as a moderating influence in the union, allowing it to be used by extremists. He knew that Binnys were determined to break the strike, and saw that the more matters escalated, the more intransigent they became. He also realised that the communal divides among the workers would be exploited by the company. He met with Binny managers secretly on 26 January and agreed that the workers should return under Binnys' conditions. In turn, they promised to withdraw the court case against him and allowed a union to be formed so long as no outsiders were involved. Wadia then persuaded the workers to return to work. In this, he had agreed to accept the dismissal of the jobbers. He had taken these decisions on his own initiative, without consulting the workers or the executive of the union. When the workers realised what he had done, they rejected Wadia and his group and turned for leadership to their nationalist rivals – Chetti, Iyer, and others. The union now became linked closely to the Congress, mobilising workers for street demonstrations. Nationalists criticised the British employers and argued that only once India was free would workers obtain justice. On 28 February, for example, many workers attended a Congress meeting during a hartal over the imprisonment of a prominent Muslim nationalist. The nationalists did not however want any further strike actions in the mills.[53]

Bad feelings continued to fester in the two mills, with the management applying disciplinary measures that were designed to humiliate and force a showdown with the workers. This led to some brief strikes in both mills in April 1921, escalating on 26 May to a lockout in the Buckingham Mill. With the waning of the post-war boom, Binnys could afford to close the mills for a time to starve the workers into submission. The workers of the Carnatic Mill struck in sympathy on 3 June. The workers believed that that the Congress would provide funds to sustain them in their action. Although the Adi-Dravidas had come out initially, by late May, many of them began to waver as they lacked the resources to sustain a long period without pay. They were also impressed that Binnys did not discriminate against them, as some Indian mill owners did, and they also felt that the position of untouchables had, in general, improved under British rule. In this, they lacked empathy with the nationalists, whether of the Congress or Khilafat. On 20 June, 700 to 800 of them resumed work. This was the first time that Adi-Dravidas who were already in the workplace had broken solidarity. Some Adi-Dravidas remained on strike and continued to support the union. They feared the consequences of breaking solidarity, especially with the Muslim workers whom they feared. Nonetheless, more and more returned to work. Some were threatened and attacked by those still on strike, despite the pleas by the unions for workers to remain nonviolent. The Adi-Dravidas defended themselves by going to work in groups armed with swords, knives and sticks. On 28 June, about sixty people attacked an Adi-Dravida slum, setting the thatched roofs of ninety-five huts on fire to chants of 'Gandhiji ki jai!'. The government arranged for the slum to be evacuated, and on 1 July 150 empty huts were destroyed by attacking crowds. Muslims were to the fore in these attacks – there was resentment among them that the Adi-Dravidas had not supported a hartal to protest the arrest of a Muslim leader in March, and there had been a fracas between them at that time in which one Adi-Dravida was killed. The union condemned the violence strongly, claiming it was the work of a few hooligan elements. Willingdon called the Congress leaders of the union and warned them that they would be held responsible for any further violence. He told them to advise the workers to go back to work. As the government had arranged for alternative accommodation for those who had lost their huts in the crowd action, the strikers claimed that it was siding with the Adi-Dravida strike-breakers. When Willingdon visited the new housing colony, he received a rousing reception from the Adi-Dravidas. A huge meeting of the union was held on 11 July, attended by top Congress leaders, and the workers were urged to work closely with Congress. Some workers threatened to invade the residential quarters of the European and Anglo-Indian mill staff, and the army had to be called in to keep the peace, as tensions simmered during that month.[54]

More and more men drifted back to work after this. Binny refused to negotiate with the union, believing that the strike would soon wane into insignificance. The workers now looked to Gandhi to help them, remembering how effectively he had intervened in the strike by Ahmedabad workers in 1918. The situation in Madras differed however, as the main mill owners were British businessmen who despised nationalists such as Gandhi. On 16 September, Gandhi addressed a large meeting of the union members on the beach in Madras that ended with a big bonfire of foreign cloth. In his speech, Gandhi sympathised with the plight of the workers, but expressed grief that they had become divided along communal lines. He condemned the force that had been used against the Adi-Dravidas. Instead, they should treat them with consideration and generosity, not looking down on them because of their low status, and in this way gain their sympathy. In fact, India did not deserve freedom while the 'curse of untouchability' remained. While they had a perfect right to demand higher wages, they had also to accept their duty to work diligently and not absent themselves from work without permission from the managers. If they remained on strike, they and their families could earn a livelihood through hand-spinning and weaving. If they wanted to support the nationalist cause, the best thing they could do was to maintain complete nonviolence, wear only khadi cloth, not gamble or steal, and 'not defile our bodies by touching wine and women'. Gandhi's prescriptions did not go down well. He was offering moral advice without any material support, and they were not impressed by his call for tolerance towards the Adi-Dravidas. The violence continued – on the day of Gandhi's speech, a policeman was killed in a fracas. On 5 October, a crowd set upon an Adi-Dravida slum after some of them had attacked a caste Hindu house. The police opened fire, killing one and injuring fifteen. Police were posted to guard these slums, which prevented further such attacks. The strike gradually petered out, ending finally on 21 October. Many found that they no longer had jobs to go back to, as they had been taken by others. Binny also refused to reinstate the strike-leaders and the local Congress rejected any responsibility for those who had lost their jobs. The strike was thus crushed with the workers gaining nothing. It was, in Arnold's words, 'a traumatic experience for the Madras workers and their Congress patrons'. Union membership dwindled to almost nothing, and when nationalists tried to revive labour agitation in April 1922, they had no success. As in Bombay, when union activism eventually revived in the late 1920s, it had no significant connection with the Congress.[55]

The Congress and Khilafat organisations in Madras were far more active in organising labour in strike actions than was the case in Bombay, actively encouraging strike action as a part of the Noncooperation Movement. Nonetheless, as in Bombay, leaders from elite backgrounds proved to have little control over the workers. Despite ostensibly controlling the union, the nationalists were unable to determine the sorts of action that workers felt appropriate, such as attacking blackleg labourers, both on their way into the factories and in their homes. There was a strong communal edge to all this, with caste Hindus and Muslims uniting against the Adi-Dravida workers. Once again, we see workers participating in the violent street politics that were a feature of their daily lives, and in this ignoring the calls of the nationalist politicians for nonviolence. Rather than provide a powerful contribution to the movement in 1920–22, the strike action in Madras spawned only bitterness and mutual disenchantment between nationalists and workers.

Bengal

In contrast to other regions of India, industrial production in Bengal was dominated by Europeans, both as owners and managers. The tensions that this gave rise to can be appreciated if we examine the production of jute fabric. This, the leading industry in Bengal, was situated almost entirely in the city of Calcutta and adjoining areas along the Hooghly River. The boom period for this industry was between 1890 and the mid-1920s, and huge profits were made during the First World War. By the 1920s there were about 300,000 workers in the jute mills, only a quarter of whom were Bengali. Well over a half originated from impoverished rural areas in eastern UP and Bihar (the Bhojpuri-language region), and they kept a close relationship with their home villages, often returning to them for several months each year to help with the harvest. About one-third were Muslim, the rest largely Hindu. They were divided by caste, language and religion, which provided a problem for union organisers. The workers were recruited by jobbers, known as *sardars* (leaders) in Bengal, these jobbers then controlled them in the city, determining where they would be employed and how they would be housed. Wages were extremely low, and for many of the women, particularly so, even when the industry was booming, and the workers lived in grinding poverty, with bad housing and poor health as the rule. They were mostly illiterate and untrained, having to learn how to operate their machines on the job. There was always a surplus of workers, and they were considered easily replaceable. This limited their bargaining power. The jobbers recruited from their own communities and based their control on community loyalties. The caste panchayats of the Hindu migrants and the Muslim ulama of the Jolaha migrants from UP were very important for the workers. According to Dipesh Chakrabarty: 'Community consciousness thus also gave to these socially marginal people psychological comfort and security.' The Muslims were better organised, being linked up with wealthy Muslims of Calcutta, whom they accepted as their community leaders, and who encouraged them to resist Hindu 'insults'. Many of these wealthy Muslims were non-Bengalis who were staunch pan-Islamists, and supporters of the Caliphate. Due to their influence, many Muslim workers supported the Khilafat Movement in 1920–22. They had a hazy notion of a great Sultan who was within a few day's march of Calcutta who would send his army to defeat the British. The Amir of Afghanistan had a similar reputation. There was a pronounced anti-British tinge to all this. The Bengal bhadralok had a limited grasp of the community politics of the mass of the workers and for many years failed to provide any meaningful leadership, except in mills with a mainly Bengali workforce. This began to change only during the noncooperation period.[56]

Working class militancy often expressed itself in strongly anti-British ways as the most visible adversaries of the workers were the managers and European superintendents, many of whom were Scotsmen from the Dundee area. They adopted a paternalistic attitude, representing themselves as 'fathers' and the workers as 'children' who had to be treated firmly. Their authority was expressed through their extravagant and ostentatious lifestyles. They were vigilant about their self-perceived 'dignity' and would flare up at any perceived slight. And they routinely kicked and beat workers with canes. In all these respects, their attitude had more in common with that of the Bengali zamindars than the modern British bourgeoisie. They were quick to respond to labour unrest, with violence inflicted either by themselves or their hired strongmen, and they obtained police support for this. Participation in any nationalist activity was regarded as a personal betrayal. If severely provoked, the workers could react in kind to this atmosphere of intimidation backed by violence. Such incidents occurred when a boss was seen to act particularly unfairly, for example in a way that violated the beliefs or honour of the workers, as when they insulted their religion or raped a female worker. Beating up or trashing the house of a manager provided a vivid rejection of his zamindar persona. In the pre-First World War period, strikes by workers were often very violent affairs, with personal vengeance being inflicted on notorious managers.[57] During the noncooperation period there was however remarkably little violence by workers during political strikes, which suggests that there was a change in attitude in this respect, albeit only temporary.

Between 1914 and 1920 there was relatively little working-class unrest in Bengal. During the industrial boom of the First World War, many villagers had moved to the cities in response to the strong demand for extra labour and somewhat higher pay than in rural areas. The factory-owners had made huge profits at this time by paying low prices for the raw jute and underpaying their workers. The boom ended in mid-1920 as the demand for manufactured goods slumped on global markets. It was considered in business circles to be the greatest economic crisis ever known in Calcutta and many workers found themselves in difficulty. Many new industrial concerns floated during the war had to close. The jute mills were hit particularly hard. During 1921 they operated only four days a week, and wages were cut accordingly. The depression continued through to 1922. This had an impact also on the lower-middle classes who had been employed as clerical workers in large numbers when the industry was prospering and who now lost their jobs.[58]

Before 1920, union organisation in Calcutta had been slow to develop; very few workers were members of trade unions and few strikes involved unions. There was no culture of joining voluntary associations and paying membership subscriptions, holding elections, and so on.[59] In 1920–21, there was a surge in strikes and union formation. In 1918–19 there had been fifty-one strikes in Bengal as a whole and seven new unions had been formed, while in 1920–21 there were 282 strikes and 102 new unions. Thereafter, the figures under both heads declined sharply, reviving again only in the latter part of the 1920s. Of the strikes in 1920–21, two-thirds started between October 1920 and June 1921, and union formation occurred largely during the same months. There were strikes by workers in jute mills, iron foundries, paper mills, engineering works, coal mines, the railways, the docks and on boats, gas works, printing presses, the postal service, the municipal council, and on trams and taxis. These were organised by a diverse range of groups, and in some cases more than one group vied for leadership. As it was, actual workers provided the bulk of leadership. Some historians have understood this labour unrest as being almost wholly due to the Noncooperation Movement, others claim that the impact of the noncooperators was minimal. As it was, the jobbers provided the leadership during many of these strikes and negotiated on behalf of the workers. Outsiders appear to have acted as leaders in only one-fifth of the strikes in Bengal between January 1918 and December 1921. Although in most cases these outsiders were noncooperator nationalists, others who opposed the agitation, such as moderate nationalists, social workers, and religious leaders, were also involved. It is clear from this that nationalists aligned with the Congress organisation in Bengal led by Chittaranjan Das were not the chief instigators and leaders of strikes at this time. Indeed, Gourlay estimated that only 15 per cent of union leaders were such nationalists, and they were generally in the top roles that had public visibility rather than in the lower leadership positions. This means that effective leadership was more likely to be in the hands of the workers, and particularly the jobbers.[60]

The outsiders who came to act in these roles in 1920–22 were largely members of the Bengal bhadralok or from the Muslim elites. As there was a huge cultural gap between them and the workers, the latter tended to rely on their own kind for leadership. The workers nonetheless looked up to these elites. There was a widespread feeling that people of status were best placed to intervene successfully on their behalf with the factory owners and managers. Rich people who lived, dressed, and deported themselves well were thus trusted as leaders. In turn, the elite union leaders tended to see themselves as philanthropists who were helping the poor as an act of charity. They often held that the poverty of the workers was due to their ignorance and immorality, and that if they learnt to act thriftily, work industriously and abstain from drink and other vices, they would improve their life situations. In general, they viewed the workers as being uncouth *merua* (a derogatory Bengali term for a Hindi-speaker), who were characteristically rowdy, noisy, unruly and so on. Being so culturally empowered, the union leaders tended to run each union as their personal fiefdom. Workers chose to align with a particular authority-figure in this respect.[61] Some young Bengalis who were inspired by Gandhi tried to implement a more Gandhian approach in such disputes. Nagendranath Gangopadhyay, a son-in-law of Rabindranath Tagore took the leading role in this in Calcutta, encouraged strongly by C.F. Andrews. The most active Gandhian union organiser in the Calcutta suburbs was Pandit Krishna Kumar Sastri, who was from Arrah district in Bihar. He preached Hindu-Muslim unity, forming arbitration courts and giving up liquor and toddy. This Gandhian union work contrasted strongly with the more militant tone of Khilafat and Congress leaders aligned with Chittaranjan Das who became involved in union organisation. The Khilafat leaders played the most active role in such organisation. They too preached Hindu-Muslim unity, giving up alcohol and social reform, but also stoked ill-feeling against Europeans in general. Khilafat agitators such as Muhammad Osman and Latafat Hussain organised unions and created volunteer groups among Muslim workers of Calcutta and its suburbs. In their rhetoric, they appealed strongly to Islamic values. At least forty nationalist leaders, including Chittaranjan Das, Jitendralal Banarji and Akram Khan (the Bengali Khilafat leader), were office-bearers in these unions during the Noncooperation Movement. Some bhadralok leaders who were active in the Calcutta Corporation joined the protest and set about organising workers in the tramways, engineering industries, the Electric Supply Company and the docks.[62] This meant that there was at this time a positive connection between the industrial action in Bengal and the Noncooperation and Khilafat Movement, even though the militancy would not have been so great had it not been for the economic crisis. In the words of a Christian missionary working among the poor who observed the waves of strikes in 1921: 'There is no doubt Gandhiism was the match that lit the fire, but the fuel was already there in the shape of a longstanding almost inarticulate sense of injustice among the workmen.'[63] The workers conducted their protests on their own terms and took outside assistance as and when it suited them. They were never manipulated by outsiders or submitted obediently to their direction.

According to Rajat Ray, a major target of attack was 'the interlinked complex of tea, jute, coal, oil, railway, steamer and engineering interests'.[64] Across all these industries, there was a firm resentment amongst Indian employees of white domination, with its strong racist underpinnings. Such an attitude was seen in a walk-out by 350 women workers at the Hooghly Jute Mill, Kidderpore, on 16 September 1920, after one of them was beaten by a European assistant manager. They demanded his dismissal, and this was granted next day. On 14 September 1920, workers at the Union (North) Jute Mill, Sealdah, went on strike, demanding a ten per cent wage rise. The manager dismissed all the workers, but they refused to capitulate, and were granted the pay rise and taken back on 20 September. On 5 November 1920, an itinerant maulvi, Ismail Emanuddin of Tippera, gave a sermon that exhorted Muslims to save the holy places while striking at European capitalists in India. He condemned these capitalists for taking all the profits from the jute industry and steamer business, leaving their clerks and coolies barely enough to live on. In May 1921, there was a rumour in Howrah District that boys were being kidnapped for sacrifice and burial in the foundations of the new Ludlow Jute Mills, then under construction. At that time, people were prepared to believe any iniquity of the Europeans. This led to rioting in two mills. There was a strike in the workshops of the Burma Oil Company at Chittagong in May, with a complete hartal that was called off only when the company surrendered to the workers. There was even a campaign to persuade domestic servants of Europeans to go on strike, leave their service, and boycott them socially. This had mixed success, but it alarmed the Europeans. In May the servants of Europeans at Akhaura in Tippera went on strike for a short time after a jute agency assistant slapped an employee. In much of this, there was a clear spirit of assertion against the racist domination of Europeans, and in the circumstances of the day this had obvious nationalist implications.[65]

This was seen also in union-inspired agitation in the coalfields of West Bengal. The workers there were mainly of adivasi origin. After the AITUC was established in 1920, a deputation was sent to these coalfields to form labour associations at Raniganj and Barakar in Burdwan District. They were helped in this by rich Marwaris who wanted to wrest control of the mines from their European owners. A bank was opened to promote Indian enterprise in the mines. Two swamis, Biswanand and Darsananand, took the lead in this work, stoking up strong racial animosity against Europeans in meetings there. Although Darsananand demanded equity between rich and poor and a large increase in wages, he also said in a speech at a meeting that the real object of the dispute was to replace European with Indian control of collieries. He advised workers to leave the European-controlled mines and work at Indian-owned ones. This resulted in strikes at eleven European-run mines involving 5,300 workers. In Ray's words: 'The strikers were tribals and low caste villagers who looked upon Darsananand as a god come to earth who would bring blindness, barrenness of women and flooding of pits unless they followed his instructions.' Chittaranjan Das visited Raniganj in July 1921 and exhorted the people of the mining area to oppose the European companies. There was also a strike at Burn & Company's Kulti Iron Works, directed by unionists who had been similarly deputed by the Congress.[66]

There was no such Congress-led instigation when the tram drivers and conductors of Calcutta went on strike from 1 October 1920. These workers had been petitioning the management from July and held a series of meetings purely on their own initiative in the previous month before acting. Only after the strike had started did some Congress activists and other outsiders become involved when the workers asked them to help negotiate with the management, which led to a settlement. A new union committee was then established with N.C. Chunder – a noncooperator – as treasurer, and N.C. Sen – a Congress nationalist who refused to give up his legal practice – as president. The secretary was an outsider with no political affiliation. These leaders were caught unawares when the tram workers demanded that there be further action in January 1921. They urged the workers to negotiate rather than strike, but were ignored by the workers, who went on strike. On 18 February, some workers attacked trams being driven by Anglo-Indians and tried to occupy the Kalighat tram depot. The police intervened to stop this, leading to a fracas in which a policeman shot dead one worker and injured two others. A meeting was quickly convened on the following day and the workers agreed to resume work while an enquiry was held into their grievance. In this instance, the violence appears to have put the workers in the wrong, and they promptly agreed to an enquiry without any guarantee that they would gain any benefit. With no concessions coming, they decided on strike action in August 1921. They determined to launch it in September, against the advice of Chunder and Sen. It was called off just before it was due to begin, much to the anger of many of the tram workers. At a meeting later in September, N.C. Sen was demoted to vice-president. There was a split in the union over this that lasted until January 1922. A strike went ahead in October to November 1921. All of this demonstrates that the noncooperators were hardly in control of industrial action throughout eastern India. In this instance, strikes and meetings were organised independently of them by union members, and the members were the ones ultimately in control.[67]

There were also strikes on the railways of eastern India that were linked to the Noncooperation Movement. Railway employment was notorious for its discriminatory and racist practices, with European and Anglo-Indian managers who lived in segregated sections of the railway colonies. Europeans had a monopoly of the top jobs, and Anglo-Indians of intermediary positions. Indian workers, or 'coolies', were employed in the lower-grade jobs. They were controlled in often violent ways. Pay was highly discriminatory, and even the most skilled 'native' Indians could not rise far in the organisation. In the words of Chandavarkar: 'The nationalism of railway workers was nourished by racial conflicts between Europeans and Eurasian [Anglo-Indian] foremen and Indian workers.'[68] The European and Anglo-Indian employees had taken the initiative in forming a union for the East Indian Railway in 1919 – the Railway Workers Association (RWA) – and branches were opened over the following year. Although this union was dominated by the European and Anglo-Indian railwaymen, Indians provided the bulk of the membership. Differences between the Europeans and Anglo-Indian and Indian employees surfaced in August 1920, as the former were not committed to having a parity in wages between the different ethnic groups. The former felt that Indians were swamping their union. A separate union for Indian railway workers was formed in October 1920 – the Eastern Railway Indian Employees Association, followed in November 1920 by the Bengal-Nagpur Railway Indian Labour Union (BNRILU) based at Kharagpur, a major railway junction in Medinipur District. In May 1921, the East Indian Railway Indian Labour Union and the Assam-Bengal Railway Employees Union (ABREU) were established. Outsiders – particularly noncooperators – were prominent in the formation and management of some of these unions, and there was firm nationalist inspiration behind their formation. The BNRILU, in particular, was formed through the initiative of noncooperators. Gandhi stopped at Kharagpur in September 1920 and advised the railway workers to form a separate union for Indian workers. He sent N.S. Marathe to encourage this, and some workers then went to Calcutta to ask for help from the noncooperators. It was then decided to form an All-India Railway Labour Union (AIRLU), with the Kharagpur union as its first branch. Chittaranjan Das chaired the advisory board for this body, and N.C. Sen was elected president. These unions satisfied a firmly held belief among Indian railwaymen that the European and Anglo-Indian dominated RWA was not representing them adequately. The new unions of Indian workers demanded parity in wages. The RWA still contained Indian workers, however. In February 1921, the RWA decided to call a strike, and this was supported by AIRLU on condition that RWA committed itself to an end to wage discrimination along ethnic lines. The RWA refused to accept this and called the strike off after a day. The AIRLU then decided to break all links with RWA. RWA subsequently declined in significance with the assertion of the Indian unions. This history reveals that the grievances were formulated in the first place by the workers themselves, and noncooperators only became involved in response. The emergence of unions along ethnic lines was caused above all by the racism of the Europeans and Anglo-Indians – the Indian unions were prepared to cooperate with them if they committed themselves to anti-discriminatory policies.[69]

On 24 May 1921, the workers of the newly-formed Assam-Bengal Railway Employees Union went on strike in sympathy with the tea plantation workers who were marooned at Chandpur and had been beaten up by Gurkhas on 21 May (this will be examined in more detail in the next chapter). The railway workers at Chandpur had wanted to strike at once after witnessing the brutality against the tea workers and had sent a deputation to the headquarters of their union at Chittagong to press for this. The president of the ABREU was the leading noncooperator, J.M. Sengupta, and he and the other office-holders tried to dissuade them from such action, arguing that it was a purely 'political' affair. Sengupta agreed however to visit Chandpur to assess the situation for himself, and after meetings there agreed to support the strike. He announced that the strike was a protest at the treatment of the tea labourers, and he demanded that the government facilitate their travel back home. The ABREU executive in Chittagong were not happy about this, and only accepted the decision reluctantly after several meetings. The steamship workers of this region also struck at the same time and for the same reason. Chittaranjan Das rushed by boat to Chandpur and took charge personally. He stated that the strikes were 'national' in character. There were calls for a national steamer service to replace the European companies. Both strikes soon centred around demands for higher wages and better working conditions. In a letter to the managers in late May, Sengupta argued that the strike was over wages and working conditions and not a political strike. He claimed that the executive had been on the point of advising the workers to strike on these issues when the Chandpur incident occurred, which precipitated it all. Talks to resolve these issues were held but failed to lead to any settlement. In July, railway workers were forcibly evicted from their quarters and new workers brought in, causing a riot when police escorting a group who had returned to work were attacked by those still on strike. There is evidence that Sengupta had instigated this. Armed police were called in to quell the disturbance. Those who remained on strike were fed and housed by the noncooperators, allowing them to sustain their action. In the case of the steamship workers, it was only when new crews were brought from Calcutta that they began to drift back to work, fearing the loss of their jobs. By mid-July their strike was effectively at an end. The railway workers continued their strike while negotiations continued, with C.F. Andrews conducting talks on behalf of the workers. Chittaranjan Das and the noncooperators encouraged them not to compromise, and he even stated in June that the strike was largely in support of the Noncooperation Movement rather than over working conditions. By the end of August, however, the strike funds were exhausted. Gandhi met the strikers on a visit to Chittagong on 31 August and advised them to take up weaving and spinning to support themselves rather than rely on Congress. This unhelpful advice was the final straw for the railway workers, and the strike collapsed in September. In general, these strikes were sustained so long because there were substantial grievances about pay and conditions, though the financial support and moral encouragement for the workers by the Bengal Congress leaders also played its part.[70]

This strike brought out the profound differences that existed between Gandhi and Chittaranjan Das over Congress support for political action by industrial workers. Writing in *Young India* on 15 June 1921, Gandhi condemned the Bengal government for its 'callous indifference' towards the tea garden labourers, but deplored the sympathetic strike by the railway and steamship workers.[71] This directive was in direct contradiction to Das, who was actively encouraging and organising the strikes in the area at that time. He and his followers were infuriated by this statement by Gandhi and considered breaking with him entirely. They were restrained from this by fear that the movement would in such a case inevitably become more violent.[72]

The atmosphere of the time, with widespread nationalist agitation, certainly fuelled working-class militancy in eastern India. Workers often shouted nationalist slogans during their industrial action, and they participated widely in nationalist activities. Many became Congress volunteers, playing a significant role in the successful boycott of the Prince of Wales on his visit to Calcutta in November 1921. Muslim workers were to the fore in all this, mobilised through their sympathy for the Khilafat cause. Although this boycott was almost entirely nonviolent, there was one exception to this rule when a jute mill manager in Howrah was attacked and badly injured after he deducted the pay of workers who had taken part in the protest.[73] The support by these workers for the campaign continued into 1922 – of the 349 volunteers arrested in Calcutta in the first week of January 1922, no less than 123, or 35 per cent were mill hands.[74] The government accused the nationalist leaders of paying mill hands to court arrest. In fact, they appear to have joined the protest largely on their own initiative. Sarkar quotes an elderly mill worker who stated that he had been driven solely by his conscience in organising support amongst his fellow workers for the hartal on 24 December.[75] Although both Gandhi and Andrews feared that the industrial strikes in support of Noncooperation would become increasingly violent over time, this did not in fact prove to be the case.[76] Violence was very much the exception in these strikes. I have come across only four such instances in the literature that I have examined and have documented above – at the Kalighat tram depot in February 1921, at the Ludlow Jute Mills in May 1921, at the Assam-Bengal railway quarters in July 1921, and at a Howrah Mill in November 1921. Nobody was killed by the workers, though one European manager was badly injured, and in retaliation one worker was killed and two injured by police. This was hardly a high level of violence. The large majority of strikes were conducted without any accompanying violence – a remarkable record, given that such disputes had in the past often been very turbulent affairs, and we have seen already that there was considerable violence in Bombay and Madras at this time. The literature is silent as to why this was the case, but it is most likely that the strong stress on nonviolence and active work by nationalists and Khilafatists committed to this principal was conducive to a largely nonviolent outcome.

We may note in this context that young Bhadralok radicals had for the past two decades been active patrons of gymnasiums, which – as Chandavarkar has reported for Bombay – could provide a meeting place between local strongmen and more elite patrons.[77] While during the Swadeshi Movement these radicals had had almost no rapport with the lower classes, a decade of organisation had allowed for greater strength in this respect. Although these radicals were earlier invested in violent revolutionary work, we know that many were prepared to give nonviolent methods a try in 1920–22. Chittaranjan Das, for example, was a founder-member of the revolutionary organisation, the Anushilan Samiti, and he was known at this time to have an understanding with the other main group, Jugantar. Young Bhadralok nationalists of these groups gained a reputation during these years for being among the most dynamic and selfless nationalists in the Congress organisation in the province. In 1920–22, they threw their support behind Gandhi and his methods.[78]

The nationalist leaders in Bengal were in general far more sympathetic to the idea of linking strike action by workers to the political struggle. At the Nagpur Congress of December 1920, Chittaranjan Das had persuaded the Congress to form a 'labour sub-committee' that would campaign for Congress to adopt programmes that benefitted workers, and which would also encourage workers to join the Congress. Das was a member of this committee.[79] He, more than any other provincial Congress leader, understood the strategic power of strike action in support of the cause. He was not overly concerned if there was some collateral violence, so long as it did not get out of hand. As it was, following this approach, the Congress in Bengal was able to ensure that there was considerably less violence in strikes in their province at that time, in comparison to Bombay and Madras. Gandhi, however, did all he could to counter this strategy, particularly when he visited Bengal in 1921 and told the workers that they had no business striking in support of the movement. In this, he failed to appreciate how much he was undermining the struggle in that province.

Conclusion

The strikes in Bombay, Madras and Bengal were by no means the only ones during this period. Sarkar mentions strikes also in the woollen mills of Kanpur (UP), on the railway at Jamalpur (Bihar), in the cotton mills at Sholapur (Maharashtra) and Ahmedabad (Gujarat) that occurred in 1919 and 1920. He sees these as creating a popular pressure that fed into the Noncooperation Movement that followed these strikes. Once the movement was fully underway, there was a wave of industrial action. During 1921, there were 396 strikes throughout India, involving 600,351 workers and a loss of 6,994,426 working days.[80]

Notable among these was the strike by workers at the Tata steel works at Jamshedpur in southern Bihar. Working conditions for the Indian employees were extremely bad. The work was dangerous, with frequent accidents. Living conditions were terrible, with poor sanitation and little provision of education. The company owned all the houses in the town and could evict anyone it wanted. Five hundred European and American supervisors were employed there in 1921.

They had permanent contracts – while Indians in the same positions had only temporary ones – and they also received higher wages. They determined whether unskilled workers remained in the positions or not, and what each of them was paid. They often beat workers to force them to work harder or stay overtime. They could dismiss them without prior notice. About 30,000 Indian workers went on strike for the first time in February 1920, demanding higher wages, regular increments, adequate housing, leave without pay and compensation for workers who died at work. Tata cut the water supply and withheld foodgrains to get them back to work. The workers had started the strike but approached outsiders to obtain negotiators and legal advisors. A Congressman, S.N. Haldar, came from Calcutta and agreed to lead the strike and establish a union, the Jamshedpur Labour Association (JLA). The Tatas said they were prepared to recognise this union so long as it cooperated with the management. Teja Singh, a leader amongst the workers who was a graduate, claimed to have met Gandhi in connection with the strike, but Gandhi merely advised the Jamshedpur workers to 'suffer in silence for Indian industry'. Other nationalists advised the workers to scale down their demands and resume work while negotiations continued. At a meeting, the workers shouted their disapproval at both the managers and the Congress leaders, while cheering their own leaders, such as Teja Singh. The management called in the army, with over a thousand troops being brought to intimidate the workers. Meetings on company property were banned – which meant in effect the whole town. Gurkhas stationed in the factory threw brickbats at workers who were returning from meetings to provoke them to violence. The strikers refused to retaliate in kind, maintaining their nonviolence. After three weeks, the management brought blackleg labourers into the factory with the help of the police and army. Protesting workers were fired on, with five being killed and ten seriously injured. This caused the workers to waver. The management then announced that it would give some concessions if they resumed work on 20 March, and it was agreed that the strike would be called off. In the following month, however, the management then largely reneged on the agreement, and sacked the strike leaders. The strike had been broken with the help of the British, who had provided the police and army to intimidate the workers.[81]

As in many other cases from this period, industrial workers who had hoped for firm support from nationalist leaders in their struggles felt let down. This was less the case in Bengal than in Bombay, Madras and Jamshedpur, for Chittaranjan Das and other leading figures in the Bengal Congress were prepared to support strikes that put pressure on the British. In this, they proved more radical than the leaders elsewhere.

To what extent was Gandhi's strategy justified this time? Was he right to refuse to allow political strikes in support of noncooperation? He had three main reasons for his stance. First, he did not trust the workers to remain nonviolent, so that their support was likely to be counterproductive. Second, he believed that workers were often manipulated by politicians against their best interests. Third, he held that the struggle was against the British, and that political strikes would alienate Indian capitalists and thus divide the movement. We may examine each of these arguments in turn.

Gandhi was not confident that the workers could or would remain orderly and nonviolent when brought out in support of political causes. His experience of the riots by Ahmedabad workers in April 1919 – a class that he believed – mistakenly – had grasped his message when he had led their strike in the previous year – showed, for him at least, that they could not be trusted in this respect. As argued in the section on Bombay, the culture of the newly emerging working-class of the big cities was one that emphasised male virility and honour, and which valorised the power of the local boss. Chandavarkar has noted that the solidarity of the emerging working class was rooted as much in the neighbourhood and local caste or religious groups as in the workplace. Employment in the mills was uncertain, and people depended on their jobbers and neighbourhood connections and protectors – such as the *dadas* – for security. Living and working together did not create working class solidarity as such – the patterns of association that emerged in the city could also divide people.[82] In such a world, it was seen to be legitimate to settle differences violently in street confrontations and even battles. Gandhi might not have fully understood how such a local politics operated, but he was witness to the results when workers were led by neighbourhood leaders in mass attacks on perceived enemies. As we have seen in the section of this chapter on Congress and the workers, Gandhi believed that such violence would diminish once workers were better educated and had a better grasp of political affairs, so that they gained a sense of ownership over industry. Against this, it can be argued that workers can be very well educated and still violent. Gandhi would have done better to have tried to understand why in some situations workers resorted to violence while in others they did not. The key elements in this respect were the people who had authority on factory floors and in the slums and chawls – people such as jobbers, local strongmen, local politicians, or religious figures. When people of this sort who already commanded the respect of the workers encouraged a violent response, the workers were likely to respond in kind. When they decided that a nonviolent reaction was more advisable, they were quite capable of enforcing nonviolent discipline – even in the face of police violence – and to sustain a peaceful protest. Leaders in such a case understand that nonviolence wrong-foots opponents by putting pressure on them to compromise in a reasonable manner and they make sure that their followers act peacefully. This was the case during the Bombay strike of January 1919, when the jobbers maintained this sort of control and thereby provided an opening for the British to intervene in favour of the workers. It is likely that this was generally the case in Bengal in 1920–22, where working class participation was noticeably less violent than in other parts of India.

Another concern of Gandhi was that the workers were in many cases being led by nationalist firebrands who did not have their real interests at heart. His belief in this respect was reinforced by what his close friend C.F. Andrews observed during the strikes in Bengal in 1921. Andrews had striven for many years to alleviate the conditions of workers throughout the British Empire, and he was carrying out such work in Bengal at that time.[83] In a polemical book that he wrote after his experience there, he accused the nationalist politicians of inciting 'the poor in their distress into meaningless strikes'. He had witnessed strike after strike that had brought nothing but misery and starvation to the workers.

> Therefore, I say most earnestly to you who are popular leaders, if you will bear with me; it will not do merely to excite the poor to strike. It will not do indiscriminately to use these strikes (in which the poor are the

chief sufferers) as a weapon to bring government to its knees. Mahatma Gandhi is the friend of the poor. He himself is the poorest of the poor and he knows that in such strikes the poor suffer most of all.[84]

Although Andrews was a firm supporter of the Indian nationalist movement, he did not believe that this was an appropriate way to take it forward. He felt that while middle class leaders could afford some privations for the cause, the poor were already on the edge, and would certainly suffer a lot more. Without denying the strength of his feeling in this respect, and even a certain validity to what he was saying, we may note that large numbers of the poor and oppressed throughout India felt at this time that it was worth their while to come out in protest, even if it might mean privation and hunger for a period. Clearly, they believed that there was more to be gained in the long term by taking such action. In most cases we have examined in this chapter, the workers – including the jobbers – took the initiative to strike and try to link their action to the nationalist cause. The real problem was, perhaps, that they were let down by leaders who failed to give them adequate support and press the advantage against the British at critical junctures. Chittaranjan Das certainly felt this about Gandhi – he was furious when Gandhi refused to support the strikes in East Bengal in mid-1921, in effect abandoning the workers who had sacrificed so much.

Thirdly, there was Gandhi's belief that as many capitalists were Indian, political strikes would set Indian against Indian, weakening the wider nationalist struggle. Indian capitalists were major donors to the Congress, and any loss of their support in this respect would undermine the ability of the organisation to carry on its work. In this, Gandhi had a hard-headed understanding of the need for finance in political campaigns. This was not however how many workers understood the matter – for them the Indian capitalists were a part of the problem of imperial rule. They experienced this each day in their workplaces, as they were bossed around by white supervisors and treated with racist condescension by white bosses, even in Indian-owned factories. They saw how white employees were paid far more than they were, even for carrying out the same functions. In the streets around their slum homes and chawls, they had to put up with daily oppression from the police led by white officers. Indeed, it was in the street that they experienced the state most directly. The police spied on their meetings, prosecuting people for using seditious language. The experience of the imperial state was particularly harsh during strikes, as the police were deployed in breaking up meetings and stopping picketing at factory gates.[85] For the workers, fighting the bosses – whether British or Indian – was to take on the imperial system that underpinned their power. They clearly saw their fight as a nationalist one. In refusing to acknowledge this, Gandhi failed to mobilise a group whose active support would have given much greater strength to his movement. By acting as he did, he was unable to gain the confidence of the workers – particularly in Bombay and Madras – which would have provided an opening for a more sustained and possibly effective application of his nonviolent principles by workers. The success of his struggle in South Africa had depended very centrally on the strike by the miners that he led personally in 1913. In this case, he had ensured that there was no violence on the part of the workers, to the eventual benefit of the cause. Seven years on, he backed away from engaging wholeheartedly with such a potent force.

5

TERRAINS OF RESISTANCE 1920–22

The Noncooperation Movement incorporated varied regional and local campaigns that challenged a range of dominant groups, from the imperial rulers, to European business interests, to various Indian elites allied to the imperial state. These campaigns braided into the wider movement. As Ravinder Kumar has pointed out: '…the agitations led by the Mahatma rested upon loose alliances reflecting the interests and aspirations of a large number of classes and communities'.[1] These protests were on the whole nonviolent. In this, we can discern eight major terrains of resistance, each of which involved a distinct relationship of domination and subordination. These were:

1. Anti-landlord movements involving refusal of rent and other impositions.
2. Industrial grievances of the working classes against British and Indian capitalists.
3. Struggles to wrest control of local government from the British.
4. Refusal to pay land tax imposed by the British and taxes imposed by local authorities.
5. Protest by peasants having their land appropriated by the state for capitalist development projects.
6. Protests against British indigo and tea planters.
7. Protests by users of forest produce against imperial forest officials.

8. Struggle for popular control of religious institutions waged against priests imposed by the imperial state.

Of these conflicts, we have already in Chapter 3 examined that of the anti-landlord struggles, and in Chapter 4 that of the industrial working classes. In this chapter, we shall look at major protests from different regions of India under each of the six other heads.

Local self-rule

From the start in 1885, those associated with the Indian National Congress had sought to gain control over local governments – notably the municipalities of several cities – to implement their agendas. Municipal politics provided a crucial arena in which would-be nationalist politicians honed their skills. They could exercise meaningful levels of power on such bodies.[2] This agenda continued to be promoted during noncooperation, despite the boycott of other forms of representative institutions. In Ahmedabad, for example, the municipality had been granted a wider franchise and the right to elect its own president in 1919, and Vallabhbhai Patel was voted into this position by nationalists who gained control as a result. In February 1921, the municipality voted to refuse government grants for schools, to boycott government educational institutions, and establish national ones instead. It was eventually suspended by the government in 1922.[3] Similarly, Congress gained control of the Surat municipality at this time and refused all government supervision and finance. It handed over Rs 40,000 from its funds to the national schools. The government similarly suspended it, after which the Congress launched a campaign to refuse to pay all municipal taxes, which effectively paralysed the municipality for several years.[4] In Nadiad in Kheda District, where no less than a quarter of the entire population of the town enrolled as Congress members at this time, the nationalist-controlled municipality refused government grants and raised its own subscriptions for nationalist schools outside government control. These funds proved inadequate for the purpose of running the two high schools and nine primary schools that had been declared 'national', and the Congress president of the municipality, Gokaldas Talati, then toured other parts of India appealing for money to pay the teachers. In the end, Talati had to admit defeat and advised the council to accept government grants once more. Seventeen councillors resigned in protest, and the people of the town refused to pay their municipal taxes. In 1922, the government annulled the council and ordered fresh elections.[5]

These campaigns provided useful experience for nationalists in using constitutional procedures to implement their programme. They also, however, demonstrated that although greater representation had been granted at this level there were still clear limits on any effective independence.

No-Tax Campaigns

Land tax

It was reported in July 1921 that there was a widespread belief in Bombay Presidency that when the 'Indian Parliament' convened in Ahmedabad at the end of that year (e.g. the annual session of the Congress) the peasants would not have to pay any land tax.[6] As it was, there was little of such protest in the presidency as a whole in 1921–22. Certain areas in Gujarat and Karnataka provided exceptions to this rule. In rural Gujarat, the Patidars of Kheda and Surat Districts supported Noncooperation with great fervour, with widespread take-up of the constructive programme and the establishment of national schools in villages. They were eager to launch civil disobedience in support of the cause by refusing to pay their land tax, but Gandhi was not prepared initially to sanction such an escalation of the struggle. It was only later in 1921 that he agreed to launch this campaign in one sub-district of Surat, Bardoli. We have examined the reasons for his choice of this area in Chapter 2. As it was, this campaign was not allowed to begin despite meticulous preparation, and it was Kheda rather than Bardoli that experienced such a protest, with the peasants in a number of villages refusing their land taxes from December 1921 onwards. They all paid up as soon as Gandhi suspended civil disobedience in February 1922.[7] Elsewhere in Bombay Presidency, there was strong support for Noncooperation in the more prosperous districts of Belgaum and Dharwar in Karnataka. The main group involved was that of the relatively well-to-do Lingayats of this region, who were both landowning peasants and traders. In some sub-districts they threatened to withhold their land taxes from as early as October 1920. In Kanara District, many village officials responded to the call by resigning from government service, and preparations were made for a no-tax campaign in 1921 that was supported most strongly by prosperous Havig cultivators of this area. Protests continued in Kanara into the middle of 1922.[8]

The coastal districts of the Andhra region in South India saw similar mobilisation in 1921–22. A new Andhra Pradesh Congress Committee (APCC) was established at the start of 1921, with Kondu Venkatappayya as its first President. A Brahman of Guntur, he had been one of Gandhi's first recruits in this area. This was a fertile region where, as in Bombay Presidency, most of the peasants paid their substantial land taxes direct to the British. The dominant Kamma, Reddy and Raju peasants were to the fore in the movement. The peasants of Pedanandipad – a large village of Guntur District – decided that they would contribute to the cause by refusing to pay their land tax and other rural cesses to the British. Their main grievance was that an already-high land tax was being supplemented with extra cesses – particularly a tax on water use that affected all farmers, even those who did not use water from government irrigation works. A middle-level peasant and rice miller who worked for the Congress called Parvataneni Chowdary acted as leader in this. He had already gained a reputation and prestige in the locality by performing Hindu religious stories (*harikatha*). Once the richer farmers were committed, poorer peasants joined the struggle, so that there was strong class unity. The campaign soon expanded to some fifty villages around Pedanandipudu. Although such civil disobedience was not on Gandhi's agenda, at that juncture, the local leaders put such pressure on the Guntur District Congress Committee that it agreed to support a no-tax campaign in mid-June 1921. It requested that the AICC accept this at its next meeting, which was held at the end of July. It would however not agree to such a protest before Gandhi had first launched a no-tax campaign in Gujarat. Throughout 1921, Venkatappayya continued to put strong pressure on the all-India leaders to agree to sanction it formally. Meanwhile, the villagers were already refusing their tax-demands, and when the APCC met in early January 1922, three thousand peasants turned up and made such a clamour that the committee agreed to sanction their campaign. It ruled that each district Congress committee could lead its own no-tax movement if it felt the conditions were right. The campaign was to include non-payment of land tax, water rates and income tax. In addition, many village officials resigned their posts. The movement was strongest in Guntur, Kistna and Godavari Districts. This led to a dramatic decline in government collections, particularly in Guntur District, where up to a hundred villages were now refusing their taxes. In January 1922, only Rs 400,000 of the Rs 1,473,000 due from land tax of this region had been collected.[9]

Gandhi, however, had reservations about this campaign. Writing to Venkatappayya in January 1922, he acknowledged the strength of protest in the region, but informed him that they were not yet ready for tax refusal, as untouchability was rife in the area, not enough khadi was being produced, and an insufficient proportion of the population was 'accustomed to ways of non-violence'. They should refrain from any such a campaign 'till the masses have undergone the necessary discipline and self-purification'. Otherwise, such protest 'will be not *civil* but *criminal* and will, therefore, render us unfit to conduct our own affairs as an orderly civilised nation'.[10] Venkatappayya replied that the campaign was already well advanced in Guntur District, and that large numbers of untouchables had in fact joined the movement, and that the practice of untouchability was disappearing. Also, self-sufficiency in khadi was well advanced. Property was being attached forcibly in lieu of tax, the military had been touring the area in armoured cars and lorries, local leaders were being arrested, and still the people were submitting peacefully.[11] In an article in *Young India* towards the end of January, Gandhi reiterated once more that 'civil non-payment of taxes is a privilege capable of being exercised only after rigorous training.' It was the very last stage in Noncooperation. He nonetheless acknowledged that such a campaign was already at an intensive stage in Andhra and said that if the leaders there were convinced that the people were adequately prepared then he did not wish to dampen their ardour. He concluded: 'God bless the brave Andhras.'[12] The Guntur District Congress Committee met on 27 January 1922, along with leading peasants from different talukas. The peasants reported that the campaign was thriving despite government coercion, though they accepted that they had not fulfilled all of Gandhi's conditions adequately, e.g. in removing untouchability. Also, in 'one or two cases' there had been a failure to conform rigorously to the principles of nonviolence. They also noted that the Madras authorities were stepping up their repression, with emergency legislation to hasten the process of confiscation of property and land. The authorities had found that when such land was put up for auction, no one would bid for it out of solidarity with the movement. The proposed solution was to give it away to members of the depressed classes. Commenting on this on 29 January, Gandhi assured the people of Andhra that even if they lost their land and property, they would get it back once swaraj was gained. He condemned the way that the depressed classes (e.g. the untouchables) were being used 'as pawns in the game by the government'. He exhorted the cultivators of Andhra to put their faith in God and remain firm, even if the military fired on them. 'The Andhras are a virile people proud of their traditions. They are a devoutly religious people capable of sacrifice. Much is expected of them by the country and I have every hope that they will not be found wanting.'[13] The campaign was however called off by the APCC on 10 February after civil disobedience in general was halted by Congress in response to Chauri Chaura. The British claimed that the peasants of Andhra were already by then having second thoughts about their opposition, and there is evidence that the arrest of the most inspirational of the village leaders was undermining the determination of many peasants. Nonetheless, it was the decision by Congress at the all-India level that caused the movement there to quickly disintegrate.[14]

Local Taxes

In some cases, the taxes that were refused were those levied by local authorities. The most impressive of these campaigns occurred in Medinipur District, West Bengal. This was a zamindari area in which landlords collected rents from tenants. Unlike in much of East Bengal, Awadh and Bihar, most tenants in this district enjoyed security of tenure. Many – known as *jotedars* – rented large amounts of cultivable land. In some cases they farmed this land personally, as well as with hired labour, and were relatively prosperous. They also controlled the local market in agrarian produce, and also sub-rented much of their land to poor sharecroppers, known as *bhagchasis*. In Medinipur, the majority of both the *jotedars* and *bhagchasis* were members of the Mahisya caste. This was the most numerous Hindu caste in Bengal with a population in 1921 of 2,210,684. Some were employed in trade and manufacture, with a good number living in Calcutta by the early twentieth century. As with the Patidars of Gujarat, there was a stratum in this caste that, by the early twentieth century, was educated in English. They sought positions in respectable professions, but often found it hard to compete with the entrenched bhadralok. In Medinipur, the Mahisyas made up almost one-third of the population of the whole district, but about three-quarters of the population in the eastern areas around Kanthi that provided the mass support for the no-tax campaign of 1921–2. The Mahisyas had exerted a lot of energy in previous decades in claiming to be a respectable caste – something not recognised by Brahmans. They had a caste association, the Bangiya Mahisya Sabha, and a caste journal, *Mahisya Samaj*, that praised agriculture as a worthy way of life and held that it was wrong to stigmatise manual labour, as the high castes often did. They asserted that they nurtured society, unlike the parasitical bhadralok of Bengal. In all this, they were ideal recruits for the Gandhian movement.[15]

The Swadeshi Movement had had relatively little impact on the masses of Medinipur, though there were revolutionary terrorist cells active there whose members were largely from the bhadralok. The elites of the area were involved in a protest that was launched in response to an announcement by the British in 1915 that the district would be partitioned as it was unmanageably large. Kanthi would become a separate district. Some Congress leaders claimed that the measure was designed to undermine the nationalists, as with Curzon's partition of 1905, and they called for a sustained agitation against the proposal. Between 1915 and 1919, the campaign was confined largely to the elite method of petitioning the government. It was only with noncooperation that genuine mass mobilisation began in the district. The main leader who emerged in 1920 was a Mahisya lawyer called Birendranath Sasmal. Born in 1881, he was from a rich landowning family of Kanthi that had embraced English education from the mid-nineteenth century and had pursued professional careers. The family was known for its philanthropy. He was educated in Calcutta and was the first Mahishya to travel to England and qualify as a barrister; arriving back in 1904 and he practised initially in the Calcutta High Court, and then from 1907 in Medinipur, where he built an extensive practice. Sasmal developed an interest in nationalist politics during the Swadeshi Movement and served on local government institutions in the district. He gained a reputation through his social work in the area between 1913 and 1920, particularly during floods when he single-handedly organised relief works, and he wrote articles in local newspapers that revealed the suffering of the people. This brought him into direct confrontation with the local administration, as it had been tardy in providing relief, particularly during the floods of 1913 and 1920. He asserted that the British had lost their moral right to rule. A particularly direct and emotional speaker, he was able to sway an audience to marked effect. Sasmal boycotted the Bengal council elections of 1920, following the Congress decision in this respect. He enjoyed strong support from Chittaranjan Das, who was then forging links with local activists in building a campaign that reached all parts of Bengal, and in July 1921 was appointed the secretary of the Bengal Provincial Congress Committee. In early 1921 he gave up his legal practice to focus on organising the movement in Medinipur. Some lawyers and teachers of the district resigned their positions to join the movement. Many young people and students became volunteers and toured the villages to spread the message of Noncooperation. There was widespread implementation of Gandhian constructive work. The Congress workers told the villagers that the British were responsible for ruining local industries and for the huge price rises of recent years, and swaraj was the answer. These appeals had a powerful impact in the district.[16]

The issue that soon became the focus for the campaign was the Bengal Village Self-Government Act of 1919 that established local union boards with nine members – six elected and three nominated. The British Divisional Commissioner and District Magistrate had ultimate control over the boards, being able to annul any measures that they disagreed with and order new elections to the boards at any time. The boards were to be responsible for sanitation and water supply. They had to maintain local roads, bridges and waterways, and could start medical dispensaries; they were meant to promote cottage industries, were required to pay the salaries of village watchmen (*chaukidars*) who were attached to local police stations. The watchmen, as government employees, had to report on the movement of 'bad characters' in an area and could arrest those committing offences. The boards were required to raise money for all of this through taxes imposed on property owners or occupiers of buildings to a maximum of Rs 84. This meant that local taxes were increased significantly. Those who failed to pay the tax were liable to have property confiscated. As it was, the funds available through local taxes were inadequate for any meaningful local work. Most of the sums went on paying staff salaries, leaving very little for any welfare work. In general, the act gave an appearance that the government was supporting local development while providing insufficient funding to facilitate this in practice.[17]

The boards came into existence in Medinipur in April 1921. Initially, the people of the area were positive about them, hoping they would alleviate some local problems. However, once the tax arrangements became known there was immediate protest, as they were already having problems paying existing taxes. Many petitions were sent demanding that the measure be revoked. In some places there was violence – in a village in Ramnagar Thana of Kanthi the houses of two union board members were burnt down. Sasmal had not initially wanted to take this issue up, but the discontent forced his hand. He requested that Gandhi allow a campaign of civil disobedience against the union board. Gandhi refused to provide All India Congress Committee backing for this on the grounds that the technique for such a campaign was complex and subtle, and he himself wanted to experiment with applying it. He told Sasmal that he could start the movement on his own initiative, so Sasmal went ahead without securing the permission of the AICC. He launched the campaign by asserting that the poor were being taxed in oppressive ways and the extra demands would make the people more vulnerable to bad harvests. Arguing that new taxes were being imposed on a zamindari area, he said that this went against the spirit of the permanent settlement of 1793. As a lawyer, Sasmal's argument had considerable force. He maintained that the poor health and high death rates of the people were not caused so much by poor sanitation as by poverty and starvation, and ridiculed the idea that people should be made to pay for privies. In one speech, he claimed that 'the establishment of union boards would not only destroy the villagers' traditional right to settle their internal affairs at the level of the village and on their own initiative… [it would] …intrude into the privacy of their family life'. The government, he asserted, would use the village watchmen to snoop on them and collect information about all that was going on in the villages. He opposed the 'evil design to modernise our village social life which is already in a process of disintegration'. In this way, Sasmal and his fellow Congress activists built a strong movement. Without their leadership, the protest would not have been as effective. Sasmal was widely respected as being a person of good family and wealth, with a lucrative legal practice in Calcutta that he had given up to serve the people. People had great trust in him. Other Congress leaders of this area also sacrificed their jobs, such as teaching in schools and colleges, to lead the movement.[18]

The problem was essentially a sectional issue of the dominant peasantry, as it was the control of the upper strata of cultivators over the internal affairs of the villages that was being threatened above all. Nonetheless, a broad range of peasant classes supported the campaign. Its anti-British aspect helped here. The poor crops of the 1920–21 season also meant that the tax was widely resented. There was accordingly a wide-scale refusal to pay the union board tax. By May 1921, most presidents and members of the union boards had resigned, and those who initially hesitated were subjected to much pressure, including social and economic boycott, and soon they mostly came around too. There was a particularly strong social boycott of Krishnananda Das, the Panskura union board president, after he helped the police to attach property. He was branded a 'traitor'. Posters were put up in Kanthi town threatening the remaining union board members with sanctions if they insisted on collection. The movement was strongest in Kanthi sub-division, with very little of the tax being collected there. Many people enrolled as Congress volunteers and were trained in campaign organising. They collected donations and subscriptions, and organised meetings and demonstrations. Meetings were held frequently to encourage such unity, with many being held in private houses so that women could participate. Women accordingly supported the movement strongly. The volunteers worked with village leaders, travelling from place to place and coordinating the protest. They instructed the villagers to surrender their belongings peacefully but refuse to cooperate with the officials when they tried to take away the confiscated goods. Although official reports claimed that there was some violence, this was denied by the people. For example, one official who went to a village left when he heard the people making a lot of noise that he believed was directed against him – in fact they were singing religious songs loudly. The people often performed such congregational worship when they knew that officials were coming to collect the tax or confiscate property.[19]

Officials toured the villages trying to persuade the people to change their stance, to no avail. Crowds gathered around them to debate the matter in a vigorous and sometimes heated way. In some cases, government servants were abused and denied shelter. Nonetheless, even those who showed some respect to the officers refused to pay the tax. The government escalated its drive to force people to pay in mid-September 1921. Within one month the property of four thousand defaulting families was seized. The people remained peaceful and handed over objects of their own accord. The officials were unable to obtain any labour to carry the goods away to Kanthi town, and in the end had to use their own vehicles. The property was put up for auction in the town, but nobody bid even at ludicrously low prices, and the effort had to be abandoned. This happened time and again. Rural government servants resigned or refused to work. In Tamluk and Ghatal subdivisions the *chaukidars* were reluctant to assist the authorities in attaching property. They complained that they were being threatened but refused to say who was responsible. Some of those who had resigned agreed to resume their service after much persuasion, though the authorities were uncertain as to whether they would in fact return to work. In general, the *chaukidars* refused to carry anything for fear of being boycotted socially if they did so. In the end, the government had to give up attaching property because of this.[20]

By November 1921, it was clear to the British that the local government initiative had failed badly in this area. They were concerned that the movement might soon address other issues and spread, and it was best to withdraw the union boards in Medinipur to prevent this.

They realised that this represented a loss of face but could not see any other way out. This measure was implemented in December and the confiscated goods were returned to the people. In all, the movement had greatly consolidated the Sasmal-led Congress in the district. He had led, with great success, an overwhelmingly peaceful protest to powerful effect. During the entire campaign, only one isolated act of violence was reported – an assault on a white settlement officer in Bogra. Otherwise nonviolent discipline proved exemplary.[21]

There was similar noncooperation in a municipality of Guntur District in coastal Andhra. The government had established a new municipality in early 1920 that incorporated four villages of Baptala Taluka of Guntur District, the largest two of which were Chirala and Parala. The people of these villages believed that it was a ruse to raise taxes by up to ten times the amount paid previously to the local board. A rate-payer's union was formed, and the government was petitioned, to no avail. Eventually, at the end of December 1920, it was agreed that they would refuse to pay the municipal tax. All municipal councillors resigned. Duggirala Gopalakrisnayya, a prominent Congress leader of Andhra, took over the leadership and incorporated the protest into the wider Noncooperation Movement. He set up a volunteer army dressed in red that was called 'Rama Dandu', which by April 1921 had over a thousand members. It was a well-disciplined and nonviolent force. In April, Gandhi suggested that they might migrate in a block from the four villages. The exodus took place over the following months, with the entire populations of these villages – about 15,000 in all – erecting huts in the adjoining countryside in which they stayed. People of all castes and communities took part in this. They named the encampment 'Ramnagar'. Life there was hard, with little protection from the hot summer sun and then heavy monsoon rain. Many fell ill. During the second half of 1921, over forty people were prosecuted for offences cooked up by the government, with many being fined and some jailed. Some of the huts were burnt down by people who appeared to have been working for the government. Their leaders, including Gopalakrisnayya, were all arrested and jailed. Morale was gradually undermined by all of this, and after Gandhi halted the campaign in February 1922, the protest soon collapsed.[22]

Resisting Dam Construction: The Mulshi Satyagraha

There was one campaign connected with the Noncooperation Movement over an issue that was novel at that time though now commonplace in India – the building of a dam that would create a reservoir that flooded prime agricultural land appropriated against the cultivator's will. Then, as subsequently, 'national interests' were invoked as the reason, and although in this case a privately-owned Indian business corporation was carrying out the project, it received the full backing of the imperial state. The concern was the Tata Hydroelectric Power Company, which was a subsidiary of the Bombay-based Tata Group, which, more than any other Indian-owned corporation, had pioneered the development of heavy industry in the subcontinent. There was an acute need for electric power for its factories in Bombay City, and this demand could be met in part by producing hydroelectricity from new dams in the highlands to the east of the city. Twenty-two major dams were envisaged by Tata at that time, the first of which was to be built at the confluence of two rivers – the Mula and the Nila – that flowed through a valley of fertile farmland in the Mulshi Peta sub-division of Pune District. The planned reservoir was scheduled to flood 44,000 acres of this land, in an area known for its production of high-quality rice, particularly a variety called Ambemohor that was much prized by the Maharashtrian elites. Mulshi had 85 villages, in 81 of which the peasants paid taxes direct to the state. Two-thirds of the entire population were Maratha-Kunbis, the dominant caste of this region. In Mulshi, they were mostly modest farmers who cultivated their land with family labour. Many were indebted to moneylenders, with mortgages on their land.[23]

The government of Bombay granted permission for this project in March 1919. It agreed to issue official notices of acquisition on the land, which it did in June 1919. The peasants of Awalas village were the first to declare that they would fight to remain on their land. Others soon joined them, affirming that they would never surrender their motherland. One great fear of whose who had mortgaged their land was that the moneylenders – who in this area were mainly Maharashtrian Brahmans and Gujarati Baniyas – would take the compensation, leaving them destitute. While they retained their land – even if mortgaged –

there was hope that one day they would be able to redeem it. In this, the poorer, heavily indebted peasants, were particularly firm in their support for the campaign. At this stage, the moneylenders supported the movement, as they wanted the best possible compensation on their mortgaged land. Between March 1919 and April 1921, twenty petitions were sent to the Bombay government, twenty-eight to various officials, and up to twenty telegrams to the Viceroy and other high officials. In a petition to the Duke of Connaught of 28 January 1921 the peasants stated: 'The Bombay government have backed up the Capitalists to cause discontent. 15,000 persons have to part with their beloved land permanently and they have to wander about anywhere else. This is a calamity for them and they are approaching His Royal Highness to get out of it.'[24]

The campaign now came to the notice of Vinayak Bhuskute, a reporter for the Pune newspaper *Loksangraha*, and in December 1920 he went to Mulshi to investigate. He was a strong admirer of Gandhi, and quickly assumed the role of activist rather than mere reporter. He addressed meetings in three villages that were attended by people from surrounding areas. He argued that a private company was building the dam in the interests of capitalists and of Bombay City, and told them how Gandhi had devised a new method of resistance that they could use called satyagraha. Until that moment, the peasants of the area had never heard this term, but it now entered their vocabulary. Bhuskute agreed to act as a leader for them in such a satyagraha. After he published his report, N.C. Kelkar – the leading nationalist in Maharashtra after the death of Tilak earlier that year – agreed to tour Mulshi with Bhuskute. Kelkar addressed a meeting of people from some seventy villages at which he promised wider support if they launched a satyagraha. He publicised the matter at the Nagpur Congress in December 1920 and won a vote of support for the campaign.[25]

By that time, Tata had already started work on the project, even before the compensation terms had been agreed to. Labourers began constructing the foundations of the dam and boundary posts were erected and the peasants denied access to their land. When the Tata workers were challenged by the peasants to explain what they were up to, they were threatened and, in some cases, beaten up by Pathan guards hired by the company. In some cases, their property was looted, and their standing crops and trees destroyed. The government stood by the company in this. In one case in late 1920, the peasants of a village went in a large body to try to stop the construction work. The village leaders of Mulshi and some other peasants met in Pune on 23 January 1921 and agreed to sign a pledge to launch a satyagraha against the Tatas. In response, the Collector of Pune District issued a statement that the needs of the many of Bombay City outweighed that of a relatively small number of peasant farmers. However, the landowners would be compensated generously in cash or kind, and they would be helped, if possible, to acquire alternative land – though this could not be guaranteed. He also warned them that if they broke the law in protest they could be punished, and if they wanted help from the authorities, they would be best served by not obstructing the building of the dam. Bhuskute held a meeting in Pune with some other Congress workers to plan the satyagraha. Some prominent people from Mulshi also attended. They decided that their priority was to stop the construction work. Bhuskute then spent three weeks touring Mulshi gauging support. A meeting was held at the Jyotirupeshwar temple to take an oath of satyagraha. They pledged not to sell their land to the company and refuse compensation from the government in cash or kind. Even some of the Brahman and Gujarati moneylenders participated and took the oath. The oath included a commitment to nonviolence, and Bhuskute explained the principles of satyagraha, stressing that they had to be careful not to retaliate in the face of violence by the company employees. The meeting ended with shouts of 'Mahatma Gandhi *ki jai*!' They adopted the slogan '*jan kinwa jamin!*' (land or life!) and declared that they would prefer to drown rather than leave their land. Bhuskute toured the villages with two local youths explaining the principles of satyagraha to the peasants.[26]

At this juncture, N.C. Kelkar began to backtrack. In common with many of the older Maharashtrian nationalists who considered themselves followers of Tilak and his legacy, he resented the way that Gandhi had taken over the movement, in the process displacing the Maharashtrian Brahmans who had hitherto dominated the Congress in western India. They were doubtful about the Noncooperation Movement, feeling it was unlikely to bring swaraj.

They stood above all for the interests of the Brahmans of the region, many of whom had interests in rural moneylending, and their main concern was that they receive good compensation. They had adopted a radical rhetoric initially to try to gain maximum compensation for landowners – which included the moneylenders who had lent on mortgages to peasants of the Mulshi area. Accordingly, at a meeting in March 1921, they stated that the protest should be delayed until after the end of the monsoon – e.g. September to October 1921 – to give everyone concerned time to reach a compromise. Another meeting was held in Pune soon after, attended by 250 people of Mulshi itself. They insisted that satyagraha be launched immediately. Kelkar asked them whether they wanted him or Bhuskute as their leader – the peasants replied Bhuskute. Kelkar walked out in a huff, followed by other members of the committee. The peasants complained that the Brahmans had suggested to them the idea of 'satyagraha' – something they had never heard of before – and now that the time had come for them to launch it, many of these Brahmans were deserting them. Bhuskute then stepped in and said that they should launch the satyagraha on Ramnavami day (birthday of Lord Ram) in April. Kelkar then went on to conduct negotiations with Tata and the government and agreed in May 1921 to accept the building of the dam and the displacement of the peasants so long as replacement land was found for all those who wanted it. Those who preferred cash compensation would be given it. This 'agreement' was rejected firmly by the peasants of Mulshi.[27]

An important new leader now emerged – Pandurang Mahadeo Bapat. He was born in 1880 into a lower-middle class family of Chitpavan Brahmans of Parner in Maharashtra. After graduating from the Deccan College in Pune, he won a government scholarship to study mechanical engineering at Edinburgh University in 1904. While there, he became inspired by the Savarkar brothers and other revolutionary nationalists of India and learnt to make bombs and use a revolver. He returned to India in 1908 and worked underground, travelling about the subcontinent instructing revolutionaries on bomb-making. He was arrested in 1912 and spent time in jail. On his travels, he had found that the mass of the people had no idea about nationalism, and he realised that violent revolutionary activity would get nowhere while this was the case. He decided to focus on raising consciousness among the people. From 1915–18 he worked as a journalist at Tilak's Pune-based newspaper, the *Mahratta*, after which he was employed in a project to compile an encyclopaedia in Marathi. He resigned from this post in 1921 so that he could work full-time in Mulshi. He very quickly became the effective leader of the entire campaign. He did not believe in nonviolence as an ethic, but could appreciate its tactical value, and therefore agreed to conform to it in this case.[28]

On 10 April 1921, Bapat and three other leaders met Gandhi in Bombay to discuss the protest. Gandhi gave his full support, arguing in *Young India* that the dam project had no value at all for India if it was built at the expense 'of even one poor man'. He pointed out – referring to his own experience as a lawyer who had dealt with many land-acquisition cases – that the compensation never reflected the value of something that the owners' whole life, self-identity and sentiment was invested in. Their cause was wholly just, and he had no doubt that if they maintained strict nonviolence they would gain their objective.[29]

A Satyagraha Mandal (association) was established to lead the protest, and it was launched formally at a large meeting on the banks of the Mula in Mulshi on 16 April 1921. The leaders explained the need for peace, perseverance and determination. The people now declared that they would refuse to vacate their land and accept no compensation. Some leading peasants from twenty-five villages issued a statement: 'Bury us under these walls and bury our women and our cattle, too. When we lie dead there then you can build your reservoirs unhindered. Tell this to the government and to the Tatas as well.' A camp was established near the dam as a base, and the satyagrahis were divided into units, each headed by its own leader. There were among them about five hundred women. The site of the dam, and a road that was used to bring construction material to the dam, had already been occupied by protestors, so that work had been stopped. On the first day they marched to the site of the dam carrying a saffron flag with 'Satyagraha' written on it. Jets of hot water were sprayed on the satyagrahis, to no avail. The work had to be called off for that day, and the protestors returned to the place of the meeting in triumph. Next day, they again marched to the site of the dam before work could start. At night the satyagrahis gathered in the camp to sing devotional songs and heroic Maharashtrian ballads – *bhajan, kirtan* and *powada*. The obstruction continued over the following days, with interludes while the Tata company tried to negotiate, all to no avail. As the Maharashtrian labourers on the dam now refused to work, Kanarese and Tamil workers were brought in by the company. Female labourers were employed to make it appear that the protestors were abusing women, but they merely prostrated themselves before these women to prevent them from working. On 26 April, the chief engineer on the dam agreed to stop work until 7 November. He hoped that this would defuse the movement during the period of the monsoon, when construction work was in any case impossible. The people of Mulshi told him that if work began on that date, they would continue the protest until the work was abandoned. They were prepared to go to jail if necessary.[30]

Although work on the dam had been halted, Tata continued to build a railway to the dam site. The people of Shere village, which was on this stretch, objected and launched a satyagraha on 1 May 1921, led by the headman of the village. From 19 May, they pulled up rails, and the labourers put them back. Initially, there were no arrests. On 5 June, they sat on the tracks of the Chinchwad-Mulshi railway section, holding up a train. The satyagrahis were forcibly removed by company workers hired from outside Maharashtra. There appears to have been some attempt by the peasants of Shere to grab the implements of the Tata workers by force. Bapat and Bhuskute happened to be passing through Shere at the time and intervened to prevent the protest from escalating violently. Bapat then led a satyagraha to block the passage of the construction train at Paud and they removed two stretches of rails. The police held an enquiry and framed charges against twenty of the protestors. The court reached a verdict on 19 October 1921, acquitting four and fining the rest. Bapat received the highest fine, of Rs 100. Two paid, while the majority opted to go to jail for 15 days. Bapat, and two other leaders refused bail and were sentenced to six months' imprisonment. In this way, the authorities removed them from the scene before the satyagraha was due to resume. In September 1921, Tata hired four hundred Pathan strongmen from Sindh who they intended to use to break the forthcoming satyagraha. They were prepared to use violence.[31]

During the first week of November, the Tatas asked the prominent moderate nationalist M.R. Jayakar to mediate on the issue. After studying the problem he concluded that the real issue was about justice for the peasants, and if they were given generous compensation, alternative cultivable land and other facilities, the problem could be solved. There was no further construction work over the following months while compensation details were negotiated and put into place. Eighty-thousand rupees was distributed in compensation, with a bonus being promised to peasants who willingly accepted the awards by 15 March 1922. In January 1922, there was a protest at the site of the dam, with the engineer-in-charge of the work acting aggressively towards the satyagrahis. His dog bit Bhuskute on the leg, and his labourers beat up the satyagrahis. The satyagrahis acted with great self-restraint. A case was taken out against sixteen protestors, who were arrested on 27 January. Bhuskute was among them. The company resumed work on the dam in March 1922. The protest resumed accordingly, with work being blockaded in late March. At that time, only about 15 per cent of the landowners had accepted compensation, amounting to less than 10 per cent of the amount that was being offered. On 1 April, Bhuskute and three other leaders were sentenced to six months imprisonment. The others were released after paying fines.[32]

From 6 April 1922, work on the dam was obstructed in relays. Satyagrahis were arrested, with some being jailed. Cordons were placed around the workers by the company – the satyagrahis tried to break through and were beaten when they did so. Women participated strongly in the protest. They were led by Jaibai Bhoin of Vadusta, who was jailed for three months in late April 1922. The women had their saris and hair pulled at by Tata's guards. This harassment received much publicity in the Marathi press. In one cartoon in *Mauj* newspaper, Duryodhana, the villain of the Mahabharata, was shown as a Parsi disrobing Draupadi in front of a person wearing a crown, who symbolised the British rulers. It was alleged that labourers had stood nude in front of the women to insult them – something the government denied, stating that women and children had been deliberately put in front during the protest, and that there had been cases of fighting between the women and some women employed by the company, and that these slight skirmishes were blown up by the press out of all proportion. The satyagraha continued into May 1922, with around five-hundred local people and one-hundred-and-fifty outside volunteers taking part led by Bapat, who at this time was given the title 'Senapati' – or 'army commander' – an honorific by which he was known for the rest of his life. Satyagrahis were beaten up by the labourers, some being left unconscious, but they remained disciplined, self-controlled and strictly nonviolent under Bapat's close guidance. By 20 May, 198 persons had been arrested and jailed, including some of the leaders.[33]

Bapat published a circular on 3 May 1922 stating that he envisaged ten thousand Maharashtrians going to jail, one hundred lives being sacrificed, and the campaign continuing for five years. He asked people to volunteer from outside Mulshi and donate funds. He said that work on the dam would be obstructed, and that they would plead with the labourers to stop work. They were prepared to damage any completed work. He thus considered the destruction of property as a legitimate part of the nonviolent satyagraha. He also said that when all reasonable efforts had failed, they would launch what he called '*shuddha* (pure) satyagraha', which allowed the use of limited violence of a largely ritual sort. This statement proved highly controversial. The *Bombay Chronicle*, which had until then supported the protest, reconsidered its position on 18 May 1922, stating that Bapat was deviating from the Gandhian position, as Gandhi did not permit the destruction of property. It also said that it could not support the idea of so many dying for the cause. The issue should be discussed by the All India Congress Committee. Bapat sought to make the satyagraha an all-Maharashtra affair and based himself in Bombay to work for this. He gave speeches, published handouts and raised funds. An all-Maharashtra conference on Mulshi was held in Bombay in June 1922, attended by eight hundred people. The president of the conference was the old Tilakite and Hindu nationalist B.S. Munje. He supported the destruction of property, stating that Hindus and Muslims were not expected, like Christians, to turn the other cheek. Hindus were permitted by their religion to employ violence to vindicate their rights. This was an argument that nationalists of his ilk had long deployed against Gandhi. Bapat then spoke, arguing: 'We must fight the obvious adharma [immoral act] being committed before us. It is not adharma, to take recourse to any means permissible by religion to reinstate saddharma [true religion, or the truth]. Nothing is to be achieved by tying ourselves down by artificial means.' He said, however, that he would maintain strict nonviolence for the time being. It was resolved that the satyagraha would continue for three years, with three thousand volunteers being mobilised and Rs 300,000 collected. The Tatas now strengthened their stand in the knowledge that the satyagrahis no longer enjoyed the firm support of the Gandhian wing of the Congress.[34]

The campaign was suspended during the monsoon of 1922, resuming on 2 September. Bapat led the satyagraha on that day, filling the foundations of the dam with rocks. He and thirty-six others were arrested and prosecuted. Bapat and two colleagues were jailed for six months, and twenty-nine others to one to three months. Bhuskute was released on 2 October and took over the leadership. He found that there was some demoralisation, as the resolve of the Tatas had clearly not been shaken, and many more local landowners had accepted compensation. It was estimated that eighty per cent had capitulated during 1922, on top of the fifteen or so per cent who had done so during 1921. Construction on the dam was going ahead full steam. Volunteers were mobilised from all over India to participate, most coming from the Tilak Vidyalaya School in Nagpur. Protests were staged on four days in each month and there were further arrests and sentences of imprisonment. The peasants themselves were busy with their harvest and did not participate. The government issued an order prohibiting Bhuskute from entering Mulshi Peta, which he violated, leading to a one-year jail sentence.

Other volunteers were sentenced to between three to six months. Women and children were fined, or in default given three months in jail. All opted for jail. The campaign was now depending largely on outside volunteers. Several newspapers argued that the time had come to abandon the protest as it was failing. Imprisoned in Yeravda jail in Pune, the satyagrahis suffered harsh and discriminatory treatment. The European officers in the jail ordered the satyagrahis to operate the hand mill, pull carts, and clean the drains. They followed orders without resistance, but – with the coarse prison diet – their health soon suffered. Cases of chest pain, giddiness and loss of consciousness were reported. They were often caned and verbally abused. Bhuskute was handcuffed and made to stand up even when he was suffering from dysentery. The newspapers received reports of this and publicised it all critically.[35]

When the leaders were jailed, the peasants had felt discouraged. There was not a single person among them who could provide similarly effective leadership. After his release from jail on 6 March 1923, Bapat realised that the peasants who remained loyal to the satyagraha had suffered most loss, and he therefore released them from their pledge not to accept compensation. This required considerable moral courage on his part. He stated that he intended to carry on the satyagraha nonviolently and called for volunteers. There was a satyagraha on 23 March, with protestors being arrested and jailed. At the end of March, Bapat said that the satyagraha would continue even if all the landowners had accepted compensation. It was, he said, now mainly a Maharashtrian rather than local struggle. They might not stop the dam, but satyagraha was in itself valuable in promoting spiritual and national uplift. It was an important part of education for students in nationalist schools, grooming them for later struggles. In effect, this meant an end to the campaign as a mass struggle. It dragged on as a kind of testing-ground for would-be satyagrahis of Maharashtra, who were able to test their nonviolent resolve in the face of the violence of the Tata's hired thugs. For example, Visnupant Apte of Ratnagiri stated after his release from jail for participating in the protest that it had allowed him to free himself from fear. He said that they were fortunate to have Senapati Bapat as their leader – a Krishna-like figure. 'Jail was their battlefield and volunteers should fill up the jails under the leader of their Senapati.' Bapat toured Maharashtra making speeches and raising funds.[36]

In October 1923 Bapat announced that the time had come for an escalation towards 'shuddha satyagraha'. He declared: 'The proper ways of protest must always be tried first. But when these prove ineffective, we have to resort to destruction of property and use of violence. I believe in both violence and non-violence, depending on the circumstances. But there should not be indiscriminate faith in either. We must not perpetrate pointless violence which serves no purposes. You must be prepared some day either to kill or to die.' The police immediately served an arrest warrant on him – but he fled before it could be served, but a few days later offered himself up to the police.

He was sentenced to one year in prison for making seditious speeches. The satyagraha came practically to a halt with Bapat's imprisonment in Yeravda jail.[37]

In this case, a movement that was initially a part of the Noncooperation Movement continued long past its collapse, becoming a part of what developed into the 'no-changer' phase in which Gandhian radicals waged a series of satyagrahas in different parts of India that served to maintain morale and train activists. In this case, Bapat – a leader who had never believed in nonviolence as a moral principle – advocated a more confrontational and possible violent form of 'satyagraha'. He did not however take his colleagues in Maharashtra with him in this. After his release in 1924, Bapat called for volunteers for his 'shuddha satyagraha', but only five came forward. They were all admirers of him as a former underground revolutionary, and two in particular were fascinated with violence and were already armed with pistols and swords. In December 1924, they blocked a railway line in Mulshi and then attacked the labourers who came to remove the obstruction. Bapat had a pistol, which he fired, wounding a railwayman in the leg. They then surrendered, as planned. At the trial, Bapat stated that they had deliberately only caused superficial wounds to the workers, as the violence was intended to be more symbolic than real. He was sentenced to seven years' imprisonment. As for Bhuskute, who was released from jail in July 1924, he denounced the whole idea of 'shuddha satyagraha' and joined with other leaders in a declaration that they would never endorse such violence. He and these others now carried the Gandhian flag in Maharashtra. In this way, the Mulshi Satyagraha created a cadre of Gandhian activists in Maharashtra who did not identify with Tilak and his Hindu nationalist legacy. However, in marked contrast to some of the other movements of dominant peasants in other parts of India, the people of Mulshi itself – who had initiated the protest in the first place – failed to produce any notable leaders who were committed to Gandhian principles.[38]

To conclude, the old Congress stalwarts of Maharashtra had developed cold feet at an early stage of this movement, leaving the leadership in the hands of a younger and more radical group of young Maharashtrian nationalists. They adopted nonviolent strategy on pragmatic grounds and organised a powerful and admirable campaign along such lines. Gandhi embraced their movement with enthusiasm, as he was opposed in principle to capitalist development projects that conflicted with the interests of rural folk. Although the campaign did not stop the building of the dam and formation of a reservoir that flooded prime land, it helped to build the Gandhian movement significantly in Maharashtra and win support for nonviolent strategies.

Protests against Indigo and Tea Planters

Indigo Planters of Bihar

The campaign against indigo planters was, as before, strongest in north Bihar on estates where white planters – known as '*gora sahebs*, or 'white gentlemen' – rented land from zamindars and princes. Though the position of such planters was in general weakened considerably by the satyagraha of 1917,[39] some who were renting land on long-term leases managed to maintain their position through various exactions. They demanded higher rents on the land that they sub-let to peasants, extra payments for timber use, rents for the land on which the peasants had built their houses, new payments in kind, such as cattle hides, and a variety of cesses. The people in such areas soon realised that their exploitation had hardly abated, and from 1919 onwards began to refuse rents to the planters. In March 1919, three activists even claimed that Gandhi had told them to refuse their rent – advice of which the Mahatma himself was unaware. The protests intensified during the Noncooperation Movement, particularly in the districts of Muzaffarpur, Champaran and Purnea districts. The nationalist leaders in Bihar were now actively involved in promoting this campaign, linking it up with the wider movement. There were demonstrations, boycotts of indigo factories and planters' *haats* (weekly markets) – with the setting up of alternative markets – refusal of rents and strikes in the indigo factories by contract labourers. Though this was all conducted largely nonviolently, there were a few cases of violence and some arson.[40]

Many peasants in these three districts enrolled as volunteers. A notable local organiser was a *mahant* (chief priest) of a temple at Paharchak called Raghunath Gir, who became President of the Bariapur

Taluka Noncooperation Sabha in Muzaffarpur District. He promised that once swaraj came he would become headman of Bariapur, and he would divide the land of the local Motipur factory among the peasantry. They would pay only a very low rate of two annas per *bigha* (around a quarter of a hectare of land) to the government. Tenants were persuaded to pay no rent or supply labour or carts to the Motipur factory. The factory labourers were told to stop work and threatened with social boycott if they did not comply – and this was enforced with washermen and barbers refusing to serve those who remained in their jobs. As a result, many of the largely low caste workers resigned their positions and joined the movement. The planter managed to employ some new rent collectors (*amlas*), but when two of them tried to collect rents in Paharchak they were abused and then beaten to death by a crowd. In the same district, there was opposition also to the Belsand planter, who controlled one thousand bighas of rented land. A large crowd surrounded his factory on 4 January 1922, shouting 'Gandhiji ki jai!' There were similar demonstrations at other factories. The *amlas* of the Karnoul factory were threatened with assault. The sugarcane crops of the Mia Chapra factory were destroyed – the ringleaders were prosecuted. The factory was then picketed, and the factory manager boycotted.[41]

There was intense anti-planter protest also in Champaran District, with many factory workers being persuaded to give up their posts. Those who refused to do so were threatened. There was great resentment towards those *amlas* who remained in their posts trying to collect the rent and other payments. As they were visiting villages to do this without protection, they were in a particularly vulnerable position. At Madhubani village in the west of the district, for example, the protest against the Piprasi factory was led by one Baiju Gir. There was violence in June 1921 when two *amlas* assisted by a factory peon tried to confiscate a herd of around one hundred cattle that were grazing on an uncultivated tract that the planter claimed as his. One hundred villagers led by Baiju Gir intervened with the intention of releasing the cattle. The police reported afterwards that Baiju Gir had been unable to control the enraged crowd and some of them had attacked the three men, beating one of them unconscious. The other two fled. The cattle were then released. In the northwest of Champaran, an *amla* of the

Chautera factory who had tried to impound some cattle was beaten, leading to a police case against the villagers. The *amlas* of this factory, and particularly the head *amla*, Kali Singh, were notoriously oppressive and hated in the area as a result. There was also anger against some Magahiya Doms (untouchables from Magadh who handled cattle carcasses) who had been appointed as *chaukidars* (watchmen). On 1 November 1921, 150 to 200 people from the villages of Patilar and Lagunaha gathered outside the Chauterwa factory shouting 'Gandhiji ki jai!' The local panchayat head and some villagers tried to maintain order as the crowd quickly swelled to some five thousand. They surrounded the house of the *amlas*, who cowered inside. Windows and doors were broken, and the occupants challenged to come out. When they refuse to come, their houses were set on fire, forcing them out. They were attacked, and one older *amla* was beaten severely. The crowd then set other buildings on fire, causing over Rs 100,000 worth of damage. The planter's big bungalow was among those damaged. Poor peasants were the ones mainly involved in the attack. All over the district, peasants began to graze their land freely on the land that the planters claimed they had a right over.[42]

Many *haats* owned or leased by planters in Champaran were boycotted in October 1921 and alternative *haats* were established. The planters earned a considerable income from their *haats* by levying fees on merchants and vendors, and the boycott was a direct challenge to them. In the new *haats*, the fees were either much lower or non-existent. Merchants who refused to sell at the new *haats* were subject to social boycott. This was a local initiative, not coming from the Congress leaders. Indeed, they did not approve of it, and even went to the villagers that had established such markets to dissuade them from continuing. In June 1921, there was a confrontation in Dhanaha (also Champaran), between a force of mounted police that was accompanied by the local planter, Mackinnon, and his *amlas*. He was trying to ensure that the villagers supplied carts and labour. The police looted goods and money from the houses of the villagers, whereupon they were surrounded and threatened. They had to release their looted goods. There were rumours that many factories were to be attacked, though in fact there were only a few incidents of minor arson on them. A deputation of the planters met the Commissioner of the Tirhut

Division asking for firm action to stop the assaults on their factories. In late 1921, mounted police were sent to patrol the area, and a fine was ordered from the villagers as compensation for the arson and security against further such attacks. Those who had contributed to the Tilak Swaraj Fund and Khilafat Fund were ordered to pay a similar amount to the planters. The people refused to cooperate with this. The district-level Congress leaders disapproved strongly of the violence. Immediately after the attack on the Chauterwa factory, they rushed to the place to warn the people against perpetrating any more such acts, arguing that such violence undermined the chances of success for the movement. They were instructed as to the advantages of conforming strictly to nonviolence.[43]

In Purnea District, there was a strong campaign in April and May 1921 against a few planters who were known for being particularly harsh in their exactions. Their factories were boycotted, and peasants refused to cultivate indigo or pay any rent. Planters with better reputations were left alone. In May 1921, the District Magistrate agreed to meet a delegation of around 500 tenants who expressed their grievances. He also heard the factory owners put their side of the case. Two of the most notorious planters, the Shillingford brothers, agreed to reduce fees and rents, and allow the peasants freedom to grow trees on their rented lands and use them in ways not hitherto permitted. They were not to be forced to grow indigo. Once this was agreed, the peasants paid their arrears and ended the boycott of the brothers and their factory.[44]

In 1921–22, the planters found that as a rule, they were getting less support from the provincial-level authorities in acting in oppressive ways. Only if the law was broken in an obvious way was firm action being taken. The hegemony of the planters was fast being eroded, and they now felt very isolated in their factories scattered over the region. They complained of being subjected to 'race hatred' and sent a delegation to meet the Governor on 22 January 1921 to express their fears, demanding stronger action to quell what they saw as sedition, but they no longer found the government so willing to side with them. They were told that the movement was also directed against Indian zamindars, so it was not specifically anti-European. The colonial state was no longer prepared to countenance the abuses committed by the planters of Bihar and demanded that they grant concessions to the peasants.[45]

In this protest, the Congress leaders were unable to prevent some physical assaults on *amlas*, two of whom were killed. No planter was harmed in any way, though they were vulnerable to attack. There was also arson and destruction of indigo crops, though on a relatively minor scale. The extensive burning of the factory at Chauterwa was the chief exception to this rule. The foremost weapons employed by the protestors were boycott of the factories and employees who refused to resign, the non-payment of rents to the planters, and refusal to pay their demands for various fees and grazing charges. It was the strength of these nonviolent tactics that proved most successful in curtailing the oppression of the most notorious planters, rather than the relatively sporadic though more dramatic cases of violence.

Tea Planters of Assam and Bengal

The other major anti-planter agitation at this time was directed against tea garden owners and managers in Assam and North Bengal. A slump in the industry at that time had seen a reduction in wages, which caused the workers great hardship. The protest began in early 1921 in Jalpaiguri District – the area known as the Duars of Bengal – where the tea garden workers were largely Santal and Oraon adivasi immigrants from south Bihar. There were rumours that Gandhi Raj was about to replace the British raj, and that a terrible storm would destroy all those who had not declared for Gandhi. The local Muslims were also enthusiastic supporters of Khilafat. The labourers were exploited badly by Marwari shopkeepers, and on 12 February 1921 raided the shop of one such merchant-cum-moneylender. The police retaliated by searching their houses for appropriated goods, with four Santals being arrested. A crowd of Muslims, Santals and Oraons wearing Gandhi caps gathered and demanded that they be released. When the police refused to do this, the demonstrators tried to liberate the four prisoners, whereupon the police opened fire killing three and wounding some twelve others. One of the dead was found wearing a cap with 'Falakata Swaraj No. 141' on it, revealing that he had signed up to the local nationalist organisation. The protestors believed that the Gandhi caps made them immune to police bullets. *Haats* that were owned by the tea estates and which demanded various exactions were boycotted and new *haats* established under popular control. Protestors were arrested and jailed for such boycotts.[46]

The protest was then taken up by tea garden workers in Assam who were largely from peasant backgrounds in eastern UP – particularly from Basti and Gorakhpur Districts. This was an area in which the Noncooperation Movement was particularly strong, and news about it, with all the accompanying beliefs about Gandhi, quickly reached the tea gardens in which they were employed – mainly in the Chargola and Longai valleys. Strikes started in late April with demands for large pay-increases, and in May there was a sudden exodus that was prompted by a rumour that 'Gandhi Raj' had arrived, so that they no longer needed to labour for the planters, and that a golden future awaited them in their home region in UP. It was said that Gandhi had ordered them to leave and that he had chartered a steamer on the Padma River to take them on their way. Large numbers downed tools and announced that they were quitting. Although the British claimed that Congress activists had stirred this all up, Rajat Ray denies that there was any external incitement – his detailed research suggests that it all stemmed from the workers themselves. The planters then invoked the Inland Emigration Act of 1859 that required 'coolies' to obtain discharge certificates from the district magistrate if they wanted to return home, on the grounds that they had to show that they had fulfilled their contracts. These were often refused. In 1921, many plantation managers took matters into their own hands and, after citing the Act, arrested people – which in fact they were not entitled to do under the law. Most workers managed to avoid arrest, and some six to seven thousand – around half the total workforce in the plantations of that area – made their way by rail and on foot to Tippera District of East Bengal. They congregated in large numbers at Chandpur, a port on the Padma at the end of the railway line from Assam, from where they intended to proceed on the promised steamer. This failed to materialise. Faced by unmanageable crowds and with a danger of an outbreak of cholera, the divisional commissioner K.C. Dey tried to find ways for them to obtain a passage. The Bengal government, under the influence of the Indian Tea Association, promptly censured Dey and ordered that they be denied access to any boats. On 19 May, a crowd of the workers tried to force their way onto a steamer, and some nearly drowned. Because of the fear of cholera, Dey ordered that they leave their camp at the railway station for a football field outside the town. They refused to move, and a troop of armed Gurkhas was sent on 20 May, which forced them out in a brutal manner, with some being injured, though none appear to have been killed. Gandhi's old colleague C.F. Andrews, who had always taken a strong interest in the plight of migrant contract labourers throughout the British empire, went to Chandpur to observe the situation for himself. He arrived on 21 May, and seeing how critical the situation had become, travelled to Darjeeling to persuade Bengal Governor Ronaldshay and his council – who were in residence in the hill station for the summer season – to facilitate the workers' journey. He had no joy in this, such was the strong influence of the tea-planter lobby in Darjeeling.[47]

The 'Gurkha outrage' at Chandpur was now being publicised strongly in newspapers, with overblown comparisons being made with Jallianwala Bag. The East Bengal Railway Employees Union went on strike in support of the tea garden workers, with all rail services in the region stopping on 24 May. About a thousand workers were left stranded along the way. The dynamic leader of the Chittagong District Congress Committee, J.M. Sengupta, became involved as president of this union, and he took the matter up vigorously. On 27 May, the *sarongs* (sailors) on the Padma steamers also went on strike after the secretary of their union was arrested. This soon spread to the steamer ports at Goalando (which lies at the point where the Ganges and Brahmaputra Rivers converge to become the Padma, and which was the intended destination of the workers), and Barisal and Khulna. Chittaranjan Das and a large contingent of Calcutta Congress activists rushed by boat to Chandpur to take charge of the protest. They organised a series of hartals in the towns of the area, including in Chandpur.[48]

C.F. Andrews returned to Chandpur and tried to persuade the steamer and railway workers to return to work to provide transport for the tea garden labourers. He was opposed in this by the Congress activists, as they wanted to put maximum pressure on the government. He was also shunned by officials, who resented his public criticism of them after his trip to Darjeeling. He opened a subscription for the stranded workers. The Congress activists responded by launching their own separate fund raising drive. Das sanctioned the spending of Rs 150,000 from the Tilak Swaraj Fund for this purpose, and food and medical aid was provided. By early June, Andrews had raised enough from his own fund to charter a private steamer to take the workers from Chandpur to Goalundo, and by the middle of that month they were all on their way. The workers believed that Das and his colleagues were largely responsible – ignoring the role of Andrews. On their steamer journey they shouted 'Chitta Ranjan Das ki jai!' Andrews had been very concerned about what he had felt to be a highly inflammatory situation. Writing to Gandhi on 21 June he argued that: 'East Bengal is on the very border line of violence'. He had, he said, worked hard to preach *ahimsa*, and the tea garden workers had responded well – 'they have given me such treasures of love. Time after time the passion has died down as I have spoken about you'. As a result, there had been no incidents of violence on their part. Writing in *The Modern Review* in August 1921, Andrews provided a graphic account of how the refugees had arrived in Chandpur in an emaciated and starving state, moved by a firm belief that Gandhi was about to relieve them of all their sorrows and afflictions. They were sustained, he said, only by their courage, which conferred on them a 'spiritual beauty'.[49]

The protest spread to the Nepalese workers of Darjeeling District of Bengal in July 1921, with strikes in the plantations that were launched by the workers themselves rather than any nationalists. Wages were very low in the tea gardens there. Particularly militant were the workers in the Kalimpong area, where they were mobilised by a dismissed government officer called Dal Bahadur. They went to the district office and shouted 'Gandhiji ki jai!' – which revealed their sympathies for the wider movement. Meanwhile, the protest continued in the Duars area.[50]

In all these protests by tea garden workers, there was little violence. Indeed, the only occasion on which any force was used on the part of the workers was in the attempt by some Muslims, Santals and Oraons, to liberate a few arrested colleagues in the Duars in February 1921. Otherwise, the violence was all on the part of the authorities. The brutal way in which Gurkha soldiers were deployed to force the tea garden workers to leave the railway station at

Chandpur rebounded badly, with its publicity stoking outrage and the widespread mobilisation of Congress workers from other parts of Bengal to come to the area in solidarity with the workers. This led directly to the powerful strikes by the railway workers and sailors. In responding oppressively, the Bengal government soon found itself in a very difficult situation. It became a classic case of the 'backfire' that nonviolent protest aims to provoke.

Forest Satyagrahas

During the late nineteenth century and early decades of the twentieth century, the British implemented a series of forest laws and regulations that in effect deprived local people – in particular, adivasis – of the right to use forest resources freely. Previously, they had cut timber for housebuilding, fuel, and making implements, and had grazed their livestock in forests, gathered food and hunted for meat there. For the most part, they lost access to these important resources when forests were declared by the British – and then the Indian princes and big landlords – to be reserved for their own exploitation. This became a major grievance in such areas in the early years of the twentieth century.[51] It provided the basis for protests in several forest tracts that were linked to the Noncooperation Movement.

Eastern India saw the most widespread of these protests. In the border region of western Bengal and south-eastern Bihar – known as the Jungle Mahals – Santal and Mahato adivasis were mobilised, initially by Bengali nationalists from a bhadralok background. At the start of 1921, there was no nationalist organisation at all in that remote part of Bengal, so in line with encouraging protest in all parts of the province, Chittaranjan Das sent emissaries to work in this tract. One, Satcowripati Roy, travelled to Gidni, where he met an old acquaintance, the lawyer Sailajananda Sen. Roy persuaded him to work for Congress along with another member of the local elite, Murari Mohan Roy. Together, they established a local branch of the Bengal Congress. The activists contacted the adivasis through networks of Marwari traders and village headmen – groups that both resented the power of the zamindars. The activists told the people that British rule was collapsing, swaraj had come, the forests and land were theirs, and that in future they would have to pay only four annas to the Congress fund and nothing to the Midnapore Zamindari Company (MZC), a European-owned corporation that had acquired the right to exploit many of the forests of this tract and which behaved as if it had state authority there. Previously, the adivasis had not dared oppose it openly.[52]

While Das had issued strict instructions that the nationalist activists should not encourage any protest directed against zamindars, an exception was made in the case of the MZC as it was owned by Europeans. In May 1921, the bhadralok leaders organised a meeting of 700 Santals who resolved to abstain from liquor, a clear Gandhian agenda. The leaders also told the adivasis to boycott foreign goods, and particularly cloth. The adivasis told the Congress activists that their main grievance was the loss of their forests and that they wanted to take back control from, above all, the MZC. The Congress activists agreed to organise a strike by adivasi forest labourers who worked for the Company. The MZC reacted with strong-arm tactics designed to force them back to work, and in a scuffle, one of its employees was killed. Very quickly, adivasis throughout the area rebelled, refusing to respect the Company's authority. The District Magistrate tried to bring about a compromise, but Roy refused to accept it and instead established what was in effect a parallel government. The revolt in 1921–2 was thus initiated by the Congress, but quickly took on a dynamic of its own. Anonymous messages circulated exhorting the Santals to raid the weekly markets, and from November 1921, weekly markets became a target, with up to a thousand adivasis appropriating produce and destroying foreign cloth. These raids, and the goods taken, and in some cases, destroyed, were all clearly targeted and never random. Protest continued after the main movement had collapsed in February 1922. There was a second wave in August 1922 that focussed on seizing back control of the forest and fishing rights in local ponds. The rebellion covered the western part of Medinipur District, and some parts of Bankura District in West Bengal and Singhbhum District in Bihar. The scale of the revolt took the government by surprise: it deployed the police to crush it and imposed a punitive tax. Though the local Congress activists did not lead this revolt, they largely supported it and thereby retained the trust of the adivasis. The district-level Congress under B.N. Sasmal, on the other hand, did not extend any active support, though it made some feeble noises about the imposition of punitive taxes after the revolt had been crushed.[53]

In all this, the only notable act of violence occurred when an MZC employee was killed in a fracas. The raids on markets violated Gandhian principles, though they did not entail any physical harm to the merchants. In other respects, the adivasis were remarkably nonviolent. For example, on one occasion a crowd of one thousand assembled outside a court where four Congress workers were being tried and protested in an entirely peaceful manner. The case was adjoined, but an exorbitantly high bail of Rs 700 was demanded from the accused. The crowd demanded that they be released but did not try to implement this demand through force.[54]

There were similar protests among the Chero and Kherwar adivasis of Palamau District in south-western Bihar, and by adivasis in the interior regions of Andhra. In these two areas, news of the Congress calls for swaraj led many adivasis to believe that they could now take back control over their forests. In Palamau, some Kherwars enrolled as Congress volunteers and exhorted their fellows to break the law by refusing to pay various taxes and rents to landlords. They demanded the restoration of the right to collect timber and other produce from the forests. Many asserted that as swaraj had come, the land was now theirs. Trees were felled and the land cultivated under the old shifting system.[55]

In Andhra, some adivasis of the Palnadu area of Guntur District took the initiative, in February 1921, to boycott forest officials and to refuse to pay fines for breaking forest laws. They stated that their protest would be nonviolent and requested Congress leaders to help them. Wood was taken for fuel, leaf mould for compost, and cattle sent into the forests to graze, in violation of forest rules. The government increased the number of forest officers in these areas and sent police reinforcement. Congress leaders came eventually in July 1921 and helped draw up a list of demands to present to the District Collector. These were relatively mild, seeking some relaxation of forest rules to allow greater free use of the forests. The Andhra Congress refused to support civil disobedience against the forest laws at that juncture, arguing that the people should confine their protest to a boycott of forest officials. A month later, three adivasi activists were arrested on a concocted charge of ejecting two forest guards from their accommodation and soon after that the Congress leaders who had come to advise and organise the peasants were themselves arrested and imprisoned. A district-wide six-day hartal was declared, which led to the arrest of more nationalists. There were more hartals in Guntur, spreading soon to Godavari and Kistna Districts. In early August, Gandhi ordered that the hartals be called off and other militant action cease. This brought an end to the wider protest, but had no impact in Palnadu, where civil disobedience towards the forest laws instead intensified. For a time, forest administration virtually collapsed in this area. The Guntur Congress leaders had to go along with this or lose all local influence, and agreed in early September to support the campaign. In this, they were going against official Congress policy, as the regional nationalist press was quick to point out. The people of Palnadu refused to pay any grazing fees and other related taxes. Their cattle were seized and impounded, with some dying due to neglect. Those that survived were auctioned off. In a few cases, crowds of peasants tried to rescue their cattle and were dispersed by the police. There were also some confrontations in which forest officials were beaten up. During that year, fifty-eight cases of assault on forest officials were reported from Guntur District. Punitive police were stationed in the affected areas and forty people were arrested, of whom nineteen were jailed. The movement now spread to forest villages in the districts of southern Andhra – notably Cuddapah, Anantapur and Nellore. There was a major confrontation in Palnadu in February 1922 after livestock were confiscated by the police. Stones were thrown and some of the cattle recaptured. The police opened fire, killing the local Congress leader, Kannegunti Hanamanthu, his servant, and a man employed to take care of the police inspector's horse who had got caught up in the crowd. Six injured people were captured, while the rest fled. This shooting, which came at the same time as Gandhi was withdrawing civil disobedience throughout India, demoralised the people of Palnadu, and the forest protest there – as elsewhere in southern Andhra – soon collapsed.[56]

There was widespread breaking of the forest laws in the densely forested Chittagong District of East Bengal. The movement in that district had been largely an urban one until December 1921, when it spread into the forest tracts of the interior. There, the volunteers initiated a protest that the people then took into their own hands. Forest reserves were looted, forest contractors, officials and policemen were assaulted, and government buildings burnt. The anger was directed mainly at the Forest Department. This continued up until April 1922. The Congress volunteers did not direct this and had no control over the people. This proved to be the most violent of the forest protests during this time.[57]

In the mountainous Kumaon Division of Uttarakhand in the Himalayas, local elites had formed a Kumaon Parishad, in 1916, that provided a focus for nationalist activity. They were aware of the growing discontent of the peasants of this area against the forest regulations that had been introduced by the British in a relatively mild form in 1893 but had then been extended in a much harsher way in 1911. The Kumaon Parishad began to form branches in the villages. One of the major grievances was against a corvée system in which peasants were forced to provide free goods, services and labour for the forest officials when they were on tour. In January 1921, responding to the Noncooperation Movement, the Parishad leaders launched an agitation to refuse all cooperation with forest officials, and refuse any free services. The main leader was Badridutt Pande of Almora town, and he announced the start of the campaign at an annual fair that was attended by large numbers from all over the region. In a speech at the fair he asserted that Gandhi 'would come and save them from oppression as he did in Champaran'. Many were enthused and took the message back to their villages. There were at least 164 village meetings to organise resistance between then and the end of April. Key organisers in all this were ex-soldiers who had become disenchanted with British rule. The area was an important recruiting ground for the Indian army. The forest officials now found that they were being widely boycotted. The government had to abandon their use of corvée and pay the going rate in cash for such services.[58]

Inspired by the success of this movement, Pande and his colleagues took up a more radical demand, namely the right for all villagers to use the forest freely. Men and women throughout the region began to ignore the forest laws and take what they wanted. They burnt the forest floor in defiance of forest regulations. In the past, they had done this annually as it cleared the ground for the fresh grass on which they could feed their cattle. Such fires had been banned by the state as it was claimed that they damaged exploitable timber, especially pine. The fires did less damage to the deciduous trees that the villagers prized more. Over half of the protected forest floor of Kumaon was burnt in defiance of the forest officials in 1921, with many pine saplings being destroyed. In this, a subsistence economy was asserting itself against a system based on the export of timber and other forest produce – such as resin from pines – as commodities. Many were arrested and sent to prison. The protest soon spread to the other division of Uttarakhand, Garhwal, though it was never so widespread there.[59]

In mid-1921, the government set up a Kumaon Forest Grievances Committee to investigate and find a solution to this problem. As it did not have a single villager as a member, the people had little confidence that it would deliver justice. Some boycotted it, though others took the chance to voice their various grievances when the committee visited their locality. The committee eventually concluded that the forest laws were causing unnecessary friction, and that the situation could be largely resolved if certain areas of the forest were set aside for free use by the villagers. Once the new rules were implemented, there was a considerable easing of tension.[60]

To conclude this section, while forest satyagrahas were not explicitly encouraged by Gandhi or the Congress at the national level, as these protests were directed typically against British forest officials, the Congress could hardly say that they had no place within the wider movement. In some of these protests, middle-class nationalists carried out the initial mobilisation, while in others the forest-dwellers themselves took the lead after receiving news of the wider movement with its promise of imminent self-rule. In Andhra, the regional Congress wavered on this issue, but in the end had to accept the forest protests as a *fait accompli*. In Kumaon in the Himalayas, activists inspired by Gandhi took it into their own hands to encourage such resistance. They received an enthusiastic response from local peasants, and the campaign was remarkably successful, with the British conceding that their grievances were justified. In all cases, the protests took on a dynamic of their own, with local people devising their own forms of resistance, such as appropriating forest produce or grazing their livestock in forbidden tracts. In some instances, the outside Congress leaders tried to dampen the protests, to no avail. The movements were for the most part nonviolent, though there were cases of forest officials and policemen being assaulted, but in only one case lethally. The people of Chittagong District were less restrained in this respect, and it is notable that they were not prepared to accept day-to-day leadership from Congress activists.

Religious Democracy for Akali Sikhs

A remarkable movement for popular control over Sikh gurdwaras that began in 1920, provided a fine example of the practice of courageous nonviolence. It braided closely with the Noncooperation Movement. The demand was that the Sikh gurdwaras be managed by popularly elected representatives of the Sikhs rather than by the corrupt priests who were backed by the government. These priests – or *mahants* – were known for the feudal ways in which they ran the extensive temple estates that had been accumulated through generous donations of land, over the years, by devout Sikhs and for their loyalty to the imperial state. Many treated their temples as milch cows to accumulate personal wealth and lived in opulence on the proceeds. They were often found to be drunk while performing ritual functions, and they had a reputation for their sexual predation – female worshippers were frequently raped, and the honour of no Sikh woman was said to be safe in the gurdwaras. The priests often stole from the devotees and were despised by the people, demands for their reform had been voiced over the previous decades through newspaper campaigns, conference resolutions, legal challenges, and pleas to the British couched in temperate language. None of this had any success. Some boycotted the gurdwaras in protest, but the mahants could ignore them with impunity as they had enormous incomes from the estates and did not depend on the offerings of temple-goers. There was an unstated pact between them and the Punjab government that so long as they opposed all anti-British activity vociferously, they would receive strong state support against all popular opposition to their control. The mahants were particularly reviled for the way in which they had condemned the Ghadar revolutionaries of 1914–15 as 'fallen Sikhs', and for cravenly honouring General Dyer after the Amritsar massacre, even making him an honorary Sikh.[61]

The strongest challenge to the corrupt mahants came from a group of Sikhs who sought to restore the purity and moral authority of their religion. They were scrupulous in maintaining the five marks of the Sikh by wearing the *kesha* (long uncut hair), *kangi* (comb), *kada* (steel bracelet), *kachha* (long underwear), and *kirpan* (knife). Many had become lax in these respects. They also rejected the casteism that was practised by many Sikhs at that time. The reform movement had grown from the Singh Sabha movement that began in urban areas in the late nineteenth century, but which spread to rural areas after 1900. In 1920, some reformers resolved to form groups of militant volunteers known as *jathas* to occupy and seize control of the gurdwaras. By early 1921 there were ten major jathas in existence, each with between 500 and 3,000 members, who were recruited in the first instance by preachers who toured the villages. When on the march, each jatha consisted of between about fifty and a hundred men. They wore a black turban, a black band on one shoulder, dark blue clothes, and carried a long staff with a small axe mounted on top. Though carrying their symbolic axes and *kirpans* (often of sword-length), they sought to take over the gurdwaras peacefully through strength of numbers. They took the name of 'Akalis', or 'immortals' – a term used first by the tenth Sikh Guru, Gobind Singh (1666–1708), to describe those of his followers who were prepared to die for their faith in battle.[62]

In August 1920, a large congregation of such Sikhs met in Jallianwala Bagh and demanded that the government-backed manager hand over the Golden Temple. The pressure was such that he stepped down – which was a marked victory for the reformers. Despite this, the temple priests tried to stop the Sikh agitators from entering the holy place on the grounds that they could not accept the popular demand that low-caste Sikhs be admitted and accorded the full rights enjoyed by those of higher caste. In the end the holy book was consulted, and a verdict was reached that all Sikhs should be admitted, after which many of the priests capitulated. Those who continued to oppose the reformers were replaced by jatha volunteers and a new management committee was formed. The government responded by appointing a rival management committee that consisted largely of loyalists. The reformers then held an assembly of over ten thousand Sikhs from all over the region on 15–16 November 1920, that created a larger committee of 175 members named the Shiromani Gurdwara Prabandhak Committee (SGPC). Its president was Sardar Kharak Singh (b. 1868), who was from a wealthy Sialkot family. He was an admirer of Gandhi and other nationalist leaders and became the effective leader of the movement – being known as 'Betaj Badshah', or 'uncrowned king' of Punjab. Although the thirty-six members of the government-backed committee were included in the 175, they were greatly outnumbered and easily outvoted. The committee met in December and deliberated on new rules for the management of the Golden Temple. An organisation to coordinate the jathas, called the Shiromani Akali Dal, was established on 14 December. This was dominated by Sikh militants in a way that the SGPC was not. Its first target was to recruit 10,000 volunteers, and when this number was quickly reached it was increased to 30,000. Mohinder Singh has estimated the total strength of these groups in early 1922 as being 15,506. The bulk of them were from Sikh peasant families, mainly from the districts of Lyallpur, Sheikhupura, Amritsar, Jullundur and Hoshiapur. Two-thirds of them were of the dominant Jat caste. There were also Sikhs of the Khatri caste, many of whom were traders, particularly from Rawalpindi District. Fifteen per cent of the volunteers were from low castes, being employed mainly in agricultural labour. The leaders were largely of the better-educated middle classes, being lawyers, teachers and richer landowners. Throughout the struggle, there was much sympathy for these Akalis from the Hindus and Muslims of Punjab.[63]

Initially, the British were unsure how to handle what appeared to be primarily a movement for religious reform. For example, they made no attempt to stop a jatha that took control of the gurdwara at Sialkot in October 1920, reintroducing the free kitchen that had been stopped by the mahant. They stepped back also at Gurdwara Panja Sahib, which was also occupied by a jatha at this time. The chief mahant denounced the Akalis and ordered them to leave the premises, and when they refused, they were attacked by his supporters. Fresh jathas arrived as reinforcements to strengthen the occupation and the mahant was forced to relinquish control.[64]

With the launch of fully-fledged noncooperation at the end of 1920, the militant Akalis decided to link their protest firmly to this movement. They included certain aspects of the Congress programme, such a boycotting foreign cloth and wearing khadi that was dyed dark blue in the Akali style. They shunned the British courts and established an alternative system of justice. In this, they were like the Congress volunteers. They endorsed the principle that their protest should be firmly nonviolent. They began to act in a more confrontational manner. The new solidarity between the Akalis and the wider nationalist movement alarmed the Punjab officials, who could hardly believe that the solid yeoman peasantry of the province had joined the nationalist struggle in this way. They resorted to conspiracy theories, blaming urban agitators for whipping up a class that had always been loyal to their paternalistic British masters. As one such official put it: 'The Sikh peasant has been committed to a policy of "self-determination" imposed by men who are not his natural leaders, and has been induced by some mysterious process of mass psychology to enter a sphere of activity hitherto [interdicted] by all traditions of loyalty and self-interest.' Having hitherto classed this as a 'religious' affair, they now switched to classing it as a 'political' protest, which justified much stronger repression. As Richard Fox has pointed out, religion and nationalist politics were in fact entangled throughout. We can observe this in the career of one prominent Akali leader, Kartar Singh Jhabbar (1874–1962). From Jhabbar village of Sheikhupura District, he trained as a Sikh preacher at a Sikh seminary in 1906–09, after which he joined the Singh Sabha as a preacher. He was involved in the Rowlatt Satyagraha and was jailed for a time as a result. In 1920, he became active in the movement to control the gurdwaras, and was to the fore in the campaigns at Sialkot, the Golden Temple, Tarn Taran and Guru ka Bagh. For Jhabbar, as for other Akalis, there was no distinction between their religious agitation and nationalist politics.[65]

An Akali Fauj, or army, was formed that was more tightly organised than the jathas. A significant number of retired soldiers joined this organisation, and they brought a military-style discipline that distinguished its groups from other jathas. In early 1922, there were 1,269 Akali volunteers who were military pensioners or discharged soldiers, making up eight per cent of the total number of volunteers at that time. Many had fought in Europe during the First World War. They marched four abreast in ordered ranks, carrying a flag, wearing dark-blue uniforms and identifying badges, often supplemented with their old Sam Browne belts. The leaders carried whistles to blow commands. They had the air of a powerful army on the march and often took circuitous routes, allowing them to gather support in the villages as they went.[66]

The first major target during this new phase of the struggle was the gurdwara at Tarn Taran, near Amritsar that was occupied by a jatha in January 1921. The volunteers were attacked by the priests – who were about seventy in number. More volunteers were sent from Amritsar who tried to negotiate but, while taking a rest, they were attacked with great ferocity by the priests who were allegedly drunk. Some of the volunteers were badly injured in this unexpected assault with wounds from lathis, brickbats and even daggers. They refused to fight back. Two subsequently died. The District Magistrate and Police Superintendent came with the police and restored order. Because the priests had provoked the violence, they were told to leave the gurdwara, allowing the jatha to take over. This was the first time that blood had been shed in a serious way in the struggle.[67]

Much worse was to come at the gurdwara at Nankana, which was the birthplace of Guru Nanak and one of the holiest of Sikh shrines. The mahant, Narain Das, was a dissolute figure who kept a Muslim mistress, hosted dancing girls in the gurdwara, and allowed profane songs to be sung there. All of this caused outrage within the wider Sikh community. Reformers held a large meeting in October 1920 to deplore his behaviour and demand that he mend his ways. The mahant was alarmed by this growing opposition and hired about four hundred strongmen to resist any occupation. Some of them were notorious outlaws. They were armed with swords, lathis and guns. A first attempt to occupy the gurdwara in November 1920 was repulsed. A further hundred or so men – mainly Pathans – were then hired. The British, who knew exactly what was happening, encouraged the mahant to acquire more firearms and ammunition. They also passed on intelligence reports to him about the plans of the jathas. A second attempt at occupation was scheduled for 4 March 1921, and several jathas assembled for this purpose. The SGPC wanted to avoid the volunteers being hurt and sent emissaries to stop any over-enthusiastic jatha from trying to occupy the temple at that juncture. It announced instead that a large congregation of Sikhs would meet outside the gurdwara at the start of March to press the mahant to reform. All except one jatha leader agreed to delay their arrival until this congregation was held. The exception was Bhai Lachhman Singh. Born in 1886, he was from an affluent family of a village in Gurdaspur District and was a fervent Akali and jatha leader from the start of this movement. He continued to lead his 130-strong group to Nankana, arriving on 20 February 1921.[68]

Lachhman Singh decided that the jatha would go to worship at the gurdwara in a nonconfrontational way while awaiting the arrival of other jathas for the coming congregation. The mahant saw an opportunity to attack them, and promptly distributed arms and ammunition to the hired men. As soon as the worshippers entered the temple, the gates were locked. As the members of the jatha bowed before the holy book – the *Granth Sahib* – and began singing devotional songs the hired men opened fire without warning. Those who tried to flee were shot down. Some who sheltered in side-rooms were dragged out and killed. The mahant supervised the massacre, telling his men to spare no one with long hair. Every one of them died and not a single attacker was hurt in any way. The mahant ordered his men to mutilate the corpses and then pile up and burn them so that it could not be proved that none of the mahant's men had been killed. When news of this atrocity reached the British, troops were sent and the mahant and some of his men were arrested. Most of the other hired men managed to flee. The army took over the gurdwara. Other jathas resolved to march on Nankana and take control. Although ordered to turn back by the authorities, they continued on their way. Rather than try to stop them by force, and thus possibly shed more blood, the Deputy Commissioner decided to hand them the keys to the temple on condition that they form a committee to administer it. In this way they gained control, though at great cost.[69]

Once news of the massacre reached other parts of India, there was an outpouring of sympathy for the Akalis and condemnation of the mahant. Gandhi, Shaukat Ali, Lala Lajpat Rai and many prominent people of Punjab visited Nankana to offer their condolences. Gandhi arrived on 3 March and declared it to be 'a second edition of Dyerism more barbarous, more calculated and more fiendish than the Dyerism at Jallianwala'.[70] In a speech at the temple he expressed his wonder at the way in which the members of the jatha had refused to fight back, even though armed with *kirpans* and battle-axes. The event, he said, 'will live in history'. He declared that it was not just an act of the Sikhs, but of 'national bravery' in which the 'martyrs died not to save their own faith merely but to save religion from impunity'. They should dedicate the martyrdom to *Bharat Mata* (Mother India), as the Sikh people would only be liberated fully in a free India. The Sikhs had to be firm in their support for the nationalist cause and resist any attempts by the government to divide them from Hindus and Muslims. They must fight nonviolently, and even if they carried *kirpans* and battle-axes as marks of their Sikh identity, they must ensure that they were never used in anger.[71] In all this, Gandhi sought to integrate the Akali protest fully within the wider nationalist struggle.

Speaking next day in Lahore, Gandhi discussed the nonviolence of the Akali protestors in general. He had by now developed some scruples about what he saw as the over-confrontational methods used by the Akalis. Though in no way doubting their great bravery, he argued that they were in effect 'taking possession by a show of force'. By this, he meant that the large numbers who formed the jathas intimidated the temple mahants into handing over the temples, so that they did it under duress rather than through persuasion or sympathy. He held that 'entering to take possession must bear the taint of violence and as such is worthy of censure'. This was so even if no violence was 'contemplated or intended'. Because of this, he called for the suspension of the movement to take control of the gurdwaras.[72] In this, Gandhi was hardly doing justice to the Akalis. His appeal to a strictly ethical approach that won hearts rather than coerced through sheer strength of numbers was an unrealistic one in the circumstances. The mahants were unlikely to undergo any rapid change of heart, given their venality and unconscionable ways. In practice, nonviolent resistance succeeds by mobilising large numbers, so that opponents become isolated and their will is weakened whether or not they accept the truth of what the protestors are demanding. In this, there is moral coercion – but that is key to the whole process.

Writing soon after, Gandhi described what had happened at Nankana in detail, and again praised the Akalis for providing an exemplary demonstration of nonviolence. Having taken a vow of strict nonviolence, they had refused to defend themselves or retaliate, even as they were being massacred. He noted how their strict nonviolence had placed them morally in the right, and so long as they continued to act in this way they would certainly win.[73] In this he was correct. The Akalis were gaining victory-after-victory in their struggle, for even the British were unable to countenance the violence of the mahants against men who were showing such bravery in the face of death.

After an investigation, the government of India concluded that the Punjab authorities had, as in 1919, been at serious fault. The new Viceroy, Reading, pointed out how the local officials and police had stood by, in effect conniving at the violence by the mahant. If the police had intervened to maintain order, it could not have happened. The Viceroy and his council sent a letter on 6 June expressing their dissatisfaction at the way the Punjab authorities were handling the Akali issue. They had neglected their foremost duty of maintaining the peace. Despite this, no action was taken to discipline the errant officers. Although the Punjab authorities continued to try to defend what they had done, they had now to adopt a different approach; they now sought to divide the Sikhs by winning over those inclined towards loyalism towards the British through limited reforms, while clamping down on the more fervent Akali activists through arrests.[74]

Although the Akalis had gained control over the precincts of the Golden Temple at Amritsar in October 1920, they did not have the keys to the *toshakhana* (treasury), with its great wealth. The bunch of 53 keys was still in the hands of Sunder Singh Ramgarhia, the government-backed manager. Meeting on 29 October 1921, the SGPC demanded that Ramgarhia hand the keys over. To forestall this, the British sent a police force to take them into safekeeping. Jathas began to arrive from all over Punjab in early November to ramp up the pressure on the British, and meetings and congregations were held in Amritsar, Lahore and other towns, at which fiery speeches were delivered. Following their new policy of trying to split the movement, the British arrested some of the more radical leaders, on 26 November, when they were speaking to a congregation at Ajnala. The SGPC immediately adjoined its deliberations at the Golden Temple and went to Ajnala to resume the congregation. They announced that there would be a mass boycott of the Prince of Wales, and all Sikhs – including ex-soldiers who received pensions from the state – were asked to absent themselves from any function in his honour. Because of this, the scheduled visit of the prince to Amritsar was cancelled by the authorities. More radicals were arrested. When brought for trial they refused to offer any defence, on the grounds that they were noncooperators – in this following the Gandhian principle of admitting full guilt and inviting punishment. One of them proclaimed that they were 'non-co-operators and were not prepared to offer any defence as they had no regard for a foreign government, its Courts and the law'. Others made similar declarations. They were all convicted and jailed. This merely stoked the movement, with more and more Sikhs from both towns and rural areas coming forward to protest. The military reported that Sikh soldiers were becoming restless on the issue. Alarmed, the Punjab authorities tried to divide the Sikhs by getting some pro-British Sikhs to take control of the keys, but in the face of such a massive agitation not even they dared accept such an offer. The SGPC resolved, on 6 December, that no Sikh should agree to take over the keys until all the Akali prisoners had been released. On 12 January 1922, the government capitulated, agreeing to hand over the keys, and five days later, the Akali prisoners were all released. The SGPC added to the humiliation of the authorities by refusing to go to the government office to collect the keys, demanding that a leading official bring them in person. The District Magistrate of Amritsar came, carrying the keys wrapped in a red cloth, and presented them ceremoniously to Baba Kharak Singh, president of the SGPC. The victory was hailed all over India, and Gandhi sent a telegram to Kharak Singh: 'First battle for India's freedom won. Congratulations.'[75] The Akalis had succeeded by forging an alliance of a growing number of Sikhs as well as the general public as the movement escalated, thus isolating the British. The British attempt to divide-and-rule had failed for the time being. It provided a classic example of successful nonviolent strategy, with the moral high ground being held through the exemplary commitment of the Sikhs throughout to strict nonviolence. This wrong-footed the British, who had always projected the Sikhs as a very violent people. One thing that the movement had not however achieved was to bring about any change of heart among the British officials in Punjab. The British had been forced against their will to make concessions that they would try to reverse as soon as it became possible to do so.

The officials now tried to create dissent in the Akali ranks. The Sikh Maharaja of Patiala, a staunch loyalist, had already met Lord Reading and advised him that they needed to win over the more moderate Akalis. He tried to persuade Akali leaders to focus on religious reform and distance themselves from nationalist politics. He paid liberal stipends to some Akali leaders on condition that they work to counter their erstwhile colleagues. He helped the government form a rival association of loyalist Sikhs and attempted to counter the recruitment of the jathas in the rural areas, banning the subjects of his large state from participating in all such activities. He employed journalists on high salaries to carry on propaganda work against the movement. In all this, he worked closely with the Punjab police.[76]

Some militants among the Sikhs chafed against the nonviolence of the main Akali movement. Among them were demobilised soldiers, some returned emigrants from Canada who had been radicalised abroad, and ex-Ghadrites. They believed that a violent revolution, as in Bolshevik Russia, could achieve far more than Gandhian civil disobedience, and held that the latter was designed to discipline and control the discontent of the masses, so that it never threatened vested interests in a serious way. Some argued that nonviolent tactics were 'unworkable'. This group first made itself heard at a Sikh educational conference in March 1921, after which they organised a separate meeting in May of that year. Out of this emerged a rival group called the Babbar Akali Dal. They discussed plans to collect arms and ammunition, organise a mass rising, execute officials and other 'enemies' of the Sikhs, and link up with the Bolsheviks through Afghanistan. The group also plotted to assassinate all those responsible for the massacre at Nankana and drew up lists of British officials and Sikhs to be so targeted. In many respects, this represented a revival of the revolutionary movement of the secret societies of the previous two decades, particularly the Ghadr Movement. They toured Punjab, encouraging the people to rise up in arms, and 'to cut down the foreigner and purge the land of sinful deeds'; and they appealed to the violent martial tradition of the Sikhs and their battles for self-determination over many centuries. Arrests soon followed as, in common with the earlier revolutionaries, they were lax about security. Ruthless interrogations led to the conspiracy being exposed and many members were arrested. Despite this reverse, some Babbars who had remained free organised their own jathas from November 1921, as they could see that this tactic had provided an excellent means to mobilise mass support. They asserted a strong Sikh identity, appealed to the past glories of the Sikh kingdom, and made use of much religious imagery. They exhorted the Sikh peasants to abandon the nonviolence that they claimed was ineffective. The Akalis who were committed to nonviolence condemned them strongly, and overall the impact of the Babbars was limited while noncooperation was going on. Afterwards, from mid-1922 – with what appeared to be the failure of Gandhian tactics at the all-India level – the Babbars began to gain more adherents, especially in the Jullundur and Hoshiarpur area. Some local criminals and bandits also joined, hoping to obtain social legitimacy in the process. From early 1923 they began to murder Sikhs whom they classed as 'toadies'. The British quickly hit back, and most of the leading militants were subsequently killed in police encounters and many of the rank-and-file arrested and jailed. The path of violence failed to liberate the Sikh masses at that time, though it created a heroic legacy that inspired some future Sikh revolutionaries. Probably its main impact lay in making the other Akalis appear relatively moderate, which eventually helped them in their negotiations with the government.[77]

Once the all-India movement collapsed in February 1922, the Punjab authorities launched their counter-offensive. They wanted to proclaim the Akali Dal unlawful and arrest all the members of the SGPC, but this was vetoed by Lord Reading, who realised that these bodies enjoyed strong support from Sikhs throughout Punjab. Instead, there were limited and targeted arrests of certain leaders. The authorities also tried to restore the power of the mahants. The first major clash in this respect occurred at the Guru ka Bagh gurdwara in Amritsar District, which had extensive estates in the area. It had been controlled by a notoriously corrupt mahant called Sundar Das Udasi. Under pressure from the SGPC and unnerved by what had happened at the Golden Temple, Sundar Das had agreed on 31 January 1921 to work under a management committee of eleven members appointed by the SGPC. He still controlled the estates, however. In August 1922, J.M. Dunnett, the District Magistrate of Amritsar, heard that Akalis were felling dead trees on the estate to use as fuel for the communal kitchen of the gurdwara. This had been going on for some time without objection from the mahant. Dunnett realised that this could be made an issue and had five Akalis arrested for this supposed 'crime'. After a trial, they were sentenced to six months in prison and a fine of Rs 50 each. This enthused the movement, which had been a state of relative quiescence after the victories during the Noncooperation period. Jathas marched to the estates of the gurdwara to cut wood on a much larger scale. There were large-scale arrests from late August onwards. The government now had to deal with four thousand militant Akalis. It tried to stop the jathas by turning them back on the roads and at railway stations. Even supplies of provisions to the temple were also not allowed to go through. Dunnett declared all gatherings at the Guru ka Bagh illegal. Despite this, the jathas kept on coming. Many were attacked by the police armed with lathis, some mounted on horses, and many suffered severe injuries.[78]

This violence by the police against Akalis who refused to fight back in a heroic manner, even when beaten badly, caused outrage throughout Punjab and beyond. Prominent national figures, journalists and members of legislative assemblies came from all over India to verify that the violence came entirely from the side of the state. They were of all religions and wings of the nationalist movement, ranging from Hindu nationalists such as Swami Shraddanand and M.M. Malaviya, to leading Khilafatists, and Christian missionaries such as C.F. Andrews. Some of the reporters were beaten by the police as they made their notes. The police actions were filmed by an American cinematographer, who titled the resulting newsreel 'Exclusive pictures of India's martyrdom'. There was a huge rally of over 13,000 people at Jallianwala Bagh on 10 September, over which M.M. Malaviya presided at which the actions of the government were condemned in strong language. C.F. Andrews met Edward Maclagan, the Governor of Punjab, and told him that he had seen hundreds of Christs being crucified at Guru ka Bagh. The publicity caused an outcry that reached even Britain. Maclagan and his executive council visited Guru ka Bagh on 13 September and ordered the police violence to stop. He issued a statement: 'There is no doubt that these stories and the sight of these injuries have excited a large measure of sympathy for the Akalis on the part of loyal and moderate Sikhs and other persons not generally in sympathy with the Akali movement.'[79] He was also worried about the way that Sikh units of the Indian army were becoming excited on the matter. In this way, the protest was succeeding by drawing moral support away from the state, leaving it isolated as erstwhile loyalists and sympathisers were increasingly alienated. In this way, it provided a paradigmatic example of effective nonviolent strategy.

It was not yet over, for the police had only paused in their offensive. While negotiations went on between the government and the SGPC, jathas continued to march to Guru ka Bagh. The police were instructed to concentrate on hitting the Akalis in their private parts or on their legs and feet, in a way that caused maximum pain leaving them almost senseless. They were then dragged by their long hair and dumped in the fields. Large numbers were arrested. By early October the prisons in Punjab were almost full, and arrangements had to be made for temporary jail-accommodation. The jathas kept coming throughout that month, singing their sacred hymns lustily. On 25 October, a jatha of 101 army pensioners led by Subedar-Major Amar Singh was arrested and stripped, leaving them only in their underwear. Another jatha of 103 pensioners followed on 12 November, and they were treated in a similar way. Although the army authorities tried to stop news of this from reaching Sikhs on active service, photographs of the beatings were circulated among the troops, who were outraged at the way that veterans were being so humiliated. The Congress announced that it would conduct an enquiry into the police atrocities. After examining over a hundred eyewitnesses, it published a report that was highly critical of the authorities. Maclagan met Lord Reading in Simla, who – wily as ever – suggested that a way out could be found if a loyalist Sikh could take the estates on lease from the mahant and then allow the Akalis to take the wood. Sir Ganga Ram, a wealthy retired engineer, agreed to do this. The police were then withdrawn. This brought an end to this phase of the campaign. Over 1,500 Akalis had been injured, and more than 5,600 jailed during its course.[80]

The British continued trying to break the movement. In October 1923 they arrested sixty members of the SGPC and tried them for 'treason against the King-Emperor'. The Punjab authorities believed that once the head was cut off, the movement would soon wither. They were quickly proved wrong in this, for a new committee of 62 members was immediately formed to continue the agitation in a more militant way. On 7 January 1924, the Deputy Commissioner of Amritsar at the head of one-hundred armed police tried to surprise the new committee when it was meeting at the Golden Temple. Volunteers formed a human wall to stop them entering the sacred place wearing their boots, and they were forced to turn back. Instead, the committee members all presented themselves for arrest. All except two of the 62 refused to defend themselves at the trial, and they were sent to prison. In this way, they maintained the moral high ground. A third committee soon took the place of the second, and its members were also arrested but soon released as it was found that they were not leading figures in the movement. All of this led to severe criticism of the Punjab government in the nationalist press. In the end, under a new governor, Sir Malcolm Hailey, the authorities reopened negotiations with the SGPC leaders. This culminated in legislation in 1925 to establish a more democratic system of control for the gurdwaras. The SGPC was officially recognised as the representative body of the Sikhs. Hailey deliberately created splits in the body, however, by refusing to release the Akali prisoners unconditionally. Either they agreed to accept the legislation in full, or they would remain in jail. Over half the jailed leaders refused such terms. The SGPC was split over this, some members wanted to work the act, others to refuse to do so until all prisoners were set free. The moderates gained control of the committee, marginalising the radical Akalis. Once eventually out of jail, they agitated against the moderates. The unity of the early 1920s had been lost.[81] This revealed that the British authorities in Punjab were never converted to the Akali point of view in a moral sense. They had merely shifted their stance to alleviate the pressure that the movement had put on them, and then continued their tactics of divide-and-rule by other means.

The Akali campaign that began in 1920 and ended in 1925 was probably the most powerful of the regional struggles in India during this period, with about 30,000 men and women being jailed at different times, some four hundred dying for their cause, and about 2,000 being wounded. One and a half million rupees was levied in fines. It was a genuinely mass movement. The campaign provided examples of heroic nonviolence, and largely achieved its objective in gaining control over some two hundred gurdwaras. It caused serious concern to the British, as it made strong inroads into the army. Many Sikh soldiers asserted their support for the Akalis by wearing black turbans and kirpans (which were banned in the army) and refusing to salute their officers in the correct way. When a member of the 19th Punjabi Company was arrested for wearing a black turban, the rest went on hunger strike. They were court-martialled and given sentences of two years each. Some Sikh troops also refused to go abroad on service. The dissidents were all court-martialled, sentenced, and dismissed from service. Retired soldiers who supported the movement had their pensions and land-grants taken away. The movement also further legitimised the Indian National Congress in Punjab, with middle class nationalist leaders gaining great prestige amongst the peasantry. No longer could the British boast of a supposed 'proverbial loyalty' of the Sikhs towards their rule.[82]

Conclusion

The Congress under Gandhi supported only certain of these campaigns. It backed attempts by nationalists to further the Congress agenda by using their control over local government institutions. The Bengal Congress gave strong support for the campaign in Medinipur to refuse local taxes, and Gandhi did too after visiting the district in September 1921. Although refusal of land tax was on the Congress agenda, Gandhi was prepared to sanction it in only one test area initially – that of Bardoli sub-division in Gujarat. Despite this, peasants of other areas refused their taxes in support of the movement, notably in Kheda in Gujarat and Guntur, Kistna and Godavari in Andhra. In most cases, the initiative came, in the first place, from local-level leaders who were from peasant backgrounds or had close links with the peasantry. Once these peasant movements had gained a strong momentum, they were then accepted by the district and provincial leaders – sometimes rather reluctantly. Gandhi was prepared to tolerate such movements in part because they engaged the British directly (rather than Indian landlords or princes, as in areas such as Awadh and Rajasthan). Also, the regional organisers of these movements were already leading lights in their local Congress organisations and known to have a firm grasp of the basic principles of the movement. Gandhi was thus open to being reassured as to the generally nonviolent potential of these campaigns. We have seen, for example, how in his correspondence with the Andhra leader Kondu Venkatappayya in early 1922, Gandhi accepted his assertion that there was a general commitment to nonviolence by the people of this region. In general, therefore, he gave a guarded backing to the land tax protests.

The British had a rather different understanding of all this. For example, in his official report on noncooperation, P.C. Bamford claimed that in the case of the no-tax campaigns: '...it was apparent that the Congress leaders were being carried on a wave of enthusiasm, of their own raising, faster than they liked to go and much hesitation was apparent among them as to the actual introduction of this step which, they were perfectly aware, would most certainly lead to violence.'[83] In fact, Gandhi and the Congress hierarchy believed no such thing – they could see that when the dominant peasantry was mobilised in an area with a strong Congress organisation, there was a relatively low possibility of violence. In early November 1921, as we have seen in Chapter 2, Gandhi had said that he would support civil disobedience in any district in which there was an almost complete boycott of foreign cloth and widespread production and wearing of khadi cloth, and where the people were living in religious harmony and opposing untouchability. He also said he would withdraw his support if any violence was reported. In other words, Gandhi wanted the people to demonstrate a firm commitment to the movement by ending their dependence on foreign products, and by ending discrimination on grounds of religion or caste purity. He assumed there would be strict nonviolence in such places – though if he was to be proved incorrect on this score, he would immediately halt the protest. On a visit to Medinipur during the height of the anti-union board campaign in September 1921, Gandhi had been highly impressed by the commitment of the people to 'my movement', which appears to have been something of a pleasant surprise to him, given that this was Bengal. He encouraged them to keep up the good work, embrace swadeshi fully and strive for Hindu-Muslim unity.[84] Although he would not, at that time, give full Congress backing for the civil disobedience campaign there, he said that he would not oppose it.

We can observe Gandhi's thinking along these lines when he toured Bardoli preparing it for civil disobedience in the last two months of 1921. He was pleased by the very peaceful atmosphere that prevailed there and was confident in the ability of the local people to maintain nonviolence; he was impressed by the volunteers, male and female, who were carrying out excellent work in mobilising the people along such lines. Nationalist education was well advanced. He also found that there was remarkably little prejudice against untouchables,[85] but was however disturbed to find that the highly exploited labourers who were tied by debt-bonds to the rich peasants had been ignored in all this, being considered too worthless and ignorant to be included. He found that the same applied to the adivasi peasants of the eastern part of the taluka, and ordered the volunteers to rectify this defect immediately. They responded with alacrity, touring the villages telling the labourers and adivasis that a saviour called Mahatma Gandhi had arrived in their midst who would uplift and save them. By this means, they too were mobilised.[86] Similarly, in Andhra, Gandhi was concerned that untouchability had yet to be eliminated, that khadi production was only moderate, and there was little experience of nonviolent methods. The local leader, Venkatappayya, assured him that the practice of untouchability was rapidly dying out, that they were almost self-sufficient in khadi, and that the people were submitting to government repression entirely peacefully. Gandhi accepted this and blessed the campaign there.

We have noted already in the previous volume some of the reasons why such dominant peasants had by this time come to appreciate the advantages of Gandhian nonviolence in their campaigns of civil disobedience.[87] They were from a more prosperous village stratum that had relatively high rates of literacy and were exposed to the literature of the Gandhian Congress with its constant entreaties for principled nonviolence. They were able to grasp the clear strategic advantages of such an approach – one that put them morally in the right. Furthermore, they could see that such a method suited their own class needs. They were, above all, fighting for their self-determination against oppressive local bureaucracies. Although – prodded by Gandhi – they managed to mobilise the poorer peasantry behind their cause, they had no intention of surrendering any power to them at village level. Rather, they appreciated how nonviolence did not generally disturb the rural status quo. For all these reasons, the caste groups that took the lead in several of the significant campaigns of 1921–22 – whether the Patidars, Kammas, Reddys, Lingayats, Havigs, Jats, or Mahisyas – were willing at that time to make a firm effort to maintain the principles of Gandhian nonviolence.

6

BRAIDING THE NATION

In the last three chapters, we examined a wide range of local campaigns. Although focussing on specific issues, all were underpinned by the general demand for a swaraj that was regarded as either imminent or already in being. In this chapter, we shall try to delineate the ways in which these protests were braided into a cohesive national whole. This process was never secure – the threads braided for a time but then unravelled.

The concept of 'braiding' of different political domains comes from Ranajit Guha. While emphasising the differences between the elite and subaltern domains, he nevertheless insisted that they always interacted. In particular, the – in his words – 'more advanced elements of the indigenous elite' made strong efforts to integrate the domains under late British rule. When the braiding was 'linked to struggles which had more or less clearly defined anti-imperialist objectives and were consistently waged', the results could soon transcend the limits set by the elites and become 'explosive'.[1] Applied to noncooperation, we find a multiplicity of political actors from many classes and regions braiding numerous threads into a powerful demand for national 'swaraj' in a way that shook British rule to its core. In this chapter, we shall examine how the authority of the British was undermined, how an alternative nationalist message was propagated, and the sort of leadership that came to the fore to steer the movement.

Authority

Writing on the theory and practice of civil resistance, Kurt Schock has noted that although grievances 'are at the root of collective challenges to the status quo, ...rarely if ever is there a direct and unmitigated relationship between grievances and dissent'. He cites Frances Fox Piven and Richard Cloward, who have stated: 'The social arrangements that are ordinarily perceived as just and immutable must come to seem both unjust and mutable.' Doug McAdam has written similarly as to how cognitive liberation is required before there can be widespread popular mobilisation. People must start to believe that that the existing order is unjust or illegitimate, that existing conditions are not inevitable, and that they can change the whole system of oppression through their personal participation in a campaign of collective action.[2]

Was this the case in India in 1920–22, when British rule was challenged in new ways? Was a regime seen as 'just and immutable' being rejected, and if so, in what way? To answer these questions, we need to understand how the British had maintained their hold over India during the nineteenth century and initial years of the twentieth century. In what way, if any, was their rule considered legitimate? Ranajit Guha has argued that the British never enjoyed 'hegemony' – that is, that they never provided what Gramsci defined as the intellectual and moral leadership that is accepted as inevitable and even rightful by subaltern classes. Rather, they dominated through a combination of force and persuasion. Their rule continued to be viewed by many Indians as alien, and there were periods of outright revolt, as in 1857, when rebels sought to restore the rule of those considered 'their own'.[3] In my view, although British rule in India rested to a considerable extent on force, it could not have continued so long as it did without being widely accepted as having a legitimacy that derived from two sources – one conservative, the other liberal. The first was that of authority, in the sense understood by Hannah Arendt. She argued that we should understand 'authority' as being separate from both force and persuasion. Authority does not require coercion, and it does not try to rationalise its existence through argument. Rather, it assumes a hierarchy of control that is seen to be self-evidently legitimate, and within which each social group has its own stable place. The source of such authority is seen to be a force that is 'external and superior to its own power … which transcends the political realm.'[4] For many of the British in India, the transcendent force – as supposedly approved by the Christian God – was that of the rule of property and a codified law.[5] As Kipling asserted memorably in 'Recessional' (1897):

> God of our fathers, known of old,
> Lord of our far-flung battle-line,
> Beneath whose awful Hand we hold
> Dominion over palm and pine –
> …..
> If, drunk with sight of power, we loose
> Wild tongues that have not Thee in awe,
> Such boastings as the Gentiles use,
> Or lesser breeds without the Law -
> Lord God of Hosts, be with us yet,
> Lest we forget – lest we forget!

For Kipling, British rule rested on upholding 'the Law', being contrasted with the regimes of 'lesser breeds' that held to no such principle. They were, rather, the 'heathen heart that puts her trust / In reeking tube and iron shard' – in others words, peoples who ruled through force rather than through Law. He exhorted his fellows to remember their responsibilities – otherwise the Raj would lose its legitimacy and soon perish.[6] In this, the British placed themselves at the apex of a hierarchy of authority, wrapping themselves in a cloak of indomitable strength. Arendt understands such authority as being essentially pre-modern, being a principle upheld by conservative thinkers. From the eighteenth century onwards, this mindset was challenged by liberals who sought to root sovereignty not in a divinely appointed hierarchy but in the People. British liberals saw their role as that of educating subjugated peoples so that they would be in a position in time to exercise responsible government. This appeal resonated with middle class Indians, who tried to hold the imperial state to such a promise. In this, they revealed the extent to which they had been hegemonised. For the mass of the people, however, it was the authority of the British that they rejected so emphatically during the Noncooperation Movement of 1920–22.

Sumit Sarkar has noted in this respect of Bengal that while the masses there largely regarded the Swadeshi Movement of 1905–09 as a quarrel among the 'Babus' – e.g. between the British and the bhadralok – in 1920–22 they now believed that the Raj itself was doomed. There were two main causes for this. First, there was the economic dislocation caused by the First World War, with rapid inflation causing severe hardship to large numbers. This created a climate of dissatisfaction that could fuel protest. Second, and probably more important, was a popular belief time that British authority was in melt-down. This was fed through numerous rumours about the specific ways in which this was happening. People who were suffering from many oppressions and hardships were thus emboldened to take direct action.[7]

The British were now depicted as being irreligious, demonic, treacherous, and responsible for a decline in the moral character of the Indian people. British institutions such as their schools and courts were seen to crush people's souls, suppress noble ideas, instigate evil passions, and divide society. India's spiritual morality was being undermined. These sentiments led in some cases to considerable hostility towards all white 'sahebs'. Europeans were, for example, boycotted throughout East Bengal. They had stones and bricks thrown at them in Dacca and Comilla. Even those who worked for Europeans as servants were affected by the new mood, as at Akhaura in Tippera, where in May 1921 many went on strike for a short time after a jute agency assistance slapped one of them. Some very intemperate taunts were directed at the rulers. 'At a meeting in Nadia it was stated that chastity was rare among English women and Englishmen were described as sons of bastards.'[8] The climate of hostility in UP was such that the English began to suspect almost all Indians of subversion, even their servants. Their memories were of the so called 'Mutiny' of 1857, when their forebears were attacked and killed by the people, and they feared that there might be a repetition in 1921. They took to carrying revolvers around with them, and in Allahabad, plans were drawn up for a quick evacuation of the entire European community to the fort if necessary.[9]

The aura of authority around the British was fractured also at this time because they were seen – supposedly – to tremble before the power of the Mahatma. The Banaras daily newspaper *Aaj* thus reported in January 1921 how an engine-driver at Kasganj station in Etah district had dreamed that Gandhi was marching towards them to destroy all Britishers. He awoke and ran wildly to the European quarter warning its inhabitants to flee. There was – it was said – a panic, with English women being hidden away in cupboards and boxes and the Englishmen desperately trying to obtain the keys of the town armoury in the middle of the night to no avail. Next day, the Indians of the town had a good laugh. For them it showed up the imperial rulers to be a cowardly people who were mortally afraid of Gandhi. The engine-driver's dream appears to have then been reported widely, with great glee, in the provincial press.[10]

It was significant in this respect that there was widespread discontent in regions that acted as recruiting-grounds for the Indian Army. We have seen this in the case of the Akali movement in Punjab, where many Sikhs rejected the British presence in a wholly new way. Often, the experience of serving in the army during the First World War provided the catalyst. Uttarakhand, which saw a major protest against British forest officials at this time, was another such recruiting area, and many of the local leaders of the protest were ex-soldiers who had experienced the wider world of imperial rule. They were considered sophisticated people and they enjoyed considerable prestige in their villages. They felt that they had put their lives on the line for the British Empire in the Great War, and that they deserved their reward – namely, free use of the forest resources. They took the initiative in establishing local branches of the Kumaon Parishad. In a speech, one such demobbed soldier recounted how when he had been visited by the King Emperor while he lay in hospital recovering from a battle-wound he took advantage of the situation to complain that they were being oppressed in his home by petty officials and forest guards. He proclaimed: 'Government was not a Raja, but a Bania and Rakshasi Raj and the King Emperor was Ravan'. In other words, the King Emperor lacked legitimacy in his eyes, being more of a Ravan, or demon-king, than a moral authority, acting more like a money-grubbing Baniya (merchant) than honourable ruler. In this way, British rule was rejected by those who had had a particularly close experience of it. Many ex-soldiers took the initiative in burning the forest-floor in defiance of the forest officials, with their example soon being followed by their less bold fellow-villagers.[11] This loss of authority in major recruiting-areas was particularly ominous for the imperial state.

There was now an unprecedented disrespect for the law-enforcing agencies of the state – that is, the police, the courts, and the jail. The Awadh Kisan pledge of May-June 1921, point 7, stated: 'We shall not be afraid of constables. If they oppress [us] we shall stop [them]. We shall submit to no one's oppression.'[12] It was reported from the interior of Mymensingh District of East Bengal that the government had lost its authority and people were refusing to cooperate with police investigations.[13] The police found that they could no longer keep order through a token presence, but needed to show their strength in numbers, which added to the tension. Large crowds demonstrated outside courts when there were trials of nationalists, and even rescued nationalist prisoners from the clutches of the police.

People were no longer scared of jail and regarded it as a place of pilgrimage. This all became a major concern for the government. The nationalists depicted the British courts of law as places of falsehood, deceit, treachery, dishonesty and meanness, and people's tribunals (panchayats) were commonly established to provide an alternative justice. Panchayats would – it was said – provide true justice and save the honour of the people and unite rather than divide them. In Awadh, the kisan pledge of May–June 1920, point 5, stated: 'We shall not quarrel and if we do we shall settle it by panchayat. Every village or two to three villages combined will form a panchayat and disperse of matters there.' Such panchayats were set up also in Bihar in early 1921 as an alternative to the British courts. In Medinipur, the initiative came from some local lawyers and teachers who had resigned their positions to join the movement, and who urged the people to settle disputes through arbitration only. Some lawyers who had given up their practices travelled around the rural areas settling disputes in this way. In Bengal as a whole, 866 such popular courts were established during the movement, and for a time they outnumbered the government ones.[14]

The nationalists sought to replace the institutions, customs and rituals associated with British rule with alternatives of their own that the people could look up to and respect. National ceremonies replaced those of the British, with alternative meetings, processions, days of celebration and remembrance, publications, flag salutations, songs, and plays.[15] Kidambi has written of how in Bombay City, there were 'hartals, flag salutations, dawn marches, sit-downs, pickets, parades and processions'. These 'carefully choreographed rituals of resistance' served to claim public spaces as legitimate arenas for nationalist politics. The largest protest meetings were held on the sands of Chowpatty beach, which was on the border between the Indian and British-dominated localities, and which was overlooked from the residence of the Governor of Bombay Presidency on the adjoining Malabar Hill.[16] In this way, a prominent space in Bombay City was apparently 'liberated' – at least for a time – from the clutches of the British. Shunning foreign cloth and wearing khadi became a marker of the new identity, with respect being given to those who wore this national dress rather than British-style outfits, as had hitherto been the case. Liquor-drinking was branded as disreputable and giving up drink was said be a form of moral purification.

The people came to see the Congress and Khilafat as rightful authorities that would stand for them. This helped empower and build their self-respect and confidence. As an official working for a British-owned landlord agency told a Congress activist in the Jungle Mahals of Medinipur in Bengal: 'It is because of you that the peasants have the courage to carry out these wrongful deeds'. The 'wrongful deeds' that he had in mind were numerous. The peasants began to treat the Congress office in the same way that they had the government office previously, coming there with deeds for the sale and transfer of land, with Congress workers putting the Congress seal on the documents. The Congress also set up granaries for surplus rice and gave it out on loan to those in need. The local post office stopped functioning, and the Congress took over. A manager of the Midnapore Zamindari Company was even seen to take off his hat when passing the Congress office as a sign of deference.[17] In eastern UP, an alternative Gandhi currency was, for a time, used in place of official rupees. This originated in receipts handed out for donations to the Khilafat fund that bore a certain resemblance to a one-rupee note. They became known as 'Gandhi notes', and people who refused to accept them as legal tender were accused of opposing the Mahatma.[18]

The alternative authority, that was to be put in the place, was not in general a liberal-democratic one. Rather, it was a righteous authority – whether under the benign rule of a great raja, a Caliph, or a saintly Mahatma. In embracing such an agenda, the masses gained a new confidence and audacity. They stood up for themselves and shed their awe of British authority. The demand for swaraj went well beyond the areas ruled directly by the British; there were protests also in the Indian princely states that covered about one third of the land mass of the subcontinent, in which the authority of the princes was challenged. These were spearheaded mainly by the middle classes of the cities, some of whose members were developing pro-nationalist sentiments at this time, with peasants also becoming involved in a few princely states, as we have seen already in the section in Chapter 3 on anti-landlord movements.[19] Though the movement unravelled in 1922, and though there was still twenty-five years before full independence came, the rule of both the British and the princes never recovered from the profound traumas they suffered in 1920–22.

Propagation

The nationalist message was propagated in many ways, each reinforcing the others. Direct appeals were made through mass meetings, processions, and the enactment of nationalist rituals. News of the movement and instructions were communicated through newspapers, nationalist weeklies and bulletins both in English and regional languages. There were nationalist songs, poetry recitals and plays.

Huge rallies attended by thousands of people provided a powerful demonstration of the mass support enjoyed by the nationalists. Many of the leading nationalists were powerful orators who knew how to stir popular emotions. The Andhra leader Gopalakrishnayya was, for example, said to have a melodious and compelling tone that made a deep impression on his audience. In his speeches, he compared the movement to the mythical battle of Kurukshetra in the Mahabharata, with Gandhi as the Krishna figure who had come to save the people from evil rule.[20] There was of course much fluidity in the interpretation of such messages – as Shahid Amin has shown so well in his study of the interpretation of Gandhi's speech in Gorakhpur.[21] There were also smaller gatherings. In Andhra, Congress volunteers were, for example, dispatched to go from village to village giving speeches. According to government reports, they gave powerful exhortations excoriating the British and their rule.[22]

Gandhi did not trust large crowds to always remain peaceful, and he insisted that they should be carefully marshalled by well-trained volunteers. Since the time of the Swadeshi Movement, Congress had had its patriotic *karmi* (workers) or *sevak* (servants) who had sought to control crowds.[23] *Seva Samitis* (service associations) performed the same function for the Home Rule League and in the Rowlatt Satyagraha. Gandhi felt that these volunteers had not proved up to the task. They failed – he asserted – to coordinate their work, and too often got caught up in the fervour of the occasion rather than stand apart from the crowd and act as what he called 'people's policemen'. They had to be carefully trained – just as soldiers were trained before being sent into battle – and they needed a book of instruction for guidance. They should be posted at different places in crowds, rather than merely bunched around the leaders. They should signal to each other with flags and whistles. The crowds had to be taught to stand in an orderly and 'motionless' manner, not pressing forward. When welcoming a leader at a railway station, they were to stand outside rather than obstructing the platform and passage out. They should provide plenty of space for the vehicles of the leaders to proceed, lining the roadsides rather than pressing forward. They had to be encouraged to chant a limited number of constructive 'national cries' at appropriate junctures rather than keep up a discordant din. Gandhi discouraged cries that celebrated individual leaders, such as himself or the Ali brothers. Best of all was the slogan '*Hindu-Musalman ki jai*' ('Long live Hindu-Muslim unity'). The chanting should be in unison and in harmony. Indeed, silence at such times was quite appropriate and dignified. Women in the crowd should be protected and children never allowed into the middle of dense crowds. These suggestions were not, Gandhi emphasised exhaustive, but provided a guide to the sort of considerations that they needed to have in mind when developing strategies of crowd control.[24] As we have seen in previous chapters, such directions were not adhered to as much as Gandhi would have liked. Large crowds were not easy to control, and the available number of trained volunteers was normally inadequate. Despite this, most demonstrations were peaceful. We shall examine this issue more in the next chapter when we look at popular protest.

There was an eruption of nationalist publishing at this time that continued from a tradition of activist journalism in India. The first copy of Gandhi's weekly, *Young India*, appeared in October 1919, priced at one anna – low enough to be easily afforded.[25] Elsewhere, two journalists who worked with the Pune-based newspaper *Loksangraha* – Vinayakrao Bhuskute and Shankarrao Deo – became important leaders of the Mulshi satyagraha after visiting the area to investigate the grievances of the peasants. This movement received strong support throughout from Tilak's old Pune-based newspaper, *Kesari*.[26] Other journalists started new nationalist newspapers. One such person was Dasrath Dwivedi, a young nationalist of Gorakhpur district who had been employed as a journalist on the *Pratap* newspaper in Kanpur. He decided to return home to start a nationalist paper called *Swadesh* that provided detailed coverage of the Noncooperation Movement.[27] In Awadh, local newspapers were often inventive in the way that they reported Gandhi's supposed sayings and they mixed reports of actual events with rumours. The *Awadh Bhashi* published accounts of various 'miracles' associated with Gandhi, which all helped boost his popularity in the region.[28] Writing of Bihar, Lata Singh noted how local newspapers reported nationalist activity from all over India, which gave the impression that the movement was going from strength to strength. This helped to build and consolidate anti-British sentiments. In itself, the fact that such news and comment could be published, challenged the authority of the British. There were also nationalist pamphlets, leaflets, news bulletins, books, posters, and collections of songs. They were printed, cyclostyled, even handwritten. Much of this was produced in underground printing presses and distributed clandestinely. Prices were very low. The language was generally simple and easy to follow, and people would regularly gather in the house of a literate person to listen to the reading of such material.[29]

The message they put over was that it is better to die than live the life of a slave, and dying for one's country was depicted as a worthy sacrifice. Those who did not join the struggle were said to be bringing dishonour and shame on their families. India was said to be losing its spiritual values because of British rule, with Brahmans and Kshatriyas having fallen from their high pedestals. The Ramayana and Mahabharata were frequently invoked as ideals, and British rule was equated with that of the demon-king Ravan, while noncooperators were like his opponent, the deity Ram. Or, the nation was elevated to the status of a mother goddess – Bharatmata – who demanded the highest sacrifice from all. The sacred cow was said to be threatened by the British who had slaughtered hundreds of thousands. It was therefore *dharmic* (a religious duty) to join the struggle. By resisting, the people could save their religion and glorious civilisation and honour. Satyagraha was seen to be self-cleansing, failure to support it as ritually polluting. Wearing khadi was one way to cleanse oneself.[30]

Nationalist songs and music were also of great importance. Mary King has argued that: 'Music and the singing of songs is a universal feature of nonviolent struggles, binding participants together, enlivening, unburdening, helping to find a collective response to apprehension or fear, and sometimes contributing to the making of decisions.'[31] Gene Sharp, similarly, writes:

> Under appropriate conditions, singing may constitute a method of nonviolent protest – for example, singing while an unwanted speech is being made, singing national or religious songs and hymns, rival vocal programmes to compete with boycotted ones organised by the opponent, singing while engaged in a march, civil disobedience, or some other act of opposition, singing songs of social and political satire and protest.

He mentions how, in 1901, Finns had sung patriotic songs with great fervour, drowning out pro-Tsarist propaganda being preached from church pulpits.[32] Gandhi was always aware of the power of music and song, deploying it routinely in his ashram. He saw also that it was useful in crowd control, stating: 'Music means rhythm, order. Its effect is electrical. It immediately soothes. I have seen, in European countries, a resourceful superintendent of police controlling the mischievous tendencies of mobs by starting a popular song.' Nationalist volunteers – he continued – could achieve the same effect by leading the singing of nationalist songs during demonstrations.[33]

Many collections of nationalist songs and poems that could be set to music were published in response to this need. Generally considered 'seditious' by the government, they were often banned – with copies being retained in the archives, where they can be viewed to this day. The Maharashtra State Archives in Bombay, for example, holds booklets of patriotic songs and poems in Gujarati that date from this time. They were commonly priced at an affordable one anna. One by Jadulal Narandas of Nadiad was titled *Asahkar Vina* (the Lute of Noncooperation), another was published by the Ganesh Printing Press in Ahmedabad titled *Vada-Sinorno Raja ke Rakshas Yane Julamathi Prajani Luntayeli Laj* (The Demon-King of Vadasinor or the honour of the Subjects Robbed through Oppression), and another by Prabhudas Lallubhjai Thakkar of Chhapra in Kheda District titled *Laganma Khadina Gito* (Marriage Songs on Khadi). Jadulal Narandas also published a book of poems titled *Swadesh Kavya* (Poems of Self-Rule). *Asahkar Vina* and another pamphlet by Narandas were subsequently banned by the British and the author issued with a warning. The Bharuch Khadi Committee in Gujarat employed a blind poet and musician called Hansraj Harakhji Amreliwala – who was from Amreli in Kathiawad – to travel around singing songs that advocated the boycott of foreign cloth and the use instead of khadi. He was known for his melodious voice and ability to attract a crowd. He published a booklet of his songs titled *Kavya Triveni* (Poems of the Triveni – the confluence of the three sacred rivers of the Ganges, Jumna and mythical Saraswati). These were also banned.[34]

Songs such as these – which were published in all parts of India in regional languages – were on many nationalist themes. They spoke of British oppression; they lauded Gandhi and Mother India; they endorsed swadeshi, spinning on charkha, the wearing of khadi, the national flag, nationalist education, uplifting untouchables, jail-going; they advocated sobriety and a moral lifestyle, and the boycott of the British and their machinery of government.

Shahid Amin has written of the 'melodious Gandhi bhajans' that were performed to village audiences by high-caste Congress activists in Gorakhpur District, in UP in early 1921.[35] For Bihar, Singh has described how nationalist meetings generally started with the singing of such songs. They emphasised the way that India was being ruined under imperial rule. The British were condemned for destroying Indian culture – their government was irreligious, demonic, treacherous, and responsible for a decline in the moral character of the Indian people. They were accused of ruling by dividing Hindus and Muslims. British institutions such as their schools and courts were seen to crush people's souls, supress noble ideas, instigate evil passions and divide society. Courts were places of falsehood, deceit, treachery, dishonesty and meanness. The British were shown as perpetrating *jalim*, or atrocity, with Jallianwala Bagh being cited as proof of this. One song was titled 'Oppression of Dyer', and it recounted how the blood of children and women was on his hands and how he had 'spoilt the honour of dear and devoted wives'.[36]

The subject of British oppression was the theme of a Gujarati song: *Digdarshan*, or 'A Revelation', by Hansraj Amreliwala. In this, he declared how his tongue was ashamed to describe the atrocities committed by the British in Punjab, in 1919. Those 'lordly asses brayed and spat on the brave women of the sacred soil'. The British divided Hindu and Muslim brothers and derided their unity. The people of India had:

> ...to break this state of dependence, otherwise it is better to die.
> How can you still swallow the poisonous pill of slavery?
> It was better if mother had given us poison instead of giving us milk.
> That power has drugged us to sleep by means of foreign cloth.
> That power has sucked our blood to its heart's content and further added insult to injury.
> Your pulse is still throbbing, so rise with a new life!
> By good luck, a saint [Gandhi] has come to you; behold! And shake off your lethargy.[37]

In another song, he declared that they were living in a dark age in which corruption and vice flourished, to which the only answer was to fight for swaraj.[38] Similarly, Prabhudas Thakkar exclaimed in his *Laganma Khadina Gito*:

> Look O sister, how deceitful is Government;
> It has arrested the heroes of India....
> It increases the army for the sake of protection and strikes India with India's arms.[39]

The most popular nationalist song in Andhra dealt with the same theme. *Makoddi Telladoratnamu* by Garimella Satyanaryan had verses that deplored that despite abundant harvests the people lacked food to fill their stomachs, how they were forbidden by law to speak out against oppression, how young people were stopped from entering their schools if they wore a Gandhi cap, how herds of pregnant cows were slaughtered, how they should go to jail to win freedom, how the white people had committed many oppressions – such as killing Mappila rebels by suffocating them in rail wagons – and so on. In response to all this, the 'God' Gandhi and Bharat Mata had performed great *tapasya* (penances), and in response the goddess *Dharma* (religion) had appeared and said that all their desires would be fulfilled. This had put great fear in the hearts of *doras* (white people). Each of the thirteen verses ended with a chorus:

> We don't want this White Lord's rule; God
> We don't want this White Lord's rule.
> Pouncing on our lives,
> Violating our modesty
> We don't want this White Lord's rule; God
> We don't want this White Lord's rule.[40]

Some songs depicted British rule as being on the edge of collapse, so that the people of India had nothing to lose and much to gain by rebelling. Gandhi was taken as the inspiration in this respect. In the words of a nationalist song from Andhra:

> Everything filled with Gandhi – this whole world filled with Gandhi
> Disobeying – the Government laws
> Calling all – with blessing hand
> Here is *swarajya* – here is freedom
> Come, come, here – (he) called all generously.[41]

Others lauded Gandhi, conferring on him divine powers. Several songs from Andhra thus depicted Gandhi as a divinity who had come to save India. We shall examine these in the next chapter. There were songs that advocated swadeshi and khadi production and wearing. In one of his Gujarati songs, title *Chavi*, or 'Key', Prabhudas Thakkar exclaimed: 'Put on khadi, O my sister. The spinning wheel will be the destruction of those who disgraced lakhs at Jallianwala; so says Gandhiji.' The song goes on to allege that cow fat was mixed with foreign cloth and bones with foreign sugar, polluting the bodies of the Indian people.[42] In similar vein, Hansraj Amreliwala intoned:

Why do you besiege the Mother and suck her very life blood by putting on foreign clothes?
Why do you caress the poisonous and ungrateful enemy of the Mother by co-operating with him?
Guru Gandhiji has been telling us that swaraj is contained in swadeshi only,
He has put on a loin cloth and is going through the forest of difficulty.[43]

In *Digdarshan*, or 'A Revelation', Amreliwala proclaimed that wearing foreign cloth was like trampling 'on the breast of the Mother' – e.g. Mother India, or Bharat Mata. It was like taking the side of Dushasan (an antagonist of the virtuous Pandavas of the Mahabharata). It maintained the grip of 'that brutal foreign power that tramples on the head of Bharat and puts out the light of Islam' – a power that humiliated Punjab by committing atrocities in Amritsar.[44]

Set alongside these songs with a strongly Hindu content, there were ones that were designed to appeal to Muslim Khilafatist sentiments. These could be composed by Hindus such as Jadulal Narandas, one of whose Gujarati songs went:

Oh Ruler of Medina [e.g. the Prophet Muhammad] for God's sake help us;
See what sorts of oppression they are practicing upon us.
May the Khilafat remain intact until the day of judgement![45]

Poetry and song was extremely important in South Asian Muslim culture, and pro-Khilafat songs and poems composed by Muslims became a striking feature of the movement. These tended to be subtler in sentiment than the average run of nationalist songs composed by Hindus. The *musha'ira* or poetic recitation was central to elite Muslim culture, while the masses sang Islamic devotional songs at festivals and shrines. Minault has written of how poetry and song provided a means of communication between the Muslim elites and masses. It spoke to people's emotions in a way that political speeches by themselves could not. Popular poetic imagery of unrequited love and the conviviality of the assembly of believers was adapted for the political cause, with laments for a devastated garden and an end to the easy conviviality of a vanished time of Islamic rule, now replaced by a foreign oppressor.

In such songs and poems, the patriot thirsted for freedom, but was instead imprisoned in a cage.[46]

Some prominent Khilafat leaders such as Muhammad Ali, Hasrat Mohani, and others wrote powerful verse that they published in their newspapers. Often, their poems were ambiguous, so that they avoided censorship. For example, a poem in the *Zamindar*, which was the mouthpiece of Muslim activism in Punjab, went:

> The garden is restless to hear the song 'God is one'
> The time to set the nightingale free from his cage has come.

Readers would have been clear that this meant freeing India from the British cage, but it was not stated as such, and thus could hardly be branded seditious by the British. The past glories of Islam were invoked in a way that suggested present decline into an abject subjugation.

Muhammad Ali wrote poetry under the penname of Jauhar. He mainly wrote in jail when he had the leisure to do so. Being in prison, the imagery of the bird in the cage longing for the garden of freedom appears frequently in his compositions. Hasrat Mohani edited *Urdu-e-Mu'alla* from Aligarh. He was renowned more for his poetry than prose. Much of it dealt with matters of love, but he also composed political verse. For example:

> The custom of tyranny successful, how long will it last?
> Love of country in a stupor, how long will it last?
> How long will the chains of deception hold fast?
> The stymied anger of people, how long will it last?
> What tyrannies in the name of laws are passed.
> This veiled force, how long will it last?
> The riches of India in foreign hands are clasped.
> These numberless riches, how long will they last?

There was no covert imagery here – the message was direct.[47]

Forms of popular religious recital were appropriated by nationalists to convey a nationalist message. Religious songs and hymns – known as *bhajans*, *kirtans*, and *qawwali* – were sung during rites of worship, religious festivals and in processions. In the words of Murali, they expressed the 'aspirations, perceptions and world-view' of the masses. Hindu devotional songs were often sung in Andhra in *radhotsawas* – processions bearing an image of a deity on a wooden cart (*radha*, or elsewhere in India, a *rath*) – that was dragged along as participants sang their hymns of praise. During noncooperation, this was given a nationalist content, with participants interlacing religious and nationalist songs. Pictures of Gandhi and other nationalist leaders were carried on the wooden cart along with the image of the deities. It soon became a requirement for all such processions to incorporate images of Gandhi. A nationalist from Guntur noticed in June 1921 that if it was omitted, the people 'become angry and refuse to drag the *radha*'. Smaller processions that carried hand-held images of deities were known as *prabha* (meaning 'greatness' or 'glory'). Nationalist *bhajan kirtan prabha* became a major feature of the movement in Andhra. They would start in one village, with rallies being held as they passed through other villages. The number of participants swelled as they went. When the AICC session was held at Vijaywada in Andhra in March-April 1921, it was estimated that some 200,000 people came from different parts of the province in many such groups. They sang bhajans and kirtans as they went along, holding meetings in each village on their way to propagate swaraj. Although such processions were ostensibly in honour of Hindu deities, they were sufficiently incorporative to include nationalist politicians such as Gandhi and the Ali brothers. They were not seen as communally divisive, being popular celebrations in which people of all classes and religions participated.[48] In Gujarat and Bombay, early-morning processions – mainly of women – wound through towns and cities singing religious-cum-nationalist songs, both Hindu and Islamic. Previously such pre-dawn processions – known as *prabhat pheris* – had featured only religious hymns, now a nationalist content was injected into them.[49] In Medinipur in Bengal, purely religious songs were sung to maintain solidarity when officials came to collect tax or distrain property in lieu of tax. One official reported that he felt so intimidated by the strength of feeling expressed in such a performance that he left the villages without taking the intended action.[50]

Troupes of travelling players also performed specially written nationalist plays. Plays were a particularly important medium in this respect in Andhra. Damaraju Pundarikashaudu of Guntur, who wrote a series of such plays, stated in the introduction to the first of these – *Navayugarambham* (Advent of a New Era) of 1921 – that his aim was to reach 'the illiterate common people and developing political consciousness among them'. The play was full of religious imagery, with Gandhi being depicted as the saviour of Hinduism and *Bharat Mata*. The play ended with a blessing: 'Under the able leadership of Mahatma Gandhi, who believes in non-violent path and leads you with competence, all of you would become victorious. Best wishes for you. Soon you would get *Swarajya*.' Another of his plays, *Gandhi Vijayam* (Victory of Gandhi) depicted peasants discussing the burdens of British rule and looking to Gandhi to save them: 'Resolve to non-cooperate for one year; then only *Swarajya* with all miracles would come…' In another of his plays, Gandhi was depicted as being sent by Krishna to avenge the Amritsar massacre after a mother who had been humiliated by General Dyer had issued a fervent prayer to the deity. Krishna declares: 'You will have salvation by the method shown to you by Mahatma Gandhi, who is sweetly peaceful…' Krishna is reincarnated as Gandhi, who then chases General Dyer away. In all, around eighteen plays were produced in Andhra at this time to propagate the nationalist message. Some were on mythological figures or heroic warriors from the past such as the ruler of Mewar, Rana Pratap, and the Maharashtrian king Shivaji – both of whom defied the Mughal Empire – with clear parallels being drawn between what were depicted as past struggles to liberate the Motherland, and the present campaign. Several theatre groups toured the rural areas, putting on these plays to village audiences. There were hundreds of such performances, continuing even after the actual texts of these plays had been censored and banned by the government as 'seditious'. Their emotional impact was considerable. In the words of one police inspector – 'in my humble opinion even several non-cooperation meetings could not impress so well.'[51]

It is striking how much of this nationalist propaganda – in all its various forms – appealed to both Hindu and Muslim religious sentiments. At the time, each tradition managed to respect the other, so that at this juncture the two – in general – reinforced rather than undermined the movement for a united India. Neither 'Hindu nationalism' nor 'Muslim nationalism' – meaning mutually exclusive and antagonistic doctrines – were to the fore in 1920–22. There was in all this, however, the potential for more fundamentalist and exclusivist religious appeals, as was to become only too apparent in the years that followed.'[52]

Leadership

Successful protest movements require able and committed leadership at various levels. Important tasks of leaders are: to establish a clear goal for a movement; create an organisational structure; work out strategy and tactics; guide in a planned way; identify appropriate moments for different types of action; provide internal discipline; direct, motivate and interpret events to followers; show faith that a favourable result will be achieved; set an example through personal courage and sacrifice; act as the 'voice of the movement' in dealing with the authorities and media; ensure that the movement is united and coherent; and negotiate with opponents in a constructive way. It also helps to have a clear strategy in the face of repression, with plans for regrouping and maintaining the strength of the movement in adversity.

Gene Sharp has emphasised how important such leaders are when knowledge of the principles of nonviolence and nonviolent technique is not widespread – they need to educate followers in this respect. He notes how Gandhi believed in strong leadership at every level, from the top down to local cadres, as the mass of participants had – in Gandhi's view – no intelligent understanding of nonviolence, while they had a strong faith in their leaders.[53] In this, Gandhi advocated a hierarchy of leadership. While he provided the overall direction and strategy, local leaders mobilised a range of social groups around the many issues that we have examined in previous chapters. Sydney Tarrow has observed that the most powerful movements tend to draw on local networks, as this allows for stronger solidarity. In this respect, movements become coalitions held together by overarching leaders.[54]

We can distinguish three main levels of leadership during the Noncooperation Movement – the national – which Gandhi came to embody in the popular mind – the provincial, and the local. We shall look at each of these in turn. The leaders whom we examine preached nonviolence for the most part – either because they deemed it a preferable tactic at that juncture or because they adhered to it as an absolute moral principle. In winning and maintaining support for this strategy, they succeeded to greater or lesser degrees.

Gandhi

As the reader will already have grasped, it is hard to underestimate the power of Gandhi's name in 1920–22. Sumit Sarkar has described it as a new 'symbolic power centre' that provided a focus for many discontents as well as huge hope. This projection of Gandhi was exceptional; no other nationalist leader ever achieved such a level of adulation.[55] Though the Ali brothers can also be counted as national-level leaders who were in certain respects on a par with Gandhi, their reputation was on a different level.

Gandhi appealed to different people and groups for a range of reasons. The nationalist elites appreciated his unique ability to reach out to the popular masses. Others revered him as a champion of the people in their struggles against class and caste oppression and colonial rule; as a member of the upper class who had given up his professional career and wealth for the cause; as a person of great personal purity and morality; as an ethical reformer; as a messiah of an imminent earthly paradise – that of 'Gandhi Raj'; even a reincarnation of God. His name was even appropriated as a rallying cry in attacks on traders and policemen. We may examine these attributes in turn.

First, the nationalist elites appreciated him as one of their own who had a rare gift to be able to speak the language of the people. Thus Rabindranath Tagore, writing in the *Modern Review* in October 1921, set out what he believed to be so distinctive about Gandhi's leadership:

> The movement which has now succeeded the Swadeshi agitation, is ever so much greater and has moreover extended its influence all over India. Previously, the vision of our political leaders had never reached beyond the English-knowing classes… At this juncture, Mahatma Gandhi came and stood at the cottage door of the destitute millions, clad as one of themselves, and talking to them in their own language. Here was the truth at last, not a mere quotation out of a book. So the name of Mahatma, which was given to him, is his true name. Who else has felt so many men of India to be his own flesh and blood?

Writing in 1923, the communist M.N. Roy, noted how Gandhi's saintly qualities had enthused the masses. He had come to personify:

> ...the golden legend of the idealist and ascetic who has cheerfully give his whole life to the service of his fellows, upon whose personal character no faintest blemish rests, whose fearless courage and love of truth stand proven before the whole world and who combines the naïve purity and innocence of a child with the iron will and unbending principles of a man, such a character will go down to history with the same moral force upon posterity as his saintly prototypes of the past.

In this, Roy argued, he had the ability to take on the mighty British Raj.[56] Members of this elite were not always comfortable with the way that Gandhi exerted his appeal, but generally suppressed their misgivings because of his ability to link up with the masses. Jawaharlal Nehru, for example, was concerned by the way that the Mahatma was deploying religion in his politics, by, for example, invoking the deity Rama and his time of just rule. Nonetheless: 'I was powerless to intervene, and consoled myself with the thought that Gandhiji used the words because they were well known and understood by the masses. He had an amazing knack of reaching the heart of the people.'[57]

Second, Gandhi was regarded as a champion of the nation and its people. The nationalist plays from Andhra that we examined in the previous section spoke of how Gandhi was avenging the Amritsar wrong, fighting for self-rule, restoring the health of Bharat Mata, and removing the servitude and suffering of the people.[58] He was admired for standing up to the government and other oppressors. In Bengal, for example, the people wondered at the way that Gandhi had taken on what was known as the great 'Burra Lord Sahib' (e.g. the British rulers), in a fearless way, defeating it time and again.[59] Throughout Awadh, the peasants regarded Gandhi as their champion due to the reputation he had gained for taking on the white planters in nearby Champaran. A British police officer who toured Awadh for a month in late 1920 to evaluate the mood of its people reported that:

> The currency which Gandhi's name has acquired even in the remotest village is astonishing. No one seems to know who or what he is, but it is an accepted fact that what he orders must be done. He is a Mahatma or sadhu, a Pandit, a Brahman who lives in Allahabad, even a Deota [deity].

> One man said he was a merchant who sells cloth at three annas a yard. Some one had probably told him about Gandhi's shop (the new Swadeshi store in Hewett Road). The most intelligent say he is a man who is working for the good of the country … [nonetheless] … the real power of his [Gandhi's] name is perhaps traced back to the idea that it was he who got the *bedakli* [eviction] stopped in Partabgarh. … The reverence for Gandhi is undoubtedly partly due to the belief that he has great influence with the Government.[60]

In Bahraich District it was commonly believed that Gandhi was endorsing lower rents, and – encouraged by this – large groups of tenants went around the district calling for the abolition of rent in grain. Some in Awadh believed that he was antagonistic only to the zamindars and not the government, and even said that they supported Gandhi and the Sarkar (government) against the landlords.[61] In north Bihar, Gandhi's visit to that region in December 1920 had coincided with a fall in the price of essential commodities, and many believed that he was responsible for this.[62]

Third, Gandhi was admired as a great renouncer. On 11 November 1920, the *Swadesh* newspaper of Gorakhpur exhorted its readers: '… cast your eyes towards Mahatma Gandhi. This pure soul has sacrificed everything for you. It is for your good that he has taken the vow of renunciation, gone to jail and encountered many a difficulty and suffering. Despite being ill, he is at this moment wandering all over [the country] in the service of your cause.'[63]

Fourth, Gandhi's demands for moral and ethical reforms struck a chord with many. We shall see in the next chapter how such moves towards ritual purity fed into existing low caste movements of self-assertion, and in this respect, Gandhi was pushing at an open door. Nonetheless, the people accepted his message on their own terms. In a speech to a huge crowd of largely peasants at Gorakhpur on 8 February 1921, Gandhi exhorted them to stop gambling, smoking tobacco and marijuana, drinking alcohol and whoring, and to spin and weave. He also told them to pursue Hindu-Muslim unity, abstain from any use of lathis or taking property by force, and never use the threat of social boycott to gain support for the movement. If the people purified their way of life and methods of protest in these ways, swaraj would certainly be gained within the year. The main lessons that the people took from this – as shown by numerous reports in the local press over the following year – was that they could gain swaraj by maintaining a vegetarian diet and ceasing from lying (reforms that were not specified by Gandhi in his speech as such), as well as stopping gambling, smoking, drinking liquor and whoring. The injunctions about the use of lathis, appropriating the property of exploiters, and social boycott were ignored.[64]

Fifth, there was Gandhi's reputation as the herald of an imminent rule of justice in what was known as 'Gandhi Raj', and sixth, the belief that he was a reincarnation of God. We shall examine these aspects of Gandhi's appeal in detail in the section on millenarian and thaumaturgical beliefs in the next chapter, but here we may merely mention that Gandhi's appeal as a great prophet, a saintly person with uncanny powers, or as a reincarnation of God was very different to the sort of 'religious' approach seen with certain earlier nationalists in India. From the time of Bankimchandra Chattopadhyay and Tilak onwards, certain nationalists had sought to blend religion with the appeal to an Indian national identity. In these cases, the religion that was projected as 'national' was a Brahmanical Hinduism as followed by the higher castes, with appeals to the notion of Bharat Mata or Durga or Kali, both Mother goddesses popular in Bengal, and this in itself was potentially divisive in a sub-continent of great religious diversity. Despite this, as Sarkar has pointed out, no mass cults developed around leaders such as Tilak or Aurobindo (though later an elitist and quietist cult evolved around the latter after he had left political life for good). Gandhi's 'religious' persona was very different – he was seen by the masses as being in the tradition of the great ascetics – people 'renowned for their piety and virtue' whose following often cut across religious boundaries. These were the Hindu *sanyasi*, the Islamic *pir*, the Sikh *sant*, the Jain *sadhu* and *sadhvi*, the Christian saint, or indeed those such as Kabir who was part-Hindu, part-Muslim. Charismatic people of any background, however humble, or of either gender could become such figures. It was a form of reverence that united rather than divided. When expressed through refusal to cooperate with a worldly and 'satanic' regime and the fight for a new rule of earthly justice, it became one of revolt.[65]

Seventh, the rallying slogan of 'Mahatma Gandhi ki jai' became transformed in certain areas from a marker of nationalist support into a cry that 'struck terror into the hearts of waverers and enemies alike'. People now sought to legitimise their various actions against oppressors by invoking Gandhi's name. In this, it assumed the function of traditional calls to action such as 'Jai Mahabir' or 'Bam Bam Mahadeo'. A crowd of the low Badhik caste thus raided a market in Gorakhpur District on 15 February 1921 crying 'Mahatma Gandhi ki ji'. Sweet sellers at a fair in Bara Banki District were raided in February 1922 to cries of '*Mahatma Gandhi ki jai aur mithai le leu*' (long live Mahatma Gandhi and take the sweets).[66] In Bihar, according to Singh: 'The peasants looted bazaars in Gandhi's name; the tribals distilled liquor on "his orders", and the peasants burnt planters' factories to the 'jaikar' ['long live!] of Gandhi. In effect, the 'jaikar' of Gandhi became a militant avowal of the organised strength of peasant volunteers, a rallying cry for direct action, a cry that mobilised and struck terror in the hearts of the planters.' It was notable in all this that it was Gandhi rather than the Congress that was invoked. As yet, Congress lacked strong organisation at local level, and the name of Gandhi made up for this as the alternative to British rule.[67]

Sumit Sarkar has written of 'the extraordinarily open nature of the "reception" of the Gandhian message'. Gandhi's name became what Roland Barthes described as 'a text without an author'.[68] Shahid Amin has written similarly of the way that the idea of the 'Mahatma' became a free-floating sign that could be 'thought out and reworked in popular imagination'. There was little that either Gandhi or other Congress leaders could do to alter such beliefs.[69]

Regional-level Leaders

The top regional-level leaders generally came from upper-middle class and professional backgrounds. These were men such as Motilal and Jawaharlal Nehru, M.M. Malaviya, Lala Lajpat Rai, Rajendra Prasad, Chittaranjan Das, Vithalbhai and Vallabhbhai Patel, C. Rajagopalachari, and Konda Venkatappayya. They had thrown their support behind Gandhi and noncooperation in late 1920, and now acted as the dynamic leaders of the provincial Congress organisations based on linguistic areas that were formed in the new Congress constitution that came into being at the end of that year. Many were successful and prosperous barristers working in the provincial-level high courts who renounced their practices at this time, causing themselves considerable financial hardship. They subjected themselves, moreover, to jail-going, thus sacrificing their erstwhile lives of luxury for the privations of prison cells. They came to be popularly revered for their self-sacrifice in this respect and for – it was said – their devoting of their lives to the service of the people. Though several of these leaders lacked any strong religious beliefs and did not appeal to religion in their speeches and writing, their renunciation of worldly values and adoption of a simpler way of life was seen by many as a form of religious commitment.[70] Some, such as Malaviya and Lajpat Rai, were more obviously religious in their approach. Rai was a leading Arya Samajist who had linked this form of Hindu revivalism strongly with the nationalist cause. Malaviya was a leading light in the Hindu Mahasabha, an organisation that had been created with the intention of providing a Hindu counter to the Muslim League. Secular leaders such as Motilal Nehru disliked the organisation, which they viewed as a narrowly communal body.[71] Malaviya advocated using religious appeals for the mobilisation of those he considered 'illiterate people'.[72]

Many of the top Khilafat leaders had come similarly from highly educated, professional backgrounds, and in many cases had not previously shown any strong religious proclivities. Now, they began growing beards and conforming to the outward practices of Islam; in this winning the sympathy and support of the Muslim masses.[73] One such person was Mazharulal Haq, a leading lawyer of Patna who had lived in ostentatious opulence. He became a leading light in the Bihar Khilafat Committee and led the Rowlatt protests there in 1919. On the call of noncooperation, he sold off his law books and resolved never to taint his life again by working in a British court. He became, in the words of Mahadev Desai, 'a *fakir* for the cause of Swaraj and Islam'. He grew a 'silver-white beard', donned khadi and began sleeping on a thin mattress on the floor. He began to rise early to say his prayers. His former mansion was now used for public work while he lived in a separate humble dwelling. He toured Bihar extensively, giving stirring speeches on noncooperation and the Khilafat.[74]

Most provincial leaders of this sort had received high-quality education in leading English-medium schools and colleges, and in many cases had received further training in Britain. They were as a rule successful in their professional careers. Some – though not all – proved to be somewhat aloof from the masses, giving only lip-service to their demands. We have seen in Chapter 3 how Motilal Nehru and M.M. Malaviya tried to use peasant discontent to strengthen their respective political positions while at the same time not wanting to alienate the landlords unduly. Other members of the provincial elites were selective in their strategies for mobilisation. For example, Vallabhbhai Patel – the President of the Gujarat Provincial Congress Committee – focussed his attention in rural campaigning on the community that he himself stemmed from – the dominant Patidar farmers of the province – while being lukewarm towards the demands of lower social groups. In his autobiography, Indulal Yagnik recalled how in 1921 Patel refused to release Congress funds to help the famine-stricken adivasis of eastern Gujarat despite Yagnik's heartfelt pleas, as he believed that they could contribute little to the cause. Yagnik went over his head to Gandhi to get the money – much to Patel's chagrin.[75] Yagnik (b. 1892) was from a younger generation of such provincial leaders and was less calculating and cautious in his approach. Jawaharlal Nehru (b. 1889) was similarly enthused at this time, later writing: 'Many of us who worked for the Congress programme lived in a kind of intoxication during the year 1921. We were full of excitement and optimism and a buoyant enthusiasm. We sensed the happiness of a person crusading for a cause. We were not troubled with doubt or hesitation; our path seemed to lie clear in front of us and we marched ahead, lifted by the enthusiasm of others, and helping to push on others.' They acted almost recklessly, not caring if they were arrested.[76]

Some other leading provincial figures were from less elite backgrounds but managed to build a wide following by applying local idioms and appeals in their political mobilisation. They tended to be more active in the day-to-day organisation and running of protests. Baba Ram Chandra in Awadh was in this category – we have examined him in detail already in Chapter 7. Another such person was Master Tara Singh, who was from a village in Rawalpindi District of Punjab. His father was a village record-keeper. Born in 1885 as a Hindu, he was educated at a Christian mission school, but converted to Sikhism in 1902, becoming extremely fervent in his faith. He attended the Sikh Khalsa College in Amritsar and became a nationalist at the time of the Swadeshi Movement, participating in anti-British protests. In 1908, he and two others opened a school in Lyallpur District that aimed to provide education for Sikh peasants. Further such schools were opened in the following years. From 1920 he became a leading light in the Akali struggle to wrest control of the gurdwaras from the British, giving up his school-teaching work to focus on the movement. He became the editor of two pro-Akali daily newspapers, one in Punjabi and one in Urdu, and was appointed secretary of the leading Akali campaigning group, the Shiromani Gurdwara Prabandhak Committee. He was arrested and jailed more than once during this struggle. He was always careful to stress the importance of the agrarian grievances of the Sikh peasantry alongside the demand for control over the gurdwaras and insisted that the Akali movement was for democratic rights and an end to rural oppression. He saw it also as being integral to the nationalist movement led by Gandhi, stressing that the exemplary nonviolence of the Akalis revealed their firm adherence to this wider cause. He was keen to promote a new leadership of the Sikhs by educated younger men who were not from the landlord backgrounds common amongst earlier community leaders – people, in other words, like himself. As a result of the Akali movement, he came to be regarded as a major spokesperson for the whole Sikh community.[77]

Local-level Leaders

This category included a wide range of local activists with varying degrees of adherence to the Congress and Khilafat hierarchies. Some regarded themselves as the agents of Gandhi, the Ali brothers and the provincial leaders, and they did their best to conform to their directions and guidance. These were people such as Birendranath Sasmal in Medinipur and J.M. Sengupta in Chittagong – we have looked at their activity already in Chapter 4. Others claimed to be acting in the name of Gandhi and Congress/Khilafat but were very much loose cannons. This was the case with people such as Motilal Tejawat in the Rajasthan/ Gujarat border region. Some of these leaders had carried out social and political work in an area for many years, others were sent by the provincial bosses to mobilise a locality.

Kunvarji Mehta, the leading nationalist activist of Bardoli Taluka in South Gujarat provides a good case study of a local activist who had worked for many years in an area and was also closely integrated into the Congress. He was born in 1886 into a Patidar family from a village near Surat. His father was peasant farmer, village headman, businessman and schoolteacher. He followed his father in becoming a teacher in a government vernacular school, where he taught in Gujarati (he never mastered English). At the same time, during the time of the Swadeshi Movement, he developed strong nationalist sentiments, attending the Surat Congress at Surat in 1907, where he supported Tilak and the extremist nationalists. Later, he protested at Tilak's arrest, and was punished by being transferred to a school in Bardoli Taluka. In 1908 he founded an association – the Patidar Yuvak Mandal (Patidar Youth Association) – that campaigned for social reform, education and caste unity. He established a hostel in Surat where young Patidars could stay while attending government schools in the city. Mehta believed that the Patidars could assert themselves best through firm support of the nationalist cause, and as early as 1912 was in touch with Vithalbhai Patel – then one of the leading Gujarati nationalists. He started a magazine called *Patel Bandhu* that publicised the work of Gandhi in South Africa. When Gandhi returned to India in 1915, Kunvarji went to Bombay to meet him and invited him to come to South Gujarat to see his work. Gandhi did so in 1916, and he spoke warmly about the Patidar community. In 1920, Kunvarji threw his support behind noncooperation, advising Patidars who were village officials or in other official posts to resign. He himself had already resigned as a government teacher. He started a Congress Committee for Bardoli Taluka – the heartland of the South Gujarat Patidars – and acted as its president. He recruited about forty volunteers who toured the taluka encouraging the peasants to support the movement. In less than a year, nearly four-fifths of the schools of the taluka had renounced their government grants and became nationalist schools. He made use of the many contacts he had built up in the area through his school teaching and facilitating young Patidars in obtaining a good education. They in turn responded to his calls to throw their support behind the movement.[78]

In mid-1921, Kunvarji approached Gandhi and announced that Bardoli was ready to advance to civil disobedience. Gandhi agreed to visit the taluka, which he did in October. He was much impressed by what Kunvarji had achieved in this sub-district and agreed to make it the first place in India for a Congress-approved campaign to refuse land tax. Kunvarji told Gandhi that the taluka was one-hundred per cent ready to launch the campaign. Gandhi challenged him: how many of the local adivasis – known there as the 'kaliparaj', or 'black people', who made up about half the population – had been mobilised? Kunvarji had to admit that this was a major lacuna in their work. Gandhi ordered them to rectify this before civil disobedience started. Kunvarji recruited a group of Congress volunteers to go to the adivasi villages. The adivasis of the area were exploited ruthlessly by Parsi liquor dealers-cum-landlords, and these Parsis threatened to beat the activists up if they tried to enter the villages that were under their control. The Parsis were known to be strongly loyal to the British. Kunvarji countered the threat by insisting that the volunteers tour in groups. As they went, they sang bhajans and shouted slogans – but were ignored by the people. A local Ayurvedic doctor who had worked in this area for some time told them that rather than sing bhajans that appealed to the religious sensibilities of the upper castes, they would do best to shout the '*jai*' – or 'long live' – of the adivasi deity Simariyo Dev. They began to do this, and in this way attracted some sympathetic attention. Kunvarji then gave speeches that associated Gandhi with Simariyo Dev, claiming that he had come to save the adivasis after their deity's powers had begun to wane. This struck a chord, as they had indeed suffered severely over the past four decades from the growing encroachments of the Parsis. Kunvarji told them: 'In our country Ram and Krishna were avatars. Gandhi is such an avatar. He has come to uplift us'. He taught them to shout in Gujarati 'Mahatma Gandhi ni jai'.[79] In this way, Kunvarji proved to be an adept mobiliser of all classes in Bardoli behind the cause, though – as we will see in the next chapter – Gandhi did not at times appreciate the way in which he so manipulated local beliefs.

In other cases, a city-based activist was dispatched by a provincial leader to mobilise the people in a locality. They had to build up local contacts who could give them insights into the local situation and ways in which a mass base could be built. Thus, in early 1921,

Chittaranjan Das sent volunteers charged with this task to different parts of Bengal. One such person was Satcowripati Roy, who was sent from Calcutta to the Jungle Mahals of Medinipur District. We have already examined in Chapter 5 the protest that he led there. Here, it is enough to note that he started by contacting members of the local bhadralok elite, one of whom was a relative, who then put him in touch with Marwari traders and village headman, who both resented the power of the Midnapur Zamindari Company. In this way, he was able to organise a strike by adivasis who worked for the Company. The adivasis had never dared protest in such a way previously but felt empowered under the leadership and guidance of the elite activists. Once the movement ended, Roy returned to his home in Calcutta and became a prominent member of Das's Swaraj Party, showing that he had no long-term commitment to the Jungle Mahals and its people. The members of the local bhadralok elite who he had mobilised continued to fight for the rights of the adivasis under a nationalist banner, however.[80]

The MZC also held estates in the area along the Ganges in central-western Bengal, and Chittaranjan Das sent another young bhadralok activist called Someswarprasad Chaudhuri to organise resistance there also. He had left his studies as a medical student in Calcutta after joining the educational boycott. Das insisted that he mobilise only the tenants of the MZC and not those of other mainly bhadralok landlords – in other words British and not Indian zamindars. Someswarprasad contacted Marwari traders who dealt with the peasants on a day-to-day basis and the village headmen and collected details of the major grievances of the tenants. He then focused on a campaign to refuse *begar*, or free labour, for the company. The movement soon spread nonetheless to the tenants of Indian landlords – including one who was at the time hosting a top Congress leader. Someswarprasad came to be regarded by the peasants as a guru-figure who provided what they understood as the *mantra* of *dharmaghat* (strike). It was said that his orders had the force of God's commands, and it was claimed popularly that the death in an accident of powerful village headman who had opposed the movement had been brought about through divine wrath. In this case, a young outsider started a campaign that rapidly went beyond his somewhat inexperienced control.[81]

There were significant numbers of local leaders whose personas were that of holy men – *sadhus*, *swamis*, *babas* and *fakirs*. According to Kapil Kumar, writing on Awadh: 'The militant rural intelligentsia, often represented by the *babas* and *fakirs*, played a vital role in building up anti-landlord and anti-colonial sentiment.' He goes on to note that such people were grounded in local realities, were mobile, and devoted all their time to the task. They were able to deploy local religious and cultural traditions for a peasantry who understood the world through their religion. They were able to summon a large crowd at short notice, and the people would obey what they demanded of them.[82] One such person in Awadh, examined in Chapter 3, was Suraj Prasad, a saffron-clad self-proclaimed follower of Gandhi who became known as the *Chotta* (little) Ram Chandra. He was subsequently disowned by the Congress.

Swamis, sadhus and mullahs were also active in many parts of Bengal and Assam. Muhammad Osman used appeals to religion in mobilising mill workers in Calcutta. Swami Dinanada – formerly a professor in an engineering college – and Swami Darshanananda were to the fore in organising nationalistic strikes in the Bengal coal fields, and the latter was also involved in organising railway workers. Two sadhus called Bisamber Das Guru and Siyaram Das of Ajodhya preached to tea garden labourers in Assam, exhorting them to quit their work and leave the plantations, which they did in large numbers.[83] In Orissa a prominent local leader was Rama Das Babaji, who we have come across already in Chapter 5. He was a young man from a poverty-stricken background who had survived in his youth on charity from a landlord. Rather than show any gratitude for such munificence, he now dressed in the saffron garb of a sadhu and incited the peasants to resist the landlords as a class. An inspired orator, he soon gained a mass following.[84]

Besides the mainstream Congress leaders and godmen, there was a range of other local leaders. Many had rather tenuous links to the Congress or the Khilafat, even when they claimed to be acting in the name of Gandhi or these two organisations. We have come across a number of such people active in Awadh in Chapter 3, such as Kedar Nath and Deo Narain Pande in Fyzabad District, Pandit Ramlal Sharma in Sultanpur District, and Thakur Din Singh in Pratapgarh District. Another such figure that we have not examined so far was Phulchand

Dusadh, from the remote Kolhan belt, in Singhbhum District of southern Bihar. He became a leader of the Ho adivasis – the major group in this area. Urban nationalist leaders began to mobilise this community from April 1921 onwards. The protest took off in July with around 15,000 Hos collecting outside the jail in which a nationalist leader was imprisoned and demanding his release. By August, many more were involved, believing that British rule was on the verge of collapse. Phulchand Dusadh, a Ho of Chittimitti, emerged as their leader at this juncture. He was a vendor of Indian medicines, was educated and knew English. He toured the villages declaring that 'Gandhi Swaraj' had come. He persuaded students to leave government schools and said that under 'Gandhi Swaraj' the government and mission schools of Chaibasa town would be replaced by new schools under the orders of Gandhi. He told them to stop eating meat. No land tax would be paid under Gandhi raj, only a poll tax of two pice per head. He distributed pamphlets and pictures of Gandhi and Bharat Mata and told them that Gandhi was their raja and that they should hang the picture of Bharat Mata and worship her each day by lighting a lamp. He said:

> If the people do not obey Gandhi's orders rakshasas [demons] and devils will come, people will get no food or drink, and rakshashas, devils and worms will eat them and they will become lame...The English are leaving the country and the few Englishmen who are left behind are hiding in Chaibasa and will run away in three or four months time. 40 crores of Habsi [Arab soldiers], who are the soldiers of Gandhi, will come to Chaibasa and fight with the sahibs. The sahibs will run away to their own country.

Dusadh organised and lead a procession to the Mahadev temple each Wednesday evening chanting 'Ho Hari, Hari, Hari, Radha Gobind, Gandhiji ki jai, Hari Hari Nath'. They thumped their lathis on the ground as they marched. He and other local activists began to encourage civil disobedience, even thought this was not at that time Congress policy. Under his leadership, the authority of the British in this tract practically disintegrated at that time.[85]

In areas that sent significant numbers of peasant-recruits into the armed forces, demobilised soldiers often became local leaders. They had gained a knowledge of the wider world and an ability to organise in a discipline manner. Many who had served in the Indian army during the Great War had become disaffected by both what they had experienced abroad and a feeling that all they had given to the empire had not been reciprocated after they returned to India. Several of the leading Sikh Akalis came from such a background, and some local leaders in Kumaon, as we have seen in Chapter 5. Shahid Amin has provided us with graphic details about another such figure, Bhagwan Ahir of Chaura in Gorakhpur District. Recruits from this district had been posted to Flanders and Mesopotamia during the war, and Ahir had served as a non-combatant in Basra for two years. Now demobbed, he received a monthly pension from the government. He joined the nationalists and – dressed in his old khaki jacket – acted as a drillmaster to peasant activists. On 1 February 1922 he headed a picket of meat, fish and liquor shops at the Mundera market. When berated by a policeman for being a disloyal pensioner, he responded with a very un-Gandhian '*lund-se*' ('up your penis'), and the enraged policeman then beat him up. He and his fellow workers decided to show their strength and sent messages to the surrounding villages telling people to assemble for a big demonstration on 4 February. The disciplined march through the area provided a good display of Bhagwan Ahir's drill training from the previous months. The police were intimidated and let them pass. The crowd taunted them – the police, they cried, were 'shit-scared'. The officers retaliated by firing their guns in the air as a warning to the protestors. A cry went through the crowd: 'Bullets have turned to water by the grace of Gandhiji', and thus emboldened the crowd rushed the police, chasing them into the Chauri Chaura police station. The building was torched, and the entire police force of twenty-three men died. Bhagwan Ahir fled to the border with Nepal, but – still dressed in his khaki coat – was soon identified and captured. Though he claimed to have played no part in the actual massacre, he was disbelieved by the court and hanged in 1923.[86] In this case, we find military-style discipline being deployed in a way that culminated in great violence. Thus, while the discipline and courage of the Akali Sikh ex-soldiers who became committed to Gandhian methods made them model practitioners of nonviolence, the ex-soldier Bhagwan Ahir proved far less exemplary in this respect.

Some of the militant volunteers at Chauri Chaura were skilled wrestlers, trained at the local *akhadas* (gymnasium). This was run by a

Muslim, Nazar Ali of Chotki Dumri, who had spent time in Rangoon, returning in December 1920 and establishing a tailoring shop and *akhada*. He became a powerful presence in the area. His followers were often Hindus, who understood their practice as a form of worship of Durga, conferring *shakti* (divine power). Wrestling provided a way in which peasants could gain prestige – they were admired for being independent-minded and not easily bossed around by landlords or officials. They were celebrated both for their physical strength (*bal*) and the cunning (*chhal*) needed to out-think an opponent in combat. Wrestlers were celebrated in folklore as popular heroes, along with dare-devil herdsmen and others who defied authority. They were expected to provide leadership when called on, particularly when things turned violent.[87]

The wrestler figure thus provides us with another category of local leader, albeit not one whose ethics had much in common with those of Gandhi. Besides being important in the rural areas of eastern UP and Bihar, they were, as we have seen in Chapter 4, also active in the politics of big cities. In Bombay and Calcutta, the wrestling culture of the *akhadas* was, in most cases, an import carried by recent migrants from eastern UP and Bihar, and many of the *dada* figures of Bombay and *sardars* of Calcutta were associated with the gymnasiums. Dipesh Chakrabarty has noted how many of the Calcutta sardars attended *akharas*, developing a reputation for physical prowess and strength that was used when necessary to control their worker clients. They were both feared and admired for their mettle in this respect, and ambitious workers aspired to become such figures.[88] I have argued that the wrestler-*dadas* were likely to have been heavily involved in the rioting in Bombay of November 1921 – another of those outbreaks of violence that caused Gandhi to believe that he had misjudged the people profoundly. The same was the case at Chauri Chaura. Nonetheless, wrestlers could – if so motivated and in different circumstances – be excellent practitioners of political nonviolence.[89] It appears that in 1920–22 many were not.

Leadership in 1920–22

Gandhi believed that the exemplary leader of the sort of movement he sought to build should be an independent-minded moral agent who controlled his or her own destiny. Such people – the model *satyagrahi* – were to become the very personification of the struggle through their whole way of life and being. In standing up for their principles, they would provide moral leadership for their community. He had developed his conviction in this respect during his struggle in South Africa. In his weekly *Indian Opinion,* he extolled exemplary individuals who had transcended their own time to provide such leadership. The figures he named were generally Europeans such as Joan of Arc, Lord Nelson, Sir Thomas Munro, Mountstuart Elphinstone, and Elizabeth Fry. He maintained that in failing to produce such people, India had been subjugated by a foreign power.[90]

Gandhi made efforts to forge such leadership after he returned to India. In Champaran, he recruited a group of full-time assistants who agreed to give up other work for the duration of the campaign. He chose educated, professional Biharis, many of whom were lawyers with well-established law practices. He insisted that they change their whole way of life, giving up their servants and cooks and living simply and inexpensively. This helped to reduce the cultural gap between them and the peasants. Gandhi also inspired them with his strong work ethic and constant initiatives. He told them that, if the need was such, they should show their commitment by courting jail. Most were reluctant to go so far, but when Gandhi was arrested and due to appear in court, two of the volunteers stated that they were now willing to follow him. After he heard this, Gandhi stated: 'Now I know we shall succeed.'[91]

Many other leaders committed to the Gandhian ethos came to the fore during noncooperation – people like Kunvarji Mehta in Bardoli, Birendranath Sasmal in Medinipur, and many others elsewhere. Nonetheless, such was the scale of the movement and speed of its advance that most local leaders had at best only a rudimentary grasp of Gandhian principles. Gandhi was well aware of this, and disowned some prominent activists whom he felt lacked proper understanding of his tenets. In general, they kept on regardless. As it was, many of these local leaders were looked up to by their followers because they had renounced worldly advantage in putting themselves on the line with courage. They courted jail and went to prison applauded by their followers. What is more, most of the local campaigns that such people led were not violent in any important respect – only a very small minority of local nationalist leaders advocated violence against their opponents. Thus, although Gandhi was unable to control most of the key local activists in what he considered a satisfactory manner, they in turn led what were in general highly effective nonviolent campaigns. These conformed to a popular form of nonviolence that I shall analyse in the next chapter.

The fact that there was such a spirit of nonviolence was revealed when local leaders were arrested and jailed. Only in a few cases did this result in violence by enraged followers, and when this did happen, the movement was crushed by the authorities with varying degrees of speed and ruthlessness. New leaders frequently emerged to take the place of the arrested ones. This was the case, for example, in Orissa, where the inspired leader Rama Das Babaji was jailed in September 1921. The provincial Congress Committee sent a worker to take charge of the protest, and he was joined by other local activists. Two leading figures in this respect were schoolteachers who had been dismissed for nationalist activity. Others had peasant backgrounds or were disaffected employees of the landlords. They started up several peasant *sabhas* (associations) and enrolled peasants as four-anna members of Congress. Peasants then started sabhas on their own initiative. The no-rent movement and no-tax movement was at its height between January and April 1922. Thus, although the nonviolent movement was initiated by an agitator who was arrested early on, it continued to grow and become more militant under a burgeoning new leadership.[92]

In observing the relationship between leaders and followers in hierarchical societies such as India, several historians have argued that the masses lack the confidence to take the helm in mass movements. They frequently quote Karl Marx, who claimed that this was a feature of the peasantry in general. As he wrote in *The Eighteenth Brumaire of Louis Bonaparte*: 'They cannot represent themselves, they must be represented. Their representative must at the same time appear as their master, as an authority over them.' Quoting this passage, Dipesh Chakrabarty has argued that this was a feature of the subaltern classes of early twentieth century India, including the subject of his own study, the Calcutta working class. Although union leaders were meant in that city to be the elected representatives of the workers, their authority was in practice rooted in deference and hierarchy. This was revealed through body-language, dress, speech – an entire semiotics of domination and subordination. Rich people were trusted more as leaders, particularly if they had renounced their wealth to work in the interests of the poor. There was a belief here that people of status were best placed to fight for them against the mill owners and managers.[93] It is thus possible to argue that when the position of the British in Indian society was challenged in 1920–21, large numbers promptly transferred their allegiance to an alternative elite – namely that of the Congress and Khilafat leaders. Although the ideal nationalist leader was meant to be a humble servant of the people, in practice – it may be argued – the masses regarded their new leaders as their superiors. Not only that, they loaded them with huge expectations, as the 'master' was believed to have superior powers that could benefit loyal and trusting followers. It is possible to observe this effect in the way that people venerated Gandhi. Also, as in Awadh, where the peasant leaders were regarded as the new rajas while their followers were depicted as their *praja*, or people/subjects. This was reflected in the popular saying during the Kisan Sabha Movement of 1921: '*Baba Ram Chandra ke rajwa, praja maja urawe na*', meaning 'In the Raj of Baba Ram Chandra the *praja* will make merry'.[94]

There is some truth in this argument. We see it, for example, in an example from Awadh, when a group of tenants had in 1921 raided the property of their taluqdar. Jawaharlal Nehru rushed to the place and convened a meeting of the peasants at which he accused them in harsh tones as having brought shame on the movement. He ordered those involved in this 'crime' to raise their hands, and some two dozen did so. The police who were watching promptly arrested them, and they subsequently received lengthy jail sentences. The government took advantage of this to arrest many more people. Many later died in prison. In his autobiography, Nehru expressed his regret at having exposed what he called 'these foolish and simple folk' to such suffering.[95] In this case, the peasants had followed the order of an elite figure whom they trusted as having power to protect them – to disastrous effect.

Despite this, the masses were by no means always deferential towards authority, however perceived, in 1920–22. Leaders could take their followers only so far. If they demanded that they abandon strongly held beliefs or social conventions, they were likely to be ignored or even disavowed. In this, leaders generally had to work with the grain of local belief. Attempts by Gandhians to include untouchables in nationalist activity could, for example, be opposed strongly by caste Hindu peasants. This was the case in Chikhodra village of Kheda District in Gujarat when untouchables were included by Congress workers in a meeting to launch a no-land tax campaign in December 1921. The Patidar peasants were so infuriated that they promptly abandoned the campaign.[96] Also, the peasantry and working classes did produce their own leaders. There were dynamic and resourceful peasants and worker-leaders – notably the jobbers – who had an ability to crystallise the feelings of their fellows and lead them in a range of campaigns. Indeed, the movement could only have been so powerful in 1920–22 because there was such leadership in depth at that time.

7

ASAHYOG ANDOLAN

THE NONCOOPERATION OF THE PEOPLE 1920–22

In his book *Civil Resistance*, Michael Randle has argued that mass civil resistance became a significant political force only in the nineteenth century. This was, he argues, due to a convergence of forces. One of these was the spread of industrial capitalism and the various social and political developments that went with it. Urbanisation and the concentration of manufacture in factories gave workers a new power to work in concert to achieve their goals. Dislocation, impoverishment and exploitation made concerted action more necessary for these classes. Increased literacy also played its part. The period also saw the growing assertion of an articulate professional and manufacturing middle class that demanded a greater say in government and utilised improved methods of organisation and mobilisation to press for this. This class linked up with artisans and workers to demand a broadening of the electorate and constitutional reform. The eighteenth and nineteenth centuries also saw the consolidation of the modern bureaucratic state and the rise of nationalism. The modern nation was built on the idea that the polity was an expression of the will of the people, and that the people thus had a right to dissent if they felt that the state was not working in their interests. In many cases, nationalist struggles overlapped with liberal constitutional struggles against authoritarian governments. Both were spearheaded by the middle classes, with support from other classes. Civil resistance thus evolved out of various emancipatory struggles of that time.[1]

Although this argument makes much sense in the European and American contexts, it does not explain why there were such powerful campaigns in India – a largely preindustrial country. Literacy, for example, had hardly been a determining element in the participation of many poor people in Gandhi's campaigns. By contrast, it has been suggested by others that Indian nonviolence grew from its unique culture and history.[2] Either Randle's argument is Eurocentric and does not apply here – or perhaps it does in a way that needs modification. In this chapter we shall examine the forms that mass resistance took, during what was popularly known as '*asahyog andolan*' (Noncooperation Movement) of 1920–22, to determine how we may understand it in this respect. I shall deal with the issue under four main heads: solidarity, forms of protest, purification, and the supernatural. In a final section, I shall end the chapter with some observations on the forms that popular nonviolence – in contrast to popular violence – took in 1920–22.

Solidarity

Sumit Sarkar has written of how discontent in early-twentieth century Bengal could be directed against anyone perceived as being outside the local 'moral community'. This might be expressed in religious terms, as when Muslim tenants rejected their Hindu landlords, or in caste terms, as when the Namasudras – a Dalit group – rejected higher caste *jotedars* (rich peasants), or the Mahisyas peasants – a caste that included poor sharecroppers, middle and rich peasants – united as a community against British officials. In the adivasi areas along the border with Bihar, the people united against outsiders, such as Bengali land-grabbers, Marwari traders and usurers, and British officials who enforced the oppressive forest laws. When resisting these perceived enemies, they often spoke of a 'golden age' when 'all jungles were free'.[3]

In some cases, the community invoked was that of the peasantry in general against their oppressors. In such solidarity, the more powerful and prosperous members of the group stood side-by-side with their poorer neighbours. In Awadh, peasants of a wide range of castes were mobilised against the landlords – some being from middle-level groups such as the Kurmis and Ahirs, and others from lower or untouchable castes, such as the Pasis and Chamars. In the early stages, the Kisan Sabhas were established mainly by members of these middle-range castes, but they then mobilised the lower castes.[4] In coastal Andhra, the prosperous peasants of the dominant castes took the lead, which then emboldened the poorer peasants of lower castes. When the dominant caste leaders were arrested and jailed, the poorer peasants became demoralised.[5]

In many cases, solidarity was expressed in caste terms. Lloyd and Susanne Rudolph have written of the significance of caste in the modern Indian polity:

> Caste has become a means to level the old order's inequalities by helping to destroy its moral base and social structure. In doing so, caste has helped peasants to represent and rule themselves by attaching them to the ideas, processes, and institutions of political democracy.[6]

In this way, nationalist initiatives gained a mass democratic base in many areas through the support given them by important and self-assertive local castes. This was the case with the Mahisyas of the Kanthi and Tamluk subdivisions of Medinipur District of Bengal. This caste made up nearly three-quarters of the population of this region, and while some were rich many were poor. For several years they had demanded that they be considered a respectable caste, something that was not recognised by the bhadralok. They had started a caste organisation, the Bangiya Mahishya Sabha, with its own journal, to press this demand. A few more prosperous Mahisyas began to develop an interest in English education at the start of the twentieth century and had tried to obtain positions in the local administration, the judiciary and local government bodies. They found it hard to compete here with the better-educated bhadralok. Their enthusiastic participation in noncooperation provided for them an alternative path for their self-assertion at all levels. They provided the mass support for the campaign to refuse to pay their union board taxes.[7] The same was true in Gujarat, where the Patidar peasantry provided the bulwark of the movement in the rural areas. They also had their caste organisations that were designed to raise the status of the caste, and they also supported noncooperation as a part of their movement for self-assertion. They nonetheless did so on their own terms. For example, in Sisodra village of Surat District there was strong backing by the dominant Patidars for noncooperation. The Police Patel of the village had already resigned after signing the Satyagraha Pledge at the time of the Rowlatt Satyagraha in 1919. The village school, with 125 pupils, then rejected the government grant and become a 'national' school. The Patidars took to spinning on the charka with enthusiasm. They donated Rs 3,000 to the Tilak Swaraj Fund, representing one-and-a-half rupees per head. They also expressed their willingness to refuse their land tax if called on to do so. They refused, however, to allow an untouchable boy to sit with the other children in the national school. In this, they clearly rejected an important part of the Gandhian programme.[8]

The solidarity of certain castes could lead to members of other castes being either marginalised or actively opposed. In some cases in Awadh, for example, the antagonism was in some cases directed against fellow-tenants who happened to be of the same caste as a local landlord, even though they were not themselves oppressors.[9] In Gujarat, Patidars generally scoffed at the idea of mobilising castes whom they considered their inferiors, such as the Baraiyas and the Vankars (the latter were considered 'untouchable'). The Patidars considered the nationalist movement a vehicle for their own caste betterment and resented lower caste involvement. They dressed this up in language that suggested that the lower castes were too 'backward' and 'ignorant' to be so mobilised.[10] In this respect, caste solidarity could at times be restrictive.

Religion provided another base for solidarity. In the case of the Khilafat Movement, an appeal was made to all Muslims to support a pan-Islamic grievance. The emotive language that this entailed can be seen in a circular put out in Bombay City for the First Khilafat Day on 1 August 1920. The preamble proclaimed: 'In the name of God, the merciful and compassionate. One who becomes the friends of the enemy of Islam may be considered as one of them.... Keep regard and reputation of Islam, God and his Prophet and never do any such work by which your weakness of faith might come to light and thereby the enemies of Islam will be overpowered.....' The main text went on:

> Inauguration of Tark-e-Mawalat of Adam-i-Ishtak Amal or Non-co-operation (which means severing all connections with the pledge-breaking Government) and the test of self-respect for the community of the Mussalmans of India and the test of the perseverance of the prestige of the nation and country of the Hindu brethren. Non-co-operation is a glorious act of the Mussalmans, the foundation-stone of which was laid for the first time in the year 9 A.H. and which is once more being revived (put into practice) by Islam now.

The text then stated that it was in 9 A.H. that the Prophet Muhammad ordered his followers to sever all connections with three leaders who refused to join the army to defend the Muslims from attack. They suffered severe social boycott in Medina. It was asserted that contemporary Muslims were being now forced to resort to such tactics against those who were snatching the Holy Places of Islam away from the control of the Caliph and bring the 'Jazirat-ul-Arab' (the Arabian peninsula) under the 'Christian powers [that] have done whatever they could to destroy and ruin Islam and they are still trying'. It is the 'command of God' that you should 'not make friends with those hypocrites and enemies of Islam who leave no stone unturned to bring about your downfall and disgrace...' It is 'the bounden religious duty of us Mussalmans' to resort to noncooperation. Indian Muslims who do not support this will be unable 'to show their face to other self-respecting nations, and will be condemned to suffer all calamities and difficulties in this world'. 'In short, non-co-operation is a religious obligation and a kind of *jehad*.'[11] This appeal was not that of a Muslim nationalism that demanded a separate nation-state for South Asian Muslims. Rather, it sought unity amongst Muslims as well as comradely support from all non-British people of the subcontinent whatever their religion.

In the case of Hindu beliefs and practices, Hindu nationalism – in the sense of a belief that 'Hindus' as a pan-Indian collective were fighting for their political self-determination in the face of alleged attacks by members of other faiths – was muted during noncooperation. More regional forms of Hindu belief and practice formed a basis, rather, for local cohesions. We have seen already in Chapter 3 how in Awadh Baba Ram Chandra used such local idioms to powerful effect in that struggle, and Chapter 6 examined this process in Andhra and Gujarat also. Similarly, in Maharashtra, regional religious sentiments underpinned the solidarity of the peasants of Mulshi. The dam being built by the Tatas was due to submerge several temples, including the prominent Jyotirupeshwar Mandir. Meetings were held in this and other temples of the region – both in Mulshi and Pune – giving them a sacred force. The campaign was launched formally on Ramnavami day – the birthday of Lord Ram – in April 1921. A mass rally was held that day on the banks of the River Mula, with the saffron flag of Maharashtra hoisted over the main platform. The flag had the word 'Satyagraha' added to it, and it became the ensign of the whole campaign. That night, the people sang devotional songs and heroic ballads – bhajan, kirtan and powada. During the first week of May 1921, the Maharashtra Provincial Congress conference that was held at Vasai was addressed by a Shankaracharya (head of a major Shaivite monastery), who exclaimed that this and other such conferences were in fact religious gatherings. He exhorted them: 'It is one's duty to sacrifice one's life for the struggle.' In October 1921, some of the protestors performed a religious ritual known as Rudrabhishek, involving a reading of spiritual texts. The harassment of women protestors by the guards employed by the Tatas was publicised in the Marathi press as a form of religious violation. For example, a cartoon in *Mauj* newspaper showed Draupadi, the heroine of the Mahabharata, being disrobed by the evil Duryodhana, who was depicted as a Parsi. This was played out in front of a person wearing a crown, who symbolised the British rulers.[12]

Incantations were commonly deployed to enthuse solidarity. As Baba Ramchandra later commented in the case of Awadh: 'As soon as the cry of "Sita Ram" was raised, thousands of peasants poured out in waves from the surrounding villages.' The police and landlord's men often made themselves scarce as soon as they heard the cry.[13] Projit Mukharji has pointed out how such communal singing and incantations were believed to concur divine blessing on participants in whatever endeavours they undertook. This was seen in both Vaishnavite and Shaivite forms of devotional worship, as well as in Islam. Mystical strands of Islam found all over the Muslim world had a strong tradition of *jikir* (from the Arabic *dikr*, or Urdu *zikr*), in which holy names were chanted continuously. The Prophet Muhammad had sanctioned chanting, either aloud in public or personally in one's mind or in a low voice. *Pirs* who were ambiguous in their religious affiliation were also invoked through such chants and hymns.[14]

Oaths, vows and pledges provided another important means for maintaining solidarity during the movement. Gandhi saw such pledges as key to satyagraha. He however insisted that these be given freely and voluntarily by individuals. In practice, considerable community pressure was put on people to take such oaths. In Awadh, for example, it was common for an *eka* (unity) association to be formed with a recital of a holy text by a Brahman in a village, after which people were expected to take a 13-point oath. People were told '*eka karo*' (act with unity), and those who refused faced being ostracised. Amongst other things, they were made to vow to resist illegal ejection by landlords, to pay only the recorded rent, not to perform free labour, to stop paying cesses, to refuse to tolerate insults from the landlords and their men, and to form panchayats. The oath was taken over holy water from the Ganges. In the case of Muslims, the holy scripture – the *Milad Sharif* – was deployed to strengthen the vow.[15] In Punjab, the Akali protestors took a vow of strict nonviolence, and they maintained this even when being assaulted and in some cases killed.[16] In Maharashtra, a satyagraha oath was taken at the Jyotirupeshwar temple by the people of Mulshi. They pledged not to sell their land to the Tatas and refuse any compensation in cash or kind. Even the Brahman and Gujar moneylenders participated and took the oath.[17]

Social boycotts were deployed widely to ensure solidarity. As we have seen in Chapter 2, Gandhi had many reservations about the use of such a method. His general stance was that it was wrong to inflict social boycotts in punitive and psychologically violent ways. Few conformed to Gandhi's strictures in this respect. Even in his home region of Gujarat, peasants in Kheda District were threatened with fines and a social boycott if they paid their land tax in early 1922.[18] In Awadh, people were frequently compelled to join *eka* bodies and engage in protests through threat of social ostracism. In one demonstration in Rae Bareli District of January 1921, many only participated after being told they would be boycotted socially if they failed to do so, and they were told that non-compliance was on a par with the sin of killing nine cows if they were Hindus, or eating nine pigs if they were Muslim – both infringements that would have occasioned social boycott. Landlords were also boycotted socially by washermen, barbers and sweepers.[19] In Medinipur, there was a strong social boycott of Krishnananda Das, the Panskura Union Board President, after he helped the police to attach property. He was branded a 'traitor' to the community. Social boycotts were also imposed on officials. When they tried to attach property in lieu of tax, they were threatened as they entered villages, being met by a barrage of 'profane language' and refused any shelter. Many feared to go to the villages as a result.[20] In all regions of India, the mass of the people had no moral scruples over the use of such sanctions. They did not see it – as Gandhi did – as contradicting their participation in a nonviolent movement. Indeed, for most, it was hard to see how the necessary solidarity in what they believed to be a moral cause could be maintained without the use of social boycotts.

A final method in which solidarity was maintained was through marching and drilling in a military fashion with the intent of inculcating in satyagrahis an army-style discipline in their nonviolent protests. The ethos of a squad of 'soldiers' – in which comrades stick by each other in adversity – helped forge a collective spirit. Gandhi often conceived the ideal satyagrahi as a courageous warrior who was prepared to offer even his life in support of the cause.[21] During 1921, he was particularly fulsome in his praise of the Sikh Akalis who had refused to retaliate in the face of lethal attacks by their opponents.[22] Many of them were ex-soldiers who had served in Europe in the First World War. Recently demobilised soldiers had returned home angry at the way they had been treated during the war. In their villages, they heard how the peasants had been compelled against their will to provide fixed quotas of recruits and money for the war effort, while at the same many had been interned for alleged sympathy for the Ghadar revolutionaries.[23] They joined the movement and organised themselves with military-style discipline.[24] They revealed an extraordinary capacity for heroic nonviolence, being prepared to die rather than break their oath of nonviolence.

Military-style organisation became a feature of the movement all over India, even in regions without any strong tradition of recruitment into the army. Many of the volunteer corps that were started during noncooperation incorporated such training. By mid-1921, there were about 345 nationalist volunteer corps, with 15,186 members, and 404 *seva samitis* with 15,269 members. Nearly half of the total number were from Bombay and Bengal Presidencies. They were dressed increasingly in the new Congress uniform of white khadi *kurta-pyjama* and Gandhi cap.[25] In Mulshi, the protestors marched in ranks to the site of the dam behind a nationalist flag on the day that the satyagraha was inaugurated in April 1921. Each unit had its own military-style commander. These Congress militias did not always conform to Gandhian strictures. In Bihar, many of the Congress volunteers were reported to be using undue intimidation against the police, courts, and those trying to go to courts to lodge complaints. They were applying social boycotts in the punitive ways abhorred by Gandhi.[26]

Many Khilafat volunteers took to wearing wore either para-military uniforms of khaki-coloured trousers, tunics, Sam Browne belts, leather shoes, topped by Muslim-style caps, or green Arab-style robes. They wore badges or armbands with crescents and paraded with green flags bearing a crescent moon and star, and often performed military-style drills. By late 1921, there were some 16,000 Khilafat volunteers in 36 districts in UP alone. They carried out social work and acted as a parallel 'national' police force. In Lucknow, for example, Khilafat volunteers directed traffic alongside the police in some places – often giving contrary orders. They moved around giving speeches about swadeshi and singing poems about swaraj and the arrest of their beloved leaders. They picketed cloth shops. Minault notes that rather than conform to the exemplary forms of nonviolent behaviour demanded by Gandhi, they sometimes carried swords or wooden staves in processions, which Minault considered: '…an ominous display of force among the nonviolent'. Cases were reported of Khilafat volunteers using strong-arm methods to oblige merchants to comply with strikes and boycotts. British observers claimed that most such volunteers were local trouble-makers who could call out 'mobs' but hardly ensure their nonviolence. In September 1921, an armed band of Khilafat volunteers thus tried to forcibly prevent the arrest of the Khilafat leaders Maulana Husain Madni. In Calcutta, the arrest of some Khilafat volunteers led to a riot in which the police were attacked.[27]

When the AICC met in Bombay in July 1921, concerns were voiced about the quality of many of such volunteers. In response, it was decided to establish a centrally controlled National Volunteers Corps.

Members were to take a pledge of nonviolence and obey the orders of their superiors. They were expected to carry out social service. In Bihar, for example, local corps known as the Quami Sevak Dals were formed that included both Khilafat and Congress workers.[28] It does not appear that this had much impact. In general, the nationalist militias obeyed their own rules – enforcing popular notions of justice that largely ignored Gandhi's directives. Although this could lead to rowdy confrontations with the police, there was in practice very little lethal violence. Unlike the later militias of the Rashtriya Swayamsevak Sangh (founded in 1925) – to whom they bore a superficial resemblance – the nationalist militias of 1920–22 were not conceived as street-fighting bodies that would intimidate their rivals through force.[29] In this, Chauri Chaura – where the Congress militia that was drilled by an ex-soldier took the lead in the massacre of the policemen – was the exception rather than the rule.

Although there was often a strong class base to such solidarities, they were voiced most commonly in terms of ties of locality, ethnicity, caste and religion rather than economic status as such. Even in the case of a clear class – that of tea planation labourers in north-eastern India – the fact that they were generally recruited along ethnic lines meant that there was much congruence between the two. This was a common feature of peasant solidarity in South Asia, as pointed out by Ranajit Guha in his work on nineteenth century insurrections.[30] While these forms of social identity might appear superficially to have been longstanding and 'traditional', the way that they were expressed by 1920–22 were nonetheless novel. A century earlier, for example, there had been no notion in western Bengal of a widespread 'Mahisya' caste identity, just as in Gujarat there had been no concept of a united 'Patidar' caste. These were new types of solidarity that were forged under late imperial rule as a means for the social and political self-assertion of certain landed peasant communities. Similarly, appeals to 'Hindu' values or a unified 'Islam' were novel ones – in earlier times religious identities were far more likely to be local and sectarian, so that Shaivites of one locality might believe that they had interests in common against Vaishnavites of the same area, or a local 'heretical' Sufi sect might be ranged against more orthodox Islamic rivals. Ethnicity, caste and religion were being asserted, consequently, in novel ways within the nationalist movement. In general, they involved an appeal to a group with a wide social base that would have weight within a democracy. Over and above this there were the forms of solidarity that mimicked imperial patterns of organisation, such as that of soldiers dressed in uniform whose courage was forged through marching, drilling, and obedience to the orders of a squad-leader. In this, disparate and shifting forms of solidarity underpinned the protests of these years.

Forms of Protest

Popular protest during noncooperation took five main forms that did not involve any physical harm to other humans – that of non-compliance, demonstration, pressurising, raiding, and sabotage. Although these methods of dissent could at times go beyond what Gandhi preached as acceptable forms of protest, they were believed to be legitimate by those who took part. We shall look at each in turn.

Non-compliance. The Congress and Khilafat high command set out a relatively limited programme in this respect, namely boycotts of elections to the central and provincial legislatures, government educational institutions, courts of law, and foreign goods. Refusal to comply with government tax-demands or landlord rent-demands were not on the agenda at the start and were to be sanctioned at a later stage in only very limited and controlled cases. As it was, many peasants took the initiative in refusing government demands for land tax, local government dues, or demands by landlords for rents. For example, the Eka associations that were formed in the landlord-controlled areas of Awadh devised their own forms of action, such as paying only a 'fair' rent, refusing many cesses, resisting illegal ejections by landlords, refusing to tolerate any abuse or insults by landlords and their hired men, and even laying claim to and harvesting the crops from land that the landlords delineated as their own personal holdings.[31] This agenda had nothing to do with anything that emanated from the UP Congress headquarters in Allahabad. Similarly, in forest areas, peasants refused to obey the forest-protection regulations that so often violated what they saw as their customary rights. The people often believed that Gandhi and other leaders were behind them in such protests, and we have seen already how they might succeed or fail to gain such an endorsement in practice. There were also strikes by workers in factories and on plantations that were either condemned by or received varying degrees of support from the nationalist hierarchy. In all this, there were many tensions between what the leaders saw as acceptable and what the masses believed to be intrinsic to their protests.

Demonstration. This could involve large numbers converging on a seat of government or another symbolic place. We have seen in Chapter 3 how in June 1921 around ten thousand peasants of Udaipur State marched to the capital and camped before the palace of the ruler, dispersing only after he eventually agreed to remedy some of their grievances. In Awadh, mass protests at the mansions of the landlords became a feature of the movement. There were processions, such as the *radhotsawa* processions in Andhra and *prabhat pheries* in Gujarat. Some were local, but they could cover long distances – in the manner of a pilgrimage procession – swelling in numbers as they proceeded through the countryside. There were also the regimented marches by Akalis to major gurdwaras that swelled as they passed through the villages. Mass evacuations provided a longstanding method of popular demonstration, with subjects quitting the lands of an oppressive ruler and migrating to that of a potentially more benevolent one.[32] The most striking case of this during noncooperation was the migration by the tea planation workers of Assam. This, as we have seen in Chapter 5, created great logistical problems for both the authorities and the Bengal Congress organisation – and neither reacted particularly well or compassionately, as C.F. Andrews pointed out most acerbically in his reports. In this case, unlike in earlier protest migrations, the people concerned were employees in a capitalist enterprise who were effectively downing tools by returning to their distant homes.

Rural communities tended to rally themselves for such protests in ways that differed from those of the elites. Often, they responded to messages carried by word of mouth or by other oral and symbolic means. In coastal Orissa, for example, messages were passed from village-to-village by blasts from conch-shells and *hulahuli* (ululation).[33] In the Jungle Mahals of West Bengal, Santals gave signals to collect together by sending a withy tied with a series of knots that indicated the exact number of days ahead for the gathering. These were sent from one village headman to another, and the place and purpose was communicated orally at the same time. A village headman had a duty to pass it on to the headman of the next village. It was the custom that if such a withy was passed to a village, the Santals of that place had a duty to respond, and that failure to do so would lead to severe penalties.[34]

Pressurising. This involved both obstructing and intimidating. Mass sit-downs were in the first category. One such case occurred in Awadh in December 1920, when crowds who wanted to travel home by rail after attending a massive rally in Ajodhya town were refused entry to the train by the station master. They reacted by staging a spontaneous sit-down on the railway lines for over two hours that prevented any movement into and out of the station. They were drenched with hot water from the engines and beaten by the police with lathis, to no avail. The station master caved in and allowed them on the trains. They returned to their villages filled with enthusiasm, realising the strength that they had in numbers.[35] Another instance was during the Mulshi Satyagraha in Maharashtra, when peasants obstructed the building of a railway line by removing rails as they were laid, and stopping the movement of construction trains by sitting on the track.[36]

There was in India an old method of intimidating protest known as *dharna*. This entailed sitting before the house or business establishment of someone against whom there was a grievance, the object being to shame the person into redressing the issue.[37] In 1920–22, picketing provided an updated version of such pressurising. Congress exhortations to picket retail outlets selling foreign cloth and liquor were taken up with alacrity by many urban protestors. In Bombay City, picketing began under Congress leadership in June 1921, but it quickly assumed a momentum of its own. There were widespread protests in front of liquor shops, with would-be customers having to run the gauntlet of picketers sitting with anti-drink banners. Women who resented the dire impact of drunkenness on their family lives often took the lead in this, and were encouraged to do so by Gandhi, who believed that they were less likely to retaliate against violence by thwarted drinkers or the police. The protest was driven by a strong animosity towards the shopkeepers, who were predominantly Parsis. For many, this community was seen to be one that benefited by exploiting the working classes, whether as mill-owners or merchants. They were known for their great loyalty to British rule. During noncooperation, they were abused as the 'Biryaniwallahs of Willingdon Club' (e.g. members of an elite club that indulged on rich mutton *biryanis*) who had supported the Willingdon Memorial in 1918 and in November 1921 turned out to greet the Prince of Wales with passionate enthusiasm. The British reported that Muslim picketers were more aggressive than Hindus. They abused customers, shouting at Hindus that they were drinking cow's blood, and at Muslims that they were drinking pig's blood.[38] By the end of June 1921, about 245 shops were being picketed by about 375 volunteers, most of whom were working-class Maharashtrians. The liquor protest flagged during the monsoon months but revived thereafter. By mid-November, 282 shops were being picketed and picketers being arrested and prosecuted. In all, 92 picketers were convicted, of whom one was jailed and 59 fined. The rest – apart from two found not guilty – were let off with a warning. Liquor shops formed a target for attack during the riots that then followed, with four being burnt down and 135 looted or damaged. All picketing was immediately halted.[39]

Another form of intimidation seen during noncooperation was the large gathering outside courts or police stations that was intended to put on pressure for arrested or under-trial protestors to be freed. This happened in Awadh when leaders were arrested and brought to trial. For example, after Baba Ram Chanda and 32 Kisan Sabha activists were arrested on trumped-up charges in late August 1920, a crowd of four to five thousand peasants went to the court at Pratapgarh when the case was about to be heard there. They stood outside shouting *Baba Ram Chandra ki jai*. The trail was then held in the jail to avoid the prisoners being brought to the court. As soon as they realised what was happening, the crowd rushed to the jail and resumed their protest there. To defuse the situation, the trial was postponed for ten days. This merely gave time for an even bigger crowd to assemble on 10 September, the day that the case was to be resumed. Although they were encouraged in this by some prominent UP Congressmen, such as Jawaharlal Nehru and Gauri Shankar Misra, these leaders made no attempt to go to Pratapgarh themselves and soon distanced themselves from the agitation. The message went around the district that Pratapgarh jail had become a shrine where the *darshan* (auspicious view) of the saint could be obtained. Large numbers turned up on the day. Rumours flew that Gandhi was himself about to appear to secure Baba Ram Chandra's release. The people demanded to see their leader but were kept at bay by armed police. The stand-off continued for thirty-eight hours. The authorities eventually tried to defuse the situation by surreptitiously driving Ram Chandra in a car to a nearby village, where he was released. The cases against the other 32 were later withdrawn as it was realised that they were too flimsy to stand up to any scrutiny.[40] There were similarities here with the court appearance of Gandhi in Champaran in 1917, with an equally triumphant outcome for the agitators. After this, the authorities began increasingly to hear the court cases of nationalist leaders outside their areas to avoid demonstrations at the courts. When, for example, three Kisan Sabha leaders of Sultanpur District were arrested in early February 1921, they were taken to Lucknow for trial, which was a considerable distance away. Their trial was accompanied by a wave of repression in the district itself, and there were no such demonstrations at the Lucknow court.[41]

Forcing profiteering shopkeepers to sell at a fair price was another type of pressurising seen during noncooperation. There were strong moral expectations that merchants should not profiteer at the expense of those in need and charge only reasonable prices for essential commodities. In Awadh, for example, crowds gathered in front of shops in 1921, demanding that the merchants sell at a fair price. To take one case, a crowd of 300 to 400 peasants of Fursatganj in Rae Bareli District protested on 6 January in front of the shops of local traders, shouting 'Ram Chandra Maharaj Ki Jai', 'Mahatma Gandhi Ki Jai', and Shaukat Ali Muhammad Ali Ki Jai'. They were protesting about the high price of grain and cloth and the tyranny of the taluqdars. The crowd soon swelled to 8000 to 10,000. The Baniya traders were accused of profiteering and they were told to sell at a fair price.[42] Similarly, volunteers in Gorakhpur District picketing the meat, fish and liquor shops at Mundera Bazaar in January 1922 tried to force the merchants to sell the meat and fish at a just price. The police came and beat them up.[43] Such action could involve the boycott of entire markets that sold at exploitative prices. In Bihar, many weekly markets owned or leased by indigo planters were boycotted in October 1921 and alternative ones were established. The planters earned a considerable income from these markets by levying fees on merchants and vendors, and the boycott was a direct challenge to them. Fees were either much lower or non-existent in the new markets. Merchants who refuse to sell at them were subject to social boycott. This was a local initiative, not coming from the Congress leaders. Indeed, they did not approve of it, and even went to the villagers that had established such markets to dissuade them from continuing.[44]

Raiding. This was a form of protest directed at profiteering shopkeepers, landlords, or those who hoarded essential commodities at a time of need. Historians writing on the Noncooperation Movement have generally described this as 'looting'.[45] This term, however, suggests an action that motivated primarily by either greed or narrow economic need. It is useful in this context to refer to E.P. Thompson, who pointed how in eighteenth-century England attacks on profiteering merchants were often depicted as mere 'rebellions of the belly' that lacked any political content. He argues that in almost all cases such attacks were believed by the perpetrators to be legitimate. They saw themselves as defending ancient rights and customs that were being ridden over roughshod by unscrupulous merchants. Their belief was, in Thompson's words, 'grounded upon a consistent traditional view of social norms and obligations, of the proper economic functions of several parties within the community, which, when taken together, can be said to constitute the moral economy of the poor. An outrage to these moral assumptions, quite as much as actual deprivation, was the usual occasion for direct action.'[46]

Using the term 'raid' rather than 'looting' suggests a form of direct action that is rooted in moral expectation. It may be objected that the English word 'loot' comes directly from the Hindi '*lūt*', and that it was a term used at the time. 'Loot' is defined in *The Oxford English Dictionary* as: 'Goods (esp. articles of considerable value) taken from an enemy, a captured city, etc. in time of war; also, in wider sense, something taken by force or with violence; booty, plunder, spoil; now sometimes *transf.*, illicit gains, 'pillage' (e.g. by a public servant). Also, the action or process of looting.' In Hindi, similarly, '*lūt*' means 'plundering', and the assumption is that it is both criminal and immoral. In the latter respect, it was often used to describe the excessive prices demanded by profiteers, with *lūtka māl* being the term for extortionately-priced goods. In other words, it was seen to violate the moral economy. The term *lūt-mār* is defined in a leading Hindi-English dictionary as 'plundering and killing, looting and violence'.[47] This, therefore, is a term that in both languages has strong overtones of immoral behaviour and violence. The 'raid' is, on the other hand, an accepted method in nonviolent resistance. Gene Sharp, in his work on such protest, discusses what he calls the 'nonviolent raid', and mentions in this context raids that occurred during the Civil Disobedience Movement in India in 1930–31, when protestors tried to gain entry to salt depots and Congress offices that had been seized by the government. He also describes, as another case, action against eight Boston merchants who were defying the boycott of imported merchandise in 1770. Over one thousand people had proceeded in an orderly manner to the houses or stores of the merchants and demanded that their goods be shown to them for inspection. Sharp argues that such actions were mainly symbolic, the main aim not being so much as to gain possession so much as to challenge authority.[48] Thompson likewise emphasises the discipline of the crowd in eighteenth-century raids in England. The main aim was not to sack granaries and bread-shops but to set a fair price. When unopposed, the crowds proceeded nonviolently. He notes: 'It is the restraint, rather than disorder, which is remarkable…' Often produce was deliberately spoiled or thrown away rather than taken for consumption.[49]

In the case of appropriation of hoarded goods, and unlike the cases of nonviolent raiding cited by Sharp, crowds during noncooperation tended to punish the exploiters by taking the goods away. In Awadh, for example, about forty persons went to Deeh Bazar in the Tiloi estate on 5 January 1921 and requested a Baniya cloth merchant to sell cloth at four annas a yard. When the merchant refused, they raided his shop. On 12 January, the landlords of Dankara village in Faizabad District were attacked and their houses raided. There were further raids on other landlords, rich peasants, Baniyas and goldsmiths of that district on 13 and 14 January. The most common targets were the grain stores of Baniyas and other traders. The raiding was carried out by crowds of between one and five thousand people, with women following the men and carrying off goods. Some upper caste women were subject to humiliation, maltreatment and abuse by groups of oppressed women. Armed police arrived on 15 January, and along with the hired men of the landlords tried to recover the goods and generally punish those who had rebelled. 346 were arrested and much of the produce recovered. It was officially estimated that 114 places were raided in 31 villages.[50] In some cases, as we have seen in Chapter 3, gangs of criminals took advantage of the situation to carry out robberies while claiming to be in solidarity with the Kisan Sabha activists. The Kisan Sabha leaders denounced these gangs and promised to work with the government against them. In some cases, for example in Rasulpur and Arkha villages in Rae Bareli, the Kisan Sabha Panchayats themselves insisted that goods taken from the landlords should be returned.[51] They understood that appropriating property for personal use negated the political point that they were trying to make.

In Gorakhpur District, a crowd of the low Badhik caste raided a market in Gorakhpur District on 15 February 1921 crying 'Mahatma Gandhi ki ji'. In another incident, sweet sellers at a fair in Bara Banki District were raided a year later to cries of '*Mahatma Gandhi ki jai aur mithai le leu*' (long live Mahatma Gandhi and take the sweets). An official commented on such raiding of markets in north Bihar in early 1921 that those involved believed that Gandhi had given orders that prices of rice, vegetables, cloth and other products should be reduced to around a quarter of what was being asked at that time. When going to the markets, they first enquired what the prices were and then told the trader that Gandhi had ordered a much lower one. When the trader refused to sell at such a rate, they were abused and beaten, and their shops raided. In citing these cases, Shahid Amin argues that the peasants deployed the name of Gandhi to validate direct action that they believed to be just and fair. Their 'Gandhi' was not as he really was, but a figure who in their imagination supported such action.[52]

In Bengal, high prices had brought an increase in such raiding by distressed peasants from the closing years of the First World War onwards. During noncooperation, however, the raids were driven more by the political rather than economic climate. In areas with large adivasi populations in north-western Medinipur district, Santhals and Mahatos raided weekly markets and destroyed liquor shops in January 1922 to cries of 'Gandhi Maharaj Ki Jai'. While searching for foreign cloth they seized all sorts of textiles and also forbad the export of rice but did not take anything away with them – showing that they were making a point rather than trying to obtain goods free of cost. In April 1923, there was a wave of raiding of fishponds by adivasis along the borders with Bihar in Medinipur and Bankura Districts, on the border with Bihar. Crowds of up to 5000 Santals and other low caste people raided the ponds in broad daylight. They stated that in the times of their fathers all ponds were open to the public and believed that by such action this 'natural right' would be restored. When a British official tried to stop them, he was chased away.[53]

We may argue also that taking possession of a place against the wishes of those who controlled it in abusive or exploitative ways was another form of 'raiding'. The Sikh Akali jathas provide a case of this – with bands of protestors taking possession of gurdwaras against the wishes of their corrupt owners. Although Gandhi praised their nonviolence and deplored their brutal repression, he expressed reservations about such a method. He stated that 'entering to take possession must bear the taint of violence and as such is worthy of censure'. This was so even if no violence was 'contemplated or intended'.[54] As it was, Gandhi continued to praise the Akalis for their exemplary actions even after questioning their full conformity to his methods. Later, in 1930, Gandhi expressed no such reservations when his followers carried out raids on salt depots during the salt satyagraha. In general, raiding was regarded by Congress leaders as questionable when it involved what they saw as 'looting' – a criminal act. The popular raids of 1920–22 often involved the appropriation and carrying-away of goods in a way that could be so classified, and they were accordingly condemned. As it was, most such action was relatively restrained, with nobody being hurt in the process. Indeed, the mass of the people regarded such direct action to enforce a 'moral economy' as being a perfectly legitimate part of the nationalist protest.

Sabotage. Besides raiding, there were a few cases of sabotage. In Awadh, the crops of landlords were occasionally destroyed or forcibly harvested. Such sabotage was not however a major form of protest there at that time.[55] It was more common in Bihar, where the crops of indigo planters were destroyed and there were some arson-attacks on their property as well as the houses of their employees. Sabotage of this sort was in some cases opposed by leading peasants who realised that it could be counterproductive. District-level Congress leaders disapproved strongly of this sort of action. For example, after an attack on one indigo factory, the leaders of Bettiah District rushed to the place and warned them that such action undermined the chances of success for the movement. They impressed on them the advantages of conforming strictly to nonviolence.[56] Little in the way of sabotage was carried out elsewhere in India, and we can hardly consider it a significant feature of noncooperation, in contrast to the Rowlatt Satyagraha of 1919 when much government property was targeted or the Quit India Movement of 1942, when there was widespread arson, bombing and destruction of communications. Sabotage directed at property rather than people has been considered by some activists as a legitimate form of nonviolent protest but condemned by others. Brian Martin points out that sabotage against objects lies on the border between violence and nonviolence. It may be included in a nonviolent movement in certain cases – e.g. smashing weapons that are designed to be used for aggressive purposes. An act that entailed a grave risk to human life would on the other hand be classed as violent. As it is, the boundaries are a matter of constant debate in nonviolent movements.[57] Gene Sharp does not consider that 'acts of demolition directed against machinery, transport, buildings, bridges, installations and the like' are 'violent' unless they cause injury or death to humans, or threaten to do so. He notes, however, that although such sabotage has accompanied some predominantly nonviolent movement, it has the potential to escalate into violence against people, and that it is generally discouraged by the leaders of such struggles.[58] This was certainly the case during noncooperation, when not only the Congress leaders but in some cases village leaders did their best to stop such acts.

Purification

One notable feature of the popular movement was that many participants took it as a call to purify their lives. They responded by refusing to eat meat and fish, drink alcohol or take drugs, to stop gambling, and to renounce other vices, such as extra-marital sex. Such reformed ways of life were seen to be a mark of higher social status, and the nationalist movement became a vehicle for such advancement. In this way, a new purer polity could be forged in an India free from imperial rule. The call to give up liquor was also popular with many women in India, as they were often the victims of drunken assaults by husbands – and household money was frequently squandered by male members on drink. Many women therefore participated with enthusiasm in the picketing of liquor shops.

In the decades before the Noncooperation Movement, there had been many movements by middle and low caste groups, as well as Muslims, all over India to purify their daily habits. While local elites generally resisted such attempts by such groups to raise their status, middle-class nationalists had in general regarded this as a commendable means towards promoting a fresh, untainted mass culture for the new Indian nation. This issue therefore had great potential in forging solidarity between such elites and the masses during 1920–22.

In Gorakhpur District, for example, almost all Hindus of the area, even Brahmans, ate meat and fish until the closing years of the nineteenth century. Only very devout people abstained, and they were in a very small minority. During the early decades of the twentieth century, people began to embrace such a lifestyle at a much wider level. Besides stopping the consumption of meat, fish and alcohol, moves were made to bring an end to animal sacrifice as an act of worship and to prevent female caste-members doing demeaning work that gave rise to sexual exploitation, such as performing free services for landlords or government officials or working as housemaids. Chamars, considered an untouchable caste, resolved to give up processing the carcasses of dead animals, which was their traditional, much-despised calling. Caste-members who broke the various new rules were made to pay substantial fines. In early 1921, a widespread boycott of meat and fish was reported due to the preaching of 'a Bengali sadhu'. Amin understands this as a 'reversal of the signs of subordination'. The refusal to carry out demeaning work for superiors provided a particularly unambiguous challenge in this respect. Gandhi was seen to endorse all this, though on his visit to the district on 8 February 1921 he only spoke of boycotting. As it was, the picketing of meat and fish shops were more important in the area in 1921–22 than the picketing of foreign cloth shops. It was even believed that those who broke these resolutions could be punished supernaturally by Gandhi, as we shall see in a later section of this chapter.[59]

Similar campaigns for purification that became linked to the nationalist movement were seen all over India in 1920–22. This became a notable feature of the movement in the Chhota Nagpur region of southern Bihar. The population of this area was predominantly adivasi, and – as in Gorakhpur District – there had been movements for purification in preceding years. The Tana Bhagat movement had, for example, started amongst the Oraons of Ranchi District in 1914, when the 25-year old Jatra Oraon proclaimed that he had received a divine message from Dharmes, the supreme deity of the Oraons, that he would become a king whose followers, known as *bhagats*. would share his kingdom. Those who did not join would be struck dumb. He told them to rid themselves of belief in ghosts and their exorcism, and to stop animal sacrifice and liquor drinking. They were no longer to work as coolies for others and stop paying rent to landlords. British rule had led to the strengthening of an Oraon elite during the nineteenth century who had been given privileged positions, and the movement challenged their power directly. It was prophesied that the whole area would be cleansed of high caste exploiters, Muslims, missionaries, policemen and officials. The looked to the Germans to help their movement, crying: '*Angrez ki kshai, German ki jai*' (Destruction to the English, victory to the Germans). It was said that the 'German Baba' would attack non-believers with bombs from the sky. The movement spread fast in 1915. Many declared themselves as bhagats and stopped consuming chickens, pigs and liquor. They were told to avoid red objects such as chillies, as red represented the British, whom they hated. If the British tried to shoot them, their bullets would, it was said, turn to water. They took their children out of the missionary schools. By 1916, the movement had spread to migrant Oraons working in the Jalpaiguri tea gardens of Bengal, taken there by labourers who had visited their villages while on leave. Jatra faded as leader after 1918, being replaced by Sibu Bhagat, who claimed that he had the ability to mete out divine punishment on those who opposed him. Huts in his camp were whitewashed, a white flag was flown, and the Tanas came to be associated with the colour white, symbolising purity. Sibu demanded that followers take a bath twice a day, wear the sacred thread, keep women in purdah, and purify themselves if they stepped on the shadow of a non-Hindu. They did not, however, employ Brahmanical ceremonies in their worship. From 1921, the bhagats began to carry the Congress flag and take vows in Gandhi Maharaj's name. Myths grew around Gandhi and his *charkha* and swaraj. Sacrifice, violence and meat-eating were condemned, and they were charged to embrace austerity and abstemiousness and to practice pure thought and speech. Embroidered clothes and ornaments were discarded in favour of simple white garments made of khadi. The British reacted by arresting Sibu, but this had no impact on the movement.[60]

Elsewhere in Chhota Nagpur, there was a strong anti-liquor movement in Palamau District, where Cheros and Kherwars boycotted and picketed liquor shops and raided and destroyed cottage distilleries. There was a similar protest in the Santhal Parganas. The reformist Kherwar movement had swept through this area in the late 1860s under the leadership of Bhagirath Manjhi, who had declared that he was ordained by God to redress the grievances of the Santhals, to fight for their rights, and lead them as a king. He proclaimed that the land belonged to them and that no government could impose any taxes on them and he established what he styled as a new 'Santhali Raj'. He banned the slaughter of pigs and fowls, and prohibited drinking and dancing. Anti-liquor sentiments came to the fore again during 1921–22, with many Santhals participating in the nationalist movement by picketing liquor shops. This was the main form of protest in this area at that time. The government auction of liquor licenses could be held at Dumka only with very tight security that prevented any Congress activist from going anywhere near the town. There was a drastic reduction in excise revenue in the district.[61]

There was a strong anti-liquor movement in Madras Presidency. Arnold considers this to have been the most striking example of the mass movement in the province in 1921–22. For at least the past twenty years, a range of middle-level caste associations in the Tamil and Telegu regions had been propagating abstinence to enhance their social status. In Coimbatore District, for example, this had been for some years a major element in the programme of the caste association of the dominant rural caste, the Gounders. In 1921, Gounder caste leaders organised the picketing of liquor shops and the annual auctions of liquor-selling licences. Local Gounder panchayats and village headman ensured solidarity in this. Between September and December 1921, about a hundred activists were arrested for such protests. In Salem town, the leaders of the Devanga Chettis – a weaver caste – were firm advocates for temperance, and as the main nationalist leaders of the town were of this caste, they made this issue central to the protest. Not all caste leaders of the province were however pro-Congress and thus supporters of this campaign. The Nadars of Ramnad and Madurai had also been seeking for many years to raise their status through abstinence. Their top caste leaders were however supporters of the Justice Party – a provincial opponent of the Congress – and only a minority of the more influential members of the caste supported the anti-liquor protest in 1920–22. Despite this, the anti-liquor movement often took off without waiting for any guidance from such leaders. The government of Madras, which derived a quarter of its revenues from liquor, soon noticed a sharp fall in its income from both the Tamil and Telugu regions. The provincial Governor, Lord Willingdon, anticipated in February 1922 that there would be a deficit of Rs 650,000 in provincial income as a result. The financial secretary considered increasing taxes in other areas to balance the books but feared that Congress would make such tax-rises a major grievance.[62]

There were similar anti-liquor protests in other provinces. In Gujarat, Patidar caste leaders had for many years been preaching abstinence in a bid to raise their social status, and they made this an important part of the campaign in 1920–22. In Surat City, auctions of liquor licenses were picketed with the slogan: 'Give up sinful money, depend on money that is pure'. 175 protestors forced the bidders to cower inside the government office at the time of the 1921 auction, and the sum raised by the government was substantially less than in previous years. The lower classes of the city were however largely lukewarm on the issue – in marked contrast to nearby rural areas.[63] In Punjab, liquor revenue fell by Rs 300,000.[64] There was wide-scale picketing of liquor shops by activists in north Bihar.[65] In Calcutta, some union activists in Calcutta preached abstinence,[66] and elsewhere in Bengal Dalit groups vowed to give up liquor, leading to fraternisation between them and high caste Congress leaders. In March 1921, for example, a Congress leader of Rajshahi publicly embraced a sweeper who had renounced alcohol.[67] In May 1921, the Congress organised a meeting of 700 Santals of Medinipur District who resolved to abstain from liquor.[68]

The Supernatural

Popular noncooperation was informed in many cases by a belief that the movement enjoyed divine blessing, and that Gandhi was blessed by God with supernatural power. Beliefs in this respect can be divided into three main categories, the devotional, millenarian and thaumaturgic. While the first is my own category, the second two are taken from Sumit Sarkar, who in an article of noncooperation in Bengal has distinguished between popular millenarian beliefs that society is about to be transformed in a sudden and sweeping way and thaumaturgic beliefs that focus on following the nationalist cause as a means towards the 'healing of specific ills' through supernatural means.[69]

The Devotional

Gandhi was regarded widely throughout India to be a reincarnation (*avatar*) of deities such as Rama and Krishna, so that following him became a form of devotion to the divine (*bhakti*). This notion varied in quality in different regions and for different classes of followers. For many amongst the higher castes, he was seen more as a saintly teacher infused with the divine spirit. In Gujarat, for example, he enjoyed widespread support from higher caste groups and dominant Patidar peasants who regarded him as a man of unsurpassed morality who was based in his ashram with his disciples and who travelled the land preaching a new nationalist ethic that his supporters were meant to follow. Indian nationalism became a form of religious duty (*dharma*) that incorporated *satyagraha*, *ahimsa*, *tapas* (self-suffering), *tyag* (renunciation of worldly pleasure), *atmashuddhi* (self-purification), *seva* (service to the people), and self-respect. Ardent Gandhians expressed their devotion (*bhakti*) through their willingness to provide – in Hindu devotional terms – a sacrifice (*bhog*) of their bodies, minds and wealth (*tan, man,* and *dan*) for the cause.[70]

We can observe this sort of devotional feeling in the case of the prominent Patidar nationalist of South Gujarat, Kunvarji Mehta. During noncooperation, he informed Gandhi to his face: 'Bapu, in 1908, since I saw your photograph in *Indian Opinion*, I have believed you to be a god. Since that time, I realised that you were an avatar born to set India free. Day-by-day my belief has become stronger.' As proof of this he argued that rough Patidars such as himself could never otherwise have purified their ways and become his followers. Gandhi chided him for this – he was a human like any other – and he ordered Kunvarji to stop propagating such beliefs immediately. Kunvarji said he would obey but told him that in his heart he would always be an avatar. On meeting again later, Gandhi asked him if he still adhered to his mistaken belief – Kunvarji replied that his views had not changed a bit. Gandhi told him that he was free to think what he liked, but he should not go around stating it to others.[71]

Gandhi came to know about all this after he had been told that Kunvarji was projecting him as an avatar in speeches to local adivasis. The informant was D. B. Kalelkar, who had attended one such meeting and had complained to Gandhi about what he saw as a dubious manipulation of the sentiments of the poor and oppressed. Kalelkar was a Maharashtrian Brahman who had studied at Fergusson Collage in Pune where he had developed a rationalist approach to religious belief, holding that it was absurd to believe that God answered prayers by interceding in the daily affairs of human beings. He adhered, rather, to a mystical Vedantism of a sort popular among well-educated high-caste nationalists of the time. He had been attracted to Gandhi by his nationalism and his spiritual qualities, and in 1915 he joined his new ashram in Ahmedabad, where he was placed in charge of education. He became a leading figure in promoting national education during noncooperation.[72] He clearly believed that propagating the notion that Gandhi was an avatar was doing him and the movement no favours – a view that was shared by Gandhi himself. Kalelkar nonetheless revered Gandhi in a way that had its own devotional quality.

Despite all his denials, Gandhi was regarded widely throughout India as an avatar. Several songs from Andhra depicted Gandhi as a deity who had come to save India. He was said to be a reincarnation of Vishnu/Krishna or Rama. In the words of one such song:

> Gandhi Mahatma is the saviour of the world,
> All of you people, know (it);
> To establish *dharma* in the world,
> *Hari* (*Vishnu*) was born as Gandhi.[73]

He was depicted as a saviour who could single-handedly bring prosperity to the people, as stated in a song from Andhra titled 'Mahatma':

> To save us you have appeared on the Earth – Mahatma Gandhi
> To save us you have appeared on the earth
> When all the crops were destroyed – hearing the prayers of ryots,
> Who couldn't pay taxes, (you) saved (them); listening
> To the prayers of Kheda people (you) saved (them).[74]

Gandhi's visit to Bihar in December 1920 was preceded by a rumour that he was not an ordinary human, but an avatar who had come to relieve their suffering. It was said that the British had arrested Gandhi and he escaped miraculously from jail in an invisible state. Newspapers reported such rumours. One claimed that a cloud had been sighted that at first represented the four-armed Vishnu, after which it changed into Gandhi before disappearing. There were monthly 'Gandhi days' to keep all this fresh in people's minds. Gandhi's great qualities were proclaimed in meetings held on these days – on 'how much he loved people, bore sufferings for them, worked for the upliftment of the downtrodden and the removal of animosity and differences among the people'. 'Gandhi was said to be firm in truth, did not fear death and looked upon his body as trifling.' Stories were recounted of his life to illustrate his greatness. These often became morality tales. He was compared with Lord Rama and said to be the epitome of *dharma*. The movement was said to be a *dharmic yudh* (religious war). It was said that he opened the door of heaven for his followers. He was turning the *kaliyug* (age of darkness) into *satyuga* (age of truth) and giving them *amrit* (divine nectar). He was – it was held – the repository of knowledge, showing the light to a people cast in darkness and ignorance. With Gandhi as their guide, they would become brave and strong. A song that appeared in a proscribed publication titled '*Sri Gandhi Updesh Bhajanvali*' exhorted the people to sing the praises of Gandhi in bhajans and pray for his long life. In this way, through devotion to him, his fame would be spread throughout the world and people everywhere would follow his way. He was eulogised also through *chalisa* – a form of popular recital and morality tale that attributed divine qualities to a person – with a 'Gandhi *chalisa*' that illustrated his greatness. One, titled '*Shri Gandhi Chalisa*' ('Prayer to Gandhi') went:

> Make a gift of the dust of your feet to me. O great leader of India, ocean of learning, wise one and destroyer of vanity. O crown of India, destroyer of crooked policies save the wretched persons from ignominy and establish (the peace of) the rule of Rama… I bow low, with all reverence, to Gandhi who is the home of kindness, whose fame is eternal and who is the dispeller of darkness of ignorance.

It was said that by so singing his praises, his fame would be spread throughout the world and people everywhere would come to follow his way. This all helped to ensure that Gandhi's authority in Bihar was superior to that of the British and existing elites, breaking the deference that people had hitherto given to them.[75]

For many, the belief that Gandhi was a divine avatar led to a belief that he had the power to act in ways that transcended the laws of nature. Lord Ronaldshay noted in his diary entry for 17 March 1921 that it was said in Bengal that Gandhi 'has been shot by the British but has appeared again and again … has been thrown into prison but … the locks fall from the door and he walks out'.[76] A story circulated in Champaran that when soldiers fired a volley at Gandhi the bullets had bounced off without harming him.[77] Calcutta workers repeated a story that when soldiers threw a bomb at Gandhi it had melted away from his body like snow.[78] The Ali brothers were on occasion included with Gandhi in such accounts. It was said in Bengal that Gandhi and

Muhammad Ali had bestowed a heavenly bread that when hung in a mosque by a pious maulvi doubled itself by the following Friday.[79]

Because so many believed that Gandhi had divine qualities of this sort, they flocked to have his *darshan* – an auspicious viewing that brought blessings on the observer – and make appropriate offering to him, as they would to a deity in a temple. Gandhi's secretary, Mahadev Desai, provided a graphic account in his diary of Gandhi's tour of Bihar in December 1920. Their train stopped at every station along the line, and at each there were hundreds of people out to see him. Many who could not reach a station stood close to the railway track hoping to catch a glimpse of the Mahatma as the train sped past. 'Even women, who never stir out of their homes, did not fail to present themselves so that they could see and hear him.' People brought jewellery, which they offered to him as an act of devotion. *Sanyasis* came and put their rosaries in his lap. One person brought a tiger skin, and addressed him, devotionally, as 'Maharaj', stating: '...this is my feat of strength. The tiger was a terror to our people; I am giving the skin to you.' Even policemen came to salute Gandhi or touch his hand. One, from the Criminal Investigation Department – a body that regularly snooped on nationalists – stated: 'We have taken this dirty work for the sake of the sinning flesh, but please do accept these five rupees'.[80]

Two months later, in February 1921, Gandhi toured Gorakhpur District. Before he came, the local nationalist paper, *Swadesh*, exhorted the *sadharan janta* (ordinary people) to come from all corners of the district to have his *darshan*. 'There will be no end to the joy of the people when they are able to feast their eyes on the Mahatma.' As Gandhi proceeded rapidly through the area by train, vast numbers came out to catch a glimpse of him. *Swadesh* reported: 'Some, overcome with their love, were seen to be crying.' At Chauri Chaura station a sheet was spread out before the Mahatma that was soon covered with money-donations in the way that worshippers offered money before the *murtis* (representations) of deities. 'Outside the Gorakhpur Station the Mahatma stood on a high carriage and people had a good darshan of him for a couple of minutes.' After he had left, the local press talked of the 'fantastic flow of *bhakti*' (devotion) occasioned by the visit, claiming that up to a quarter of a million people had received 'the darshan of the Mahatma' on that occasion. One report stated: 'The janta [people] came with devotion (*bhakti*) in their hearts and returned with feelings and ideas (*bhav*)'. Amin comments on this that the idea of *bhav* also suggested a resolve to act on what they understood to be the directives issued by Gandhi on that day.[81]

Mahadev Desai, in his diary, observed the disorderly way in which these crowds of would-be devotees met Gandhi as he proceeded through Gorakhpur. 'Hordes and hordes of people began to rush upon our compartment and create a row from the very next station after Gorakhpur.... At every station peasants with long lathis and torches in their hands would come to us and raise cries loud enough to split the very drums of our ears.' Desai went out on the platforms of several stations and fell at the feet of the people begging for calm. They moved back, but once he returned to their compartment would surge forward once more and resume their shouting. At Bhatni, which the train reached at midnight, the crowd demanded Gandhi's *darshan*, and when told it was too late stood on the track to stop the train moving forward. Desai told them that they should be ashamed of themselves for disturbing the Mahatma in this way. They responded: 'We have come for the *darshan* of the Lord. How ever can we feel ashamed of it?' In some places, Gandhi had to get up – even in the early hours of the morning – but his pleas for the crowd to stop harassing him were met merely by 'sky-rending shouts of victory to him'. In one case, Gandhi fell at their feet and beat his head on the ground imploring them to go away, which had the desired effect. At some stations, people even broke into their compartment demanding: 'Who is Mahatma Gandhiji'? To spare Gandhi, Desai told them that he was. They then bowed down to him and left the carriage. While Desai wondered at their 'untainted love' he could not, he noted, to be 'enchanted' by it.[82] Gandhi, in common with many celebrity-figures, was experiencing the threatening quality of mass-adulation.

The Millennial

The millennial entails the notion that there is going to be a sudden, total, and imminent transformation of life on earth that will be enjoyed by a collective group. It is miraculous, as it is brought about by a supernatural power. It was often associated with the coming of a messianic saviour – often seen as an incarnation of a deity or sacred figure – who would proclaim this coming event and empower those who believed that it was imminent.[83] Many took Gandhi's promise for swaraj in a year to mean that there would be a sudden and dramatic change of this sort, and saw Gandhi as the saviour.

During noncooperation, the millennial was often expressed through the idea of *Ramraj* (the rule of Rama), with British rule being equated with Rama's great foe – the demon-king, Ravan. We have seen in Chapter 3 how in Awadh Baba Ramchandra developed a language of national resistance that was rooted in popular religious idioms, particularly those from the *Ramayana*. The new order would be that of 'Ramraj', or the rule of Ram and his consort Sita. 'Sita Ram' became the rallying-cry of the movement. Baba Ramchandra thus encouraged people to greet each other with the salutation 'Sita-Ram' or 'Jai Ram' (long live Ram), rather than *śalaam* – which was a deferential form of address associated with the greeting of a superior by an inferior. In contrast to the sharp hierarchies enforced under British rule, all would now be of equal status under Ram and Sita. Many supposedly 'respectable' high caste people complained loudly when they found themselves so addressed at that time.[84] There was frequent slippage between the idea of 'Ramraj' and 'Gandhi Raj', the two being seen to be of a similar quality. In Awadh, the peasants were also told to consider Gandhi as their new raja.[85]

Strong millennial beliefs were expressed throughout eastern UP and neighbouring parts of Bihar in 1921 and early 1922. Naujadi – the wife of one of those accused of rioting at Chaura-Chaura who was interviewed many years later by Shahid Amin – remembered Gandhi's visit in early 1921 as being heralded by celestial apparitions – a snake-like figure and other objects appeared in the sky.[86] The Gorakhpur newspaper *Gyan Shakti* reported in April 1921 that:

> One night people from all the villages kept awake and roamed over five villages each. That night it was impossible to get any sleep. They were shouting 'Gandhiji ki jai'. They had *dhol, tasa, jhal, majiras* (kettledrums and cymbals) with them. The din they caused was unbearable. People were shouting, this is the drum of swaraj (*swaraj ka danka*). Swaraj has been attained. The English had taken a bet with Gandhiji that they would grant Swaraj if Gandhi could come out of fire [unhurt]. Gandhiji took hold of

> the tail of a calf and went through fire. Now Swaraj has been attained. It was also announced that now only four annas or eight annas a bigha would have to be paid in rent. We have also heard that some peasants are insisting that they will not pay more than eight annas a bigha as rent.

Starting in Gorakhpur District, this belief in the imminent advent of a new order spread over the border into north-western Bihar, where it was modified into a story that Gandhi, a cow, a Brahman and an Englishman had taken the ordeal by fire, and only the Englishman had been burnt.[87]

The massacre of twenty-three policemen at Chaura Chaura on 4 February 1922 took place in the context of millennial enthusiasm. The judges who heard the appeals of those convicted of this crime commented that the people there understood Swaraj 'as a millennium in which taxation would be limited to the collection of small cash contribution or dues in kind from fields and threshing floors, and [in] which the cultivators would hold their lands at little more than nominal rents'. They also noted that it was remarkable: '...how this name of 'Swaraj' was linked, in the minds of the peasantry of Gorakhpur, with the name of Mr Gandhi. Everywhere in the evidence and in statements made ... by various accused persons ... it was 'Gandhiji's Swaraj', or the 'Mahatma's Swaraj' for which they were looking.' A witness at the trial stated that he had been told in early February 1921 that 'Gandhi Mahatma's Swaraj had been established, that the Chaura thana [police station] would be abolished, and that the volunteers would set up their own thana'. The peasant volunteers who marched to the police station claimed that they were 'going to hold a Gandhi Mahatma Sabha' that would bring 'Gandhi Swaraj'. Many people in the area believed that the burning of the police station at Chauri Chaura and the killing of all its policemen signalled the coming of Gandhi Swaraj. After the Chauri-Chaura massacre, a sadhu led a group of twenty people across the Ghagra River into Gorakhpur, where he declared that Gandhi Raj had been established. During the trial of the rioters, the district Congress and Khilafat leaders strongly denied that they had propagated any such beliefs. This is borne out by statements printed at the time in the local nationalist press that denounced such beliefs as misguided.[88]

In Bengal, according to Sumit Sarkar, there was 'virtually total disavowal of British authority by peasants fired by a conviction that Gandhi raj was coming or even already in existence'.[89] The Governor, Lord Ronaldshay, reported to Montagu on 9 February 1922: 'it is being widely stated in the villages that Gandhi raj has come and that there is no longer any necessity to pay anything to anybody. They are consequently not only refusing to pay rent and taxes but also repudiating their debts.'[90] In Calcutta, many Calcutta millhands believed that their day of deliverance – that of 'swaraj' – would come suddenly on 24 December. Oriya porters in Calcutta refused to carry loads of foreign cloth for Marwari merchants under a similar conviction. This belief penetrated even into the jails of Rajshahi, Barisal and Midnapur, where criminals broke out inspired by rumours that swaraj had been established outside by 'Maharaj Gandhi', that the British Raj was over, and notes and coins were being coined in the name of Gandhi.[91]

In Assam, the tea garden labourers and their families left the estates to find the swaraj that Gandhi was said to have already established in their home regions. C.F. Andrews reported in an article titled 'Oppression of the Poor', in *Modern Review,* August 1921, how these migrants arrived in Chandpur in East Bengal in an emaciated and starving state, but moved by a firm belief that Gandhi was about to relieve them of all their sorrows and afflictions. They were sustained, he said, only by their courage, which conferred on them a 'spiritual beauty'. He went on:

> The poor of India, who have been so terribly oppressed by governments and priestcrafts, by landowners and profiteers, have cried to God for deliverance. They are becoming more and more certain, that the hour of their freedom is at hand. During the past few months, it has been my lot to travel over almost every part of the North India, from East to West and from West to East, – to places as far distant from one another as Sindh and East Bengal. On these journeys, I have seen strange happenings and witnessed a new spirit. This new spirit, I am convinced, goes far deeper than the political movement of our times. It has its own initial impulse from the poor... The one thing that has impressed itself upon my mind and heart lately, more than any other, is this. The countless millions of the poor in India are astir... They have symbolised their yearning for deliverance in the person of Mahatma Gandhi.... This is not happening

in one place only. Time after time, recently, I have been in the company of the poor and the outcast and the destitute; I have been to gatherings, where the untouchables and others have flocked together in crowds to meet me and I have listened with intense pain to the story of their afflictions. They appear now to be everywhere taking the courage in their both hands as they have never done before.[92]

In Andhra, Gandhi Swaraj and *Ramraj* were considered almost synonymous. A song titled 'If the Gandhian Movement is Victorious' printed in *Andhra Lakshmi*, a Telugu-language monthly for women published from Berhampor in Ganjam District described the new order:

If the Gandhian Movement is Victorious
Crores of Hindu *coolie* people
Adopting *charka* as their work
Would get plenty of cloth and food

If the Gandhian Movement is Victorious
Hindus and Muslims become well-wishers (of each other)
Muslims end cow slaughter thinking it
As horrible; we retain our cattle wealth

If the Gandhian Movement is Victorious
Burden of taxes being less, production increases
Famine leaves motherland faster
Pleasures of prosperity would blossom and thrive

If the Gandhian Movement is Victorious
Toddy shops would slowly disappear
Widely spreading making people poor
The *Abkari* [excise] department; would it not meet its end?

If the Gandhian Movement is Victorious
Hard working weavers' labour ultimately
Bear fruit and would get them
So much food and money (prosperity) for ever

If the Gandhian Movement is Victorious
All the skills of handicrafts increase
All the daily necessities become cheap;
Making noble ideals flourish

With honourable and simple life style
People would thrive in prosperity
/
If the Gandhian Movement is Victorious.[93]

The Andhra nationalist T. Prakashan, visited Pedanandipad in 1922 at the time of the no-tax campaign. He was told by the peasants that their local leader, Veeraiah Chowdary, had informed them that swaraj was coming and that under 'the Gandhian Government' they would no longer be required to pay any tax. This had inspired their protest.[94]

Muslims tended to understand the millennium in terms of a saviour coming to restore Islam. For example, in May 1919, the Governor of Bengal, Lord Ronaldshay, was informed about an Islamic prophecy that if the infidel seized Constantinople, a Mahdi would come to save Islam. The *hijrat* (migration) movement of Muslims of Sindh and the Northwest Frontier Province to Afghanistan in 1920 that has been mentioned in Chapter 1 had strong millenarian underpinnings. Similar beliefs circulated among the Mappila Muslims during their revolt in 1921, for example the notion mentioned in Chapter 2 that the Amir of Afghanistan was coming to help them in their revolt. Otherwise, the pan-Islamism of the Khilafat Movement does not appear to have given rise to a millenarianism of a similar density to that of many Hindus at that time.

Although millennial fervour had the potential to turn violent, the times when inspired crowds attacked the police with reckless or murderous impunity were few and far between. Though exceptional, these cases were nonetheless emphasised at the time by nationalist leaders who went out of their way to condemn such behaviour – particularly in the case of Chauri Chaura – as well as subsequently by historians. In most cases, millenarian sentiments empowered predominantly nonviolent protests.

The Thaumaturgic

The prime meaning of 'thaumaturgic' provided in the *Oxford English Dictionary* is that of a force 'that works, or has the power of working, miracles or marvels; wonder-working'. It provides a demonstration of divine support for an individual or set of beliefs, and it can take the form of either conferring boons on believers or bringing misfortune to non-believers. In India, all religious traditions have sought to validate themselves through thaumaturgic revelations, and there was no doubt amongst the mass of the people, and indeed many amongst the elites, of the all-embracing validity of such demonstrations of divine power. William Crooke emphasised the widespread prevalence of such a belief in his book published in 1894 on the popular religion of northern India. In it, he described the holy men who were seen to manifest 'divine energy acquired by his virtue and self-devotion.... These saints have wrested from the reluctant gods, by sheer piety and relentless austerity, a portion of the divine thaumaturgic power...' Such people, who revealed their status through a wide range of miracles, could be within both the Hindu and Muslim religious traditions, and the same person could attract followers of both religions. Crooke mentions saintly figures who were active in the nineteenth century, such as Gauhar Shah of Meerut, who had prophesied that a windmill belonging to a Britisher called Smith would stop working – which it promptly did.[95]

By far the best study of thaumaturgic beliefs during noncooperation is by Shahid Amin, writing on Gorakhpur District. He found many reports on this in the files of the Gorakhpur-based nationalist newspaper *Swadesh*. He has placed them in four main categories: (1) testing the power of the Mahatma, (2) misfortunes inflicted on those who opposed the Mahatma, (3) misfortunes that befell people who opposed the Gandhian creed – in particular over dietary, drinking and smoking taboos, and (4) boons and miracles granted for those who accepted Gandhi's power. Thus, in the first category there were reports that peasants who had asked for various miracles in the name of the Mahatma had seen them fulfilled before their eyes. Peasants asked, for example, that their crop should change from one variety to another, that sweets should rain down from heaven, that their house roofs levitate, that an image of a deity should appear in their field. The newspaper claimed that all these things had then happened. This, Amin argues, shows that there was considerable debate going on in the villages at that time as to whether people were wise to put their trust in Gandhi and his message, with the miracles providing a powerful resolution of this conundrum.[96]

In the second category, people who doubted or disparaged Gandhi, or tried to hinder the progress of the nationalist cause, suffered physical ailments or became polluted. They might find their eyelids stuck together, their body covered in excrement, become mad, or suffer the spoiling of their meals or stocks of food. The misfortunes were generally reported as being reversed after the person had repented. Amin reports a case in which a local sadhu who was said to have slandered Gandhi found that his body began to stink. Only after he had repented did the stench diminish, and he then arranged for a sacrifice to complete the process. This, he argues, shows that godmen could not invariably manipulate the peasantry in the crude ways often claimed by the British – if their message was not acceptable, they might become the brunt of such disparaging beliefs and rumours. Landlords who opposed the movement might also receive a divine reprimand. It was thus reported that after a landlord had threatened to fine his tenants five rupees if they talked about Gandhi or became his followers, a huge apparition appeared before the people and stated that he was a follower of Shiva and that they should worship the deity. He is said to have commanded the landlord to cease making such threats and follow the Gandhian creed. Writing in the local press, the landlord dismissed this story, arguing that it had been concocted by promoters of the cult of Shiva. His tenants, according to Amin, are likely to have read it as a godly rebuke to their overlord.[97]

Thirdly, ordinary people who opposed the Gandhian creed and failed to change their way of life suffered similar misfortune. Those who thus refused to spin on the *charkha*, broke promises, told lies, ate meat or fish, drank liquor, imbibed tobacco or marijuana, or gambled were inflicted with physical ailments and illness, spoiling of the forbidden food before their eyes, sudden damage or loss to property, injury or death of livestock, even deaths in the family. They might be warned to desist from their evil ways through a marvellous sign, such the spontaneous movement of an image of a deity. In some cases, the misfortune was said to have ended once the person had repented and embraced the Gandhian way. In turn, such accounts could persuade a wider public to observe the creed. Even the pro-British newspapers that reported such stories in order to disparage them inadvertently gave them a wider currency. For example, the loyalist *Gyan Shakti* reported a belief among 'the illiterates of the town' of Deoria that the house of a local lawyer had become infested with excrement after he had reneged on a promise to give up his practice after attending the Congress session in Calcutta. The filth, which was seen by his wife, was regarded by these 'illiterates' as a divine punishment. The paper both reported the story and printed a denial from the lawyer, who stated that had not attended the Congress session and had never said he would give up his practice – nobody had cursed him, and he remained well and in fine health. The excrement that was seen by his wife was, he said, not a curse by Gandhi, but the mischief of a ghost. Interestingly, the loyalist paper did not deny that there had been a supernatural occurrence – it sought merely to interpret it differently as the act of an apolitical sprite. Amin argues that these stories reveal once again the debates going on throughout the region – with testing of what exactly was the message of the Mahatma.[98]

In the final, and fourth of Amin's categories miracles and boons were granted to those who vowed to follow and honour the Mahatma if a difficulty was overcome. In this way, people suddenly recovered lost property, livestock, and cash, or recovered their health. Trees that had been axed or fallen over righted themselves and came back to life; empty wells were replenished; foul-smelling well-water became suddenly fragrant; or in one instance caught on fire. This all conformed to the common practice of taking a vow to offer a donation to a god or saint if they removed an affliction or misfortune. If this happened, money or goods were offered up before the deity or saint. In these cases, the satisfied Gandhi-devotees donated money to national schools or other nationalist causes.[99]

Amin poses the question as to whether these stories of Gandhi-miracles were concocted and spread by local nationalists in an attempt to manipulate popular feelings. His source for most of them was after all a local nationalist newspaper, *Swadesh*. Yet, a local loyalist newspaper, *Gyan Shakti*, also felt that the stories had to be reported, even if the intention in this case was to disparage them or claim that they had no nationalist content. It seems, therefore, that the stories had been generated popularly before the local press took note of them. The act of reporting them, of course, spread them yet further – with an appearance of greater veracity now that they were in print. In turn, the printed reports – as read aloud to the illiterate or semi-literate – gave rise to further oral communication. They were spread above all because they accorded with existing beliefs about the authenticity of such signs.[100]

The local Congress and Khilafat leaders of the area made no attempt to disparage these miracle-stories. It was left to the provincial-level Congress leaders to attack them, using their mouthpiece, the *Pioneer* newspaper. The editor of *Swadesh* retaliated with a spirited defence of their policy: his paper, he claimed, was merely the messenger of the people (*janta*), and who was he to doubt popular belief in the matter? Prayer that was moved by faith and belief had a known efficacy. Miracles had happened in the time of the Buddha, Mohammad and Christ, and there was no reason to believe that they could not take place also in the time of Mahatma Gandhi– a person who now had in India the prestige of a Ram or Sita. There was, in all, nothing wrong with having such faith in Gandhi.[101]

In Awadh, Gandhi gained a similar reputation among the peasantry in 1920–21. Rumours as to his miraculous powers were spread, as in Gorakhpur, through reports in local newspapers. The *Awadh Bhashi* thus printed four of his miracles in its issue of 19 April 1921. A blind man had his sight restored after revering Gandhi; a policeman who tried to arrest a noncooperator was struck miraculously by a brick and injured; a man who purchased foreign cloth was cursed by his wife and his food turned to excrement; and a fire suddenly engulfed the house of a rich Muslim who hosted a performance by dancing girls in defiance of Gandhi's commands. Other reports told of how there was a rumour that Gandhi was to appear miraculously from the river at Ajodhya, after which hundreds of peasants rushed to the spot. In another, it was said that a six-metre tall figure dressed in white appeared in a temple and then vanished after disclosing that his name was on everybody's lips – it was assumed that it was Gandhi.[102]

We have less knowledge about the prevalence of such beliefs elsewhere in India during noncooperation, though there is some scattered information. In Bengal, Gandhi was said to have the power of turning people to stone by breathing on them. In *Dhorai Charitmanas*, Satinath Bhaduri's novel about Bengali sharecroppers that was set during this period, one peasant is converted to the Gandhian way after seeing

'Gandhi-Bawa's' face appearing in a pumpkin. He gives up eating meat and fish and smoking tobacco, starts washing every day, and refuses to work for the 'babus' on Sundays.[103] It was reported from South Gujarat that the adivasis regarded Gandhi as a deity with thaumaturgic powers. Childless couples were, for example, taking vows to give offerings to Gandhi if they were blessed with offspring. When Gandhi later went to the area, he was surprised to find adivasis placing babies in his lap that he was told had been born through his divine blessing. Women offered coins, garlands of threads and coconuts to Gandhi – as they would before a deity in a temple or shrine. Though he then ordered the local leaders to stop such preaching, the belief about his divine power had by then taken on a life of its own.[104] The adivasis continued to believe that Gandhi was a deity, and this belief soon fed into a powerful movement for social reform and self-assertion that started in late 1922 and which incorporated numerous Gandhi-miracles that I have studied in detail elsewhere.[105] Despite the relative paucity of evidence from other areas, it is likely that thaumaturgic beliefs about Gandhi and his movement were experienced in most parts of India in 1920–22.

Enchanted Resistance

In 1922, C.F. Andrews travelled to Punjab to witness at first hand the agitation against the custodian of the Guru ka Bagh gurdwara in Amritsar District. His report was later published in the *Manchester Guardian*:

> It was a sight which I never wish to see again, a sight incredible to an Englishman. There were four Akali Sikhs with black turbans facing a band of about two dozen policemen, including two English officers. They had walked slowly up to the line of police just before I had arrived and they were standing silently in front of them at about a yard's distance. They were perfectly still and did not move further forward. Their hands were placed together in prayer and it was clear that they were praying. Then, without the slightest provocation on their part, an Englishman lunged forward the head of his lathi [staff] which was bound with brass. He lunged it forward in such a way that his fist which held the staff struck the Akali Sikhs, who were praying, just at the collar bone with great force. It looked the most cowardly blow as I saw it struck and I had the greatest difficulty in keeping myself under control. The blow which I saw was

sufficient to throw the Akali Sikh and send him to the ground. He rolled over and slowly got up and at once faced the same punishment again. Time after time, one of the four who had gone forward was laid prostrate by repeated blows, now from English officers and now from the police who were under their control. The brutality and inhumanity of the whole scene was indescribably increased by the fact that the men who were praying to God had already taken a vow that they would remain silent and peaceful in word and deed. The Akali Sikhs who had taken this vow, both at the Golden Temple and before starting and also at the shrine of Guru-ka-Bagh were largely from the army. They had served in many campaigns in Flanders, in France, in Mesopotamia and in East Africa. Some of them at the risk of their own safety must have saved the lives of Englishmen who had been wounded. Now they were falling to the ground at the hands of the English officials serving in the same government which they themselves had served. I saw no act, or look of defiance. It was a true martyrdom, a true act of faith. There has been something far greater in this event than a mere dispute about land and property. It has gone far beyond the technical questions of legal possession or distraint.

A new heroism, learnt through suffering, has arisen in the land. A new lesson in moral warfare has been taught to the world. It reminded me of the shadow of the Cross. It was very rarely that I witnessed any Akali Singh, who went forward to suffer, flinch from a blow when it was struck. Apart from the instinctive and slight shrinking back, there was nothing, so far as I can remember, that could be called a deliberate avoidance of the blows struck. The blows were received one by one without resistance and without a sign of fear.[106]

In his reference to the 'shadow of the Cross', Andrews related the courage of the Akali Sikhs to the death of Jesus – both being offered through firm faith in a higher power and destiny. In such a worldview, God is seen to respond to the faith of the devotee by intervening to determine the outcome of a struggle. This may be revealed through certain signs and wonders. Throughout India, as we have seen in this section of the chapter, the strength of the protest and commitment to nonviolence was time and again underpinned by such faith in divine agency. This is an important element of nonviolent resistance that is largely ignored in the literature on the subject. Although the significance of such faith in protests in pre-modern societies is sometimes acknowledged,[107] it is not as a rule seen as important in modern times. It is acknowledged that religious institutions can in some cases facilitate association and mobilisation and provide a powerful rhetoric of struggle. Sharp, for example, cites in this respect the Civil Rights Movement in the USA in the 1950s and 1960s with its 'appeals to nonviolent discipline on religious grounds', and the Pashtu resistance to British rule in the North-West Frontier Province in the 1920s and 1930s, which 'invoked religious language and pleas'. Nonetheless, although Sharp acknowledges that Gandhi's nonviolence had strong moral and religious underpinnings, he holds that this was not crucial in what was above all his 'heavily political' work.[108] These two pages provide the only references to the 'religious' in this 600-page book on the subject. In another of his books, *The Politics of Nonviolent Action*, Sharp mentions religious processions and pilgrimages in support of political causes, the use of the pulpit for political statements, statements of support for protests by church leaders, interdicts and orders of excommunication by church leaders in support of political demands, providing sanctuary in churches and mosques for political dissidents, and so on. These are all analysed in terms of mechanics of protest, with no attempt being made to address the ways in which belief in a higher power may have motivated and given courage to the people concerned.[109] A more recent intervention by Carinne Luck, an activist from New York, focuses on the way that spiritual faith leaders have provided: 'nourishment, inspiration, and consolation to those on the frontlines of the struggle. They have served as living proof that another world is possible even while reckoning with the realities of the world here and now.' She focuses on the networks of connection that faith groups enable, the use of religious ritual in movements, the way that religion can provide a vision of a better and more compassionate future society, and the emotional support that their leaders provide for people engaged in often difficult action.[110] While these are all valuable interventions, they are nonetheless silent on the matter of supernatural agency in such resistance.

And yet, what we find in the case of India is Gandhi – its preeminent political leader in the first half of the twentieth century – embracing a belief in divine agency. He had in the initial years of that century forged a new form of protest that melded existing techniques of passive resistance with what he understood as an Indian spiritual culture, the result being 'satyagraha' – the force that comes from Truth/God. Adherence to nonviolence with sincerity, in itself, attracted divine favour, granting compelling power to the practitioner. Gandhi applied his new technique in the cause of nationalism – a form of 'imagined political community' that – as Benedict Anderson has shown so persuasively – is a relatively modern phenomenon.[111] In India, however, this involved a process of braiding with what are often depicted as 'pre-modern' forms of belief and practice, one of which was the faith that divine favour was gained through the practice of nonviolence.[112] This sort of braiding has continued in India to this day – even though it can be considered in most respects to be a functioning 'modern' democracy with a strong bureaucracy and civil society. For example, saintly figures such as Vinobe Bhave – who sought to change the hearts of hardened exploiters through an appeal to a higher morality – have often proved inspirational forces in the political life of post-independence India, as emphasised in 1964 by one of the most insightful of authorities on modern Indian politics, W.H. Morris-Jones.[113] Since he wrote, such people and matters of belief have – for good and ill – continued to occupy an important place in the Indian polity. Despite this, the relationship between belief in supernatural force and popular mobilisation is something that most theorists continue to struggle with in their materialistic and secularly oriented schemas.

In India, the large majority believed that deities and spirits had agency – a belief that was at times shared by the British too. Projit Mukharji cites accounts from India in which supernatural forces not only provided a challenge to British rule but were perceived even by the imperialists to have a genuine power. In one such case from 1850–51, a young peasant woman claimed to have met Shiva, who entered her body and spoke and acted through her. She was said to be able to charge objects with supernatural power and came to be revered as a goddess by villagers of all castes. They paid a tribute to her, which was regarded by the East India Company as a challenge to its tax-raising authority. She was jailed – with some difficulty, as several state employees refused to carry out the order to arrest her lest they incurred her divine wrath. Once imprisoned, she refused to take any food, yet her physical state remained unchanged. A British officer called Walhouse talked to her and – satisfied that she had a genuine power that was comparable in his words to that of the Sibyls, the oracles of ancient Greece – had her released. In another case, a holyman of Banaras who could heal people miraculously was jailed repeatedly by the British. Despite being guarded around the clock, he always strolled free. Such was his impunity that he even went to the local magistrate and asked for a cup of tea. Cases such as these posed immense problems for the British, as their Indian subjects were meant to be a docile population that was content to be governed. Yet, on occasions the British had little choice but to accept the authenticity of a supernatural force that defied their control in such spectacular ways.[114]

Dipesh Chakrabarty has argued that in India such beliefs are rooted in a sense of community of which deities – who reveal themselves in many ways in everyday life – are a part. For example, certain epidemic diseases are understood not as the unfortunate afflictions of individuals but as a wrath inflicted on an entire group by a disease-goddess who has a grievance against the shared community, the cure being through her propitiation in a variety of communal ceremonies. These have been reported from all over India. He cites the work of Ralph Nicholas on worship of the smallpox goddess, Sitala, in Bengal, who observed how people in even deeply-divided villages would come together in worship of these deities – and indeed routinely perform ceremonies in disease-free times to keep them content. In this way, according to Nicholas, the peasants forgot 'at least for a while... the pursuit of selfish ends'. It is considered imperative that the needs of the community override the pettiness of everyday life. Chakrabarty states: 'The language that is expressed by the symptoms and signifying power of this social body is complex and varied,' and that it covers experiences of 'class, caste, and family'. He notes how in this respect the body is understood as a social entity, in contrast to the sense of the body as something owned by the individual – a construct that emerged in its modern form in seventeenth-century Europe. It often involves a process of bodily possession by a spirit of deity. 'These performances speak of a mentality in which the mundane and heavenly times and worlds become entangled. Mortal beings enter into the stories of immortal gods.'[115] Once the will of a deity is perceived in all these ways, it must be engaged with and placated lest the community as a whole suffer.

Modern secular and materialist thought, by contrast, has generally sought to banish the supernatural from its analysis – the body is conceived as a machine that is driven by a scientifically observable physical and chemical energy. The spirit and the soul disappear. Religious belief is at best analysed as a matter of 'belief' – thus a matter of human psychology – rather than a force that acts in ways that are mysterious from a rational scientific perspective. Although such 'beliefs' are accepted as being important – as they have social consequences – they are not seen in themselves to be forces that have historical agency – only people with their multitudes of beliefs can have this. Despite this a widespread belief in the supernatural survived in the west within the sphere of 'religion', and some scholars continued to see divine agency in the working of human affairs.[116] The durability of such belief in western societies suggests, perhaps, why certain imperial officials were prepared to accept the validity of divine inspiration and possession. Such beliefs were reinvigorated in the late nineteenth century by spiritualists and theosophists who believed in an intangible, disembodied soul.[117] Gandhi and many other elite Indian nationalists were both impressed and informed by this strand in western thought, adapting it to Indian conditions.[118] By so doing, they facilitated the braiding of the different streams of Indian politics that occurred within the nationalist movement. Although Gandhi disavowed the idea that he was an avatar, his strong spirituality and firm belief that his was a divine mission gave license to the popular belief in his supernatural power. Many saw God in Gandhi and believed that in following him they were obeying God's commands.

The belief in the historical agency of supernatural forces was confined not only to nonviolent protest in India. It has been a feature also of some important campaigns of this sort elsewhere over the past century. There was a strong faith among many of the participants in the Civil Rights Movement in the USA in the 1950s and 1960s that God was working through the bodies of the nonviolent protestors. This gave the movement great power and moral authority. Martin Luther King saw his work as being inspired by Christian love, or *agape*, which he defined in 1957 as a 'creative, redemptive good will for all men'. This was, he said, central to the whole movement, being 'the love of God working in the minds of men. It is an overflowing love which seeks nothing in return'. In this respect, there was a greater power that stood with them in the struggle: 'That there is something unfolding in the universe whether one speaks of it as an unconscious process, or whether one speaks of it as some unmoved mover, or whether someone speaks of it as a personal God. There is something in the universe that unfolds for justice and so in Montgomery we felt somehow that as we struggled we had cosmic companionship. And this was one of the things that kept people together....'[119] Some sympathetic observers even witnessed what they saw as signs of divine blessing on the movement. One such person was Charlie Jackson, an African-American police officer who provided security for Martin Luther King during the March on Washington in 1963 and stood next to him while he delivered his famous 'I have a dream' speech. Jackson later told his family that he had looked up and seen that 'the clouds in the sky actually formed a cross. There was a cloud going this way and a cloud going that way and they met, and ... it must be a sign from God ... because the speech was so powerful that Martin was giving'.[120] Such faith has not withered within the African-American struggle. There is a well-known photograph taken in July 2016 by Jonathan Backman of a nonviolent protest organised by Black Lives Matter – an organisation that campaigns against violence by the police and vigilantes against African-Americans – that shows Iesha Evans, an African-American nurse and mother, standing in a calm and dignified manner before two police officers in riot gear in Baton Rouge, Louisiana. The police, according to the journalists who commented on the photograph: '...seem to stop, to yield, held back by something that radiates from her inner composure, her possession of the truth. In the instant that Bachman has caught for ever, the two officers appear confused, paralysed, even defeated by her decorous protest. Their bodies arch backwards, away from her, recoiling in recognition of her power. The officer nearest to the camera looks truly nonplussed, out of his depth, his meaty white hands flailing.' Commenting afterwards, Evans herself stated: '...this is the work of God. I am a vessel'.[121]

It is not only African-American activists who are so inspired. The white American activist Skyhawk has noted that while what she calls 'magic and ritual' is often deployed by those with power as a means towards domination, it can also call forth a 'power-from-within' that seeks to shatter domination. She defines the deployment of supernatural belief in the latter respect as 'the art of changing consciousness at will'.[122] In other words, the 'universal truths' propounded by the dominant are countered by the alternative universals of the people. Interviewed at a moment just after the 9/11 attack on New York when George W. Bush was threatening war, she argued:

> The images that we hold in our mind and the energies that we put out do have an impact on the consciousness around us. We can help to shape that by the energies that we put out consciously, by the intentions that we hold and by the words that we use.
>
> It's especially powerful if we're out there taking the action ourselves: doing it on both the outer and inner level. The other thing is that the magic and the ritual can really help sustain our spirits, and that's something we all really need right now.

She went on to assert that in this respect there was a special potency in a mystical embrace of nonviolence:

> I have a deep faith that there is a great creative force in the universe that is ultimately stronger than the forces of violence, and that if we align ourselves with that creative force, then we have that energy to draw on.[123]

Many of those who participated in the nonviolent movement against Ferdinand Marcos in the Philippines in 1980s believed that God was working with them to remove the dictator from power. The Catholic Church played a leading role in this. It sought help from the ecumenical pacifist organisation, the International Fellowship of Reconciliation, in nonviolent training. Bishops, clergymen, nuns and lay people all took part in these sessions from 1984 onwards. Their commitment to nonviolence was above all based on their faith that it was blessed by God. A local chapter of this body that was set up at this time held training sessions in thirty provinces and ten cities where there were mass prayers and fasting alongside training in nonviolent methods. A Tagalog term was coined for such protest – *alaydangal*, or 'to offer dignity' – that was modelled directly on Gandhian satyagraha. Gandhi, with his deep spirituality, was an inspirational force for the

Catholic participants. This enthused Christian protestors with the courage to stand up to the violence inflicted by the police and armed forces. Stephen Zunes writes:

> There was a strong spiritual fervour during these days, a sense that participants were caught up in something stronger than the sum of their numbers. Many described it as being a part of a 'miracle of God'. Indeed, there were several precipitous incidents which some participants took as signs of divine support, such as a large-scale tear gas attack that was halted when the wind suddenly shifted direction.

Marcos' position became untenable after troops refused his order to fire on unarmed crowds, and air force pilots refused to strafe the camps of the protestors from the air. One pilot said that he could not open fire as he noticed from the air that the crowds below formed the shape of a cross. After soldiers began defecting in large numbers and joining the protest, the dictator had no choice but to flee the country. Many believed that he had been defeated – in the words of one young participant – by 'the spiritual power that resides in the people'.[124]

The Solidarity movement against the communist regime in Poland was similarly enthused, with the Catholic Church providing strong support throughout. The strikers who occupied the shipyards in Gdansk in 1980 maintained a strict moral discipline – banning alcohol, for instance, from the yards – and holding regular prayer sessions and services led by priests. When mass was celebrated, thousands came from other parts of the city to express their solidarity with the workers. A picture of the Pope was displayed, and a wooden cross was consecrated at the spot where workers had been killed in an earlier protest in 1970. A reproduction of the most sacred relic in Poland, the Black Madonna of Czestochowa – believed to have been painted by St Luke – was attached to this cross. Her devotees sang:

> Mary, the Queen of Poland,
> I am by Your side, I remember,
> I am by Your side, I am staying up.

Lech Walesa, the leader of Solidarity, always wore an image of this Madonna on his lapel. She was renowned for her many miracles, and her devotees believed that with Her on their side, they would eventually be victorious. One commentator, Adam Michnik, has seen in all this a 'Polish messianism'.[125]

In all these cases, protestors were emboldened and enthused by their faith that a higher power affirmed their campaign. The Black Lives Matter activist DeRay Makesson has written with insight into how such a belief can braid in constructive ways within movements with a secular mentality that he calls 'hope'. He states:

> Faith is the belief that certain outcomes *will* happen and hope the belief that certain outcomes *can* happen. So when Dr. Martin Luther King Jr. says, "The arc of the moral universe is long, but it bends towards justice," he is speaking from a place of faith. He is confident that justice is inevitable even if it may come in another lifetime. Faith is often rooted in the belief in a higher power, in God. Hope, on the other hand, would mean reframing his statement to say, "The arc of the moral universe is long, and it will bend towards justice *if we bend it*." Faith is rooted in certainty; hope is rooted in possibility – and they both require their own different kinds of work.[126]

He goes on to observe that faith requires surrender to forces unseen and that it may at times waver. Hope is an optimistic stance and is 'the precursor to strategy'. In practice, those who have faith also understand that they must play an active role in achieving a better future. In this respect, faith and hope are companions. 'When my faith is challenged, it is the belief that things can change that keeps me moving forward. And when hope feels futile, I rely on faith to push forward and help reclaim that certainty.'[127]

In this respect, we may argue that Gandhian 'Truth' was reached through a complex dialogue, in which reasoned argument was reinforced with faith and hope, as well as gut feeling and political contingency. Gandhi knew that reason by itself rarely persuaded, for people tend to be guided as much as by emotional belief as by rational argument.[128] In this, Gandhi showed much greater self-awareness than the activist who tries to portray his or her moral stance as a form of objective rationality – for it is in fact based upon a belief in righteousness that is taken as a given.

As it is, large numbers in India – as elsewhere – were driven by a belief in the divine, by which I mean the psychic experience of an essence that cannot be confirmed through materialistic observation. Such an experience is for large numbers a deeply empowering passion, and it cannot – I contend – be understood as self-delusion or self-alienation. It exists in a dialogical relationship with our experience in the world and our logical understanding of it. This was understood by Max Horkheimer when he adopted a dialectical approach to religion, arguing that it is wrong to see it purely as false consciousness, as it preserves a belief in future justice, something that bourgeois atheism cannot be so certain about.[129] What matters are the actions and politics that faith gives rise to. While it is pointless to question any faith – whether it is secular or religious – we can certainly engage in debate with its manifestations. This, I would hold, provides some of the grounds for a more fruitful engagement with the world of the subordinated.

It is my argument that in the case of popular nonviolent resistance in India, faith in a higher power was of central importance and was deeply empowering, and that in this, India was not an exception – it is something that has been experienced in many nonviolent struggles, and it can give them an efficacy that cannot be understood in purely materialistic and secular terms.

The Nonviolence of the People

In this chapter, we have seen how popular nonviolence in India during noncooperation was rooted in strong local solidarities, in methods of protest with great local potency, and in structures of belief about purification and the supernatural. These diverse forms of protest were braided together by a nationalist leadership, in the way that we have set out in the previous chapter.

I have already argued in the previous volume that a popular nonviolence was becoming an increasingly important feature of the politics of the peasantry in the years before the start of the Noncooperation Movement, and that this became apparent in the campaigns in Bijoliya, Champaran and Kheda that became linked to the nationalist movement led by Gandhi.[130] This politics came into its own during noncooperation in a mass movement that was predominantly nonviolent. In this, there was a widespread belief that nonviolence was morally superior to violence. As Bondurant has pointed out, *ahimsa* is valorised strongly in the Hindu tradition and that the aphorism found in the Mahabharata: *ahimsa paramo dharmah* (nonviolence is the greatest religion or duty) is 'known in every village in India.'[131] In other words, nonviolence was regarded as not merely a superior strategic choice, but as a moral force that was blessed by God, and thus of particular potency.

Although such popular nonviolence was empowered by the nationalist movement led by Gandhi, it had a life of its own. It was not, as Ranajit Guha argued, something imposed on the people from above that ran counter to their real class interests. Guha's general position here was that in a semi-feudal society such as India – in which power was derived from the end of a *lathi* and barrel of a gun – there could be no radical change without violence, and that in seeking to stifle this, Gandhi was acting in the interests of the elites.[132] In this, Guha failed to appreciate the great revolutionary potential that popular nonviolence has for transforming even the most violent and oppressive of societies.

It is of course true that in some cases popular action involved violence. This was the case at Chauri Chaura, with the rioters in Bombay of November 1921, and with the Mappilas of Malabar. We see this also in the Rampa-Gudem hill tracts of Andhra, where the charismatic leader, Alluri Sita Rama Raju, claimed to have been inspired by Gandhi. Although he wore khadi, preached temperance and encouraged the people to settle disputes through their own panchayats, he also believed that the British could be removed only through violence, and he also carried a pistol tucked into a Sam Browne belt. The revolt he led began just after Gandhi halted the movement in February 1922, continuing through to May 1924, when Rama Raju was captured and summarily executed by the police. The Andhra Pradesh Congress Committee disowned this revolt.[133] These cases were however exceptions to the rule. In general, the Noncooperation Movement of 1920–22 was a remarkably nonviolent struggle.

To conclude, many different groups were involved during this period in agitations on a wide range of issues. In this, there were two types of braiding: that between elite and subaltern politics; and that of a variety of popular political practices. Some of the latter were rooted in feudal-style polities, others engaged with the practices of the imperial system, some represented imaginative responses to nationalist initiatives. Projit Mukharji provides us with a useful way of approaching this issue in his discussion of Indian medical history during the colonial period. He argues that rather than focus on the engagement between two supposedly monolithic forms of medical practice – the 'western' and the 'Indian' – we need to look at the way that different threads within a wide range of practices from both Europe and India became braided into new and unstable forms.[134] In the case of the Indian people, it would be wrong to try to delineate any single structures of either elite or subaltern politics that came together in the Noncooperation Movement. Rather, a range of disparate threads in both streams became intertwined in varying ways for limited but disruptive periods before they then unravelled. The process nonetheless changed future social relations and politics in important respects. In this, we cannot distinguish any uniform 'mode of popular resistance', for there were clearly many differences in the ways that people participated – depending on class, community, religion, region and so on.

Nonviolent forms of resistance cannot therefore be categorised as either coming predominantly from modern, western society, or – alternatively – from 'eastern' practices and spiritual values. They are, rather, the product of a history in which many diverse strands have braided in always unstable and ever-evolving ways.

CONCLUSION

The events of February-March 1922 left the movement in a state of collapse, as was recognised in the post-mortems that followed. In his autobiography, Jawaharlal Nehru recalled how both he and his father Motilal were left angered and deeply frustrated by Gandhi's Bardoli decision. He believed that a movement that had been going from strength-to-strength was halted in its tracks, causing great damage to their cause. Chauri Chaura was no doubt a 'deplorable occurrence and wholly opposed to the spirit of non-violence', but it was a 'remote village' where 'a mob of excited peasants' had got out of hand. Should such an incident be allowed to assume such huge importance? Did it reveal a grave flaw in Gandhi's whole strategy – namely that it could be hijacked by one act of violence? Was it really possible to train a population of three hundred million to be perfectly nonviolent at all times? Did this not give a green light to *agents provocateurs* to instigate violence in a way that would undermine all such movements? If so, 'the non-violent method of resistance would always fail'. The Congress had adopted Gandhian nonviolence because it was believed to be the most effective strategy. Nehru quoted at some length Gandhi's 1920 article 'the Doctrine of the Sword' and recalled how he and his colleagues had been truly inspired by its logic. They had learnt to resist the British by deploying the nonviolent method with great courage: 'But what was the use of the bravest and the strongest if a few odd persons – maybe even our opponents in the guise of friends – had the power to upset or end our movement by their rash behaviour?' He concluded that it was better in future if they regarded nonviolent resistance as a political method to be deployed in appropriate circumstances and be subject to review in the light of its successes or failures, rather than as 'a religion or an unchallengeable creed or dogma'.[1] Nehru, in other words, had come to the conclusion that the technique should be deployed in future as a matter of expedience rather than ethics.

The Khilafat leaders had a different and very serious concern, namely that the alliance between westernised Muslims and the ulama would be destroyed by Gandhi's Bardoli decision and that this would have severe repercussion for the Hindu-Muslim unity that they had built so laboriously. The Ali brothers, A.K. Azad, Hakim Ajmal Khan and Abdul Bari had all based their political careers on such unity, and they knew that its breakdown was likely to marginalise them politically and open the ground for populist Muslim separatists. They had done their best to keep the radical ulama within the fold, and they had managed it mainly through the promise that the movement was escalating in increasingly radical directions. They now they feared that all that they had achieved would be destroyed as the ulama deserted them. Not wanting to break with Gandhi there and then, Hakim Ajmal Khan had wired his assent to the Bardoli decision but was upset that Gandhi had not called for advice from a wider group first. The Kanpur Khilafat Committee refused however to abide by the decision at the urging of the radical ulama Hasrat Mohani and Maulana Azad Subhani. The Jamiat al-Ulama called a special session in Ajmer on 3 March to consider its position. Gandhi attended this meeting. Abdul Bari sided with the radical ulama by stating that 'there is general depression all over' and said that Gandhi was like a paralysed person, and that he would lose influence as a result. He asserted that nonviolence had failed, and that Muslims should adopt a separate advanced programme to obtain their demands. In his speech, Mohani made the wildly exaggerated claim that during the Noncooperation Movement 99 per cent of those who had resigned from government service and 95 per cent of those arrested were Muslims, and that Muslim protestors had been let down by Hindus. M.A. Ansari, Ajmal Khan and Chotani spoke out against this, and Ansari criticised Abdul Bari as being 'brainless, insincere, and a notoriety hunter'. The movement was thus splitting between the Khilafat Muslim nationalists whose priority was inter-denominational unity, and the radical ulama, who were obsessed with sharia law and a fundamentalist Islamic agenda. Abdul Bari later issued a more reasoned and moderated statement of his opinion. He accepted that he had overstated his case at Ajmer but said that he had spoken as he did due to his depression at the withdrawal of civil disobedience. He had nonetheless only endorsed Gandhian nonviolence for the sake of Hindu-Muslim unity. Such unity was essential in the fight against British rule and for ensuring that there be a peaceful and successful government once independence was gained. Unfortunately, he concluded, he had misgivings about the chances for continuing Hindu-Muslim unity now that Gandhi was in jail.[2]

In Bengal, Chittaranjan Das regarded Gandhi's calling-off of civil disobedience as the culmination of a long series of tactical blunders committed by the Mahatma. What had been in mid-1921 an irritation at – as he saw it – Gandhi's overbearing leadership and mishandling of the movement had escalated during the last two months of 1921 into a state of increasing anger. He felt that Gandhi was indecisive over launching civil disobedience, and still worse, had failed dismally to press the advantage in late 1921. Das had pushed during November 1921 for civil disobedience to start immediately but failed to get his way. Lloyd, the Governor of Bombay, wrote to Montagu on 3 December that 'Das and his colleagues desire to get rid of Gandhi under whose dictatorship they chafe and whose tergiversations, apologies and fasting embarrass them'. Soon after that, Das was jailed. In his recollections, Subhas Chandra Bose – who was very close to Das at that time – claimed that on the eve of the arrival of the Prince of Wales in Calcutta Lord Reading had made Das an offer: if he agreed to call off the boycott of the Prince he would in turn withdraw the notice that declared Congress volunteers illegal, release all those arrested under the notice, and convene a round table conference. A promise was made that the Ali brothers would be released also, though not immediately. According to Bose, he and the younger activists strongly opposed such a compromise. Nonetheless, Das managed to convince them that such a concession by the British would mean that they could claim by the end of the year to have forced the British into a retreat – even if they had not achieved 'swaraj in a year' as such. Even if the conference failed, they could resume the fight with their prestige intact. Bose says he was brought round by this 'irrefutable' logic, and a telegram was sent to

Gandhi in the name of both Das and A.K. Azad recommending that he accept the terms set out by the Viceroy. Gandhi, however, sabotaged all this with continuing to insist that the Ali brothers be released. Bose stated that Das was 'beside himself with anger and disgust. The chance of a lifetime, he said, had been lost'. Bose held – somewhat arrogantly – that with most of the other main leaders in jail, 'none of the outstanding intellectual stalwarts was in a position to advise the Mahatma as to the proper course for him to adopt'.[3] In a speech two years later, Das railed against Gandhi:

> You [Gandhi] bungled it and mismanaged it... The proudest Government did bend to you. The terms came to me and I forwarded them to the headquarters because at that time I was in jail. If I had not been in jail I would have forced the country to accept them. After they had been accepted you would have seen a different state of things.[4]

In all this, Das and Bose misrepresented the actual sequence of events and source and scope of conciliatory offers at this time. The feelers for a round table conference and Gandhi's rejection of the proposal happened before the arrest of the Bengali leaders, and it was Das who later in December offered a truce from jail in exchange for the release of political prisoners – an offer that Reading rejected. Also, it is unlikely that Reading would have been able to have made good the idea that was being floated of a round table conference due to opposition from both the Cabinet in London and the majority of provincial governors.[5] It also appears that Reading was mainly playing for time as a means to defuse the protest against the Prince of Wales and that he had little intention of allowing anything substantial to come of the negotiations.[6] Be all this as it may, Das clearly believed himself to have been the superior tactician, and his anger with Gandhi was very real.

The Bardoli decision of February 1922 compounded Das's feelings in these respects. Gandhi had, he believed, abandoned the movement without gaining any constitutional concessions. In Bengal, the British were losing control in many areas by early 1922, providing the conditions for radical change. This was now all in abeyance. Das was not particularly concerned if there was violence – it would all add to the pressure on the British. He was not at all impressed with Gandhi's moral considerations about violence.[7] In his autobiography, Bose went on to report Das's subsequent verdict on Gandhi, that 'the Mahatma opens a campaign in a brilliant fashion; he works it up with unerring skill; he moves from success to success till he reaches the zenith of his campaign – but after that he loses his nerve and begins to falter.' Bose went on to make some observations of his own. Firstly, the Congress had been mistaken to place too much power and responsibility in the hands of one person – Gandhi. This led to a situation in which 'the entire intellect of the Congress has been mortgaged to one man, and those who dare to think freely and speak out openly are regarded by the Mahatma and his disciples as heretics and treated as such.' Secondly:

> ...the promise of 'Swaraj' within one year was not only unwise but childish. It made the Congress appear so foolish before all reasonable men. No doubt the Mahatma's disciples have tried subsequently to explain away the point by saying that the country did not fulfil the conditions and so Swaraj could not be won in one year. The explanation is as unsatisfactory as the original promise was unwise – because arguing in the same way, any leader can say that if you fulfil certain conditions you can be free in one hour. In making political forecasts, no leader worth the name should impose impossible conditions. He should estimate what conditions are likely to be achieved in a given set of circumstances.

Thirdly, Bose argued, it had proved to be a mistake to try to carry on a campaign that was linked to the Khilafat issue. If the Khilafat groups had joined the Congress and come under its discipline, much more could have been achieved.[8]

Das and Gandhi had, it is clear, very different aims, and in the end they proved irreconcilable. Following in the tradition set by Aurobindo, Das wanted to put pressure on the British using any means appropriate. Although nonviolent resistance provided the most effective tactic at that juncture, he would not rule out the use of violence if necessary. He sought to generate a state of continuing escalation until British authority was effectively destroyed. His main target was the seizure of constitutional power regardless of the extent to which society might be transformed at a deeper level. Indeed, it benefited members of the Bengal bhadralok if society was not shaken up too deeply before they replaced the British. Gandhi, as we have seen, had radically different views on these matters. The tensions in these respects between the Mahatma and the 'outstanding intellectual stalwarts' of Bengal would continue to fester over the following decades.

Claude Markovits has argued that Gandhi was a far better tactician than strategist. He had a great capacity to innovate and catch the British by surprise. He knew how to exploit a given situation, combining agitation and propaganda in a most effective way. 'Gandhi proved to be a genius of "agitprop"; he was good at attracting the attention of the media upon his actions and on the movements he led.' He failed, however, to secure his retreats or prepare positions of withdrawal.[9] This judgement is borne out by the events of 1920–22. It is hard to argue that Gandhi handled the political demands of that time astutely. He created a momentum with huge skill, and up to the end of 1921 had managed to keep the Congress radicals on his side, gradually win over Indian moderates, and step up the pressure on the British. But then, in February 1922 his decision over Chauri Chaura swept the feet from under the campaign, causing it to collapse disastrously. Worst of all, he profoundly alienated the Khilafat leaders, who felt abandoned in jail. Never again was there to be firm Hindu-Muslim unity in a campaign against the British, with severe consequences for the eventual integrity of the sub-continent. Gandhi had, we may argue, proved a poor nonviolent strategist in his first major all-India campaign, and the Indian people were to pay a dreadful long-term price.

This does not mean that the movement achieved nothing of consequence – far from it. It had led to the transformation of the Congress from being little more than a debating society into a campaigning organisation with a permanent executive and a system of representation that stretched down to village level. In this respect, it established a parallel system of government – and Gandhi indeed regarded the Congress as being more like a parliament that provided a forum for people of differing opinion to debate and decide on policy, with the executive being in the role of a cabinet with collective responsibility.[10] So far as Gandhi was concerned, the existence of such a flourishing body meant that a parallel authority had been created, and in this respect an important element of 'swaraj' had been achieved. Chenoweth and Stephan have pointed out the strategic advantage for movements in creating such systems of authority. It creates the impression amongst hitherto uncommitted people that the opposition is a viable alternative to which they can safely gravitate. This, the two authors argue, played an important role in the eventual success of the pro-democracy movements in Chile, the Philippines, and Eastern Europe in the late twentieth century.[11] Noncooperation can be seen in retrospect as the great democratic moment in modern South Asia, with people of all classes throughout India understanding that they could play an active role in a civic life that stretched beyond their localities to incorporate the nation as a whole. Things were never the same again in the subcontinent. The Congress now had a vibrant and durable base in many localities of India through the constructive programme – providing a focus for future campaigns. Many of the regions in which such bases were created in 1920–22 proved to be major sites of protest in 1930–31 and 1942. We may also note that in these localities, the Congress provided a vehicle for the assertion of local communities against both the British and Indian elites. This process saw authority at the local level being gradually wrested from the existing status quo, with the classes and communities that supported the movement often becoming politically dominant in that area once independence was won in 1947.[12] There were other major shifts at this time, with a new Indian identity being forged that was expressed in matters such clothing and allegiance to a new national flag. The movement brought considerable self-confidence for many Indians, and a corresponding loss of authority for British rule. Gandhi also gained a reputation for his principled commitment to nonviolence whatever the cost, sending out a strong message to the world in this respect. These were all major achievements.

We leave the scene in 1922, with another twenty-five years of struggle stretching ahead before independence was at last gained in 1947. The pace of the Indian nationalist movement fluctuated greatly during these years, and it took many forms. Often, it involved local battles in which imperial power was disputed in satyagrahas over grievances such as high land taxes, rents and water-rates, punitive taxes, oppressive forest regulations, control over religious places, bureaucratic corruption, or the right of Indians to fly the national flag in public places. In many cases, these struggles involved social groups that had been mobilised initially between 1917 and 1922. As such challenges were local rather than all-India, the imperial state was in general more willing to compromise to isolate the discontent. There were four other national-level campaigns – the Simon Commission boycott of 1928, the Civil Disobedience Movement in its two phases from 1930–31 and then 1932, the Individual Satyagraha Campaign of 1940–41 (though 'individual, about 20,000 people broke the law, and were arrested and jailed), and the Quit India Movement of 1942. With the partial exception of the last, these campaigns were predominantly nonviolent, and when stray outbreaks of violence by nationalists occurred, Gandhi did not call off struggles as in 1922. In 1942 – the most violent of these movements – Gandhi and the Congress high command were all jailed at the start and were in no position to intervene to prevent the violence or call the protest off. In these campaigns, the support base fluctuated considerably over time. Apart from briefly during the Quit India Movement, fewer social classes participated than in 1920–22. The mass support of Muslims – such an important feature of noncooperation – was also missing in the subsequent campaigns – a grave loss to the national cause that was to culminate in the Pakistan Movement of the late 1930s and 1940s and the partition of the subcontinent in 1947.

Although nonviolent nationalist protest severely undermined the legitimacy of imperial rule, and managed to wrest certain compromises, it never broke the regime as such. Thus, although the Simon Boycott of 1928 rendered this commission a dead letter, the protest failed to obtain a promise of dominion status for India in the following year – leading to the launch of Civil Disobedience in 1930. This campaign was fought on a twelve-point programme, and a few concessions were gained in this respect from the British in 1931. Perhaps the main achievement was that the Viceroy, Lord Irwin, negotiated with Gandhi on a one-to-one basis in the Viceregal palace – a great symbolic victory for the nationalists. The second phase of Civil Disobedience was repressed harshly, leading to rapidly dwindling support and its effective collapse long before 1932 was out. Little concrete was gained beyond a feeling of national martyrdom. It was however followed by significant constitutional reforms that for the first time gave elected Indians significant control at the provincial level. Congress consolidated its position by winning the elections of

1937 in many provinces. The demand of Individual Civil Disobedience in 1940–41 was that the British promise to hand over power at the centre once the war was over. The British refused to give any such commitment, and the protest petered out. The Quit India Movement of 1942 was launched at a time of severe British setbacks in the war, with a feeling that the Axis powers could prevail, leading to India's occupation by the Japanese. The demand was that the British leave India immediately, leaving the Indian people to deal with Japan themselves. The movement – which brought an explosion of protest – was crushed with great violence by the army. This was the situation at the end of the war in 1945, against a background of British victory in the war and imperial rule being re-established in its colonies in Southeast Asia and elsewhere. Would the British do their best to hang on in India too? Their record suggested that they might.

As it was, they transferred power to the nationalist leaders in 1947. The reasons for this shift have been much debated. Writers on nonviolent strategy have given the impression that freedom was brought about primarily through nonviolent Gandhian protest. Few historians accept this as a sole or even primary cause. Clearly, the defeat of a Conservatives Party led by the arch-imperialist Churchill in the British election of mid-1945 and the formation of a Labour government under Clement Atlee played an important role in this, as since 1934 Atlee had been arguing that India should be granted Dominion Status within the Commonwealth. The Labour Party manifesto for 1945 stated that its goal was 'the advancement of India to responsible self-government', with the intention that India remain within the Commonwealth.[13] Negotiating a quick transfer of power was thus a party commitment. Some have argued that the British withdrew primarily because they had been weakened economically and politically by the Second World War, making the retention of the empire in South Asia no longer viable. While in the past India had owed large sums of money to Britain, by 1945 Britain was in debt to India, so there was no financial incentive to retain India. By that time also, most of those who served in the elite Indian Civil Service were Indians, making it in effect a self-governing colony. It has also been pointed out that elements in the army had shown themselves disloyal during the war, and this was followed by a naval mutiny in 1946. The penultimate Viceroy, Lord Wavell, felt that Indian would no longer be governable by the British if there was future widespread civil disobedience of the turbulent and often violent sort seen in 1942 that would have to be suppressed by troops with questionable loyalty, and that power must be handed over to Indians as soon as possible.[14] The possibility of protest was thus an important consideration, and whether it would have been more violent than nonviolent is an open question, given the prominence by that time of more radical groups, such as the communists, who had no principled commitment to nonviolence. We cannot therefore tell whether the threat of Gandhian nonviolence swayed the British government of the day. Atlee himself was alleged to have stated long after the event that his main consideration in granting independence was that the British could no longer rely on the loyalty of the Indian army after the revolts of the Indian National Army in the Second World War and the Royal Indian Navy mutiny of 1946, and that Gandhi's nonviolent protests had a 'minimal' impact on his decision.[15] What this perhaps indicates is that Atlee anticipated that the authorities could no longer be confident of being able to maintain order in the face of widespread revolts led by more radical – rather than Gandhian – nationalists.

The reasons for the British transfer of power are thus complex. Furthermore, the terrible violence associated with independence and partition shows that nonviolence was not a particularly potent force in the subcontinent at that juncture. The history thus raises awkward and difficult questions for those who study nonviolent strategy. All that can be done if we are working in this field is to provide studies that situate nonviolent protest in a clear historical context, analysing both the successes and failures of the method, as well as the contested understandings of what it entailed. This is something that I have – I hope – managed to provide to the best of my ability for the period 1905–22 in these two volumes.

In my introduction to the first volume, I set out the main arguments of *Subaltern Studies* on the Indian nationalist movement.[16] I want to end by proposing some alternatives ways of understanding the movement that are based both on my own findings and those of other historians in subsequent years. In this, it will be clear that although I accept several elements of the approach that was developed in *Subaltern Studies*, I now dissent from it in significant ways.

Subaltern Studies argued that the leading contradiction within the movement was between elite and subaltern. It held that the Indian elite sought, predominantly, to win constitutional power along liberal-democratic lines as in Britain, and at times deployed agitation to this end in pragmatic ways. A contrast was drawn between this liberal-constitutional approach in which agitation was deployed to gain concessions from the British, and the more radical objectives of the masses, who were fighting above all for their own social and political self-determination. In this they sought to overturn oppressive structures of power and bring into being a very different type of society. Although this argument is suggestive at a certain level, it takes no account of the important divides that existed amongst leading nationalists and their competing strategies, or the fact that these shaped the whole movement. We may say that the Indian nationalist movement was one in which different strategies came to the fore at different junctures, each having their moments. The five main ones were those of constitutionalism, strategic nonviolence, ethical nonviolence, theatrical acts of violence that invited martyrdom, and religious mobilisation. Each sought to forge links with subaltern classes in varying ways – some much more than others.

In the early period from 1885 to 1905, and again from 1910 to 1918, the movement was dominated by liberals who sought constitutional power. Strategic nonviolence – in which violence was not ruled out if tactically appropriate – was theorised first by Aurobindo Ghose, and it was in the ascendency for a brief period from 1905–09. Those committed to this strategy were prepared to work in the councils as and when nationalist agitation was in abeyance, e.g. in 1923–29, 1933–39, and from 1945 to 1947. They sometimes even worked in clandestine ways with revolutionary nationalists, with their secret cells that plotted acts of dramatic violence against British officials and symbols of imperial power, in the process courting martyrdom. Despite inspiring many fellow-Indians, the revolutionaries never enjoyed great influence within the overall movement. Perhaps their most important role lay in providing a pretext for British repression of nationalists of all persuasions, as in the notorious Rowlatt Acts of 1919. This could generate a backfire that strengthened the nonviolent nationalists – as in 1920–22 – but it could also bring brutal repression that hampered the wider movement.

Gandhi, who came to the fore in 1919, was a critic of the British form of liberal democracy, demanding an alternative form of democracy that was rooted in local communities that enjoyed powers of self-governance. To this end, he sought to build local power through his constructive programme. He believed that social and political reconstruction should be carried through in strictly nonviolent ways, as this provided both an ethical and more durable base for a just society. Though Gandhi was able in this respect to reach out to the subaltern in important ways, he was often suspicious of the people, distrusting them at some key junctures in ways that undermined what he was trying to achieve. His influence was at its peak from 1919 to 1932, and again in 1940–42. His method was also asserted in perhaps its most exemplary form in certain local-level campaigns, such as the Bardoli Satyagraha of 1928.

Those committed to strategic nonviolence generally worked together with the Gandhians, with much cross-fertilisation between the two. Though associated in its purest form with figures such as Chittaranjan Das and Subhas Chandra Bose, strategic nonviolence continued to be a guiding principle for other nationalists who in their dress and demeanour may have appeared to be Gandhians, and who were no doubt inspired by Gandhi, but regarded nonviolence essentially as a pragmatic method. Leaders such as Vallabhbhai Patel and Jawaharlal Nehru were in this category.

The final strategy was that of religious nationalism, in which people were mobilised and inspired according to their religious affiliations. This was associated with organisations such as the Arya Samaj, Hindu Mahasabha, the Rashtriya Swayam Sevak Sangh, the Khilafat and the Muslim League. Other nationalists were also drawn to this approach to varying degrees. It provided one powerful element within the Noncooperation Movement of 1920–22 – being then committed ostensibly to nonviolence – but it re-asserted itself again in more violent forms after 1937 – with the burgeoning of para-military groups such as the *shakhas* of the Rashtriya Swayam Sevak Sangh and the Muslim National Guards of the Muslim League – having its day in 1946–48, when it underpinned the brutal religious genocides of Partition.

The nationalist leaders, whatever their approaches, claimed that they had the interests of the subaltern at heart, which in some cases – notably with that of strategic and ethical nonviolence – gave rise to a braiding of the different streams. The braiding was strongest during protests, tending to unravel thereafter. Subaltern groups that had supported nationalist protest at one juncture might become disillusioned by the failure of the nationalist leaders to redress their grievances and refuse to participate in future protests. The subaltern always chose whether they should or should not link up with the nationalist movement. The self-assertion of the subaltern took many and various forms, as we have seen in Chapters 3-5. Nonetheless, it conformed as a rule to certain principles, and in this we can learn much from themes developed in *Subaltern Studies*. While some historians have depicted subaltern protest as 'pre-political' – in that it was not concerned directly with winning political power at a constitutional level – we may argue against this that it had its own political ambitions, being in this respect just as 'political' as the nationalism of the middle class. Although their politics was forged from their own histories, they only featured in middle-class nationalist narratives when their politics braided for limited periods with that of the Indian National Congress, Khilafat, Muslim League and so on. As their histories were not accorded much coherence in the writings of nationalist historians, we learn only about 'fragments' of subaltern history from such texts. By contrast, historians who have adopted a subalternists approach in their analysis and writing, have sought to understand the agendas, consciousness, and history of the masses. They have found that mobilisation was generally carried out through horizontal linkages, typically those of community. Community could be conceived in terms of class, caste, territory, or religion, and the boundaries could shift dramatically at different junctures. Subaltern consciousness was rooted typically in a subaltern mindset that blended understanding of their material life with a belief in supernatural powers. Gandhi was often perceived to possess miraculous powers. While from one perspective this can be depicted as a form of 'false consciousness', their faith in such higher realities allowed them to resist with great courage, it gave them a vision of a better future, and it should be respected and valued.

In all this, the Noncooperation Movement – the subject of this volume – stands out as one in which people committed to four of the five strategies worked together with many subaltern groups in a sometimes-uneasy alliance for its duration. Only the liberal constitutionalists refused to participate. In this degree of unity, it proved unique in the history of the whole movement.

Nationalism can be a malevolent force, preaching hatred of 'foreigners' and repression of those perceived to be the 'enemy within'. Nationalism of this sort is top-down, prescriptive and oppressive, and it invariably advocates violence to achieve its ends. It serves generally the interest of small cliques, who use it to both gain power and then to hold on to it. Nonviolent nationalism of both the strategic and ethical varieties, by contrast, seeks mass support by reaching across divides, and it is inherently tolerant, willing to engage in dialogue, and is prepared to compromise so as maintain the goodwill of adversaries. It seeks, at its best, to rouse the people-nation to struggle to assert themselves on their own terms. It is a potentially more democratic approach, and it lays a firm base for a functioning democracy once freedom is won. The Indian nationalist movement saw a mix of these two sorts of nationalist assertion, each pushing and pulling the other.

Although this legacy is a very mixed one, and it ended in great tragedy, there were, I believe, many positive sides to it. The ethical strategy, in particular, provided a compelling moral template for Indian self-determination that continued to re-assert itself even in the darkest of times – as when Gandhi put his life on the line to prevent communal violence in the final two years of his life. It meant that India became for many a beacon to the world – as was seen in the way that Gandhian method was taken up, adapted and amplified at a global level in the years after his assassination by a fanatical religious nationalist in January 1948. Above all, it revealed what the human spirit is capable of at its best, and – however grim may be our present situation – it provides a light from the past that may illuminate our future struggles.

NOTES

INTRODUCTION

1. David Hardiman, *The Nonviolent Struggle for Indian Freedom 1905–1919*, Hurst, London 2018.

1. KHILAFAT

1. Gail Minault, *The Khilafat Movement: Religious Symbolism and Political Mobilisation in India*, Columbia University Press, New York 1982, pp. 7-9, 18-27; Rakhahari Chatterji, *Gandhi and the Ali Brothers: Biography of a Friendship*, Sage Publications, New Delhi 2013, pp. 24-37.
2. Minault, *Khilafat Movement*, pp. 16-24 (photo of Muhammad Ali in 1913 facing p. 48); Chatterji, *Gandhi and the Ali Brothers*, pp. 52-74.
3. Minault, *Khilafat Movement*, pp. 1-7; Ayesha Jalal, *Partisans of Allah: Jihad in South Asia*, Harvard University Press, Harvard 2008, pp. 179-91.
4. Minault, *Khilafat Movement*, pp. 30-6, 46.
5. Ibid., pp. 38-45; Jalal, *Partisans of Allah*, pp. 192-3.
6. Ibid., pp. 46-8.
7. Ibid., pp. 51-3.
8. Ibid., pp. 54-8.
9. Ibid., pp. 68.
10. Hamza Alavi, 'Ironies of History: Contradictions of the Khilafat Movement,' *Comparative Studies of South Asia, Africa and the Middle East,* Vol.17, No. 1, pp. 2, 3, 6.
11. Faisal Devji, *The Impossible Indian: Gandhi and the Temptation of Violence*, Hurst and Company, London, 2012, pp. 21, 28-9. On the growing communal divide, see Gyanendra Pandey, *The Construction of Communalism in Colonial North India*, Oxford University Press, New Delhi, 1990.
12. Faisal Devji, 'A Practice of Prejudice: Gandhi's Politics of Friendship', in Shail Mayaram, M.S.S. Pandian and Ajay Skaria, *Subaltern Studies XII: Muslims, Dalits, and the Fabrication of History*, Permanent Black, New Delhi, 2005, pp. 78-98.

13. Minault, *Khilafat Movement*, pp. 60-2, 72-3.
14. Ibid., pp. 60-2, 69-73. On Gandhi's misgivings over the tone of the rhetoric adopted by the Muslim radicals, see M.K. Gandhi to O.S. Ghate, 8 May 1919, *Collected Works of Mahatma Gandhi*, 1st edition (henceforth *CWMG*) Vol. 15, p. 290.
15. Alavi, 'Ironies of History', p. 1.
16. Judith Brown, *Gandhi's Rise to Power: Indian Politics 1915–1922*, Cambridge University Press, Cambridge, 1972, p. 265.
17. *Bombay Chronicle*, 5 October 1920, p. 7, and 7 October 1920, p. 8; B.G. Kunte (ed.), *Source Material for a History of the Freedom Movement in India: Non-Co-Operation Movement in Bombay City 1920–1925*, Vol. 6, Gazetteers Department, Government of Maharashtra, 1979, pp. 25-6.
18. Brown, *Gandhi's Rise to Power*, p. 276.
19. Erica Chenoweth and Maria J. Stephan, *Why Civil Resistance Works: The Strategic Logic of Nonviolent Conflict*, Columbia University Press, New York, 2011, pp. 39-40.
20. In 1921, there were nearly 69 million Muslims in India, out of a total population of 316 million. They made up 21.74% of the population. J.T. Marten, *Census of India, 1921*, Vol. I, Part II, *Tables*, Government Printing, Calcutta, 1923, pp. 40, 43.
21. Minault, *Khilafat Movement*, pp. 63, 73-8.
22. Ibid., pp. 84-6, 92-3.
23. Ibid., pp. 86-90. Photo of Muhammad Ali in London facing p. 88.
24. Ibid., pp. 105-7.
25. Ibid., pp. 90-1.

2. STRATEGIES OF RESISTANCE 1920–22: ETHICAL OR EXPEDIENT?

1. On this, see Kurt Schock, *Civil Resistance Today*, Polity Press, Malden, MA, and Cambridge, 2015, pp. 183-4. The conflict between these two approaches is mentioned frequently in the literature, e.g. John Rawls, 'The Justification of Civil Disobedience', in Hugo Adam Bedau (ed.), *Civil Disobedience: Theory and Practice*, Pegasus, Indianapolis and New York, 1969, pp. 247-8; Gene Sharp, *The Politics of Nonviolent Action*, Porter Sargent Publisher, Boston, 1973, pp. v-vi, 455; Staughton Lynd and Alice Lynd (eds.), *Nonviolence in America: A Documentary History*, Orbis Books, Maryknoll, New York, 1995, pp. xl-xliii; Peter Ackerman and Jack Du Vall, *A Force More Powerful: A Century of Nonviolent Conflict*, Palgrave, New York, 2000, pp. 5-7; Howard Clark, *Civil Resistance in Kosovo*, Pluto Press, London, 2000, pp. 206-10.
2. M.K. Gandhi, *An Autobiography, or the Story of My Experiments with Truth*, Vol. 2, Navajivan Press, Ahmedabad, 1929, pp. 537-9. Also see M.K. Gandhi, 'Speech at Khilafat Conference, Delhi', 24 November 1919, *CWMG*, Vol. 16, pp. 307-12.
3. Minault, *The Khilafat Movement*, p.77.

4. Richard Gordon, 'Non-cooperation and Council Entry 1919 to 1920', in Gallagher, Johnson, and Seal (eds.), *Locality, Province and Nation: Essays on Indian Politics, 1870–1940*, Cambridge University Press, Cambridge, 1973, pp. 131-3, 139-40; Bob Overy, *Gandhi the Organiser: How he Shaped a Nationwide Rebellion: India 1915–1922*, Irene Publishing, Sparsnäs, Sweden, 2019, pp. 200-03.
5. All quotations in this and the next two paragraphs from M.K. Gandhi, 'Non-co-operation', 4 July 1920, *CWMG*, Vol. 18, pp. 5-7.
6. Overy, *Gandhi the Organiser*, pp. 208-12.
7. M.K. Gandhi, Abul Kalam Azad, Shaukat Ali, Ahmed Haji Siddick Khatri, Saifuddin Kitchlew, Fazul-ul-Hassan Hasrat Mohani, and Mahomed Ali, 'Hartal on First August', 21 July 1920, *CWMG*, Vol. 18, pp. 78-9; Brown, *Gandhi's Rise to Power*, pp. 251-2.
8. Gordon, 'Non-cooperation and Council Entry 1919 to 1920', pp. 132-3; Brown, *Gandhi's Rise to Power*, pp. 254-9; Richard I. Cashman, *The Myth of the Lokamanya: Tilak and Mass Politics in Maharashtra*, University of California Press, Berkeley, 1975, p. 204. Gordhanbhai Patel claims that Tilak had assured Gandhi of his enthusiastic support for noncooperation – see his *Vithalbhai Patel: His Life and Times*, R.A. Moramkar, Bombay, 1950, p. 40. Ravinder Kumar, on the other hands, claims that Tilak did not support such a protest – see his 'From Swaraj to Purna Swaraj: Nationalist Politics in the City of Bombay, 1920–32', in D.A. Low (ed.), *Congress and the Raj: Facets of the Indian Struggle 1917–47*, Heinemann, London, 1977, p. 83. As Tilak died before he had to make his position clear, it is hard to know which claim is correct.
9. Brown, *Gandhi's Rise to Power*, pp. 264-71 (quote by her on p. 271); Gordon, 'Non-cooperation and Council Entry 1919 to 1920', pp. 143-7; Subhas Chandra Bose, *The Indian Struggle 1920–1942*, Oxford University Press, New Delhi, 1997, pp. 46-7.
10. Pandit Motilal Nehru, M.K. Gandhi, V.J. Patel, 'Report on Draft Instructions for Congress Organizations', 22 September 1920, *CWMG*, Vol. 18, pp. 279-84; Patel, *Vithalbhai Patel*, p. 444.
11. Brown, *Gandhi's Rise to Power*, pp. 272-3 (Dwarkadas and Besant quotes on p. 273, Natesan on p. 274); Gordon, 'Non-cooperation and Council Entry 1919 to 1920', pp. 147-9.
12. Rajat Kanta Ray, *Social Conflict and Political Unrest in Bengal 1875–1927*, Oxford University Press, New Delhi, 1984, pp. 228-30.
13. Ray, *Social Conflict and Political Unrest in Bengal*, pp. 230-33.
14. Ibid., pp. 242-46.
15. Ibid., pp. 246-48.
16. Ibid., pp. 249-55.
17. Ibid., pp. 257-59.
18. Brown, *Gandhi's Rise to Power*, pp. 291-3; Ray, *Social Conflict and Political Unrest in Bengal*, pp. 261-2.
19. 'Congress Resolution on Non-Co-operation', Nagpur, 30 December 1920, reprinted in *CWMG*, Vol. 19, pp. 576-8; Brown, *Gandhi's Rise to Power*, pp. 294-5.

20. M.K. Gandhi, 'Swaraj in One Year', *Young India*, 22 September 1920, *CWMG*, Vol. 18, pp. 270-3.
21. Overy, *Gandhi the Organiser*, pp.251-2..
22. Brown, *Gandhi's Rise to Power*, pp. 294-7; Gopal Krishna, 'The Development of the Indian National Congress as a Mass Organisation, 1918–1923', *The Journal of Asian* Studies, Vol. 25, No. 3, May 1966, pp. 413-30; Ray, *Social Conflict and Political Unrest in Bengal*, pp. 262-3.
23. Ray, *Social Conflict and Political Unrest in Bengal*, pp. 259-60.
24. M. Nehru, M.K. Gandhi, V.J. Patel, 'Report on Draft Instructions for Congress Organizations', 22 September 1920, *CWMG*, Vol. 18, p. 284.
25. M.K. Gandhi, 'Letter to Chairman, A.I.C.C.', 25 September 1920, *CWMG*, Vol. 18, pp. 287-90.
26. Gordon, 'Non-cooperation and Council Entry 1919 to 1920', pp. 134-5.
27. 'Congress Constitution Adopted at Nagpur Session', December 1920, *CWMG*, Vol. 19, pp. 190-98; Krishna, 'Development of the Indian National Congress as a Mass Organisation', pp. 414-19.
28. Hardiman, *Nonviolent Struggle for Indian Freedom*, pp. 31-49.
29. Peter Heehs, *The Lives of Sri Aurobindo*, Columbia University Press, New York, 2008, pp. 123, 324.
30. On this, see Karuna Mantena, 'Another Realism: The Politics of Gandhian Nonviolence', *American Political Science Review*, Vol. 106, No. 2, May 2012, pp. 464-6; Overy, *Gandhi the Organiser*, pp. 138-62.
31. Ranajit Guha, 'Discipline and Mobilise', in Partha Chatterjee and Gyanendra Pandey (eds.), *Subaltern Studies VII: Writings on South Asian History and Society*, Oxford University Press, New Delhi, 1992, pp. 78-89.
32. M.K. Gandhi, 'Instructions to Volunteers', 17 April 1918, *CWMG*, Vol. 14, p. 350.
33. M.K. Gandhi, 'Letter to Dr. M.B. Velkar', 3 April 1919, *CWMG*, Vol. 15, p. 176.
34. M.K. Gandhi, 'Letter to the Press', 7 March 1920, *CWMG*, Vol. 17, pp. 74-5.
35. M.K. Gandhi, 'Non-Co-operation', 28 April 1920, *CWMG*, Vol. 17, p. 352.
36. M.K. Gandhi, 'Social Boycott', 8 December 1920, *CWMG*, Vol. 19, pp. 82-3.
37. M.K. Gandhi, 'Social Boycott', 16 February 1921, *CWMG*, Vol. 19, pp. 367-8.
38. M.K. Gandhi, 'My Notes', 22 May 1921, *CWMG*, Vol. 20, pp. 119-20.
39. Guha, 'Discipline and Mobilise', pp. 93-4.
40. Gandhi, 'The Doctrine of the Sword', *Young India*, 11 August 1920, *CWMG*, Vol. 18, pp. 131-34.
41. Heehs, 'Lives of Sri Aurobindo', p. 324.
42. M.K. Gandhi, 'Speech at Rawalpindi', *Navajivan*, 15 August 1920, *CWMG*, Vol. 18, pp. 64-66.
43. M.K Gandhi, 'Speech at Idgah, Karachi', 22 July 1920, *CWMG*, Vol. 18, pp.80-1.
44. M.K. Gandhi 'Democracy "versus" Mobocracy', in *Young India*, 8 September 1920, *CWMG*, vol. 18, p. 240.
45. M.K. Gandhi, 'Some Illustrations', 22 September 1920, *CWMG*, Vol. 18, pp. 273-4.

46. Gandhi 'Democracy "versus" Mobocracy', pp. 240-44; M.K. Gandhi, 'Three National Cries', 8 September 1920, *CWMG*, Vol. 18, pp. 244-5.
47. Guha, 'Discipline and Mobilize', p. 107.
48. Ibid., pp. 107-10.
49. Brown, *Gandhi's Rise to Power*, pp. 309-12; Kumar, 'From Swaraj to Purna Swaraj', pp. 86-7.
50. Brown, *Gandhi's Rise to Power*, pp. 314-5;
51. Minault, *Khilafat Movement*, pp. 132-5.
52. Ibid., p. 131.
53. Philip Woods, *Roots of Parliamentary Democracy in India: Montagu Chelmsford Reforms, 1917–1923*, Chankaya Publications, Delhi 1996, pp. 145-8; Brown, *Gandhi's Rise to Power*, p. 308.
54. M.K. Gandhi, 'Hinduism,' *Young India*, 6 October 1921, *CWMG*, Vol. 21, p. 248.
55. M.K. Gandhi, 'Speech at Bardoli Taluka Conference', 29 January 1922, *CWMG*, Vol. 22, p. 292.
56. M.K. Gandhi, 'Speech at Vadtal, 19 January 1921, in Mahadev Desai, *Day-to-Day with Gandhi: Secretary's Diary*, Vol. 3, Sarva Seva Sangh Prakashan, Varanasi 1968, p.227.
57. J.T.F. Jordens, *Swami Shraddhananda: His Life and Causes*, Oxford University Press, New Delhi, 1981, pp.107-9.
58. M. K. Gandhi, 'Hinduism,' *Young India*, 6 October 1921, *CWMG*, Vol. 21, 248-9.
59. Minault, *Khilafat Movement*, pp. 130-2, 138-9.
60. Overy, *Gandhi the Organiser*, pp. 297-8.
61. Minault, *The Khilafat Movement*, pp. 139-40.
62. M.K. Gandhi, 'Ethic of Destruction', 1 September 1921, *CWMG*, Vol. 21, p. 43; Overy, *Gandhi the Organiser*', pp. 301-2.
63. Minault, *The Khilafat Movement*, pp. 145-6.
64. Ibid., p. 146, & ft 123, p. 249; K.N. Panikkar, 'Peasant Revolts in Malabar in the Nineteenth and Twentieth Centuries', in A.R. Desai (ed.), *Peasant Struggles in India*, Oxford University Press, New Delhi 1979, pp. 616-26.
65. Ibid., pp. 147-9.
66. Woods, *Roots of Parliamentary Democracy in India*, pp. 148-55.
67. Ibid., pp. 149-55.
68. M.K. Gandhi, 'Notes', 3 November 1921, *CWMG*, Vol. 21, p. 382.
69. Patel, *Vithalbhai Patel*, pp. 457-60; *Secret Bombay Presidency Police Abstracts of Intelligence*, CID Office, Mumbai, 1921, p. 1798.
70. P.C. Bamford, *Histories of Non-Cooperation and Khilafat Movements*, Government of India Press, Delhi, 1925, p. 40.
71. Overy, *Gandhi the Organiser*, pp. 308-9.
72. B. Pattabhi Sitaramayya, *The History of the Indian National Congress (1885–1935)*, Congress Working Committee, Madras, 1935. p. 372; M.K. Gandhi, 'Letter to Dayalji and Kalyanji', 17 November 1921, *CWMG*, Vol. 21, p. 461; M.K. Gandhi, 'A Deep Stain', 18 November 1921, *CWMG*, Vol. 21, pp. 462-5; D.A. Low, 'The

Government of India and the First Non-Cooperation Movement – 1920–1922', *The Journal of Asian Studies*, Vo. 25, No. 2, February 1966, pp. 247-8.

73. Ray, *Social Conflict and Political Unrest in Bengal*, pp. 292-4.
74. Jawaharlal Nehru, *Jawaharlal Nehru: An Autobiography*, Allied Publishers, New Delhi, 1962, pp. 79-80; Minault, *The Khilafat Movement*, pp. 116, 165.
75. For an explanation of this term, see Hardiman, *Nonviolent Struggle for Indian Freedom*, pp. 171-2.
76. Woods, *Roots of Parliamentary Democracy in India*, pp. 159-60.
77. Ibid., pp. 158,160-7; Jagannath Prasad Misra, *Madan Mohan Malaviya and the Indian Freedom Movement*, Oxford University Press, New Delhi, 2016, pp. 128-9.
78. Ray, *Social Conflict and Political Unrest in Bengal*, pp. 294-6.
79. Minault, *Khilafat Movement*, pp. 181-2; Brown, *Gandhi's Rise to Power*, pp. 335-6.
80. Woods, *Roots of Parliamentary Democracy in India*, pp. 169-72.
81. Shahid Amin, *Event, Metaphor, Memory: Chauri Chaura 1922–1992*, Oxford University Press, New Delhi, 1995, pp. 15-16.
82. M.K. Gandhi, 'Speech to Congress Workers, Bardoli', 10 February 1922, *CWMG*, Vol. 22, p. 377; Misra, *Madan Mohan Malaviya*, pp. 135-7.
83. 'Working Committee's Resolution at Bardoli', 12 February 1922, *CWMG*, Vol. 22, pp. 377-81.
84. Low, 'First Non-Co-operation Movement', pp. 254-5.
85. Woods, *Roots of Parliamentary Democracy in India*, pp. 172-4 (Butler quote ft. 121, p. 173).
86. Ibid., pp. 174-84.
87. All quotations and other material in this and the next paragraph from M.K Gandhi, 'The Great Trial', 18 March 1922, *CWMG*, Vol. 22, pp. 110-120; Narayan Desai, *My Life is My Message*, Vol. II, *Satyagraha (1915–1930)*, Orient Black Swan, New Delhi, 2009, pp. 244-52.
88. D. G. Tendulkar, *Mahatma: Life of Mohandas Karamchand Gandhi*, Vol. 2, *1920–1929*, Vithalbhai K. Jhaveri and D.G. Tendulkar, Bombay, 1951, pp. 135-6.

3. STRUGGLES AGAINST LANDLORDISM

1. Kapil Kumar, *Peasants in Revolt: Tenants, Landlords, Congress and the Raj in Oudh 1886-1922*, Manohar, New Delhi, 1994, p. 177.
2. For accounts of the taluqdari system in Awadh, see Kumar, *Peasants in Revolt*, pp. 1-70; M.H. Siddiqi, *Agrarian Unrest in North India: The United Provinces (1918–22)*, Vikas, New Delhi, 1978, pp. 1-100; Gyan Pandey, 'Peasant Revolt and Indian Nationalism: The Peasant Movement in Awadh, 1919–22', in Ranajit Guha (ed.), *Subaltern Studies I: Writings on South Asian History and Society*, Oxford University Press, New Delhi, 1982, pp. 145-7.
3. Kumar, *Peasants in Revolt*, pp. 71-81; for the reputation of Kurmis as excellent cultivators, see C.A. Bayly, *Rulers, Townsmen and Bazaars: North Indian Society in the Age of British Expansion,* Cambridge University Press, Cambridge, 1988, p. 478.

4. Kumar, *Peasants in Revolt*, pp. 82-3.
5. Ibid., pp. 83-90; Nehru, *Autobiography*, pp. 51-3; Siddiqi, *Agrarian Unrest in North India*, pp. 112-3. Siddiqi notes how Ram Chandra's reputation as a proponent of the legend of Ram initially lulled the landlords, as they too were immersed in this story – though they prided themselves as being – like Ram – benevolent Rajas, with peasants as their dutiful subjects *(praja)*. At first, they even sponsored his recitals. Only gradually did they realise that Ram Chandra was using the legend in a subversive way.
6. Kumar, *Peasants in Revolt*, pp. 71-2, 82, 90-93, Siddiqi, *Agrarian Unrest in North India*, pp. 110-11.
7. Nehru, *Autobiography*, pp. 51-2.
8. Kumar, *Peasants in Revolt*, pp. 94-5.
9. Ibid., pp. 95-7.
10. Ibid., pp. 97-102, 136.
11. Ibid., pp. 103-7, 114-15.
12. Ibid., pp. 107-10.
13. Ibid., pp. 110-14; Siddiqi, *Agrarian Unrest in North India*, pp. 138-40.
14. M.K. Gandhi, 'Speech on Non-co-operation, Allahabad', 28 November 1920; 'Speech at Women's Meeting, Allahabad', 29 November 1920; *CWMG*, Vol 19, pp. 43-5; Kumar, *Peasants in Revolt*, pp. 114-5.
15. Kumar, *Peasants in Revolt*, pp. 115-17.
16. Peter Reeves, 'The Politics of Order: "Anti-non-Cooperation" in the United Provinces, 1921', *The Journal of Asian Studies*, Vol. 25, No. 2, Feb. 1966, p. 263; W.F. Crawley, 'Kisan Sabha and Agrarian Revolt in the United Provinces 1920 to 1921', *Modern Asian Studies*, Vol. 5, No. 2, 1971, p. 106.
17. Kumar, *Peasants in Revolt*, pp. 123-7.
18. Ibid., pp. 126-7.
19. Ibid., pp. 127-31; Siddiqi, *Agrarian Unrest in India*, pp. 158-9, 215; Nehru, *Autobiography*, pp. 60-1, Crawley, 'Kisan Sabha and Agrarian Revolt', pp. 100-1.
20. Kumar, *Peasants in Revolt*, pp. 131-4.
21. Crawley, 'Kisan Sabha and Agrarian Revolt', p. 102; Kumar, *Peasants in Revolt*, pp. 136-7; M.K. Gandhi, 'Telegram to Abdul Bari', 15 January 1921, *CWMG*, 19, p. 231.
22. Kumar, *Peasants in Revolt*, pp. 141-4; Crawley, 'Kisan Sabha and Agrarian Revolt', pp. 102, 105; Nehru, *Autobiography*, p. 61.
23. Nehru, *Autobiography*, pp. 61-2.
24. Kumar, *Peasants in Revolt*, pp. 138-41.
25. Ibid., pp. 145-7.
26. Ibid., pp. 147-8; Siddiqi, *Agrarian Unrest in North India*, pp. 169-70. The British claimed in their report of this incident that the crowd had hurled brickbats at the police before they opened fire – a common trope in official accounts that sought to justify police violence.
27. Kumar, *Peasants in Revolt*, pp. 154-6, 158.

28. Kumar, *Peasants in Revolt*, pp. 155, 157-6; M.K. Gandhi, 'Speech at Town Hall, Banaras', 9 February 1921; 'Speech at Fyzabad', 10 February 1921'; 'Instructions to UP Peasants', reproduced in *Young India*, 9 March 1921, *CWMG*, Vol.19, pp 344-5, 352, 419-10.
29. Reeves, 'Politics of Order', p. 264; Kumar, *Peasants in Revolt*, pp. 151-4, 171-3.
30. Crawley, 'Kisan Sabha and Agrarian Revolt', p. 95. On p. 99 he expresses surprise that violence did not occur in the villages in which the Kisan Sabha had first begun – as if this was an aberration in what he depicts as a general campaign of terror against the landlords.
31. Siddiqi, *Agrarian Unrest in North India*, pp. 150-63.
32. Pandey, 'Peasant Revolt and Indian Nationalism', p. 143,177-8, 181-2, 185. Pandey examines Gandhi's response to the supposed 'violence' of the peasants on pp. 152-7.
33. For examples of such usage see Pandey, 'Peasant Revolt and Indian Nationalism', pp. 180-81.
34. Pandey, 'Peasant Revolt and Indian Nationalism', pp. 181-2.
35. Kumar, *Peasants in Revolt*, pp. 165-9.
36. I would like to note that in critiquing Pandey's emphasis on supposed peasant violence, the criticism is also of my earlier writings, as I adopted a similar view at that time. See for example David Hardiman, *Peasant Nationalists of Gujarat: Kheda District 1917–1934*, Oxford University Press, New Delhi, 1981, pp. 253-4. Otherwise, I am fully in accord with Pandey's argument on pp. 151-61 that this was a popular political movement (rather than apolitical 'social' upsurge) that originated from the peasantry, one that was based on very real grievances, and one which in the final analysis was abandoned by the top nationalist leaders not so much because it was violent but because it conflicted with their pro-landlord agenda. I shall use his analysis in this respect in the rest of this section.
37. I shall examine this issue in detail in Chapter 7. It may be noted that in some cases, for example in Rasulpur and Arkha villages in Rae Bareli District, the Kisan Sabha panchayats insisted that property taken from landlords should be returned. See Crawley, 'Kisan Sabha and Agrarian Revolt', p. 99.
38. Kumar, *Peasants in Revolt*, pp. 229-30.
39. The sixth of his rules for UP peasants was: 'It should be born in mind that we want to turn zemindars [sic] into friends.' M.K. Gandhi, 'Instructions to UP Peasants', reproduced in *Young India*, 9 March 1921, *CWMG*, Vol.19, p. 419. Pandey has pointed all this out most succinctly in his 'Peasant Revolt and Indian Nationalism', pp. 160-1.
40. Pandey, 'Peasant Revolt and Indian Nationalism', p. 186.
41. Ibid., p. 187.
42. Siddiqi, *Agrarian Unrest in North India,* pp. 126 notes the ways in which Motilal Nehru sought to prevent what he saw as 'uncouth' peasants from having any influence in the UP Congress.
43. Nehru, *Autobiography*, p. 62.

44. Kumar, *Peasants in Revolt*, pp. 190-94, 206; Siddiqui, *Agrarian Unrest in North India*, pp. 201-3.
45. Ibid., pp. 199-200, 206-11; Siddiqui, *Agrarian Unrest in North India*, pp. 204, 207; Pandey, 'Peasant Revolt and Indian Nationalism', pp. 183-4.
46. Ibid., pp. 199-204, 209-10; Siddiqui, *Agrarian Unrest in North India*, pp. 205-6; Pandey, 'Peasant Revolt and Indian Nationalism', pp. 184-5.
47. Stephen Henningham, *Peasant Movements in Colonial India: North Bihar 1917–1942*, Australian National University, Canberra, 1982, pp. 70-89.
48. Sumit Sarkar, 'The Conditions and Nature of Subaltern Militancy: Bengal from Swadeshi to Non-Co-operation, c. 1905–22', in Ranajit Guha (ed.), *Subaltern Studies III: Writings on South Asian History and Society*, Oxford University Press, New Delhi, 1984, pp. 300, 302.
49. Ray, *Social Conflict and Political Unrest in Bengal*, pp. 306-7.
50. Ibid., pp. 298-300
51. Ibid., pp. 298-300.
52. Ibid., pp. 302-3.
53. Biswamoy Pati, *Resisting Domination: Peasants, Tribals and the National Movement in Orissa 1920–50*, Manohar, New Delhi, 1993, pp. 62-9.
54. Hardiman, *Nonviolent Struggle for Indian Freedom*, pp. 115-27.
55. Pema Ram, *Agrarian Movement in Rajasthan 1913–1947 AD*, Panchsheel Prakashan, Jaipur 1986. p. 26; British Library, Oriental and India Office Collection, Fortnightly Report for Rajputana, ending 31 December 1921.
56. Accounts of this movement come from records in the Indian National Archives, New Delhi; Premsinh Kankariya, *Bhil Kranti ke Praneta: Motilal Tejavat*, Rajasthan Sahitya Academy, Udaipur, 1985 (in Hindi); Prakash Chandra Jain, *Tribal Agrarian Movement: A Case Study of the Bhil Movement of Rajasthan*, Himanshu Publications, Udaipur, 1989, chapters 3 and 4; Hari Sen, 'Popular protest in Mewar in the Late-Nineteenth and early Twentieth Centuries,' unpublished Ph.D. thesis, University of Delhi, 1996, Chapter 6; Denis Vidal, *Violence and Truth: A Rajasthani Kingdom Confronts Colonial Authority*, Oxford University Press, New Delhi, 1997, Chapter 5.
57. Jain, *Tribal Agrarian Movement*, pp. 87-8; Sen, 'Popular Protest in Mewar', p. 317.
58. For details of the Bhagat Movement in this region, see David Hardiman, *Missionaries and their Medicine: A Christian Modernity for Tribal India*, Manchester University Press, Manchester, 2008, pp. 57, 60-9, 83-7.
59. R.E. Holland, Agent in Rajputana, to Foreign and Political Department, 30 September 1922, National Archives of India, Foreign and Political Department, 428-P (Secret – Printed) of 1922-23 (Henceforth NAI file on Motilal Tejawat).
60. M.K. Gandhi, 'Notes: The Malaviyas', *Young India*, 12 January 1922, *CWMG*, Vol. 22, pp. 164-5.
61. M.K. Gandhi, 'Notes: Danger of Mass Movement', *Young India*, 2 February 1922, *CWMG*, Vol. 22, p. 315.
62. Vidal, *Violence and Truth*, pp. 145-55.

63. R.E. Holland to J.P. Thompson, 28 March 1922, NAI file on Motilal Tejawat.
64. Interview with Roop Singh Bhil, Udaipur, 18 December 1997. As a report on a gathering of Bhils at a fair in this area had once noted: 'Every man and boy was armed with the unfailing bow and arrows, and I specially noticed that the bow was invariably carried strung, while besides a couple of dozen arrows fastened in the waist cloth, four or five were held loose in the hand to be ready at a moment's notice.' Major W.A. Salmon, Acting Political Agent, Mahi Kantha, to government of Bombay, Ahmedabad, 26 July 1881, in *Mahi Kantha Annual Administration Report 1883–84*, Oriental and India Office Collection, V/10/1542, p. 9.
65. For Pathik's views on Motilal's political acumen, and doubts about his ability to control his followers, see Pathik to Holland, 26 March 1922, NAI file on Motilal Tejawat.
66. Sir George Lloyd to Lord Reading, 2 March 1922, NAI file on Motilal Tejawat.
67. Motilal Tejawat to Gandhi, 11 February 1922, *Navajivan*, 26 February 1922, p.203 (translated from Gujarati by author).
68. M.K. Gandhi, 'My Notes', *Navajivan*, 26 February 1922, *CWMG*, 22, pp. 476-7.
69. For example, when some years before, a Mewar state official had asked some rebellious Bhils whether they obeyed the Maharana or the British, they had replied: '...of the British Government as all the Rajas now-a-days are under their supremacy'. Mitharam, 28 April 1881, in National Archives of India, Foreign Department, Pol. A, 313-11 August 1881.
70. This movement is described in N.K. Singhi, 'A Study of Jains in a Rajasthan Town', in M. Carrithers and C. Humphreys (eds.), *The Assembly of Listeners Jains in Society*, Cambridge University Pres, Cambridge, 1991, p. 156; Maya Unnithan-Kumar, *Identity, Gender and Poverty: New Perspectives on Caste and Tribe in Rajasthan*, Berghahn Books, Providence and Oxford, 1997, pp. 244-6.
71. Holland to Sir John Wood, Political Sec. F.& P. Dept of G. of I., 29 September 1921; Holland to G. of I., 3 January 1922, NAI file on Motilal Tejawat. Fortnightly Report for Rajputana ending 31 December 1921.
72. Holland to F.& D. Dept., G. of I., 21 February 1922, NAI file on Motilal Tejawat.
73. Pol. Sec. to G. of I., F. & D. Dept. to Holland, 26 February 1922, NAI file on Motilal Tejawat.
74. Lloyd to Reading, 2 March 1922, NAI file on Motilal Tejawat.
75. Reading to Lloyd, 3 March 1922, NAI file on Motilal Tejawat.
76. Major H.G. Sutton (Commandant of the Mewar Bhil Corps) to Political Agent, Mahikantha Agency, 7 March 1922; Memo. from F. & P. Dept. to India Office, 15 March 1923; V.S. Pathik to Holland, 26 March 1926; Statement of Tek Chand, son of Ratan Lal Brahman, resident of Baroti under Para at present residing in Koliari, Mewar, age 40 years, occupation beggar. Reproduced in Holland to J.P. Thompson, 28 March 1922; NAI file on Motilal Tejawat. I have examined the popular interview-based accounts in detail in my 'A Forgotten Massacre: Motilal Tejawat and his Movement among the Bhils 1921–2', in

David Hardiman (ed.), *Histories for the Subordinated*, Permanent Black, New Delhi, 2006, pp. 29-56.

77.. Fortnightly Report, Rajputana, 31 March 1922, NAI file on Motilal Tejawat.

78. He remained free until 1929, when he was arrested and sent to Mewar, where he was jailed until 1936. Subsequently he became a leading figure in the Mewar Praja Mandal, being jailed again from 1942-5. He continued with his political and social work amongst the Bhils till his death in 1963.

79. Political Sec. Foreign and Political Dept., G. of I. to Private Sec. to Viceroy, 13 April 1922; report by H.R.N. Pritchard, 14 April 1922; press communiqué from F. & P. Dept, G. of I., 7 May 1922; report by H.R.N. Pritchard, 13 May 1922, NAI file on Motilal Tejawat.

80. M.K. Gandhi, 'Non-Payment of Taxes', *Young India*, 26 February 1922, *CWMG*, Vol. 22, p. 265.

81. 'Working Committee's Resolutions at Bardoli, 12 February 1922, *Young India*, 16 February 1922, *CWMG*, Vol. 22, p. 378.

4. POLITICAL ACTION BY INDUSTRIAL WORKERS 1920–22

1. Gene Sharp, *The Politics of Nonviolent Action*, Porter Sargent, Boston, 1973, pp. 257-60, 277-8.
2. Sharp, *Politics of Nonviolent Action*, pp. 257-60, 269-74.
3. Michael Randle, *Civil Resistance*, Fontana, London, 1994, p. 42; April Carter, *People Power and Political Change: Key Issues and Concepts*, Routledge, Abingdon, 2012, pp. 16-17; Sharp, *Politics of Nonviolent Action*, pp. 275-8.
4. Anindita Ghose, *Claiming the City: Protest, Crime, and Scandals in Colonial Calcutta c. 1860–1920*, Oxford University Press, New Delhi, 2016, pp. 284-5.
5. A.R. Desai, *Social Background of Indian Nationalism*, Popular Prakashan, Bombay, 1948, p. 193.
6. Dilip Simeon, 'Work and Resistance in the Jharia coalfield', *Contributions to Indian Sociology* (NS), Vol. 33, Nos 1 & 2, 1999, pp. 44-5.
7. Rajnarayan Chandavarkar, *The Origins of Industrial Capitalism in India: Business Strategies and the Working Classes in Bombay, 1900–1940*, Cambridge University Press, Cambridge, 1994, pp. 79-81; Nandini Gooptu, *The Politics of the Urban Poor in Early-Twentieth Century India*, Cambridge University Press, Cambridge, 2001, pp. 2-3.
8. G.K. Sharma, *Labour Movement in India (its Past and Present)*, Sterling Publishers, New Delhi 1971, pp. 13, 20.
9. Chandavarkar, *Origins of Industrial Capitalism in India*, pp. 75-7.
10. Dipesh Chakrabarty, *Rethinking Working-Class History: Bengal 1890–1940*, Princeton University Press, Princeton, 1989, pp. 8, 14, 33-4.
11. Chandavarkar, *Origins of Industrial Capitalism in India*, pp. 88-9.
12. Simeon, 'Work and Resistance in the Jharia coalfield', pp. 46-7.
13. Amiya Kumar Bagchi, *Private Investment in India 1900–1939*, Cambridge University Press, Cambridge, 1972, pp. 8, 130, 161-215, 291-7; Chandavarkar,

Origins of Industrial Capitalism in India, pp. 68, 418; Ravinder Kumar, 'The Bombay Textile Strike, 1919', *Indian Economic and Social History Review*, Vol. 1, No. 1, 1971, pp. 15-17; E.D. Murphy, 'Class and Community in India: The Madras Labour Union, 1918–21', *Indian Economic and Social History Review*, Vol. 14, No. 3, July-September 1977, p. 293; Simeon, 'Work and Resistance in the Jharia coalfield', pp. 46-7.

14. Murphy, 'Class and Community in India', pp. 305-6. Similar racial tensions between managers and workers were found in the Calcutta jute mills, leading to physical assaults of white overseers. See Sumit Sarkar, *The Swadeshi Movement in Bengal 1903–1908*, People's Publishing House, New Delhi, 1973, pp. 189 and ff.
15. Chandavarkar, *Origins of Industrial Capitalism in India*, p. 102.
16. Vinay Bahl, 'TISCO Workers' Struggles: 1920-1928', *Social Scientist*, Vol. 10, No. 8, August 1982', pp. 35-6, 39.
17. Chandavarkar, *Origins of Industrial Capitalism in India*, pp. 94-5, 100-2, 110, 125, 197-8.
18. Sharma, *Labour Movement in India*, pp. 60-5.
19. Ibid., pp. 41, 58-9, 62, 76-7, 83; Kumar, 'Bombay Textile Strike, 1919', p.3; S.D.P., 'Obituary: N.M. Joshi', *The Economic Weekly*, 4 June 1955, p. 667.
20. B.P. Wadia, *Labour in Madras*, S. Ganeson, Madras, 1921, pp. 34-8; Murphy, 'Class and Community in India', pp. 304-05.
21. Sharma, *Labour Movement in India*, pp. 74-8.
22. Sanat Bose, 'Industrial Unrest and Growth of Labour Unions in Bengal, 1920–1924', *Economic and Political Weekly*, Vol. 16, Nos. 44/46, Nov. 1981, pp. 1854-5.
23. Sharma, *Labour Movement in India*, pp. 78-84; Bipin Chandra, Mridula Mukherjee, Aditya Mukherjee, K.N. Pannikkar, Sucheta Mahajan, *India's Struggle for Independence 1857–1947*, Penguin Books, New Delhi 1989, pp. 215-6; S. Bhattacharya, 'Swaraj and Kamgar: The Indian National Congress and the Bombay Working Class, 1919–1931', in Richard Sisson and Stanley Wolpert (eds.), *Congress and Indian Nationalism: The Pre-Independence Phase*, University of California, Berkeley, 1988, pp. 230-31; Wadia, *Labour in Madras*, pp. xvi-xvii; Rajnarayan Chandavarker, *Imperial Power and Popular Politics: Class, Resistance and the State in India, c. 1850–1950,* Cambridge University Press, Cambridge, 1998, p. 281; Cashman, *Myth of the Lokamanya*, p. 186.
24. Chandavarker, *Imperial Power and Popular Politics*, pp. 281-2.
25. M.K. Gandhi, 'Speech at Indian Association, Jamshedpur, 8 August 1925, *CWMG*, Vol. 28, pp. 46-7; Chandavarker, *Imperial Power and Popular Politics*, pp. 282-4.
26. Chandavarker, *Imperial Power and Popular Politics*, pp. 284-7.
27. M.K. Gandhi, 'Hartal on First August', *Young India*, 21 July 1920, *CWMG*, Vol. 19, Vol. 18, p. 78. Abbreviation added.
28. M.K. Gandhi, 'The Satyagraha Week', *Navajivan*, 20 March 1921, *CWMG*, Vol. 19, p. 452.

29. M.K. Gandhi, 'Strikes', *Young India*, 16 February 1921, *CWMG*, Vol. 19, pp. 365-7.
30. M.K. Gandhi, 'The Lesson of Assam', *Young India*, 15 June 1921, *CWMG*, Vol. 20, p. 228.
31. Kumar, 'The Bombay Textile Strike, 1919', pp. 8-9; Chandavarkar, *Origins of Industrial Capitalism in India*, pp. 81-6.
32. Kumar, 'Bombay Textile Strike, 1919', pp. 2-7.
33. Ibid., pp. 18-20.
34. Ibid., pp. 20-3.
35. Ibid., pp. 23-6.
36. Hardiman, *Nonviolent Struggle for Indian Freedom*, pp. 182-5.
37. Kunte, *Source Material: Non-Co-Operation Movement in Bombay*, pp. 8, 55-6; Bhattacharya, 'Swaraj and Kamgar', p. 227.
38. Kunte, *Source Material: Non-Co-operation Movement in Bombay City*, pp. 78-9.
39. Gandhi arranged meetings with groups of Parsis on four occasions in 1921 to try to persuade them to support noncooperation. Although he reminded them of the great nationalists that the community had produced in the past, he was met in a frosty manner. Mahadev Desai recorded how at one such meeting held in Bombay on 18 July 1921 some Parsis told Gandhi that they would only support him if he declared his loyalty to the Empire. They declared that British rule was best for both India and the Parsi community. Desai, *Day-to-Day with Gandhi*, Vol. 3, pp. 294-95.
40. Kunte, *Source Material: Non-Co-operation Movement in Bombay City*, pp. 73, 85, 91-2; M.K. Gandhi, 'Speech at Public Meeting, Bombay', 17 November 1921, and 'To Co-Workers', 22 November 1921, *CWMG*, Vol. 21, pp. 459-61, 477-8; Bhattacharya, 'Swaraj and Kamgar', pp. 227-8; Chandavarkar, *Origins of Industrial Capitalism in India*, p. 418; Mark W. Frazier, 'Seeing Like a Nation: Nationalist Political Persuasion and Positioning in Shanghai and Bombay during the 1920s and 1930s', paper presented at the annual meeting of the American Political Science Association, Chicago, 28 August-1 September 2013. Online at: https://www.icsin.org/uploads/2019/01/17/8fcf3e555a8d8a50c5cb7330d8831d42.pdf (downloaded 8 April 2019).
41. M.K. Gandhi, 'Letter to Dayalji and Kalyanji', 17 November 1921, and 'A Deep Stain', 18 November 1921, *CWMG*, Vol. 21, pp. 461-65.
42. M.K. Gandhi, 'Appeal to Bombay Citizens', 19 November 1921, and 'Statement before Breaking Fast', 21 November 1921, *CWMG*, Vol. 21, pp. 466-7, 475-7; Krishnadas, *Seven Months with Mahatma Gandhi: Being an Inside View of the Non-Co-Operation Movement (1921-22)*, Vol. 2, Rambinode Sinha, Dighwara, 1928, pp. 21-2.
43. Chandavarkar, *Origins of Industrial Capitalism in India*, pp. 197-201, 401.
44. In his comments on these disturbances, Gandhi characterised the Anglo-Indians as 'Christians', demanding that there be a 'heart union between Hindus, Mussulmans, Parsis, Christians and the Jews' of Bombay. He did not use the term 'Anglo-Indian'. In this, he highlighted the communal rather than racial

divides of Bombay. M.K. Gandhi, 'To Co-Workers', 22 November 1921, *CWMG*, Vol. 21, pp. 477-9.

45. Chandavarkar, *Origins of Industrial Capitalism in India*, pp. 215-17.
46. Ibid., pp. 217-8. A similar link between the local Congress organisation and *dada*-figures has been observed for Ahmedabad City. See Rukmini Barua, 'The Textile Labour Association and Dadagiri Power and Politics in the Working-Class Neighbourhoods of Ahmedabad', *International Labour and Working-Class History*, No. 87, Spring 2015.
47. Kumar described the strike as 'a species of working class *Jacquerie*', and he analyses it in such terms. Kumar, 'Bombay Textile Strike, pp. 2, 7.
48. Satyabrata Rai Chowdhuri, *Leftism in India 1917–47*, Palgrave Macmillan, Basingstoke, 2007, p. 60.
49. Kumar, 'From Swaraj to Purna Swaraj, pp. 93-4.
50. Murphy, 'Class and Community in India', p. 306.
51. Ibid., p. 307; David Arnold, *The Congress in Tamilnad: Nationalist Politics in South India 1919–1937*, Curzon Press, London 1977, pp. 69-70.
52. Murphy, 'Class and Community in India', pp. 299, 307-10.
53. Ibid., pp. 310-11.
54. Ibid., pp. 311-16; David Arnold, 'Industrial Violence in Colonial India', *Comparative Studies in Society and History*, Vo. 22, No. 2, April 1980, p. 252.
55. Ibid., pp. 316-18; Arnold, '*Congress in Tamilad*, pp. 70-1; M.K. Gandhi, 'Speech to Labourers, Madras', 16 September 1921, *CWMG*, Vol. 21, pp. 131-5.
56. Chakrabarty, *Rethinking Working-Class History*, pp. 8-9, 14, 33, 91-7; Dipesh Chakrabarty, 'Communal Riots and Labour: Bengal's Jute Mill-Hands in the 1890s', *Past and Present*, 91, May 1981, pp. 152-4, 160, 166-7; Ira Mitr, 'Growth of Trade Union Consciousness among Jute Mill Workers, 1920-40', *Economic and Political Weekly*, Vol. 16, Nos. 44/46, Nov. 1981, p.1839.
57. Dipesh Chakrabarty, 'On Deifying and Defying Authority: Managers and Workers in the Jute Mills of Bengal circa 1890–1940', *Past and Present*, No. 100, August 1983, pp. 125-29, 140-41; Chakrabarty, *Rethinking Working-Class History*, pp. 166-67, 173-85.
58. Ray, *Social Conflict and Political Unrest in Bengal*, pp. 269-72.
59. Chakrabarty, *Rethinking Working-Class History*, pp. 116, 118.
60. S.N. Gourlay, 'Nationalists, Outsiders and the Labour Movement in Bengal during the Non-Cooperation Movement 1919–21', in Kapil Kumar (ed.), *Congress and Classes: Nationalism, Workers and Peasants*, Manohar, New Delhi, 1988, pp. 34-9.
61. Chakrabarty, *Rethinking Working-Class History*, pp. 32, 136, 141, 146-7.
62. Ray, *Social Conflict and Political Unrest in Bengal*, pp. 269, 275; Sumit Sarkar, *Modern India 1885-1947*, Macmillan, New Delhi, 1983, p. 219; Sumit Sarkar, 'Conditions and Nature of Subaltern Militancy', p. 293; Mitr, 'Growth of Trade Union Consciousness', pp. 1840-1.
63. Quoted by Gourlay, 'Nationalists, Outsiders and the Labour Movement in Bengal', p. 54. The notion, however, that the workers were 'almost inarticulate'

is both patronising and incorrect. They could well voice their feelings to anyone prepared to listen.

64. Ray, *Social Conflict and Political Unrest in Bengal*, p. 272.
65. Ibid., pp. 272-6; Bose, 'Industrial Unrest and Growth of Labour Unions in Bengal, p. 1851.
66. Ray, *Social Conflict and Political Unrest in Bengal*, pp. 276-7.
67. Gourlay, 'Nationalists, Outsiders and the Labour Movement in Bengal', pp. 41-4; Bose, 'Industrial Unrest and Growth of Labour Unions in Bengal', pp. 1851-2.
68. Chandavarkar, *Imperial Power and Popular Politics*, pp. 307-08.
69. Gourlay, 'Nationalists, Outsiders and the Labour Movement in Bengal', pp. 44-8.
70. Ibid., pp. 48-53; Ray, *Social Conflict and Political Unrest in Bengal*, pp. 279-86.
71. M.K. Gandhi, 'The Lesson of Assam', *Young India*, 15 June 1921, *CWMG*, Vol. 20, pp. 227-8.
72. Ray, *Social Conflict and Political Unrest in Bengal*, pp. 284-5.
73. Mitra, Growth of Trade Union Consciousness', p. 1841.
74. Sarkar, *Modern India*, p. 219.
75. Sarkar, 'Conditions and Nature of Subaltern Militancy', p. 295, ft. 99.
76. Andrews wrote to Gandhi on 21 June 1921 from East Bengal predicting such an outcome, claiming that the area 'is on the very border line of violence'. Quoted in John Broomfield, *Elite Conflict in a Plural Society: Twentieth Century Bengal*, California University Press, Berkeley, 1968, pp. 218. Gandhi shared his concern in this respect.
77. Chandavarkar, *Origins of Industrial Capitalism in India*, pp. 215-16.
78. Manini Chatterjee, *Do or Die: The Chittagong Uprising 1930–34*, Picador, New Delhi, 2010, pp. 38-9.
79. Ira Mitr, 'Growth of Trade Union Consciousness', pp. 1840-41.
80. Sarkar, *Modern India*, pp. 199, 208. The Kanpur strike of 1919 is analysed by Vinay Bahl, 'Attitude of the Indian National Congress towards the Working Class Struggle in India 1918–1947', in Kapil Kumar (ed.), *Congress and Classes: Nationalism, Workers and Peasants*, Manohar, New Delhi, 1988, pp. 17-18.
81. Bahl, 'TISCO Workers' Struggles', pp. 35-8.
82. Chandavarkar, *Origins of Industrial Capitalism in India*, pp. 237-8.
83. For Andrew's work in this respect, see Hugh Tinker, *The Ordeal of Love: C.F. Andrews and India*, Oxford University Press, Oxford, 1979.
84. C.F. Andrews, *The Oppression of the Poor*, Ganesh and Co., Madras 1921, pp. 108-10.
85. Chandavarkar, *Origins of Industrial Capitalism in India*, pp. 400, 409.

5. TERRAINS OF RESISTANCE 1920–22

1. Kumar, 'From Swaraj to Purna Swaraj', p. 77.
2. Prasant Kidambi, 'Nationalism and the City in Colonial India: Bombay, c. 1890-1940', *Journal of Urban History*, Vol. 38, No. 5, 2012, pp. 954-7.

3. Kenneth L. Gillion, *Ahmedabad: A Study in Urban History*, University of California Press, Berkeley, 1968, pp. 169-70.
4. Douglas Haynes, 'From Avoidance to Confrontation? A Contestory History of Merchant-State Relations in Surat 1600–1924', in Douglas Haynes and Gyan Prakash (eds.), *Contesting Power: Resistance and Everyday Social Relations in South Asia*, University of California Press, Berkeley, 1991, p. 276.
5. Hardiman, *Peasant Nationalist of Gujarat*, pp. 144-7.
6. *Secret Bombay Police Abstracts of Intelligence*, 1921, p. 1037.
7. Hardiman, *Peasant Nationalist of Gujarat*, pp. 155-6.
8. Simon Epstein, *The Earthy Soil: Bombay Peasants and the Indian Nationalist Movement 1919–1947*, Oxford University Press, New Delhi, 1988, pp. 46-8.
9. Atlury Murali, 'Civil Disobedience Movement in Andhra 1920-22: The Nature of Peasant Protest and the Methods of Congress Political Mobilization', in Kapil Kumar (ed.), *Congress and Classes: Nationalism, Workers and Peasants*, Manohar, New Delhi, 1988, pp. 167-73, ft. 107, p. 207; Christopher Baker, 'Non-Cooperation in South India', in C. Baker and D. Washbrook (eds.), *South India: Political Institutions and Political Change 1880–1940*, Macmillan, Delhi, 1975, pp. 132-4; Sarkar, *Modern* India, p. 214.
10. M.K. Gandhi to K. Venkatappayya, 17 January 1922, *CWMG*, Vol. 22, pp. 211-12.
11. K. Venkatappayya to M.K. Gandhi, 17 January 1922, *CWMG*, Vol. 22, p. 228, ft. 1; Murali, 'Civil Disobedience Movement in Andhra 1920–22', p. 174.
12. M.K. Gandhi, 'Non-Payment of Taxes', *Young India*, 26 January 1922, *CWMG*, Vol. 22, p. 265.
13. M.K. Gandhi, 'Awakening in Andhradesha', 29 January 1922, *CWMG*, Vol. 22, pp. 281-6.
14. Baker, 'Non-Cooperation in South India', p. 134; Murali, 'Civil Disobedience Movement in Andhra 1920–22', pp. 176-8.
15. Hitesranjan Sanyal, 'Congress in Southwestern Bengal: The Anti-Union Board Movement in Eastern Medinipur, 1921', in Richard Sissons and Stanley Wolpert (eds.), *Congress and Indian Nationalism: The Pre-Independence Phase*, University of California Press, Berkeley, 1988, pp. 354-6; Bidyut Chakrabarty, *Local Politics and Indian Nationalism: Medinipur 1919–1944*, Manohar, New Delhi, 1997, pp. 61-6.
16. Sanyal, 'Congress in Southwestern Bengal', pp. 357-9; Chakrabarty, *Local Politics and Indian Nationalism*, pp. 70-6, 83-4.
17. Sanyal, 'Congress in Southwestern Bengal', pp. 359-62: Chakrabarty, *Local Politics and Indian Nationalism*, pp. 85-7.
18. Sanyal, 'Congress in Southwestern Bengal', pp. 359-62: Chakrabarty, *Local Politics and Indian Nationalism*, pp. 85-9.
19. Sanyal, 'Congress in Southwestern Bengal', pp. 366-7: Chakrabarty, *Local Politics and Indian Nationalism*, pp. 88-90.
20. Sanyal, 'Congress in Southwestern Bengal', pp. 367-8; Chakrabarty, *Local Politics and Indian Nationalism*, pp. 87-91.

21. Sanyal, 'Congress in Southwestern Bengal', pp. 368-9; Chakrabarty, *Local Politics and Indian Nationalism*, pp. 90-1; Sarkar, 'Conditions and Nature of Subaltern Militancy', p. 298.
22. Murali, 'Civil Disobedience Movement in Andhra', pp. 153-6.
23. Rajendra Vora, *The World's First Anti-Dam Movement: The Mulshi Satyagraha 1920–1924*, Permanent Black, Ranikhet 2009, pp. 3, 7, 21-5; Livi Rodrigues, *Rural Protest in Western India*, Oxford University Press, New Delhi 1998, pp. 108, 125, ft 32.
24. Vora, *The World's First Anti-Dam Movement*, p. 31; Rodrigues, *Rural Protest in Western India*, pp. 111,120, 124, ft 27,133, ft 108.
25. Vora, *The World's First Anti-Dam Movement*, pp. 37-40.
26. Ibid., pp. 32, 36-7, 42-4, 46-8, 61; Rodrigues, *Rural Protest in Western India*, pp. 110-15.
27. Vora, *The World's First Anti-Dam Movement*, pp. 32-42, 55-7; Rodrigues, *Rural Protest in Western India*, pp. 114-21.
28. Cashman, *Myth of the Lokamanya*, pp. 190-1, 194; Vora, *The World's First Anti-Dam Movement*, p. 3; Rodrigues, *Rural Protest in Western India*, pp. 112, 127, ft 48.
29. M.K. Gandhi, 'Satyagraha at Mulshi: Notes', *Young India*, 27 April 1921, *CWMG*, Vol. 20, pp. 40-1.
30. Vora, *The World's First Anti-Dam Movement*, pp. 58-9, 62-4.
31. Ibid., pp. 65-7, 73; Rodrigues, *Rural Protest in Western India*, p. 115.
32. Vora, *The World's First Anti-Dam Movement*, pp. 75-6, 91-2.
33. Ibid., pp. 96-9.
34. Ibid., pp. 100-04.
35. Ibid., pp. 104-09, 113, 154.
36. Ibid., pp. 109-14.
37. Ibid., pp. 114-5.
38. Ibid., pp. 117-20, 133, 136.
39. See Hardiman, *Nonviolent Struggles for Indian Freedom*, pp. 127-34.
40. Singh, *Popular Translations of Nationalism*, pp. 155-6, 159-60, 168.
41. Ibid., pp. 160-1.
42. Ibid., pp. 162-3.
43. Ibid., pp. 162-6.
44. Ibid., pp. 166-68.
45. Ibid., pp. 168-70.
46. Ranajit Das Gupta, *Economy, Society and Politics in Bengal: Jalpaiguri 1869–1947*, Oxford University Press, New Delhi, 1992, pp. 113-5.
47. Bamford, *Histories of the Non-Co-operation and Khilafat Movements*, pp. 60-61; Amalendu Guha, *Planter Raj to Swaraj: Freedom Struggle and Electoral Politics in Assam 1826–1947*, Indian Council of Historical Research, New Delhi, 1977, pp. 137-9; Ray, *Social Conflict and Political Unrest in Bengal*, pp. 277-80; Broomfield, *Elite Conflict in a Plural Society*, pp. 214-6; Sarkar, *Modern India*, pp. 217-8.

48. Broomfield, *Elite Conflict in a Plural Society*, pp. 216-7; Bamford, *Histories of the Non-Co-operation and Khilafat Movements*, pp. 61-2; Ray, *Social Conflict and Political Unrest in Bengal*, pp. 277-9.
49. Broomfield, *Elite Conflict in a Plural Society*, pp. 217-19; Ray, *Social Conflict and Political Unrest in Bengal*, pp. 280-2, 308.
50. Ray, *Social Conflict and Political Unrest in Bengal*, p. 277.
51. This is all analysed in depth in Ramachandra Guha, *The Unquiet Woods: Ecological Change and Peasant Resistance in the Himalaya*, Oxford University Press, New Delhi, 1987, pp. 43-61.
52. Swapan Dasgupta, 'Adivasi Politics in Medinipur, c. 1760-1924', in Ranajit Guha (ed.), *Subaltern Studies IV: Writings on South Asian History and Society*, Oxford University Press, New Delhi, 1985, pp. 124-5; Sarkar, 'The Conditions and Nature of Subaltern Militancy', p. 299; Ray, *Social Conflict and Political Unrest in Bengal*, p. 288.
53. Dasgupta, 'Adivasi Politics in Medinipur', pp. 125-35; Shrilata Chatterjee, *Congress Politics in Bengal 1919–1939*, Anthem Press, London, 2002, pp. 100-1.
54. Chatterjee, *Congress Politics in Bengal*, p. 101.
55. Singh, *Popular Translations of Nationalism*, pp. 191-3.
56. Murali, 'Civil Disobedience Movement in Andhra 1920–22', pp. 159-67; M.K. Gandhi, 'Notes: People of Andhra', *Young India*, 4 August 1921, *CWMG*, Vol. 20, pp. 460-1.
57. Ray, *Social Conflict and Political Unrest in Bengal*, p. 301.
58. Guha, *The Unquiet Woods*, pp. 110-4.
59. Ibid., pp. 114-9.
60. Ibid., pp. 120-2.
61. Mohinder Singh, *The Akali Movement*, Macmillan, Delhi, 1978, pp. 15-18, 159, ft. 44, 160, ft. 59; Mridula Mukherjee, *Peasants in India's Non-Violent Revolution: Practice and Theory*, Sage, New Delhi 2004, pp. 32-4.
62. Richard Fox, *Lions of the Punjab: Culture in the Making*, University of California, Berkeley, 1985, pp. 82, 169-72; Singh, *The Akali Movement*, pp. 93-5; M.K. Gandhi, 'Sikh awakening', *Navajivan*, 13 March 1921, *CWMG*, Vol. 19, pp. 421-2. On the issue of casteism, Singh p.159, ft 36 mentions that low-caste Sikhs were only permitted to worship at the Golden Temple at Amritsar at special fixed times, so that high-caste Sikhs would not be exposed to their 'impure' presence. They were not permitted to carry out the full range of worship either.
63. Singh, *The Akali Movement*, pp. 20-3, 87-8, 90, 92, 95, 97-101, 177-8, ft 18.
64. Singh, *The Akali Movement*, pp. 19-20.
65. Fox, *Lions of the Punjab*, pp. 84-6, Mukherjee, *Peasants in India's Non-Violent Revolution*, p. 33; M. L. Peace, *S. Kartar Singh Jhabbar: The Spearhead of the Akali Movement*, Peace and Rattan Kaur, Jullundur, 1968.
66. Fox, *Lions of the Punjab*, pp. 88, 95-9; Singh, *The Akali Movement*, pp. 95-6.
67. Singh, *The Akali Movement*, pp. 23-5. See p. 37 for the British claim that there was a 'riot' at Tarn Taran in which people on both sides were hurt. This is not

how the Akalis remembered the incident – for them the attack was entirely one-sided.

68. Singh, *The Akali Movement*, pp. 28-31, 36-8, 159-60, fts. 46, 54, 55. For the figure of 130 members of the jatha, p. 162, ft. 85. Other estimates ranged from 20 by the Deputy Commissioner of Amritsar to 150 by Gandhi. The Punjab government later accepted the figure of 130.
69. Singh, *The Akali Movement*, pp. 31-4.
70. M.K. Gandhi, 'Message to Lahore Sikhs on Nankana Tragedy', 4 March 1921, *Young India*, 16 March 1921, *CWMG*, Vol. 19, p. 399. Gandhi stated here that all the jatha members – almost 150 in number – were killed.
71. M.K. Gandhi, 'Speech at Nankana Saheb', 3 March 1921, *Young India*, 16 March 1921, *CWMG*, Vol. 19, pp. 396-8.
72. M.K. Gandhi, 'Message to Lahore Sikhs on Nankana Tragedy', 4 March 1921, *Young India*, 16 March 1921, *CWMG*, Vol. 19, pp. 400-01.
73. M.K. Gandhi, 'Sikh Awakening', *Navajivan*, 13 March 1921, *CWMG*, Vol. 19, pp. 21-5.
74. Singh, *The Akali Movement*, pp. 39-41.
75. Ibid., pp. 43-8.
76. Ibid., pp. 81, 83-4.
77. Singh, *The Akali Movement*, pp. 113-25; Mukherjee, *Peasants in India's Non-Violent Revolution*, pp 35-6.
78. Singh, *The Akali Movement*, pp. 49-52, 102-03.
79. Ibid., pp. 52-4.
80. Ibid., pp. 54-61.
81. Ibid., pp. 105-12.
82. Ibid., pp. 137-46.
83. Bamford, *Histories of the Khilafat and Non-Cooperation Movements*, p. 67.
84. As he stated: 'From the nature of my reception at Midnapore I cannot persuade myself to believe that the educated folk of Bengal have been estranged from me or have discountenanced my movement or the attainment of swaraj.' M.K. Gandhi, 'Speech at Medinipur', 13 September 1921, *Amrita Bazar Patrika*, 15 September 1921, *CWMG*, Vol. 21, p.97.
85. M.K. Gandhi, 'Notes: Bardoli', *Young India*, 12 December 1921; 'Bardoli', *Navajivan*, 11 December 1921, *CWMG*, Vol. 21, pp. 533-4, 560-63.
86. Report by Collector of Surat, J.R. Martin, 7 December 1921, Maharashtra State Archives, Mumbai, Home Dept. (Special), 584 of 1921-22; Babubhai Vaidya, *Rentima Vahan: Shri Kunvarji V. Mehta Ajhadni Ladatna Samsmarno*, Sastu Sahitya Vardhak Karylalaya, Ahmedabad 1977, pp. 165-6 (in Gujarati).
87. Hardiman, *Nonviolent Struggle for Indian Freedom*, pp. 109-57.

6. BRAIDING THE NATION

1. Ranajit Guha, 'On some Aspects of the Historiography of Colonial India', in R. Guha (ed.), *Subaltern Studies I: Writings on South Asian History and Society*,

Oxford University Press, New Delhi, 1982, p.6. This approach provides, I believe, an effective counter to the assertion made by critics such as Rajnarayan Chandavarker that historians of the *Subaltern Studies* group sought to delineate an autonomous subaltern mentality and politics that was based on – it was asserted – stereotypes about the lower classes of India. Chandavarkar saw this as a fundamental fault with the whole *Subaltern Studies* project. Such a critique ignores the idea of braiding. Chandavarker, *Imperial Power and Popular Politics*, pp. 271-3.

2. Schock, *Civil Resistance Today*, pp. 97-8. Schock cites here Frances Fox Piven and Richard Cloward, *Poor People's Movements: Why they Succeed, how they Fail*, Pantheon, New York, 1977, p. 12; Doug McAdam, *Political Process and the Development of Black Insurgency, 1930–1970*, University of Chicago Press, Chicago, 1982.
3. Ranajit Guha, 'Dominance Without Hegemony and its Historiography', in Ranajit Guha (ed.), *Subaltern Studies VI*, Oxford University Press, New Delhi, 1989, pp. 210-309. For Gramsci on 'hegemony' see Antonio Gramsci, *Selections from the Prison Notebooks*, Lawrence and Wishart, London, 1971, p. 12.
4. Hannah Arendt, 'What is Authority?', in Hannah Arendt, *Between Past and Future*, Penguin, New York, 2006, pp. 92-3, 97.
5. On the rule of property, see Ranajit Guha, *A Rule of Property for Bengal: An Essay on the Idea of Permanent Settlement*, Mouton, Paris, 1963.
6. Arthur Quiller-Couch (ed.), *The Oxford Book of English Verse: 1250–1900*, Clarendon, Oxford, 1919, poem 867.
7. Sarkar, 'Conditions and Nature of Subaltern Militancy', p. 305.
8. Ray, *Social Conflict and Political Unrest in Bengal*, pp. 274, 298.
9. Nehru, *Autobiography*, p. 71.
10. Shahid Amin, 'Gandhi as Mahatma: Gorakhpur District, Eastern UP, 1921-2', in Ranajit Guha (ed.), *Subaltern Studies III: Writings on South Asian History and Society*, Oxford University Press, New Delhi, 1984, pp. 25-6.
11. Guha, *The Unquiet Woods*, pp. 119-20.
12. Pandey, 'Peasant Revolt and Indian Nationalism', p. 173.
13. Ray, *Social Conflict and Political Unrest in Bengal*, p. 274.
14. Pandey, 'Peasant Revolt and Indian Nationalism', p. 173; Singh, *Popular Translations of Nationalism*, p. 43; Sanyal, 'Congress in Southwestern Bengal', pp. 358-9; Sarkar, 'The Conditions and Nature of Subaltern Militancy', p. 291.
15. For the development of Congress rituals around the newly-invented national flag, see: Arundhati Virmani, 'National Symbols under Colonial Domination; The Nationalization of the Indian Flag, March-August 1923', *Past and Present*, No. 164, August 1999, pp. 169-97; Sadan Jha, *Reverence, Resistance and Politics of Seeing the Indian National Flag*, Cambridge University Press, Delhi, 2016.
16. Kidambi, 'Nationalism and the City, p. 959.
17. Dasgupta, 'Adivasi Politics in Midnapur', pp. 126-7.
18. Amin, 'Gandhi as Mahatma', p. 51.

19. For nationalist movements in the Indian princely states, see Robin Jeffrey (ed.), *People, Princes and Paramount Power: Society and Politics in the Indian Princely States*, Oxford University Press, New Delhi, 1978, passim.
20. Murali, 'Civil Disobedience Movement in Andhra 1920-22', pp. 185.
21. Amin, 'Gandhi as Mahatma'.
22. Murali, 'Civil Disobedience Movement in Andhra 1920-22', pp. 185.
23. Guha, 'Discipline and Mobilize', p. 112.
24. Gandhi 'Democracy "versus" Mobocracy', 8 September 1920, *CWMG*, Vol. 18, pp. 240-44; M.K. Gandhi, 'Three National Cries', 8 September 1920, *CWMG*, Vol. 18, pp. 244-5.
25. *Young India*, Ahmedabad, 8 October 1919.
26. Vora, *The World's First Anti-Dam Movement*, pp. 32,37-8, 48.
27. Amin, 'Gandhi as Mahatma', pp. 17-18.
28. Kumar, *Peasants in Revolt*, pp. 162-63, 206.
29. Singh, *Popular Translations of Nationalism*, pp. 36-8.
30. Ibid., pp. 38-42.
31. Mary Elizabeth King, *Gandhian Nonviolent Struggle and Untouchability in South India: The 1924–25 Vykom Satyagraha and the Mechanism of Change*, Oxford University Press, New Delhi, 2015, p. 132. On this and the preceding page, King quotes some nationalist songs sung in Malayalam at the time of the Vykom Satyagraha in Kerala.
32. Sharp, *Politics of Nonviolent Action*, p. 149.
33. Gandhi 'Democracy "versus" Mobocracy', pp. 241-2.
34. Maharashtra State Archives, Mumbai, Home Department Political, Files 109, 130, 139, and 188 of 1923.
35. Amin, 'Gandhi as Mahatma', p. 16.
36. Singh, *Popular Translations of Nationalism*. pp. 38.
37. Hansraj Harakhji Amreliwala, 'Digdarshan' (A Revelation), *Kavya Triveni*, Shri Saraswati Press, Bhavnagar 1922, pp. 118-19, Maharashtra State Archives, Mumbai, Home Department Political, File No. 109 of 1923.
38. Amreliwala, '*Kavya Triveni*, p. 121.
39. Prabhudas Lallubhjai Thakkar, Song No. 5, '*Kapadnu Pokal*' (The Clothes of Falsity), *Laganma Khadina Gito* (Marriage Songs on Khadi), Kheda Vartaman Press, Kheda 1923, p. 5, Maharashtra Sate Archives, Mumbai, Home Department Political, File No. 139 of 1923.
40. Murali, 'Civil Disobedience Movement in Andhra 1920-22', pp. 187-9.
41. Murali, 'Civil Disobedience Movements in Andhra', pp. 190-91.
42. Thakkar, Song No. 4, '*Chavi*' (The Key), *Laganma Khadina* Gito, pp. 4-5.
43. Amreliwala, *Kavya Triveni*, p. 113.
44. Amreliwala, 'Digdarshan' (A Revelation), *Kavya Triveni*, pp. 118-9.
45. Jadulal Narandas, *Swadesh Kavya*, Saraswati Press, Umreth, no date, p. 10, Maharashtra State Archives, Mumbai, Home Department Political, File 188 of 1923.

46. Minault, *Khilafat Movement*, pp. 155-6.
47. Minault, *Khilafat Movement*, pp. 155-63.
48. Murali, 'Civil Disobedience Movements in Andhra', pp. 192-4.
49. Douglas E. Haynes, *Rhetoric and Ritual in Colonial India: The Shaping of a Public Culture in Surat City, 1852-1928*, University of California Press, Berkeley, 1991, pp. 234, 270.
50. Sanyal, 'Congress in Southwestern Bengal', p. 367.
51. Murali, 'Civil Disobedience Movement in Andhra 1920-22', pp. 180-3.
52. This later development is analysed well in the case of Hindu nationalism by William Gould, *Hindu Nationalism and the Language of Politics in Late Colonial India*, Cambridge University Press, Cambridge, 2004.
53. Sharp, *Politics of Nonviolent Action*, pp. 461-3. Sharp also observes that if nonviolent principles are well understood by participants, centralised leadership may not be required.
54. Sidney Tarrow, *Power in Movement: Social Movements and Contentious Politics*, Cambridge University Press, Cambridge, 1998, p. 136.
55. Sarkar, 'The Conditions and Nature of Subaltern Militancy', pp. 305-07, 314.
56. Tagore and Roy quotes from Ray, *Social Conflict and Political Unrest in Bengal*, pp. 251-2.
57. Nehru, *Autobiography*, p. 72.
58. Murali, 'Civil Disobedience Movement in Andhra 1920-22', pp. 181-4.
59. Ray, *Social Conflict and Political Unrest in Bengal*, p. 251 quotes C.F. Andrew's remarks to this effect.
60. P. Biggane, Asst. to D.I.G., C.I.D., Allahabad 7 January 1921, NAI, HD, Political Branch, Deposit, February 1921, No. 13. Full report quoted as an appendix by Pandey, 'Peasant Revolt and Indian Nationalism', pp. 196-7.
61. Kumar, *Peasants in Revolt*, pp. 162-3, 206.
62. Singh, Popular Translations of Nationalism, pp. 33-5, 48.
63. Amin, 'Gandhi as Mahatma', p. 15.
64. Ibid., pp. 21-23.
65. Sarkar, 'The Conditions and Nature of Subaltern Militancy', pp. 314-15. On cults of renowned ascetic-figures, see William Crooke, *Religion and Folklore of Northern India*, Oxford University Press, Oxford, 1926, pp. 152-3.
66. Amin, 'Gandhi as Mahatma', pp. 53-4.
67. Singh, *Popular Translations of Nationalism*, pp. 235-6.
68. Sarkar, 'The Conditions and Nature of Subaltern Militancy', pp. 313-4.
69. Amin, 'Gandhi as Mahatma', pp. 1-2, 24.
70. Sarkar, 'The Conditions and Nature of Subaltern Militancy', p. 315.
71. Misra, *Madan Mohan Malaviya*, pp. 144-45.
72. Vaidya, *Rentima Vahan*, p. 169. This Gujarati book records an instance in which Malaviya gave such advice to a leading local activist on a visit to Gujarat during noncooperation.
73. Nehru, *Autobiography*, p. 72.

74. Desai, *Day-to-Day with Gandhi*, Vol. III, pp. 143-4; Singh, *Popular Translations of Nationalism*, pp. 15-22.
75. IndulalYagnik, *Atmakatha*, Vol. 3, Ravani Prakasan, Ahmedabad, 1956, pp. 13-21 (Gujarati).
76. Nehru, *Autobiography*, p. 69.
77. Jaspreet Kaur, *Master Tara Singh and Sikh Politics (1920-47)*, Kindle edition (no place or date provided), Ch. 2.
78. Interviews with Kunvarji Mehta, Malad, Bombay 2 September and 9 December 1980, and 28 February 1981; Anil Bhatt, 'Caste and Political Mobilisation in a Gujarat District', in Rajni Kothari (ed.), *Caste in Indian Politics*, Orient Longman, New Delhi, 1970, pp. 301-8, 312-3, 320, 325; G. Patel, *Vithalbhai Patel*, Vol. 1, pp. 457-8.
79. Vaidya, *Rentima Vahan*, pp. 165-8.
80. Dasgupta, 'Adivasi Politics in Midnapur, pp. 125-9.
81. Sarkar, 'The Conditions and Nature of Subaltern Militancy', pp. 299, 311.
82. Kumar, *Peasants in Revolt*, pp. 215, 221-2, 147.
83. Sarkar, 'The Conditions and Nature of Subaltern Militancy', pp. 293-4.
84. Pati, *Resisting Domination*, p. 63.
85. Singh, *Popular Translations of Nationalism*, pp. 181-7.
86. Amin, *Event, Metaphor, Memory*, pp. 15-16, 38-9, 80-1.
87. Amin, Event, Metaphor, Memory, pp. 123-5.
88. Chakrabarty, *Rethinking Working-Class History*, pp. 108,111.
89. For example, in Ahmedabad City in 1942. See David Hardiman, 'The Quit India Movement in Gujarat', in David Hardiman, *Histories for the Subordinated*, Permanent Black, New Delhi, 2006, p. 151.
90. S. Maureen Swan, *Gandhi: The South African Experience*, Ravan Press, Johannesburg, 1985, pp. 114-5.
91. Overy, *Gandhi the Organizer*, pp. 33-5.
92. Pati, Resisting Domination, pp. 63-5.
93. Chakrabarty, *Rethinking Working-Class History*, pp. 132, 144, 150-52.
94. Siddiqi, *Agrarian Unrest in North India*, p. 113.
95. Nehru, *An Autobiography*, pp. 61-2.
96. *Secret Bombay Presidency Police Abstracts of Intelligence*, 1921, p. 1935.

7. *ASAHYOG ANDOLAN*: THE NONCOOPERATION OF THE PEOPLE 1920–22

1. Randle, *Civil Resistance*, pp. xiii, 8, 10, 20-22.
2. Dharampal, *Civil disobedience and Indian tradition with some early nineteenth century documents*, Sarva Seva Sangh Prakashan, Varanasi, 1971.
3. Sarkar, 'The Conditions and Nature of Subaltern Militancy', pp. 305-07.
4. Pandey, 'Peasant Revolt and Indian Nationalism', pp. 167-8.
5. Murali, 'Civil Disobedience Movement in Andhra 1920-22', p. 178.
6. Lloyd I. Rudolph and Susanne Hoeber Rudolph, *The Modernity of Tradition: Political Development in India*, University of Chicago Press, Chicago, 1967, p. 19.

7. Sanyal, 'Congress in Southwestern Bengal', pp. 355-6; Ray, *Social Conflict and Political Unrest in Bengal*, p. 290.
8. Mahadev Desai, *Young India*, 22 June 1921, p. 195.
9. Pandey, 'Peasant Revolt and Indian Nationalism', pp. 179.
10. Interviews in Kheda District in 1972.
11. Kunte, *Source Material: Non-Co-Operation Movement in Bombay City*, pp. 34-6.
12. Vora, *The World's First Anti-Dam Movement*, pp. 32, 46, 55, 63, 67-8, 74, 99.
13. Pandey, 'Peasant Revolt and Indian Nationalism', pp. 169-70.
14. Projit Bihari Mukharji, *Doctoring Traditions: Ayurveda, Small Technologies, and Braided Sciences*, University of Chicago Press, Chicago, 2016, pp. 277-81.
15. Kumar, *Peasants in Revolt*, pp. 192-3.
16. M.K. Gandhi, 'Sikh Awakening', *Navajivan*, 13 March 1921, *CWMG*, Vol. 19, pp. 21-5.
17. Vora, *The World's First Anti-Dam Movement*, p. 146.
18. *Secret Bombay Presidency Police Abstracts of Intelligence*, 1922, p. 202.
19. Kumar, *Peasants in Revolt*, pp. 128, 192-3.
20. Chakrabarty, *Local Politics and Indian Nationalism*, p. 90.
21. Ajay Skaria has written with insight on this aspect of Gandhian theory and practice in *Unconditional Equality: Gandhi's Religion of Resistance*, University of Minnesota Press, Minneapolis, 2016, pp. 20-22.
22. For example, M.K. Gandhi, 'Speech at Maharashtra Provincial Conference, Bassein', 7 May 1921, *CWMG*, Vol. 20, pp. 67-8.
23. Singh, *The Akali Movement*, p. 144.
24. Ibid., p. 54.
25. Brown, *Gandhi's Rise to Power*, p. 316.
26. Singh, *Popular Translations of Nationalism*, p.35.
27. Minault, *The Khilafat Movement*, pp. 119-20, 163-5.
28. Singh, *Popular Translations of Nationalism*, pp. 35, 56.
29. For a discussion of the differences between Gandhian and RSS militias, see Arafaat A. Valiani, *Militant Publics in India: Physical Culture and Violence in the Making of a Modern Polity*, Palgrave Macmillan, New York, 2011, pp. 54-8.
30. Guha, *Elementary Aspects of Peasant Insurgency in Colonial India*, pp. 169-88.
31. Kumar, *Peasants in Revolt*, p. 192.
32. Cases of this are reported from Mughal times. See Irfan Habib, *The Agrarian System of Mughal India 1556–1701*, Asia Publishing House, Bombay 1963, pp. 328-36. We find similar protest-migrations in the nineteenth century. For one such case from Saurashtra see India Office Library, R/2/668/18.
33. Pati, *Resisting Domination*, p. 43.
34. Dasgupta, 'Adivasi Politics in Midnapur', pp. 130-3.
35. Kumar, *Peasants in Revolt*, p. 117.
36. Vora, *The World's First Anti-Dam Movement*, pp. 65-7, 73; Rodrigues, *Rural Protest in Western India*, p. 115.
37. Joan Bondurant, *Conquest of Violence: The Gandhian Philosophy of Conflict*, Princeton University Press, Princeton 1958, p. 118.

38. Chandavarker, *Imperial Power and Popular Politics*, pp. 312-3.
39. Kunte, *Source Material: Non-Co-Operation Movement in Bombay City*, pp. 70-73; Chandavarkar, *Origins of Industrial Capitalism in India*, p. 416.
40. Kumar, *Peasants in Revolt*, pp. 98-102, 136.
41. Ibid., pp. 150-1.
42. Ibid., pp. 126-7.
43. Amin, *Event, Metaphor, Memory*, p. 14.
44. Singh, *Popular Translations of Nationalism*, pp. 165-6.
45. For example, Kumar, *Peasants in Revolt*, pp. 123, 126-7, 142-3; Singh, *Popular Translations of Nationalism*, pp. 235-6.
46. E.P. Thompson, 'The Moral Economy of the English Crowd in the Eighteenth Century', *Past and Present*, 50, February 1971, pp. 76-9.
47. R.S. McGregor, *The Oxford Hindi-English Dictionary*, Oxford University Press, Oxford and Delhi 1993, p. 899.
48. Sharp, *The Politics of Nonviolent Action*, pp. 380-1.
49. Thompson, 'Moral Economy of the English Crowd', pp. 108-14.
50. Kumar, *Peasants in Revolt*, pp. 123, 141-3.
51. Crawley, 'Kisan Sabha and Agrarian Revolt', pp. 106, 99.
52. Amin, 'Gandhi as Mahatma', pp. 53-4.
53. Sarkar, 'The Conditions and Nature of Subaltern Militancy', pp. 291-2, 301-3, 306-7.
54. M.K. Gandhi, 'Message to Lahore Sikhs on Nankana Tragedy', 4 March 1921, *Young India*, 16 March 1921, *CWMG*, Vol. 19, pp. 400-01.
55. Kumar, *Peasants in Revolt*, pp. 110, 123.
56. Singh, *Popular Translations of Nationalism*, pp. 160-5.
57. Brian Martin, 'How Nonviolence is Misrepresented', *Gandhi Marg*, July-September 2008, p. 237.
58. Sharp, *The Politics of Nonviolent Action*, pp. 608-11.
59. Amin, *Event, Metaphor, Memory*, p. 102; Amin, 'Gandhi as Mahatma', pp. 12-14.
60. Sangeeta Dasgupta, 'Reordering a World: The Tana Bhagat Movement, 1914–1919', *Studies in History*, 15: 1 n.s., 1999, pp.2-7, 31-3.
61. Singh, *Popular Translations of Nationalism*, pp. 43, 187-9, 191-2.
62. Arnold, *Congress in Tamilnad*, pp. 65-8.
63. Haynes, *Rhetoric and Ritual*, pp. 210, 229, 246.
64. Sarkar, *Modern India*, p. 209.
65. Singh, *Popular Translations of Nationalism*, pp. 32, 43, 66.
66. Ray, *Social Conflict and Political Unrest in Bengal*, p. 275.
67. Sarkar, 'The Conditions and Nature of Subaltern Militancy', p. 313.
68. Dasgupta, 'Adivasi Politics in Midnapur', p. 127.
69. Sarkar, 'The Conditions and Nature of Subaltern Militancy', pp. 309-10. Sarkar states that he has taken this distinction from Bryan Wilson, *Magic and the Millennium: A Sociological Study of Religious Movements of Protest among Tribal and Third World Peoples*, Heinemann, London, 1973, pp. 18–30. As it is, Wilson list seven categories of what he describes as religious movements, one of which is

the thaumaturgic. Others include the 'revolutionist' and the 'utopian' – both of which encompass aspects of what we are calling here 'millennial' beliefs.

70. Haynes, *Rhetoric and Ritual*, pp. 205, 223, 227-9.
71. Quotations translated from the original Gujarati. Vaidya, *Rentima Vahan*, pp. 176-9.
72. Madho Prasad, *A Gandhian Patriarch: A Political and Spiritual Biography of Kaka Kalelkar*, Popular Prakashan, Bombay, 1965, pp. 17, 33-4, 134, 150-2, 165, 190-200.
73. Murali, 'Civil Disobedience Movement in Andhra 1920–22', p. 190.
74. Ibid., p. 190. The reference to Kheda is of the Kheda Satyagraha of 1918.
75. Singh, *Popular Translations of Nationalism*, pp. 33-5, 48, 235-6.
76. Quoted in Sarkar, 'The Conditions and Nature of Subaltern Militancy', p. 310.
77. Ibid., p. 310.
78. Ibid., p. 311.
79. Ibid., p. 311.
80. Desai, *Day-to-Day with Gandhi*, Vol. 3, pp. 142-6.
81. The quotations are all from *Swadesh*, 6 & 13 February 1921, reproduced in Amin, 'Gandhi as Mahatma', pp. 18-9.
82. Desai, *Day-to-Day with Gandhi*, Vol. 3, pp. 262-4.
83. Norman Cohn, *The Pursuit of the Millennium. Revolutionary Millenarians and Mystical Anarchists of the Middle Ages*, Oxford University Press, Oxford, 1974, p. 15; Maria Amelia S. Dickie, 'Millenarianism' in Peter B. Clarke, *Encyclopaedia of New Religious Movement*, Routledge, Abingdon, 2006, pp. 403-5.
84. Pandey, 'Peasant Revolt and Indian Nationalism', p. 169.
85. Kapil Kumar, *Peasants in Revolt,* p. 145.
86. Amin, *Event, Metaphor, Memory*, p. 163.
87. Amin, 'Gandhi as Mahatma', pp. 52-3.
88. Amin, 'Gandhi as Mahatma', pp. 51-3; Amin, *Event, Metaphor, Memory*, pp. 44.
89. Sarkar, 'The Conditions and Nature of Subaltern Militancy', p. 291.
90. Ibid., p. 300.
91. Ibid., pp. 312-3.
92. Ray, *Social Conflict and Political Unrest in Bengal*, pp. 307-9.
93. *Andhra Lakshmi*, Vol. 1, No. 3, March 1922, pp. 3-4. Translated and quoted by Murali, 'Civil Disobedience Movement in Andhra 1920-22', p. 192.
94. Ibid., p. 194.
95. William Crooke, *An Introduction to the Popular Religion of Northern India*, Government Press, North-Western Provinces and Oudh, Allahabad, 1894, pp. 112-3, 120.
96. Amin, 'Gandhi as Mahatma', pp. 27-9.
97. Ibid., pp. 31-4.
98. Ibid., pp. 34-41.
99. Ibid., pp. 41-7.
100. Ibid., pp. 48-9.

101. Amin, 'Gandhi as Mahatma', pp. 49-50.
102. Kumar, *Peasants in Revolt*, pp. 162-3.
103. Sarkar, 'The Conditions and Nature of Subaltern Militancy', p. 311, 313.
104. Vaidya, *Rentima Vahan*, pp. 173-5.
105. Hardiman, *The Coming of the Devi*.
106. Report by Charles Frere Andrews, *The Manchester Guardian*, 15 and 24 February 1924.
107. See for example Mark Kurlansky, *Nonviolence: The History of a Dangerous Idea*, Jonathan Cape, London, 2006, pp. 10-12, 19-40, 47-55, 59-65.
108. Gene Sharp, *Waging Nonviolent Struggle: 20th Century Practice and 21st Century Potential*, Porter Sargent, Boston, 2005, pp. 344-5.
109. Sharp, *Politics of Nonviolent Action*, pp.121-2, 155-6, 191-3, 204-10, 469.
110. Carinne Luck, 'Three Ways Faith and Spiritual Leaders are Shaping Movements Today', *Minds of the Movement: An ICNC Blog on the People and Power of Civil Resistance*, 18 June, 2019. https://www.nonviolent-conflict.org/blog_post/three-ways-faith-and-spiritual-leaders-are-shaping-movements-today/ (accessed 25 June 2019).
111. Benedict Anderson, *Imagined Communities: Reflections on the Origin and Spread of Nationalism*, Verso, London, 1983.
112. As Ramachandra Guha has pointed out, in India nation-building at the popular level was carried out often in supposedly 'pre-modern' ways. He argue, for example, that oral communication was as important in India as the print media that Anderson saw as being critical to this process. Ramachandra Guha, 'The Last Polymath: Benedict Anderson as Scholar and Human Being', *Economic and Political Weekly*, Vol. 51, No. 3, 16 January 2016, p. 39.
113. W.H. Morris-Jones, *The Government and Politics of India*, Hutchinson, London 1964, pp. 59-61. For Bhave, see Geoffrey Ostergaard and Melville Currel, *The Gentle Anarchists: A Study of the Leaders of the Sarvodaya Movement for Non-Violent Revolution in India*, Clarendon Press, Oxford, 1991.
114. Mukharji, *Doctoring Traditions*, pp 265-6, 284-6. A similar emphasis if found in books by Ruy Blanes and Diana Espirito Santo (eds.), *The Social Life of Spirits*, University of Chicago Press, Chicago, 2013, and David M. Gordon, *Invisible Agents: Spirits in a Central African History*, Ohio University Press, Athens, 2012.
115. Dipesh Chakrabarty, 'Community, State and the Body: Epidemics and Popular Culture in Colonial India', in David Hardiman and Projit Bihari Mukharji (eds.), *Medical Marginality in South Asia: Situating Subaltern Therapeutics*, Routledge, Abingdon, 2012, pp. 44-6. The quote from Ralph W. Nicholas, 'The Goddess Sitala and Epidemic Smallpox in Bengal', *Journal of Asian Studies*, Vol. 41, No. 1, 1981, p. 39.
116. Leopold von Ranke, who is often considered the founding-figure for the modern discipline of history, understood God as the 'vital principle' that imbues all life, so that His working could be revealed through the study of history. See Georg G. Iggers, 'Introduction' to Leopold von Ranke, *The Theory and Practice of History*, Routledge, New York, 2011, pp. xxviii-xxxi.

117. Mukharji, *Doctoring Traditions*, p. 265.
118. The young Jawaharlal Nehru was for example tutored in his youth by a European theosophist who introduced him to Indian scriptures and made him conscious of spiritual power. He was then initiated as a theosophist at the age of thirteen by Annie Besant. Sarvepalli Gopal, *Jawaharlal Nehru: A Biography*, Vol. 1, *1889–1947*, Jonathan Cape, London, 1975, pp. 18-9.
119. Martin Luther King, *A Testament of Hope: The Essential Writings of Martin Luther King Jr.*, (ed. James M. Washington), Harper Collins, New York, 1986, pp. 13-4.
120 Melanie Eversley, 'Witnessing the Dream', *USA Today*, http://usatoday30.usatoday.com/news/nation/martin-luther-king-dream-speech/index.html (accessed 28 April 2017).
121. Jonathan Jones and Nell Frizzell, 'The Baton Rouge Protestor', *The Guardian: G2 section*, 13 July 2016, pp. 8-11.
122. Starhawk, *Dreaming the Dream*, Beacon Press, Boston, 1982, p. 13.
123. Starhawk, 'A Moment in Human History', interview by Erin George, 24 September 2001, https://nettime.org/Lists-Archives/nettime-bold-0109/msg00811.html (accessed 14 May 2017).
124. Stephen Zunes, 'The Origins of People Power in the Philippines', in Stephen Zunes, Lester R. Kurtz, and Sarah Beth Asher, *Nonviolent Social Movements: A Geographical Perspective*, Blackwell, Malden, 1999, pp. 138-43, 149-50, 153.
125. Peter Ackerman and Christopher Kruegler, *Strategic Nonviolent Conflict: The Dynamics of People Power in the Twentieth Century*, Praeger, Westport, Connecticut (CT), 1994, pp. 287, 289, 293, 304; Ackerman and Du Vall, *A Force More Powerful*, p. 146; Foundation Mary Pages, 'The Apparitions of the Blessed Virgin Mary: Crowned Queen of Heaven', http://www.marypages.com/Czestochowa.htm (accessed 30 April 2017); Adam Michnik, *Letters from Freedom: Post–Cold War Realities and Perspectives*, University of California Press, Berkeley, 1998, p. 78.
126. DeRay Mckesson, *On the Other Side of Freedom: Race and Justice in a Divided America*, Oneworld Publications, London 2018, p. 6.
127. Mckesson, *On the Other Side of Freedom*, pp. 7-8.
128. On this, see my *Gandhi in His Time and Ours*, Permanent Black, Delhi, 2003, pp.51-2.
129. Martin Jay, *The Dialectical Imagination: A History of the Frankfurt School and the Institute of Social Research 1923–1950*, Little, Brown and Company, Boston, 1973, p. 56. Jay cites in this context M. Horkheimer, *Dämmerung*, written under the pseudonym 'Heinrich Regius', Zurich, 1934, p.116.
130. Hardiman, *Nonviolent Struggles for Indian Freedom*, pp. 112-15.
131. Joan Bondurant, *Conquest of Violence*, p.111. For more details about how *ahimsa* was popularly understood in India, particularly by those influenced by the *bhakti*, or devotional, tradition, see David Hardiman, '*Ahimsa*: Shifting Meanings in Indian History', in David Hardiman (ed.), *Nonviolence in Modern Indian History*, Orient Blackswan, New Delhi, 2017, pp. 8-33.
132. Guha, 'Discipline and Mobilise', pp. 69-120.

133. David Arnold, 'Rebellious Hillmen: The Gudem-Rampa Risings 1839–1924', in Ranajit Guha (ed.), *Subaltern Studied I*, Oxford University Press, New Delhi, 1981, pp. 134-40.
134. Mukharji, *Doctoring Traditions*, p. 257.

CONCLUSION

1. Nehru, *Autobiography*, pp. 81-4.
2. Minault, *Khilafat Movement*, pp. 181, 186-8.
3. Bose, *The Indian Struggle*, pp. 74-5.
4. *The Leader*, 22 December 1923, quoted in Misra, *Madan Mohan Malaviya*, p. 131.
5. See Woods, *Roots of Parliamentary Democracy in India*, p. 167.
6. Misra, *Madan Mohan Malaviya*, p. 130.
7. Brown, *Gandhi's Rise to Power*, p. 338; Ray, *Social Conflict and Political Unrest in Bengal*, pp. 304-5.
8. Bose, *The Indian Struggle*, pp. 77-79.
9. Claude Markovits, *The Un-Gandhian Gandhi: The Life and Afterlife of the Mahatma*, Permanent Black, New Delhi, 2003, p. 108.
10. On this, see Krishna, 'Development of the Indian National Congress as a Mass Organisation, pp. 413-430.
11. Chenoweth and Stephan, *Why Civilian Resistance Works*, p. 43.
12. I have noted how this process operated in one locality in Gujarat in my *Peasant Nationalists of Gujarat*, pp. 250-1.
13. F.W.S. Craig (ed.), *British General Election Manifestos: 1918–1966*, Political Reference Publications, Chichester, 1970, p. 105.
14. See P.J. Cain and A.G. Hopkins, *British Imperialism: Crisis and Deconstruction 1914–1990*, Longman, London, 1993, pp.194-7.
15. See Majumdar, R.C., *Jibanera Smritideepe*, General Printers and Publishers, Calcutta, 1978, quoted in Ranjan Borra, 'Subhas Chandra Bose, The Indian National Army, and The War of India's Liberation', *The Journal of Historical Review*, Vol. 3, No. 4, 1982, p. 438.
16. See Hardiman, *Nonviolent Struggle for Indian Freedom 1905–19*, pp. 3-9.

BIBLIOGRAPHY

Primary Sources

Archival Records

British Library, London, Oriental and India Office Collection, Residency records.

Criminal Investigation Department Office, Mumbai, Secret Bombay Police Abstracts of Intelligence.

Maharashtra State Archives, Mumbai, Home Department.

National Archives of India, New Delhi, Home Department, Political Branch; and Foreign and Political Department of Government of India.

Official Publications

J.T. Marten, *Census of India, 1921*, Vol. I, Part II, *Tables*, Government Printing, Calcutta 1923.

Printed Collections of Primary Materials

Mahadev Desai, *Day-to-Day with Gandhi: Secretary's Diary*, Vol. 3, Sarva Seva Sangh Prakashan, Varanasi, 1968,

M.K. Gandhi, *The CollectedWorks of Mahatma Gandhi*, Vols. 1-100, Publications Division, Government of India, New Delhi, 1958–1994 (*CWMG*).

B.G. Kunte (ed.), *Source Material for a History of the Freedom Movement in India: Non-Co-Operation Movement in Bombay City 1920–1925*, Vol. 6, Gazetteers Department, Government of Maharashtra, 1979.

Newspapers and Weeklies

Bombay Chronicle.
Manchester Guardian / Guardian
Navajivan (Gujarati)
Young India

Interviews

Roop Singh Bhil, Udaipur, Rajasthan, 18 December 1997.
Kunvarji Mehta, Malad, Bombay 2 September and 9 December 1980, and 28 February 1981.

Secondary Sources

Peter Ackerman and Christopher Kruegler, *Strategic Nonviolent Conflict: The Dynamics of People Power in the Twentieth Century*, Praeger, Westport, Connecticut, 1994.

Peter Ackerman and Jack Du Vall, *A Force More Powerful: A Century of Nonviolent Conflict*, Palgrave, New York, 2000.

Hamza Alavi, 'Ironies of History: Contradictions of the Khilafat Movement,' *Comparative Studies of South Asia, Africa and the Middle East,* Vol.17, No. 1, pp. 1-16.

Shahid Amin, 'Gandhi as Mahatma: Gorakhpur District, Eastern UP, 1921-2', in Ranajit Guha (ed.), *Subaltern Studies III: Writings on South Asian History and Society*, Oxford University Press, New Delhi, 1984, pp. 1-61.

———, *Event, Metaphor, Memory: Chauri Chaura 1922–1992*, Oxford University Press, New Delhi, 1995.

Benedict Anderson, *Imagined Communities: Reflections on the Origin and Spread of Nationalism*, Verso, London, 1983.

C.F. Andrews, *The Oppression of the Poor*, Ganesh and Co., Madras, 1921.

Hannah Arendt, 'What is Authority?', in Hannah Arendt, *Between Past and Future*, Penguin, New York, 2006, pp. 91-141.

David Arnold, *The Congress in Tamilnad: Nationalist Politics in South India 1919–1937*, Curzon Press, London, 1977.

———, 'Industrial Violence in Colonial India', *Comparative Studies in Society and History*, Vol. 22, No. 2, April 1980, pp. 234-55.

———, 'Rebellious Hillmen: The Gudem-Rampa Risings 1839–1924', in Ranajit Guha (ed.), *Subaltern Studies I*, Oxford University Press, New Delhi, 1981, pp. 88-142.

BIBLIOGRAPHY

Amiya Kumar Bagchi, *Private Investment in India 1900–1939*, Cambridge University Press, Cambridge, 1972.

Vinay Bahl, 'TISCO Workers' Struggles: 1920–1928', *Social Scientist*, Vol. 10, No. 8, August 1982', pp. 32-44.

———,'Attitude of the Indian National Congress towards the Working Class Struggle in India 1918–1947', in Kapil Kumar (ed.), *Congress and Classes: Nationalism, Workers and Peasants*, Manohar, New Delhi, 1988, pp. 1-33.

Christopher Baker, 'Non-Cooperation in South India', in C. Baker and D. Washbrook (eds.), *South India: Political Institutions and Political Change 1880–1940*, Macmillan, Delhi, 1975, pp. 98-149.

P.C. Bamford, *Histories of the Non-Cooperation and Khilafat Movements*, Government of India Press, Delh,i 1925.

Rukmini Barua, 'The Textile Labour Association and Dadagiri Power and Politics in the Working-Class Neighbourhoods of Ahmedabad', *International Labour and Working-Class History*, No. 87, Spring 2015, pp. 63-91.

C.A. Bayly, *Rulers, Townsmen and Bazaars: North Indian Society in the Age of British Expansion*, Cambridge University Press, Cambridge, 1988.

Anil Bhatt, 'Caste and Political Mobilisation in a Gujarat District', in Rajni Kothari (ed.), *Caste in Indian Politics*, Orient Longman, New Delhi, 1970, pp. 299-339.

S. Bhattacharya, 'Swaraj and Kamgar: The Indian National Congress and the Bombay Working Class, 1919–1931', in Richard Sisson and Stanley Wolpert (eds.), *Congress and Indian Nationalism: The Pre-Independence Phase*, University of California, Berkeley, 1988, pp. 223-49.

Ruy Blanes and Diana Espirito Santo (eds.), *The Social Life of Spirits*, University of Chicago Press, Chicago, 2013.

John Broomfield, *Elite Conflict in a Plural Society: Twentieth Century Bengal*, California University Press, Berkeley, 1968.

Judith Brown, *Gandhi's Rise to Power: Indian Politics 1915–1922*, Cambridge University Press, Cambridge, 1972.

Joan Bondurant, *Conquest of Violence: The Gandhian Philosophy of Conflict*, Princeton University Press, Princeton, 1958.

Ranjan Borra, 'Subhas Chandra Bose, The Indian National Army, and The War of India's Liberation', *The Journal of Historical Review*, Vol. 3, No. 4, 1982, pp. 407-40.

Sanat Bose, 'Industrial Unrest and Growth of Labour Unions in Bengal, 1920–1924', *Economic and Political Weekly*, Vol. 16, Nos. 44/46, Nov. 1981, pp. 1854-5, pp. 1849-60.

Subhas Chandra Bose, *The Indian Struggle 1920–1942*, Oxford University Press, New Delhi, 1997.

P.J. Cain and A.G. Hopkins, *British Imperialism: Crisis and Deconstruction 1914–1990*, Longman, London, 1993.

April Carter, *People Power and Political Change: Key Issues and Concepts*, Routledge, Abingdon, 2012.

Richard I. Cashman, *The Myth of the Lokamanya: Tilak and Mass Politics in Maharashtra*, University of California Press, Berkeley, 1975.

Bidyut Chakrabarty, *Local Politics and Indian Nationalism: Medinipur 1919–1944*, Manohar, New Delhi, 1997.

Dipesh Chakrabarty, 'Communal Riots and Labour: Bengal's Jute Mill-Hands in the 1890s', *Past and Present*, 91, May 1981, pp. 140-69.

———, 'On Deifying and Defying Authority: Managers and Workers in the Jute Mills of Bengal circa 1890–1940', *Past and Present*, No. 100, August 1983, pp. 124-46.

———, *Rethinking Working-Class History: Bengal 1890–1940*, Princeton University Press, Princeton, 1989.

———, 'Community, State and the Body: Epidemics and Popular Culture in Colonial India', in David Hardiman and Projit Bihari Mukharji (eds.), *Medical Marginality in South Asia: Situating Subaltern Therapeutics*, Routledge, Abingdon, 2012, pp. 36-58.

Rajnarayan Chandavarkar, *The Origins of Industrial Capitalism in India: Business Strategies and the Working Classes in Bombay, 1900–1940*, Cambridge University Press, Cambridge, 1994.

———, *Imperial Power and Popular Politics: Class, Resistance and the State in India, c. 1850–1950*, Cambridge University Press, Cambridge, 1998.

Bipin Chandra, Mridula Mukherjee, Aditya Mukherjee, K.N. Pannikkar, Sucheta Mahajan, *India's Struggle for Independence 1857–1947*, Penguin Books, New Delhi, 1989.

Manini Chatterjee, *Do or Die: The Chittagong Uprising 1930–34*, Picador, New Delhi, 2010.

Shrilata Chatterjee, *Congress Politics in Bengal 1919–1939*, Anthem Press, London, 2002.

Rakhahari Chatterji, *Gandhi and the Ali Brothers: Biography of a Friendship*, Sage Publications, New Delhi, 2013.

Erica Chenoweth and Maria J. Stephan, *Why Civil Resistance Works: The Strategic Logic of Nonviolent Conflict*, Columbia University Press, New York, 2011.

Howard Clark, *Civil Resistance in Kosovo*, Pluto Press, London, 2000.

Satyabrata Rai Chowdhuri, *Leftism in India 1917–47*, Palgrave Macmillan, Basingstoke, 2007.

Norman Cohn, *The Pursuit of the Millennium: Revolutionary Millenarians and Mystical Anarchists of the Middle Ages*, Oxford University Press, Oxford, 1974.

F.W.S. Craig (ed.), *British General Election Manifestos: 1918–1966*, Political Reference Publications, Chichester, 1970.

W.F. Crawley, 'Kisan Sabha and Agrarian Revolt in the United Provinces 1920 to 1921', *Modern Asian Studies*, Vol. 5, No. 2, 1971, pp. 95-109.

William Crooke, *An Introduction to the Popular Religion of Northern India*, Government Press, North-Western Provinces and Oudh, Allahabad, 1894.

———, *Religion and Folklore of Northern India*, Oxford University Press, Oxford, 1926.

Ranajit Das Gupta, *Economy, Society and Politics in Bengal: Jalpaiguri 1869–1947*, Oxford University Press, New Delhi, 1992.

Sangeeta Dasgupta, 'Reordering a World: The Tana Bhagat Movement, 1914–1919', *Studies in History*, 15: 1 n.s., 1999, pp. 1-41.

Swapan Dasgupta, 'Adivasi Politics in Medinipur, c. 1760–1924', in Ranajit Guha (ed.), *Subaltern Studies IV: Writings on South Asian History and Society*, Oxford University Press, New Delhi, 1985, pp. 101-35.

A.R. Desai, *Social Background of Indian Nationalism*, Popular Prakashan, Bombay, 1948.

Narayan Desai, *My Life is My Message*, Vol. II, *Satyagraha (1915–1930)*, Orient Black Swan, New Delhi, 2009.

Faisal Devji, 'A Practice of Prejudice: Gandhi's Politics of Friendship', in Shail Mayaram, M.S.S. Pandian and Ajay Skaria, *Subaltern Studies XII: Muslims, Dalits, and the Fabrication of History*, Permanent Black, New Delhi, 2005, pp. 78-98.

———, *The Impossible Indian: Gandhi and the Temptation of Violence*, Hurst and Company, London, 2012.

Dharampal, *Civil disobedience and Indian tradition with some early nineteenth century documents*, Sarva Seva Sangh Prakashan, Varanasi, 1971.

Maria Amelia S. Dickie, 'Millenarianism' in Peter B. Clarke, *Encyclopaedia of New Religious Movement*, Routledge, Abingdon, 2006.

Simon Epstein, *The Earthy Soil: Bombay Peasants and the Indian Nationalist Movement 1919–1947*, Oxford University Press, New Delhi, 1988.

Melanie Eversley, 'Witnessing the Dream', *USA Today*, http://usatoday30.usatoday.com/news/nation/martin-luther-king-dream-speech/index.html (accessed 28 April 2017).

Richard Fox, *Lions of the Punjab: Culture in the Making*, University of California, Berkeley, 1985.

Mark W. Frazier, 'Seeing Like a Nation: Nationalist Political Persuasion and Positioning in Shanghai and Bombay during the 1920s and 1930s', paper presented at the annual meeting of the American Political Science Association, Chicago, 28 August-1 September 2013. https://www.icsin.org/uploads/2019/01/17/8fcf3e555a8d8a50c5cb7330d8831d42.pdf (downloaded 8 April 2019).

M.K. Gandhi, *An Autobiography, or the Story of My Experiments with Truth*, Vol. 2, Navajivan Press, Ahmedabad, 1929.

Anindita Ghose, *Claiming the City: Protest, Crime, and Scandals in Colonial Calcutta c. 1860–1920*, Oxford University Press, New Delhi, 2016.

Kenneth L. Gillion, *Ahmedabad: A Study in Urban History*, University of California Press, Berkeley, 1968.

Nandini Gooptu, *The Politics of the Urban Poor in Early-Twentieth Century India*, Cambridge University Press, Cambridge, 2001.

Sarvepalli Gopal, *Jawaharlal Nehru: A Biography*, Vol. 1, *1889–1947*, Jonathan Cape, London, 1975.

David M. Gordon, *Invisible Agents: Spirits in a Central African History*, Ohio University Press, Athens, 2012.

Richard Gordon, 'Non-cooperation and Council Entry 1919 to 1920', in Gallagher, Johnson, and Seal (eds.), *Locality, Province and Nation: Essays on Indian Politics, 1870–1940*, Cambridge University Press, Cambridge, 1973, pp. 123-54.

William Gould, *Hindu Nationalism and the Language of Politics in Late Colonial India*, Cambridge University Press, Cambridge, 2004.

S.N. Gourlay, 'Nationalists, Outsiders and the Labour Movement in Bengal during the Non-Cooperation Movement 1919–21', in Kapil Kumar (ed.), *Congress and Classes: Nationalism, Workers and Peasants*, Manohar, New Delhi, 1988, pp. 34-57.

Antonio Gramsci, *Selections from the Prison Notebooks*, Lawrence and Wishart, London, 1971.

Amalendu Guha, *Planter Raj to Swaraj: Freedom Struggle and Electoral Politics in Assam 1826–1947*, Indian Council of Historical Research, New Delhi, 1977.

Ramachandra Guha, 'The Last Polymath: Benedict Anderson as Scholar and Human Being', *Economic and Political Weekly*, Vol. 51, No. 3, 16 January 2016, pp. 38-43.

Ranajit Guha, *A Rule of Property for Bengal: An Essay on the Idea of Permanent Settlement*, Mouton, Paris, 1963.

———, 'On some Aspects of the Historiography of Colonial India', in R. Guha (ed.), *Subaltern Studies I: Writings on South Asian History and Society*, Oxford University Press, New Delhi, 1982, pp. 1-7.

Ranajit Guha, 'Dominance Without Hegemony and its Historiography', in Ranajit Guha (ed.), *Subaltern Studies VI*, Oxford University Press, New Delhi, 1989, pp. 210-309.

———, 'Discipline and Mobilise', in Partha Chatterjee and Gyanendra Pandey (eds.), *Subaltern Studies VII: Writings on South Asian History and Society*, Oxford University Press, New Delhi, 1992, pp. 69-120.

Irfan Habib, *The Agrarian System of Mughal India 1556–1701*, Asia Publishing House, Bombay, 1963.

David Hardiman, *Peasant Nationalists of Gujarat: Kheda District 1917–1934*, Oxford University Press, New Delhi, 1981.

———, *The Coming of the Devi: Adivasi Assertion in Western India*, Oxford University Press, New Delhi, 1987.

———, 'A Forgotten Massacre: Motilal Tejawat and his Movement among the Bhils 1921–2', in David Hardiman (ed.), *Histories for the Subordinated*, Permanent Black, New Delhi, 2006, pp. 29-56.

———, 'The Quit India Movement in Gujarat', in David Hardiman, *Histories for the Subordinated*, Permanent Black, New Delhi, 2006, pp. 148-84.

———, *Gandhi in His Time and Ours*, Permanent Black, Delhi, 2003.

———, *Missionaries and their Medicine: A Christian Modernity for Tribal India*, Manchester University Press, Manchester, 2008.

———, '*Ahimsa*: Shifting Meanings in Indian History', in David Hardiman (ed.), *Nonviolence in Modern Indian History*, Orient Blackswan, New Delhi, 2017, pp. 8-33.

———, *The Nonviolent Struggle for Indian freedom 1905–1919*, Hurst, London, 2018.

Douglas Haynes, 'From Avoidance to Confrontation? A Contestory History of Merchant-State Relations in Surat 1600–1924', in Douglas Haynes and Gyan Prakash (eds.), *Contesting Power: Resistance and Everyday Social Relations in South Asia*, University of California Press, Berkeley, 1991, pp. 239-89.

Douglas E. Haynes, *Rhetoric and Ritual in Colonial India: The Shaping of a Public Culture in Surat City, 1852-1928*, University of California Press, Berkeley, 1991.

Peter Heehs, *The Lives of Sri Aurobindo*, Columbia University Press, New York, 2008.

Stephen Henningham, *Peasant Movements in Colonial India: North Bihar 1917–1942*, Australian National University, Canberra, 1982.

Georg G. Iggers, 'Introduction' to Leopold von Ranke, *The Theory and Practice of History*, Routledge, New York, 2011, pp. xi-xlv.

Prakash Chandra Jain, *Tribal Agrarian Movement: A Case Study of the Bhil Movement of Rajasthan*, Himanshu Publications, Udaipur, 1989.

Ayesha Jalal, *Partisans of Allah: Jihad in South Asia*, Harvard University Press, Harvard, 2008.

Martin Jay, *The Dialectical Imagination: A History of the Frankfurt School and the Institute of Social Research 1923–1950*, Little, Brown and Company, Boston, 1973.

Robin Jeffrey (ed.), *People, Princes and Paramount Power: Society and Politics in the Indian Princely States,* Oxford University Press, New Delhi, 1978.

Sadan Jha, *Reverence, Resistance and Politics of Seeing the Indian National Flag*, Cambridge University Press, Delhi, 2016.

J.T.F. Jordens, *Swami Shraddhananda: His Life and Causes*, Oxford University Press, New Delhi, 1981.

Premsinh Kankariya, *Bhil Kranti ke Praneta: Motilal Tejavat*, Rajasthan Sahitya Academy, Udaipur, 1985 (in Hindi).

Jaspreet Kaur, *Master Tara Singh and Sikh Politics (1920–47)*, Kindle edition (no place or date provided).

Prashant Kidambi, 'Nationalism and the City in Colonial India: Bombay, c. 1890–1940', *Journal of Urban History*, Vol. 38, No. 5, 2012, pp. 950-67.

Martin Luther King, *A Testament of Hope: The Essential Writings of Martin Luther King Jr.,* (ed. James M. Washington), Harper Collins, New York, 1986.

Mary Elizabeth King, *Gandhian Nonviolent Struggle and Untouchability in South India: The 1924–25 Vykom Satyagraha and the Mechanism of Change*, Oxford University Press, New Delhi, 2015.

Gopal Krishna, 'The Development of the Indian National Congress as a Mass Organisation, 1918–1923', *The Journal of Asian* Studies, Vol. 25, No. 3, May 1966, pp. 413-30.

Krishnadas, *Seven Months with Mahatma Gandhi: Being an Inside View of the Non-Co-Operation Movement (1921–22)*, Vol. 2, Rambinode Sinha, Dighwara, 1928.

Kapil Kumar, *Peasants in Revolt: Tenants, Landlords, Congress and the Raj in Oudh 1886–1922*, Manohar, New Delhi, 1994.

Ravinder Kumar, 'The Bombay Textile Strike, 1919', *Indian Economic and Social History Review*, Vol. 1, No. 1, 1971, pp. 1-29.

———, 'From Swaraj to Purna Swaraj: Nationalist Politics in the City of Bombay, 1920–32', in D.A. Low (ed.), *Congress and the Raj: Facets of the Indian Struggle 1917–47*, Heinemann, London, 1977, pp. 77-107.

Mark Kurlansky, *Nonviolence: The History of a Dangerous Idea*, Jonathan Cape, London, 2006.

D.A. Low, 'The Government of India and the First Non-Cooperation Movement – 1920–1922', *The Journal of Asian Studies*, Vol. 25, No. 2, February 1966, pp. 241-59.

Carinne Luck, 'Three Ways Faith and Spiritual Leaders are Shaping Movements Today', *Minds of the Movement: An ICNC Blog on the People and Power of Civil Resistance*, 18 June, 2019. https://www.nonviolent-conflict.org/blog_post/three-ways-faith-and-spiritual-leaders-are-shaping-movements-today/ (accessed 25 June 2019).

Staughton Lynd and Alice Lynd (eds.), *Nonviolence in America: A Documentary History*, Orbis Books, Maryknoll, New York, 1995.

Karuna Mantena, 'Another Realism: The Politics of Gandhian Nonviolence', *American Political Science Review*, Vol. 106, No. 2, May 2012, pp. 455-70.

Doug McAdam, *Political Process and the Development of Black Insurgency, 1930–1970*, University of Chicago Press, Chicago, 1982.

DeRay Mckesson, *On the Other Side of Freedom: Race and Justice in a Divided America*, Oneworld Publications, London, 2018.

R.S. McGregor, *The Oxford Hindi-English Dictionary*, Oxford University Press, Oxford and Delhi, 1993.

Claude Markovits, *The Un-Gandhian Gandhi: The Life and Afterlife of the Mahatma*, Permanent Black, New Delhi, 2003.

Brian Martin, 'How Nonviolence is Misrepresented', *Gandhi Marg*, July-September 2008, pp. 235-57.

Adam Michnik, *Letters from Freedom: Post–Cold War Realities and Perspectives*, University of California Press, Berkeley, 1998, p. 78.

Gail Minault, *The Khilafat Movement: Religious Symbolism and Political Mobilisation in India*, Columbia University Press, New York, 1982.

Jagannath Prasad Misra, *Madan Mohan Malaviya and the Indian Freedom Movement*, Oxford University Press, New Delhi, 2016.

Ira Mitr, 'Growth of Trade Union Consciousness among Jute Mill Workers, 1920–40', *Economic and Political Weekly*, Vol. 16, Nos. 44/46, Nov. 1981, pp. 1839-48.

W.H. Morris-Jones, *The Government and Politics of India*, Hutchinson, London, 1964.

Mridula Mukherjee, *Peasants in India's Non-Violent Revolution: Practice and Theory*, Sage, New Delhi, 2004.

Projit Bihari Mukharji, *Doctoring Traditions: Ayurveda, Small Technologies, and Braided Sciences*, University of Chicago Press, Chicago, 2016.

Atlury Murali, 'Civil Disobedience Movement in Andhra 1920-22: The Nature of Peasant Protest and the Methods of Congress Political

Mobilization', in Kapil Kumar (ed.), *Congress and Classes: Nationalism, Workers and Peasants*, Manohar, New Delhi, 1988, pp. 152-216.

E.D. Murphy, 'Class and Community in India: The Madras Labour Union, 1918–21', *Indian Economic and Social History Review*, Vol. 14, No. 3, July-September 1977, pp. 291-321.

Jawaharlal Nehru, *Jawaharlal Nehru: An Autobiography*, Allied Publishers, New Delhi, 1962.

Ralph W. Nicholas, 'The Goddess Sitala and Epidemic Smallpox in Bengal', *Journal of Asian Studies*, Vol. 41, No. 1, 1981, p. 21-44.

Geoffrey Ostergaard and Melville Currel, *The Gentle Anarchists: A Study of the Leaders of the Sarvodaya Movement for Non-Violent Revolution in India*, Clarendon Press, Oxford, 1991.

Bob Overy, *Gandhi the Organiser: How he Shaped a Nationwide Rebellion: India 1915–1922*, Irene Publishing, Sparsnäs, Sweden 2019.

S.D.P., 'Obituary: N.M. Joshi', *The Economic Weekly*, 4 June 1955, p. 667.

Gyanendra Pandey, 'Peasant Revolt and Indian Nationalism: The Peasant Movement in Awadh, 1919–22', in Ranajit Guha (ed.), *Subaltern Studies I: Writings on South Asian History and Society*, Oxford University Press, New Delhi, 1982, pp. 143-91.

———, *The Construction of Communalism in Colonial North India*, Oxford University Press, New Delhi, 1990.

K.N. Panikkar, 'Peasant Revolts in Malabar in the Nineteenth and Twentieth Centuries', in A.R. Desai (ed.), *Peasant Struggles in India*, Oxford University Press, New Delhi, 1979, pp. 616-26.

Gordhanbhai Patel, *Vithalbhai Patel: His Life and Times*, R.A. Moramkar, Bombay, 1950.

Biswamoy Pati, *Resisting Domination: Peasants, Tribals and the National Movement in Orissa 1920-50*, Manohar, New Delhi, 1993.

M. L. Peace, *S. Kartar Singh Jhabbar: The Spearhead of the Akali Movement*, Peace and Rattan Kaur, Jullundur, 1968.

Frances Fox Piven and Richard Cloward, *Poor People's Movements: Why they Succeed, how they Fail*, Pantheon, New York, 1977.

Madho Prasad, *A Gandhian Patriarch: A Political and Spiritual Biography of Kaka Kalelkar*, Popular Prakashan, Bombay, 1965.

Arthur Quiller-Couch (ed.), *The Oxford Book of English Verse: 1250–1900*, Clarendon, Oxford, 1919.

Pema Ram, *Agrarian Movement in Rajasthan 1913–1947 AD*, Panchsheel Prakashan, Jaipur, 1986.

Michael Randle, *Civil Resistance*, Fontana, London, 1994.

John Rawls, 'The Justification of Civil Disobedience', in Hugo Adam Bedau (ed.), *Civil Disobedience: Theory and Practice*, Pegasus, Indianapolis and New York, 1969, pp. 240-55.

Rajat Kanta Ray, *Social Conflict and Political Unrest in Bengal 1875–1927*, Oxford University Press, New Delhi, 1984.

Peter Reeves, 'The Politics of Order: "Anti-non-Cooperation" in the United Provinces, 1921', *The Journal of Asian Studies*, Vol. 25, No. 2, Feb. 1966.

Livi Rodrigues, *Rural Protest in Western India*, Oxford University Press, New Delhi, 1998.

Hitesranjan Sanyal, 'Congress in Southwestern Bengal: The Anti-Union Board Movement in Eastern Medinipur, 1921', in Richard Sissons and Stanley Wolpert (eds.), *Congress and Indian Nationalism: The Pre-Independence Phase*, University of California Press, Berkeley, 1988, pp. 352-376.

Sumit Sarkar, *The Swadeshi Movement in Bengal 1903–1908*, People's Publishing House, New Delhi, 1973.

———, 'The Conditions and Nature of Subaltern Militancy: Bengal from Swadeshi to Non-Co-operation, c. 1905–22', in Ranajit Guha (ed.), *Subaltern Studies III: Writings on South Asian History and Society*, Oxford University Press, New Delhi, 1984, pp. 271-320.

———, *Modern India 1885–1947*, Macmillan, New Delhi, 1983.

Kurt Schock, *Civil Resistance Today*, Polity Press, Malden, MA, and Cambridge, 2015.

Gene Sharp, *The Politics of Nonviolent Action*, Porter Sargent Publisher, Boston, 1973.

———, *Waging Nonviolent Struggle: 20th Century Practice and 21st Century Potential*, Porter Sargent, Boston, 2005.

Hari Sen, 'Popular protest in Mewar in the Late-Nineteenth and early Twentieth Centuries,' unpublished Ph.D. thesis, University of Delhi, 1996.

G.K. Sharma, *Labour Movement in India (its Past and Present)*, Sterling Publishers, New Delhi, 1971.

M.H. Siddiqi, *Agrarian Unrest in North India: The United Provinces (1918–22)*, Vikas, New Delhi, 1978.

Lata Singh, *Popular Translations of Nationalism: Bihar, 1920–1922*, Primus Books, Delhi, 2012.

Mohinder Singh, *The Akali Movement*, Manohar, Delhi, 1978.

Dilip Simeon, 'Work and Resistance in the Jharia coalfield', *Contributions to Indian Sociology* (NS), Vol. 33, Nos 1 & 2, 1999, pp. 43-75.

Mohinder Singh, *The Akali Movement*, Macmillan, Delhi, 1978.

N.K. Singhi, 'A Study of Jains in a Rajasthan Town', in M. Carrithers and C. Humphreys (eds.), *The Assembly of Listeners: Jains in Society*, Cambridge University Press, Cambridge, 1991.

Ajay Skaria, *Unconditional Equality: Gandhi's Religion of Resistance*, University of Minnesota Press, Minneapolis, 2016.

Starhawk, *Dreaming the Dream*, Beacon Press, Boston, 1982.

———, 'A Moment in Human History', interview by Erin George, 24 September 2001, https://nettime.org/Lists-Archives/nettime-bold-0109/msg00811.html (accessed 14 May 2017).

Maureen Swan, *Gandhi: The South African Experience*, Ravan Press, Johannesburg, 1985.

Sidney Tarrow, *Power in Movement: Social Movements and Contentious Politics*, Cambridge University Press, Cambridge, 1998.

D.G. Tendulkar, *Mahatma: Life of Mohandas Karamchand Gandhi*, Vol. 2, *1920–1929*, Vithalbhai K. Jhaveri and D.G. Tendulkar, Bombay, 1951.

E.P. Thompson, 'The Moral Economy of the English Crowd in the Eighteenth Century', *Past and Present*, 50, February 1971, pp. 76-136.

Hugh Tinker, *The Ordeal of Love: C.F. Andrews and India*, Oxford University Press, Oxford, 1979.

Maya Unnithan-Kumar, *Identity, Gender and Poverty: New Perspectives on Caste and Tribe in Rajasthan*, Berghahn Books, Providence and Oxford, 1997.

Babubhai Vaidya, *Rentima Vahan: Shri Kunvarji V. Mehta Ajhadni Ladatna Samsmarno*, Sastu Sahitya Vardhak Karylaya, Ahmedabad, 1977 (Gujarati).

Arafaat A. Valiani, *Militant Publics in India: Physical Culture and Violence in the Making of a Modern Polity*, Palgrave Macmillan, New York, 2011.

Denis Vidal, *Violence and Truth: A Rajasthani Kingdom Confronts Colonial Authority*, Oxford University Press, New Delhi, 1997.

Arundhati Virmani, 'National Symbols under Colonial Domination; The Nationalization of the Indian Flag, March-August 1923', *Past and Present*, No. 164, August 1999, pp. 169-97.

Rajendra Vora, *The World's First Anti-Dam Movement: The Mulshi Satyagraha 1920–1924*, Permanent Black, Ranikhet, 2009.

B.P. Wadia, *Labour in Madras*, S. Ganeson, Madras, 1921.

Bryan Wilson, *Magic and the Millennium: A Sociological Study of Religious Movements of Protest among Tribal and Third World Peoples*, Heinemann, London, 1973.

Philip Woods, *Roots of Parliamentary Democracy in India: Montagu Chelmsford Reforms, 1917–1923*, Chankaya Publications, Delhi, 1996.

Indulal Yagnik, *Atmakatha*, Vol. 3, Ravani Prakasan, Ahmedabad, 1956.

Stephen Zunes, 'The Origins of People Power in the Philippines', in Stephen Zunes, Lester R. Kurtz, and Sarah Beth Asher, *Nonviolent Social Movements: A Geographical Perspective*, Blackwell, Malden, 1999, pp. 129-57.

INDEX

INDEX